THE WORLD OF CREDIT IN COLONIAL MASSACHUSETTS

The World of Credit in Colonial Massachusetts

James Richards and His Daybook, 1692–1711

Edited By

James E. Wadsworth

University of Massachusetts Press

Amherst and Boston

Printed in the United States of America

ISBN 978-1-62534-287-4 (paper)

Designed by Jack Harrison
Set in Adobe Caslon Pro
Printed and bound by Maple Press, Inc.

Cover design by Jack Harrison

Library of Congress Cataloging-in-Publication Data

Names: Richards, James, 1658–1711, author. | Wadsworth, James E., 1968– editor.
Title: The world of credit in colonial Massachusetts : James Richards and his daybook, 1692–1711 / edited by James E. Wadsworth.
Description: Amherst : University of Massachusetts Press, 2017. | Includes index.
Identifiers: LCCN 2017047293 (print) | LCCN 2017048161 (ebook) | ISBN 9781613765203 | ISBN 9781613765210 | ISBN 9781625342874 (pbk.)
Subjects: LCSH: Richards, James, 1658–1711. | Account books—Massachusetts—History. | Credit—Massachusetts—History.
Classification: LCC HF5680 (ebook) | LCC HF5680 .R53 2017 (print) | DDC 974.4/02—dc23
LC record available at https://lccn.loc.gov/2017047293

British Library Cataloguing-in-Publication Data
A catalog record for this book is available from the British Library.

Dedicated to
Walter and Carolyn Tyler
for their unwavering friendship

Contents

Acknowledgments ix

Note on Transcription of the Manuscript xiii

James Richards's Abbreviations and Archaic Spellings xv

James Richards, His Daybook, and the Economic History of New England 1

The James Richards Daybook, 1692–1711 33

Notes 289

Appendix A: James Richards's Debtors, Creditors, and Associates 301

Appendix B: Glossary of Terms 325

Works Cited 331

Index 339

Acknowledgments

This remarkable document surfaced in a dusty attic in Fairhaven, Massachusetts, in 2005. When I first saw it, it had been vacuum-sealed and wrapped in an old pillowcase for protection. The rawhide cover enclosed three bundled manuscript booklets about 8.5 x 14 inches and numerous loose pieces of paper for a total of 384 manuscript pages. Two hundred and fifty-one of those pages contained the detailed accounts of James Richards (1658–1711) of Weymouth over nineteen years between March 1692 and February 1711.

For much of the eighteenth century, the descendants of James Richards kept the volumes in which he had recorded his economic activities and used the blank pages to record some of their own business dealings. Eventually, the book found its way into the hands of the antiquarian Quincy Lovell Reed (1822–1907), who was the great-great-great-grandson of Sarah Bicknell (1651–1737), the sister of James's wife, Ruth (1660–1728). Quincy Reed amassed a substantial collection of documents related to the history of Weymouth and served as the secretary to the Weymouth Historical Society.[1] His collection disappeared after his death, but the James Richards daybook apparently passed to his daughter Harriet Loud Reed and remained in the family until it fell into the hands of one of her descendants in Fairhaven.

There it remained until my friends showed it to me as a historical curiosity. One thing led to another, and I found myself using the text to train students in the challenges of colonial paleography and research in primary sources. Now, over a

1 Luis A. Cook, "Quincy L. Reed," box 8, Weymouth Historical Society.

decade later, James Richards's daybook provides a unique window into the economic, material, and social lives of the people of Weymouth at a crucial time in the development of early American culture and society.

I would like to thank the following students from Stonehill College for their work on the manuscript between January 2006 and December 2009: Matthew Studer, Michael Raposa, Katlyne Cummings, Joe Barbieri, Julie Albert, Pete Ducharme, Matthew Mckenzie, Hillary Thompson, Christopher Lyons, Jeralyn Boccuzzi, Kevin Hart, Bernard Lynch, Patrick Noonan, Patrick Derochea, Michael Gennaro, Jonathan Grenier, and Kieran Lettrich. Jeralyn Boccuzzi bravely took on the project alone during the summer of 2007 as part of the Student Undergraduate Research Experience (SURE) at Stonehill. Michael Raposa and Erin Horanzy followed her in the SURE program during the summer of 2010. All of these students contributed considerable time and effort to the project and labored over Richards's penmanship and obscure phonetic spellings. I am not sure they appreciated it at the time, but I hope they came away with a deeper respect for the challenges of historical research and for the value of primary sources.

I would also like to thank Nicole Casper and her assistants at the Stonehill Archive for giving us space to work and computers to work on. Her generosity made this project possible. Debbie Sullivan, president of the Weymouth Historical Society, has been a constant source of information and assistance. She generously made the archival collections of the society available to me, provided copies of rare printed historical materials, and performed several searches for me. John R. Coffey, Jr., of the Weymouth Historical Society also helped me locate historic photographs of the area of North Weymouth where James Richards lived. Without their kind assistance, I never could have completed this project.

Kathleen Deree, the town clerk of Weymouth, generously gave me a work space in the vault with its spiral iron staircase and shelves bending under the accumulated detritus of the lives that have been lived in Weymouth. She let me work with the 1930s copy of the original town records, which proved invaluable in understanding James Richards, his daybook, and the Weymouth of his day.

The anonymous reviewers for the University of Massachusetts Press also provided helpful and thoughtful suggestions. Margaret Hogan undertook the difficult task of copy editing the book with consummate skill and a careful eye to detail.

I would also like to thank my wife and children, who have not only lived with this project for twelve years but have dealt with the piles of books and the questions about paleography. They have also assisted in the archival and genealogical research. In many ways, this project has been a family project and a labor of love.

Last, I wish to thank my dear friends Walter Tyler, who passed away in December 2016, and his wonderful wife, Carolyn. This is their book, and I did it for them. Carolyn trusted me with this invaluable family heirloom and provided other historical documents and family genealogies. She has been a constant and wholehearted supporter of this work. I had hoped to present the final book to them before Walter passed away. I deeply regret that I was unable to do so. But I know that Walter would have read it with his usual boyish enthusiasm for all things historical. His wry wit, ready smile, and constant stories are greatly missed. When I pick up this book, I think of Walter and Carolyn.

Note on Transcription of the Manuscript

In the transcription, I have remained rigidly faithful to the original text. I have done this to avoid imposing my own cultural and historical understanding on the text. To do so would dilute the manuscript's value as a historical source and limit its usefulness to researchers and scholars who would need to consult the original wording in any case. Although the manuscript did not have any page numbers, I have not followed the convention of numbering pages 1, 1v (i.e., verso). Instead, I have simply numbered them sequentially (1, 2, 3, etc.). I hope this makes it easier for lay readers and researchers to use the text.

I treated each page as a single unit. Each line was carefully numbered and transcribed one line at a time, and the transcription has been checked four separate times by at least three separate transcribers. I have retained the original spelling, capitalization, and punctuation. I have taken few editorial liberties, and all editorial attempts to clarify illegible text have been placed within brackets. I have retained the original author's use of superscript notations and preserved the author's crossed out entries.

To make the text more accessible, I have made a few editorial decisions. I chose to leave out the large Xs that James Richards placed over most of his entries as they would have made the transcription difficult to read. James Richards also included doodling and notes on non-business-related material occasionally in the text. When these doodlings confuse the text, I have placed them in the notes.

James also placed the symbols "ll," "s," and "d" for pounds, shillings, and pence randomly throughout the text. They are squeezed in at awkward places that disrupt the flow of the text and the continuity of the daybook entries. I have pulled these out and placed them in a single column header on each page. I believe these editorial interventions make the published transcription less cumbersome to work with while still remaining faithful to the intent and meaning of the text. Although every effort has been made to check and double check the manuscript transcription against the original, any residual errors are, of course, my responsibility.

In the annotations and glossaries, I have modernized and standardized all spellings and capitalization. For personal and place names, the standard for spelling has been the person and place index produced by the Weymouth Historical Society. I have done my upmost to identify all of the individuals named in the daybook. This has not always been possible. Those for whom biographical information is available have been listed in appendix A. Women who married or remarried after James referred to them have been listed under the last name James used. The length of the entries reflects the availability of evidence, not necessarily their importance to the daybook. Rather than annotating every abbreviation or archaic spelling appearing in the daybook, I have listed those that are not immediately discernable in alphabetical order with variant spellings in the Abbreviations and Archaic Spellings section, below. Definitions for terms that may be unfamiliar to modern audiences have been provided in the Glossary of Terms in appendix B. The annotations to the actual daybook focus on clarify confusing text or providing other information essential to understanding the manuscript and the people that appear in it. I have included in the annotations very brief notes on individuals for whom I have some information but not enough to craft a full biographical entry.

James recorded his accounts in pounds, shillings, and pence. These terms descended from classical Roman currency and referred to the Latin words *librae, solidi,* and *denarii.* Modern practice is to record them as £, s, and d, which I have followed in the introduction, notes, and glossary. One pound sterling was equal to 20 shillings or 240 pence. One shilling was equal to 12 pence.

James Richards's Abbreviations and Archaic Spellings

2 ant = second
Aalling = Allen
a leven = eleven
acars = acres
acitors, exsecetors = executors
acnoledg = acknowledge
acunpt, aconpt = account
Adcisins = Adkins
ancer = anchor
Andruse = Andrews
ant, nant = aunt
Aperel = April
asines = assigns
aut = out
ayell = ale
ayers, eyers = heirs
ayght, eyght, ayt, ayte, aight, aute = eight
ayteen = eighteen

baise = baize
baken, bacen = bacon
Baniamin = Benjamin
baper = paper
bech = beach
Bedlow, Bedlo, Budlo = Badlam
belis, beles = bellies
beme = beam
benes = beans
bifes = beefs
biscake, biskeak, buskits, biskacke = biscuit
Blancher = Blanchard
blew, bluw = blue
bluwinin = blue linen
bodis = bodice
boise, boyes = boys
bonat = bonnet
boroed, baroed = borrowed
Borstoun, Bostown, Bostoun = Boston
bote = boat
botell = bottle
bouft = bought
braft = brought
Brantery = Braintree
brass cittels = brass kettles
brot, brouft = brought
brow = brew
brther = brother
bruer = brewer
brumes, proom = brooms
bulits, boolits = bullets
butens = buttons

cajin = cajun
calefe, calves, cavefes, cofe = calves

calico = calico
camllat = camlet
cared = carried
carsi, carse, carsey = Kersey (cloth)
catting = carting
centin = satin
chabigase, chabaigs, chabaige, chabbaies, cabbaies, cabges = cabbages
ches = cheese
chikins = chickens
chist = chest
cilling = chilling
cins = skins
cittels = kettles
cleedd, clered = cleared
clooth, clat = cloth
cobbard = cupboard
coms = comes
condels = candles
connon = cannon
corant = current
cortains = curtains
cosen = cousin
Cotes = Coates
cowes, couse = cows
cricking = crooking
cunstabell = constable
cuntery = country
curanall, coranor, colanor, curanall, colanal = colonel

d, penc = pence
dafter = daughter
damaresh = damask
deyget = drugget cloth
dll, dell, dlli = delivered
Dochistor = Dorchester
doune = down
Dracke = Drake
dter, det, deter, detr = debtor
dubell = double
dusand, dusen = dozen
dwe = due

e = and
esenbrigs = osnaburg, osenberg
eyre, eyr = iron

fadam, fodam = fathom
feche = vetch
feeld = field
fere, feri = ferry
ff = F (i.e., fford = Ford)
ffife, fife, fif = five
filiting = filleting
fleec = fleece
flex = flax
furst = first
fustin = fustian
fwoot = foot

Giden = Gideon
Ginny = Jenny
glasier = glazier
goon = gun
goune = gown
grace = grass

hafe = have
halef = half
Harvi = Harvey
hed = head
held = heeled
Hener = Henry
hiffers = heifers
Hingum = Hingham
hlag, hlg = hog
hobey = hobby
hogsed = hogshead
hole = whole
Holes = Hollis
hooppules = hobbles
horce, whorse = horse
houce, hows = house
Hubey = Hovey
huck = hook
hur = her

i = often used in place of J as in iuly for July.
iar = jar
indego = indigo
Ingland = England
iudg, iugg = jug

j = often used in place of I
jacote = jacket
Jcabod = Ichabod
Jenuarey, Jenewa = January
jland = island
jnsine = ensign
juni, junr, jyner = junior
jynte = joint
Jzerel = Israel

kocks = cocks

lames, lams, lambes = lambs
laning plase = landing place
lase = lace
lentwo = lean-to
lether = leather
lickerish = licorice
Lincorne = Lincoln
lining, linin = linen
ll = pound
loding = loading

mackig = making
maier, mayor, major, majer = major
malata = mulatta
Manetecut = Monatiquot
Marah, Mare = Mary
march = marsh
marchant = merchantable
Marse = Marcy
mase = mace
Mathu = Matthew
medo = meadow
Megoon = Meagan
mele = meal
met = meat
metse = meaty
moing = mowing
molt = malt
mony = money
moten = mutton
Mumford = Mountford
muzeling, museling = muslin

necaloth = neckloth
negur, niber = nigger
Nucom = Newcomb

ocum = oakum
oke, ake = oak
one = own
otes, wotes = oats
oyell, oyl, oyll, oylle = oil

paide, payde = paid
pare, peer = pair
parell = barrel, parcel
pashage = passage
pasiance = patience
peaper = paper
peeces = pieces
pees = pieces, also peas
Peetor = Peter
penath = penny weight
penece = pennies
peneworth = pennyworth
perey = pear
petecote = petticoat
Pheburarey = February
piging = pigeon
pigings = piglets, pigeons, piggins
pill = bill
pines = pins
pips = pipes
Pitey, Pitty, Petty, Pittee, Pittey = Pettee
ploock = pluck
plou = plow
pr = per
preacking = breaking

Prentis = Prentice
punpings = pumpkins

quinses = quinces

recned = reckoned
redey = ready
Rentom = Wrentham
reseved, reved = received
resons = raisins
Robbord = Robert
rumall = romal
rund = round
rundlat = rundlet

s = shilling
sarg = serge
sariant = sergeant
scin, schin, fein = skin
Scotos = Scotch
sede = side
seder, seader = cedar
sem = some
seweed = seaweed
sex = six
shep = sheep
shering = shearing
shoos = shoes
shorting = shirting
shuger = sugar
sider, sidder = cider
sieth, sith, sithe, sife = scythe
silance = silence
Simicins, Simkins = Simpkins
sinemen = cinnamon
siphes, siue = sieves
son = sun
sord = sword
sparagras, spora gras, spara = asparagus
stadum = stadium
stees = stays
Steeuen = Steven
stocken needell = stocking needle
stoure = store
suem = sum
sun, soon = son
swon = swan

talle = tally
Tantton = Taunton
tendance e duate = attendance and waiting
thare = there
Tho = Thomas
Tirdsday = Thursday
tocon, tocan = token
toun = town
Trewant = Trufant
tungs = tongues
Turell = Tirrell
turoupse = turnips
tw, tooe, too = two
twluf, twolfe = twelve

upan = upon

valaines = valance
vele, vell, veale, vel, yell, vill = veal

wait = weight
waying = weighing
weex = weeks
weving, weefin, wefeing = weaving
wido = widow
wiefe, wife, wiff = wife
wimin, wiman, wimmin, wimmens, wimings = women
winoing = winnowing
woll = wool
wont = want
Wontam = Wenham, Massachusetts
woostted mohair = worsted mohair
worming = warming
wos = was
wosted ribing = worsted ribbon

yeeres = years
yews = ewes
yower = your
Yune = June

THE WORLD OF CREDIT IN COLONIAL MASSACHUSETTS

James Richards, His Daybook, and the Economic History of New England

Sometime in 1692, at age thirty-four, James Richards, a farmer and maltster from Weymouth, Massachusetts, took up his pen and wrote the following words: "James Richards his book to keep his debters in and to give Credit." In these few words, James summarized the socioeconomic system of late seventeenth- and early eighteenth-century rural New England.

James Richards's daybook is an artifact of the credit economy that infused virtually every social and economic relationship in colonial Weymouth.[1] It is also a memorandum of debt and credit using single-entry bookkeeping to record the credit he extended to others.[2] Sometimes he kept his accounts by the item sold and other times by the individual debtor or creditor (see James Richards Daybook, page 125, lines 20–25; page 146, lines 10–15, herein, with original pagination; hereafter JRDB). When he filled a book, he transferred the balance to a new book (JRDB, page 40, line 26). James made very little distinction between farm expenditures and household and personal items, which makes this record particularly rich and useful as a case study that can humanize what otherwise might be a dry account of economic activities. He almost always recorded prices "to give book value to the goods and labor" he exchanged, even though the real prices of these goods rested in the products and labor for which they were exchanged.[3] Like many farmers of his day, he expected others to keep track of what he in turn owed them. They could then come together to reconcile accounts periodically.[4]

Reckonings could take place at any time. In the reckoning, the two parties would agree on whether the accounts had been settled or if more was due to one side. James formally reconciled and balanced accounts 192 times in the daybook (about

10 per year), but informal reckonings could also take place in which money might exchange hands in payment of previous debts. For example, on November 21, 1694, James balanced accounts with Nathaniel Ford in which he concluded, "there was due to him from me in money 1s" (JRDB, page 7, lines 26–27).

Most of the reckonings went in James's favor. About a third of the time he owed money or goods, and 12 percent of the time the accounts were balanced and cleared. For example, on February 7, 1706, James recorded, "John Bicknell debt to goods upon a reckoning upon . . . all book debts cleared excepting malt [and] barley accounts from the beginning of the world to this day, due to me 10s 7d" (JRDB, page 125, lines 20–25). Because each farmer recorded what he was owed more carefully than what he owed, the balancing of accounts required considerable trust.[5] This system of reckonings meant that James often extended credit for long periods, and many were still outstanding at his death. His probate inventory records that forty-three pounds in debt were owed his estate.[6]

James's purchase accounts are incomplete because the primary purpose of the daybook was to keep track of the credit James extended so he could monitor his "social and economic relationships." He did not record total costs or profits, and he did not record his own labor, unpaid family labor, or his own use of his tools, plow, cart, horse, and so on. He also did not record the dozens of daily casual exchanges of minor gifts or assistance that would have been part of daily life in a community.[7] His wife and children appear rarely and only when their activities assisted him in his efforts or required his attention. For these reasons, we cannot gain a complete picture of James's farming and economic activities, his household relations, or even his credit obligations. But we can see the overall patterns of his social and economic relationships.

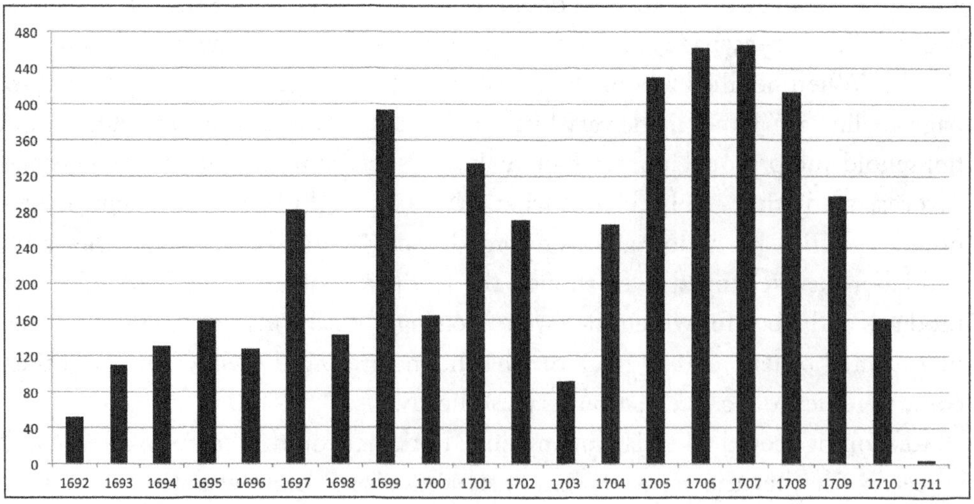

FIGURE 1. James Richards's transactions, 1692–1711 Source: James Richards Daybook

As shown in figure 1, James steadily increased his activities with occasional slumps until his most active years between 1705 and 1708. Because of failing health, his activities began to decline in 1709 before stagnating in 1710. But he continued to make entries in the daybook until a month before his death on March 8, 1711. Table 1 shows that the transactions recorded focused on providing food and clothing for his family and maintaining his farm. But the table also reveals significant commercial activities such as his textile, malt, salt, and lumber transactions, which are discussed below.

Since James Richards does not provide yearly tallies, we cannot reach any conclusions about profit and loss. But we can briefly examine the historical context that influenced the creation of his daybook and conditioned what James recorded and why he recorded it.

James Richards was born in 1658 in Weymouth, Massachusetts, to William and Grace Shaw Richards. The second successful European settlement in Massachusetts, located ten miles southeast of Boston and nestled between two inlets of Boston Harbor, the Fore and Back Rivers, Weymouth was well-situated to benefit from annual fish runs and land and water access to the growing markets in Boston.[8] The rivers provided navigation for large sea-going ships and power to run lumber and iron mills and later shoe factories.[9] Farmers and craftsmen of Weymouth developed regional contacts to market their goods and gain access to consumer products from across the Atlantic. In the 1640s, when William Richards relocated to Weymouth, and in 1692, when James Richards began his daybook, Weymouth was still a small settlement whose economy depended on fishing and agriculture and its contacts with regional markets.[10]

James married Ruth Bicknell probably in May 1682, just after the death of his father, William. The couple's first child, Benjamin, was born February 27, 1683. A few years later, their daughter Ruth was born. Their last child, Mary, was born in 1697. William had left James thirty-eight acres of land, which was held by James's mother until her death in 1692. After it passed to James, he actively expanded his landholdings.[11] By the time of his death in 1711 at the relatively young age of fifty-three, James had acquired eighty acres of land in Weymouth and ten and a half acres of salt meadow in Braintree.[12]

Compared to his contemporaries in Weymouth, James managed a comfortable independence. Unfortunately, tax valuations do not survive for this period. But a random sample of fifty-nine probates from Weymouth between 1661 and 1734 demonstrates that James's estate, valued at £850, was larger than 62 percent of his peers.[13] He also owned more land than 61 percent of them.[14]

His probate inventory is not as detailed as we might like. It does, however, include several luxury items that were relatively rare for the period, indicating a certain level of wealth, comfort, and social status. After all, "social status was determined

TABLE 1. James Richards's credits and debits, 1692–1711.

Item	# of Credits	% of Credits	# of Debits	% of Debits	Total	% of Total
Barley	107	2.6	161	17.4	268	5.3
Clothing, textiles, shoes, flax, cotton, thread, etc.	367	8.9	70	7.6	437	8.6
Currency—bills of credit, coin, bonds, etc.	413	10.0	175	18.9	588	11.6
Farm labor—hilling, plowing, carting, etc.	60	1.4	98	10.6	158	3.1
Farm—animals, tools, seeds, products	311	7.5	54	5.8	365	7.2
Food—meat, grains, dairy, molasses, sugar, vegetables, cider, spices, etc.	1,148	27.7	88	9.5	1,236	24.4
Freight	54	1.3	3	0.3	57	1.1
Household items and products	345	8.3	31	3.4	376	7.4
Household Labor	12	0.3	23	2.5	35	0.7
Lumber—clapboard, lathe, shingles, board nails, etc.	293	7.1	172	18.6	465	9.2
Malt	466	11.3	18	1.9	484	9.6
Salt	443	10.7	9	1.0	452	8.9
Taxes	43	1.0	18	1.9	61	1.2
Weapons—guns, swords, powder, shot, flints, etc.	78	1.9	5	0.5	83	1.6
Total	4,140	81.7	925	18.3	5,065	100.0

Source: James Richards Daybook

by the kinds and quantity of artifacts accumulated," as much as by the quantity of land and quality of one's credit and reputation.[15] James's inventory included three feather beds, two cupboards, a chest of drawers, and an Indian servant girl valued at thirty-five pounds. Feather beds were an expensive, prestigious item, one of the few items regularly left directly to heirs in wills. Owning three of them represented an important statement of social status. Cupboards and chests of drawers required skilled artisans to make and implied the ability to own things with which to fill them.[16] Even more rare for the time was James's servant girl. James's probate inventory also shows that he owned equipment that he could loan to his neighbors or use to produce marketable surplus, such as spinning wheels and cards, a plow and plow tackle, and a small boat.[17]

Taken together, these indicators demonstrate that James Richards was well-to-do but certainly not one of the wealthiest men in Weymouth. His contemporaries

Ephraim Hunt, who died in 1713, possessed over £2,772, and Stephen French, who died in 1718, possessed an estate valued at £2,168.[18] The fact that James's daybook represents an upper-middle-class perspective of Weymouth makes it all the more valuable.[19]

A Collaborative Undertaking: Mixed Husbandry, the Composite Farm, and the Colonial Economy

Scholars of colonial New England have created several models to explain the complexities of the colonial economy. The earliest and most persistent in popular memory is that colonial farmers were largely self-sufficient, rugged individualists who engaged in subsistence farming and had little need for, or interest in, the broader economy.[20] Following World War II, scholars began to challenge this conception with two competing visions.[21] Market historians argued that New England farmers were already capitalistic entrepreneurs in active pursuit of profit and wealth before they even stepped off the ships from England.[22] Social historians adopted a more Marxian approach and defined the rural economy as a "household mode of production" in which famers lived in communities that relied on neighborly reciprocity for labor, food, and manufactured goods.[23] In the 1980s and 1990s, a new group of scholars expanded this subsistence/market debate. One group, following a market approach, demonstrated that the vast majority of famers simply did not have the time or resources to be self-sufficient. Instead, rural famers were highly attuned to the value of their labor and products and knew that these values were intimately connected with local, colonial, and international markets.[24] About the same time, social historians, led by Daniel Vickers and Allan Kulikoff, constructed a middle ground between the market and social approaches.[25] They argued that farmers participated in commodity markets and capitalist economies while also living in communities centered on household reciprocity.[26]

More recent scholarship has tended to follow the latter approach and considered more carefully the social relationships that facilitated economic transactions and the reciprocal obligations those relationships imposed.[27] These scholars have shown that farmers throughout the North American colonies used mixed husbandry to create composite farms that "simultaneously produced for the farm family and for the market" in a society highly attuned to social relationships.[28]

James Richards's daybook demonstrates that the composite farm, based on a complex system of ecological and interpersonal relationships centered on credit, flourished in late seventeenth-century Massachusetts. The creation and maintenance of these relationships provided the motive for creating James's daybook in which he commodified even his family relationships in a multilayered subsistence, market, barter, and credit economy.[29]

Weymouth is nine miles long north to south and three miles wide east to west. Like the rest of New England, the underlying rock on which Weymouth sits is composed mostly of granite and slate. This rock is covered by glacial alluvial deposits composed primarily of clay, sand, and gravel with the northern soils near the coast being more productive then the soils further south.[30]

In the seventeenth century, nine miles of waterfront were interspersed with saltmarshes and fed by freshwater streams that flowed through low glacial hills and rock ledges into Great Pond and Whitman's Pond and thence into the Back and Fore Rivers. Mill River, Pen River, and Smelt Brook supplied fresh water and power. The mixed forest of oak, elm, beech, and walnut along the coast gave way to cedar, pine, and spruce further inland where the land leveled out from the small drumlins nearer the coast. Great Hill, the largest drumlin in the area, is 150 feet high. King Oak Hill, its nearest competitor, is 100 feet high. Swamps, meadows, rocky hillsides, flat plains, wooded ledges, safe harbors, and variegated seashores defined the Weymouth landscape. This mosaic of soils and landscapes made agriculture a challenge and regular fertilization of the cultivated fields necessary, which in turn required the use of intensive mixed husbandry.

Colonial farmers of the seventeenth century adapted the English farming practices with which they were familiar to these new landscapes, while also adopting some Native American crops to create a unique form of sustainable mixed husbandry.[31] Such husbandry combined livestock, such as cows, sheep, oxen, horses, and swine, with the cultivation of grains and fruits in a system that transferred nutrients from meadows and saltmarshes to cultivated fields and pastures.[32]

Too often we speak in condescending terms of primitive or subsistence agriculture. The mixed husbandry required of colonial farmers was anything but simple or

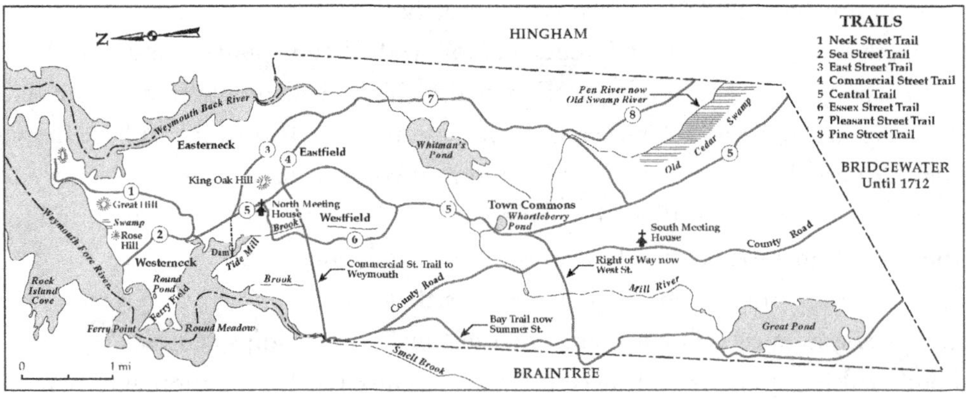

FIGURE 2. Map of the town of Weymouth, c. 1700

Map produced by Barry Levely

FIGURE 3. View of North Weymouth, early 20th century

Source: "Wessagussett: The New Sea Shore Resort, North Weymouth, Mass." Courtesy of the Weymouth Historical Society

Note: This early twentieth-century view of Weymouth shows the area where James Richards lived before it was developed. Rose Hill, which James owned, is in the center, with Great Hill to the right and Hunt's Hill to the left. The Bay Side Hotel sits on top of Rose Hill, and the Boston skyline can be seen in the distance.

primitive. It required a deep acquaintance with the lands, soils, grasses, woods, water, and weather. Mixed husbandry was not suited to monoculture. Its purpose was to create a stable, diversified system that exploited the landscape as efficiently as possible. To succeed, a farmer had to either own or have access to a variety of landscapes including salt or fresh meadows, pasturage, woodland, plow land, and, if possible, orchards within reasonable distance of each other, but not necessarily contiguous. Because cultivating land and using it as pasture results in net nutrient loss for the soil, animal manure, deposited either as the livestock grazed across the landscape or taken from the barns where the wintering livestock consumed the grasses cut from the meadows, had to be returned to the soil.

The challenge of this complicated system was that to support a family, a farmer not only needed access to the necessary landscapes; he also needed the tools and livestock to make them productive. Brian Donahue has shown that a family of eight to ten would need approximately sixty acres of orchard, pasture, meadow, woodlands, and cultivated fields to provide food, clothing, shelter, and firewood.[33] A family would also need to accumulate surplus lands and wealth to provide land for sons and dowries for daughters. To make the land productive, a farmer would need, at a minimum, several cows, a yoke of oxen, and maybe a horse and a few sheep and pigs. He would also need a barn to house his animals and process and store his grain, a plow to turn the soil in his fields, a harrow, and a cart to haul manure to his fields, grass from the meadows, and crops from the fields. He would need access to a forge and blacksmithing tools to make and repair his iron tools and shoe his horse if he had one; a sawmill to produce shingles and clapboard for his house and barn; shears, cards, spinning wheel, and loom to transform wool into cloth; a swingling knife and combs to process flax into linen for clothes, bedsheets, and tablecloths; ropes; and a grindstone to mill his grain. This list does not even consider the tools and resources required to make candles, soap, cider, leather, cheese, bacon, bread, barrels, shoes, ceramics, pewter, and many other things necessary for survival and comfort. John Worlidge's 1669 account of husbandry lists seventy-nine different tools that farmers had to master to succeed.[34]

Even families that controlled considerable acreage did not have the time, resources, or labor to produce all of this.[35] Indeed, a farmer working without the assistance of servants could probably only cultivate about twenty-five acres.[36] The system of mixed husbandry forced farmers to rely on their neighbors for access to tools, lands, livestock, skills, and labor they did not control. The key to this system was credit. Performing a service for a neighbor such as lending him a cart and horse for a day could be returned by his sons' working on your land. The mixed husbandry system and the credit relations on which it was built functioned in Weymouth and provide the context for much of what appears in James Richards's daybook.

It is difficult to estimate total acreage of farmers from wills and inventories.[37] A random sample of fifty-nine probates from Weymouth between 1661 and 1734 shows that no one owned all of the landscapes required of mixed husbandry, but all of them owned two or more different kinds. The most successful farmers owned four or five different landscapes. For example, in 1699, Samuel White owned four acres of orchard and meadow, three acres and a parcel of saltmarsh, four acres of cedar swamp, unspecified acreage in woodlands, and more acreage in Weymouth and Braintree.[38] In 1711, James Richards owned a house and a barn, with fifty adjoining acres that included an orchard, meadow, and cultivated fields; ten and a half acres of saltmarsh in Braintree; and another thirty acres of meadow on the Ferry Field near Ferry Point. These kinds of land holdings—noncontiguous acreage in varied landscapes and often different townships—were typical. Most importantly, 64 percent of them owned saltmarsh or meadow land, which was key to successful mixed husbandry.

Ownership of livestock was nearly universal. Those probates that do not list livestock are usually incomplete or do not have inventories. At least 86 percent of our sample owned cows, 64 percent owned swine, 53 percent owned a horse, 5 percent owned a bull, and 51 percent owned sheep. The average size of cow herds in Weymouth was three or four. Rarely a herd might be as large as fifteen or twenty. The system of mixed husbandry relied on livestock, especially cattle, to transform the grasses of the meadows into nutrients for the fields. Oxen and to a lesser extent horses were required to turn the soil and prepare the fields for cultivation. But only 17 percent of those in our probate sample owned a yoke of oxen and 34 percent owned a plow. Farmers needed a cart to move hay, manure, and crops to and from their fields, but only 27 percent owned one. These findings fit patterns noted elsewhere in eighteenth-century New England. Winifred B. Rothenberg found that nearly half of all farmers in Massachusetts in 1771 did not own plows or oxen.[39]

Those who did not have direct access through ownership to the land or resources they needed had several options. They could utilize the town commons, lease the necessary land or equipment, barter for or borrow it, or purchase an interest in it. The inventories reveal that Weymouth farmers held monetary interest in sawmills, farms, blacksmith shops, wharfs, grindstones, sloops, and horse carts. James Richards shared ownership in a crosscut saw with Zechariah Bicknell (JRDB, page 59, line 1). He also co-owned a sloop called *The Three Friends* with Morris Trufant and William Pratt (JRDB, page 104, lines 19–23; page 127, lines 12–15; page 243, lines 31–33; page 228, lines 26–27). In 1697, Richards recorded lending the use of his meadow and pasture to his brother-in-law Thomas Bicknell on eight separate occasions and allowed him to harvest three and a quarter acres of salt grass (JRDB, page 87, lines 29–30, 32–35). In 1702, James rented his pasture at Rose Hill to Morris Trufant (JRDB, page 84, lines 23–24). In 1698, he charged his uncle John Porter for the use of a bull on Easterneck, probably to impregnate his cows (JRDB, page 70, line 6). In 1703, Richards pastured John Vinson, Jr.'s heifer for six weeks (JRDB, page 169, line 31).

James and his neighbors also relied on each other for labor. James hired out his son, Benjamin, as a laborer and also hired other boys to work on his land. James and Benjamin helped their neighbors remove brush; break ground; plow, hill, and sow their fields; mow grass; fetch and haul corn and hay; and even store barley. In return, they helped him slaughter his animals, sheer his sheep, fan his oats and barley, mow his hay, and plow his fields. He particularly relied on John Torrey and John Green to provide him with the cart he needed to care for his land. On thirty-eight occasions, James Richards recorded hiring a cart and horse to haul hay, oats, wood, shingles, corn, dung, and salt grass to or from his lands at Rose Hill; the Ferry Field; the southern bank of the Fore River, which he called the water side; and Braintree. James arranged for Thomas Bicknell to winnow his barley and oats, Enoch Lovell to repair his shoes, James Humphrey and Nathaniel Blanchard to weave cloth, John Green to shear his sheep and slaughter his pigs, John Green's

FIGURE 4. Photograph of Great Hill, 1923 —Source: Courtesy of the Weymouth Historical Society

Note: This photograph of Great Hill was taken from Rose Hill in 1923 during the Weymouth three hundredth anniversary celebration.

FIGURE 5. Photograph of Wessagussett Yacht Club, c. 1900

Source: Courtesy of the Weymouth Historical Society

Note: This photograph of the Wessagussett Yacht Club was taken from Rose Hill in the early 1900s. It shows Rose Hill on the left where it has been leveled to allow housing construction. The long peer in the background belonged to the old Rose Hill Club, which no longer exists.

boys to hill his corn, John Torrey to mow his barely, and Ichabod Holbrook to store it.

The seasonal rhythms of mixed husbandry governed many of these activities. As shown in figure 6, James Richards remained most active April through November. Harvest time in August and September were the busiest times of the year. In March, James began preparing for the season by shoeing his horse, preparing his boat, purchasing tools, doing a bit a plowing, and selling off the extra hay he had left over from the winter. In April, he purchased barley for malting and barley seed and corn seed for planting. He sold more hay and began brushing and plowing, had the family's shoes repaired, and sold off supplies of oats and malt. In May, the sheep were sheared, calves were butchered for veal, seed was sown, fish were caught as they ran in the rivers, and lumber was shipped to Boston. In June, fields were hilled and tilled; calves and lambs were bought and sold; wool was sold; salt grass was cut and carted to the barn; lumber was shipped to Boston; and malt, salt, and sugar were sold. July looked much like June with the addition of mutton being sold and household items such as candles, lamp oil, and cheese being sold and purchased. In August, oats and barely could be harvested and winnowed, hay was cut, lambs were sold, molasses and tobacco became more available, more sheep were slaughtered for

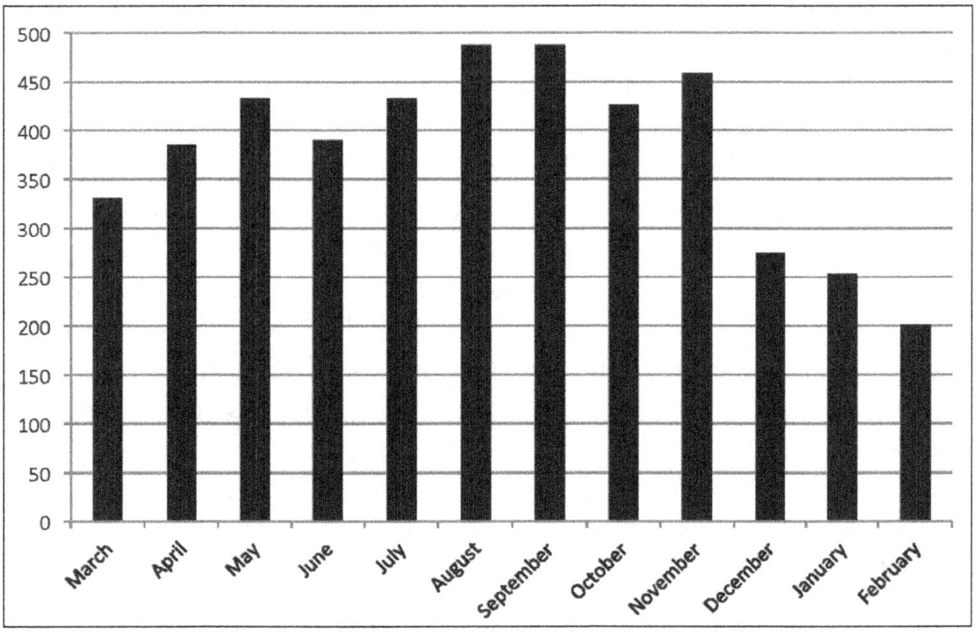

FIGURE 6. The seasonality of James Richards's transactions, 1692–1711

Source: James Richards Daybook

Note: The information in this table reflect the time of year that James Richards recorded his transactions, not necessarily the usual or only time of year to do them.

mutton and head and pluck. September, October, and November brought apples and the making of cider; the harvest of corn, oats, and garden products such as turnips and cabbages; more cutting of hay and salt grass; more slaughtering of cattle, pigs, and sheep; and the sale of salt to preserve them. As the seasonal activities slowed in December through February, James continued to sell his malt and some barely, purchased cloth, and settled in for the winter.[40]

Mixed husbandry and the seasonality of the farm allowed farmers to produce surpluses for market and develop trades that provided much needed cash and credit relationships. The probates from Weymouth and James Richard's daybook demonstrate that men established trades in weaving, surveying, carpentry, malting, cider making, barrel making, caulking, beekeeping, cordwaining, and blacksmithing. Much of this activity was simply about diversifying one's access to resources, including debtors. But it also helped iron out the "seasonal irregularities of the farmer."[41] Diversifying skill sets was a crucial strategy for family success, and it assisted local communities in overcoming the constraints of the broader economy.[42]

These activities could be most important for those who had smaller, less diversified land holdings. For example, in 1718, James Humphrey owned a horse, nine cows, two hogs, and thirty-five sheep; forty-one acres of uplands; and thirteen acres of salt and fresh marshland. But he did not apparently own orchards or woodlands, and we do not know how many acres he cultivated. He owned a plow, a horse cart, cards, looms, a considerable quantity of cloth, one quarter interest in a sloop and her cargo, beehives, and cider-making equipment.[43] Humphrey wove cloth for Richards, lent Richards his horse and cart, and sold him sheep. It seems clear that Humphrey engaged in the sustainable use of his uplands to range his sheep and cow herds while using his marshland to keep them fed over the winter. His sheep herd allowed him to sell the wool and sheep. His cow herd was large for the period and may have allowed him to produce dairy products for sale. Humphrey effectively diversified his productive activities by managing what lands he did have wisely and by using his access to essential equipment and specialized skills to offset his deficiency in land.

James Richards did the same. In 1692, at the age of thirty-four, he inherited thirty-eight acres of land from his father including six acres of "planting and pasture land," three acres of orchards, and twenty-nine acres of woodlands. As we have seen, he would later expand these holdings to ninety acres, including ten and a half acres of salt meadow and thirty acres in the Ferry Field. But when he started out, he did not own any meadow land and so his ability to practice mixed husbandry was probably restricted.

To overcome these deficiencies, James formed credit relationships with his neighbors and family members and developed several commercially viable activities that allowed him to extend his credit relationships and acquire much needed income that could later be translated into land purchases. Surpluses from normal farming activities could also be marketed. This market production could prove crucial to family success and allow people to acquire the land and resources necessary to provide sons with farms and daughters with dowries.[44]

By far, the most important commercial activity James developed was malting, which he probably learned from his father, William.[45] James and his neighbors referred to him as a maltster, a reputation he retained until the 1880s (JRDB, page 19, lines 24–26; page 86, line 25; page 190, line 4; page 201, lines 8–11).[46] Over the course of nineteen years, James purchased more than 2,065 bushels of barley, often in bulk, and sold over 1,654 bushels of malt. The malting process included soaking the barley in water, allowing it to germinate, and then drying it in a kiln, the sun, or a malt house. In 1701, the provincial legislature required that the malt be "well dryed and cleansed, by screening of it from the dust and taile which arises in the makeing."[47]

A comparison of the quantities of barley and malt purchased and sold reveals that James's commercial activities responded to the environmental and political realities of colonial New England. As shown in figure 7, James's barley purchases and sales parallel each other closely. Malt sales also followed the purchase of barley often with a slight delay. These patterns are consistent with a farmer who was purchasing the raw barley, processing it into malt, and selling the malt as a finished product.

James did not start producing malt on a large scale until 1693. He experienced severe declines in malt production in 1696–97 due to the failure of the grain harvests in 1695 and 1696. The shortage was so severe that the General Court prohibited the exportation of any grain on November 29, 1695, and reinstated the prohibition in 1696 and again in 1697.[48] The ban lasted into 1698, but by careful management of his

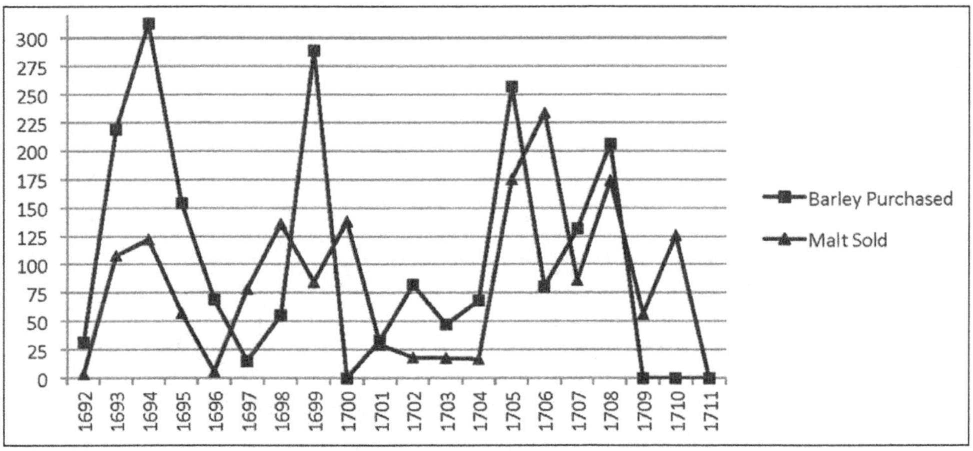

FIGURE 7. Barley purchased and malt sold between 1692 and 1711

Source: James Richards Daybook

barely and malt supplies James was able to continue selling malt. As James's health declined in the last three years of his life, he stopped purchasing barley all together and sold off much of his remaining barley and malt inventory. His last transactions in January and February 1711 were sales of barley.

As shown in figure 8, James also had far more individual transactions of malt than of barley. This happened because James frequently purchased the barley in bulk, while he sold the malt in small quantities rarely larger than one or two bushels. This practice is consistent with contemporary beer production for family consumption, which needed to be purchased in quantities that a "family could consume in a few days."[49] When James sold large quantities of malt, it was often to Boston breweries or taverns. In 1698, he sold ninety-eight bushels to Thomas Adkins for his "brew house" (JRDB, page 29, lines 1–3).[50] In 1708, he sold fifty bushels of malt to a brewer named Pemberton (JRDB, page 223, lines 1–3).

James likewise developed a healthy business in salt. Salt was crucial for local fisheries, in soap making, feeding to livestock, tanning hides, and preserving food. But colonial Massachusetts suffered from constant shortages of salt to meet the growing demand caused by increased population and the growth of the fishing industry.

Colonial authorities remained acutely aware of their dependence on salt from England or the Caribbean. Consequently, various attempts to meet the growing demand in salt surfaced periodically.[51] Despite all local attempts to ease the shortage, New England still had to import most of its salt. The Navigation Acts created an "imperial free-trade zone linking the Caribbean with North America," which meant that Massachusetts merchants, fisherman, and farmers continued to have

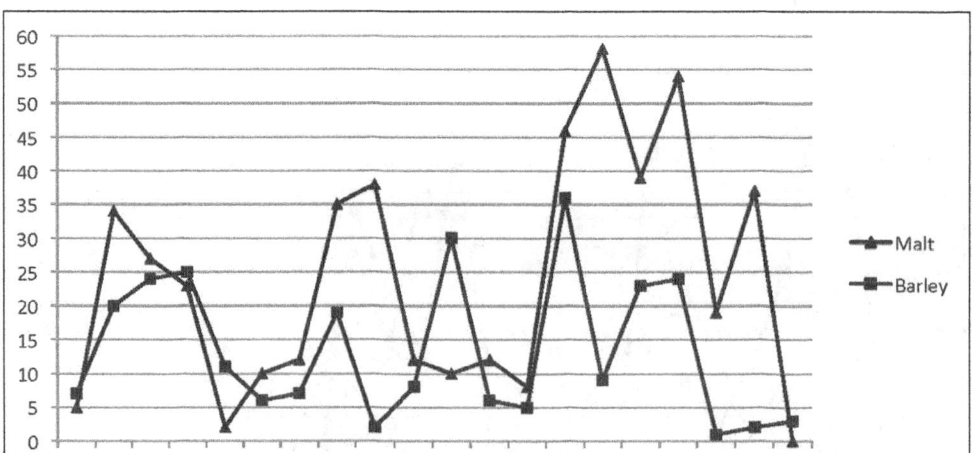

FIGURE 8. Number of transactions of barley and malt, 1692–1711

Source: James Richards Daybook

access to the salt-producing islands of Tortuga and the Wine Islands.[52] But the shortage remained a constant problem.

James responded to this shortage by selling more than 395 bushels of salt, mostly in small quantities of a peck or two. He may have been producing the salt himself from his saltmarshes in Braintree. Three methods existed at the time for extracting salt from saltmarshes. One was to form salt ponds that would produce salt through evaporation. Another, less productive method was simply to gather the salt that settled naturally on the marshland. The third was to cut the peat from the marsh and burn it to extract the salt.[53] James could have used any or all of these methods. Whatever the case, it seems clear that he was producing salt as a commercial product.[54]

He similarly dealt in a wide variety of cloth though it does not appear that he or the women in his family were weaving it themselves. Women had dominated weaving in England until the latter part of the fourteenth century when commercial production of cloth transformed weaving into a male profession with formal guilds. Seventeenth-century New England women spun but did not weave. This practice began to shift again in the first half of the eighteenth century in New England so that by the end of the century, weaving was once again women's work.[55]

This shift is not yet apparent in James's daybook. James used the lambs that he raised to produce wool, which he carded and then sold. He also purchased flax and cotton. James's wife and daughters may have spun the raw wool, cotton, and flax, but there is no evidence that they were weaving it into cloth. James's probate inventory lists spinning wheels and cards but no loom. The daybook also makes it clear that women were spinning thread, while men were weaving it. In 1705, James purchased 199 skeins of spun wool from Sarah Richards (JRDB, page 102, lines 43–44). He paid Nathaniel Ford and Nathaniel and James Humphrey to weave wool and cotton for him (JRDB, page 5, line 6; page 20, lines 24–26, 33–35; page 49, lines 38–39). Spinning and weaving were never as universal around the turn of the eighteenth century as we might think. Only 31 percent of households in our sample of probate inventories owned a spinning wheel, while only 8 percent owned looms.[56] But enough spinning and weaving were taking place in Weymouth to convince the selectmen to grant Gideon Tirrell land along the river in the town commons to construct a fulling mill in 1693.[57] Fulling cleaned and thickened woven or knitted woolen cloth through a process of washing, heating, and pounding. The process caused shrinkage of up to 25 percent, thus producing a more tightly woven, lighter cloth.

In 1699, James began to expand his commercial activities to include building supplies. Over the next ten years, he purchased and sold a considerable quantity of shingles, lathes, and clapboards. This trade flourished between 1704 and 1708. The daybook does not allow us to determine how many shingles, lathe, and clapboard

James produced himself, but he did own woodlands and had access to common land in the Old Cedar Swamp from which he might have harvested the lumber. Indeed, in 1701, Enoch Lovell hauled shingles from the swamp for James (JRDB, page 96, line 6).[58] The daybook shows that James purchased shingles, lathes, and clapboards directly from local suppliers such as John and Samuel Vinson, Joseph Pratt, Enoch and Joseph Lovell, and Abraham Shaw, and resold them to Boston (see, for example, JRDB, page 80, lines 15–22; page 162, lines 1–5).

Much of this lumber may have entered the export economy. Timber became a more common export commodity in the latter part of the seventeenth century, and export merchants had to rely on the local economy and small suppliers to fill their ships. The lumber was also used in construction projects in Boston. For example, in 1702, James sold 2,100 shingles to Robert Lash after Lash received permission in 1701 from the Boston selectmen to erect a timber building (JRDB, page 80, lines 23–24).[59] James was able to turn his access to timber into a profitable sideline as one among many small-time suppliers of lumber for city construction and for the export economy.[60]

James developed consistent business in selling sheep heads and pluck between 1696 and 1702. Pluck refers to the heart, liver, and lungs of an animal slaughtered for food, in this case mostly sheep. Most of these sales occurred between August and January, the traditional time for slaughtering animals in a society that did not enjoy the benefits of refrigeration. For example, in April 1708, James sold Samuel Bill of Boston a wether (i.e., castrated ram) for ten shillings on the condition that he return the skin and the wool after slaughter (JRDB, page 221, lines 1–3). This trade slowed to a trickle after 1702 and ended in 1709, when James was probably no longer slaughtering his own sheep or using his neighbor John Green to do it for him. The lack of sheep in his probate inventory suggests that he no longer kept them.

James's daybook demonstrates that Weymouth was connected to the interregional and international markets that brought exotic goods to town. He sold over 404 pounds of tobacco, 204 pounds of sugar, 120 gallons of molasses, and substantial quantities of cotton, calico, and muslin over the course of the time covered by the daybook. The frequency with which these commodities appear in the daybook demonstrates that the English system of trade known as the Navigation Acts functioned fairly well during this period. James had ready access to tobacco from Virginia, Maryland, and North Carolina, as well as sugar and molasses from the West Indies. Nutmeg and mace came through the Dutch-controlled island of Banda. Cinnamon came from Dutch-controlled Ceylon and cloves from the Dutch-controlled Molucca Islands. Wine probably came from northern Portugal, the Madeiras, or the Azores. Cotton came from India through the British East India Company and from southern plantations from where it was imported into Massachusetts duty-free.[61]

FIGURE 9. Map of Massachusetts Bay, c. 1700

Map produced by Barry Levely, Cartographer

As might be expected, James had to pay to move all of these goods around. Of the forty-four transactions listed involving carting, James only performed eight of them, while John Torrey and John Green moved carted goods for James in twenty-seven of the remaining thirty-six cases. James regularly charged for transporting his goods. He charged fees for moving shingles, clapboard, wood, malt, salt, molasses, veal, beef, pepper, and apples. He also carried barrels of beer and cider and seaweed. He used his boat to haul stones and wood from Grape Island and to transport products to and from Boston. He charged Lydia Thomas for bringing her a chest from Boston, Thomas Bicknell for "fetching the cannon from Boston" in 1697, Katherine Simpkins for bringing a load of wood to the Boston town dock, and Thomas

White, Jr., for bringing him some sails from Boston in 1701 (JRDB, page 132, lines 1–3; page 87, line 23; page 42, lines 3–7; page 46, line 3). James paid John Green to cart oats and Indian corn from his land in the Ferry Field (JRDB, page 17, lines 28–30). And he hired John Torrey and John Green to cart hay from Rose Hill, which was on a different portion of James's property (JRDB, page 208, lines 6–7; page 16, line 20; page 135, lines 12–13). His transport charges included moving goods over land and sea to Boston, Dorchester, and Charlestown. In this way, farmers like James facilitated the regional transportation of goods.[62]

Credit, Currency, Barter, and Exchange in James Richards's Daybook

The British Imperial system, which prohibited the exportation of currency from England and set the value of foreign monies circulating in the colonies, imposed a currency and credit famine on the colonies. The colonists resorted to five main strategies to overcome the persistent shortage of coin: credit, "barter, commodity money, overvalued coin, and paper currency."[63]

The credit system employed by New England farmers developed in sixteenth-century England and traveled across the Atlantic with them.[64] It was founded on the understanding that a household's reputation for honesty, fairness, reliability, virtue, and trustworthiness in their dealings with other people was their most valuable commodity. It "became the currency of lending and borrowing" because "individual profit and security were important, but neither could be achieved without the direct cooperation of one's neighbors, or those one traded with."[65] Credit was so important that the standard probate language of the day included credits as heritable wealth, which were often recorded as book debts owed the estate. Thirty-nine percent of the Weymouth probates surveyed included such book debts, which means that other farmers were keeping track of the credits they had extended. But credit was also a social currency that created bonds of mutual interdependence without which no family or business could prosper. The extension of credit created a social relationship of reciprocity that strengthened "communal bonds of neighborliness" while also permitting competition and profit.[66]

In these relationships, the household was the "basic unit of economic consumption and production."[67] All household members, including the wife, children, and servants, needed to uphold the good name and reputation of the family. James Richards's accounts demonstrate that wives, servants, and children actively participated in economic transactions and so contributed to the family's credit. This also helps explain why James Richards regularly mixed his household accounts with his credit accounts.

Scholars have often referred to this as a barter system, but the term oversimplifies the complexity and utility of credit. The credit system was more than the simple exchange of goods of equal value. Farmers and merchants kept running accounts of the market value of the items they traded.[68] This practice provided considerable flexibility by permitting a system of credits that allowed debts and credits to be transferred to third or even fourth parties. It also allowed second parties to place orders on another person's tab. The credits seldom had interest attached to them and so insulated both the debtor and creditor from the uncertainties of the larger economy.[69] But the system was not perfect. Accounts that remained open for years were also open to abuse, which could cause farmers financial setbacks and inflame tensions. For example, on November 26, 1710, James penned the following note: "Mr. Mouses Peneman my desire is that you would send mee the mony which I was to have of you the twentith ninth of September last past, the wont thereof is sum damage to mee."[70] The tact and appeal to emotion displayed in this plea for payment of a debt reflect the very real need to maintain amicable relations with a potential creditor, even when he was in default.[71]

Many farmers reconciled accounts by issuing credit that could be transferred to another person through a process of bookkeeping transfers.[72] More than two dozen cases occur in James's accounts where his clients placed orders or made payments on other people's accounts. For example, in 1702, James received three pigs from Joseph Pratt against Zachariah Bicknell's account (JRDB, page 34, lines 35–36, 41). Mrs. Tyler paid two shillings and six pence in cash against Samuel Bagley's account in 1698 (JRDB, page 79, lines 20–21). And in 1705, James sent a gallon of molasses to John Blancher on Ephraim Burrell's account (JRDB, page 120, lines 6–7). In 1705, Ebenezer Pratt ordered goods "delivered to Aunt Bayley upon the account of Sarah Bayley by a verbal order from himself" (JRDB, page 119, lines 1–5).

Orders could also be placed in advance of expected delivery. For example, on March 16, 1699, James Richards placed an order with Ebenezer Thare of Braintree for three heifers of "sound wind and limb" to be delivered the following May (JRDB, page 66, lines 18–22). On May 30, 1694, a man named Edward ordered two wethers, six ewes, and six lambs from James and paid a deposit of twelve shillings with the remaining three pounds due in the fall of 1695 (JRDB, page 90, lines 6–10). Sometimes the orders were given by what James called "verbal orders," which were not recorded at the time the agreement was reached (JRDB, page 76, lines 1–3; page 62, lines 1–5; page 13, lines 6–10). This system not only allowed the economy to function; it also intensified neighborhood interdependence.[73]

It is clear that the credit system James used included barter and the use of commodities as a form of payment, though it is impossible to tell how frequent this was.[74] Only forty-four transactions clearly involved formal barter and the settling of accounts in kind. James traded eggs for sugar and paid and received in payment barley, malt, corn, oats, wood, salt, sheep, wool, cabbages, and cheese. In 1701, he recorded settling an eight-shilling monetary debt to Thomas Bicknell in sheep (JRDB, page 43, lines 7–10). But since he usually assigned everything a monetary value, even when engaging in barter, it is possible that he used barter more frequently. It is also clear that mixed transactions occurred in which James received money for a portion of the transaction and commodities for the rest. This practice was common in colonial New England and was even accepted by the government. The Massachusetts General Court permitted payment of taxes in what was called "country pay," which might include lumber, wheat, corn, barley, fish, wool, or even livestock. In 1706, James Richards paid his town rate (i.e., tax) in one bushel of malt and eleven pence, which he valued at three shillings nine pence (JRDB, page 125, lines 10–13).[75]

A variety of currencies also appear in Richards's daybook, reflecting the complicated currency system of colonial New England.[76] The colonists kept track of their accounts in English pounds, shillings, and pence, but they also used foreign currency such as the Spanish piece of eight, whose value in silver in England was four shillings six pence. After 1687, Massachusetts set its value at six shillings, thus inflating the value of the coins.[77] Bills of exchange and promissory notes functioned alongside the credit system to allow economic transactions without real currency. Where the book debt functioned well at the local level in small scale exchanges, bills of exchange permitted larger scale and international transactions. But they could not overcome the need for a ready supply of cash. James used bills of credit in both local and regional transactions as currency. He wrote in his daybook, for example, "to money paid in bills of credit" (JRDB, page 173, line 26).[78] But this was rare. James only used bills of credit on twelve occasions.

In 1690, the General Court issued the first paper money in promissory notes. It took about a decade for the currency to catch on, but it eventually became the most important medium of exchange.[79] James referred to this money as "paper money," "paper bill," or "province bill." He first used it in 1692, but it never assumed a large role in his commercial transactions.

Colonists may have been short on currency, which made large-scale international trade difficult, but local folks found ways around this, and a surprising number of them had coin on hand when they died. James's daybook and the Weymouth probates demonstrate that the various forms of currency were available. James regularly borrowed and lent money and paid and received money directly for all kinds of goods, labor, and services. Sometimes payment of an account might be split between money and goods.[80] Nearly half of the probates from Weymouth show that individuals possessed cash on hand when they passed away. This mixed economy not only functioned in Weymouth but also in Boston (JRDB, page 244, lines 20–21). It provided the flexibility needed to lubricate the wheels of local and international commerce and the interpersonal relationships built on credit. It was a complicated system, no doubt, but it worked.

Obligatory Reciprocity: Networks and Personal Relationships

James Richards's practice of mixed husbandry and composite farming entangled him in networks of obligatory reciprocity with individuals and families. It is difficult to reconstruct these relationships out of the bare bones of a daybook. But it is evident that James embedded himself in a variety of networks that allowed him to get work done on his farm, to maintain and expand his property, to produce surplus, to acquire artisanal goods he could not make himself, to provide for the next generation, and to protect himself against economic uncertainties. These networks extended beyond his family and neighbors to broader markets. Still, credit networks were not enough. Constant "involvement in community affairs" also provided "social benefits in the form of status and reputation" that could create real opportunities.[81]

We can see the complexity of these relationships in the large number of people with whom James interacted. In the month of August 1705 alone, James dealt with thirty separate individuals in fifty-nine transactions, twenty-six separate commodities, three types of labor, and two types of currency.[82] James exchanged credit with or indebted himself to at least four hundred separate individuals. Almost 50 percent of them formed part of his immediate kin network, either directly or through marriage. In addition, James mentioned another two hundred individuals to whom he delivered goods or who participated in his transactions but were not debtors or creditors.[83] Consequently, Richards's daybook reveals a complicated series of social networks, many of which were facilitated by the obligations of kinship. These networks linked him to neighboring towns and to merchants in Boston in an era when credit relationships were both social and economic and based on trust.

The complicated family connections found in the daybook stem from the fact that James and his wife, Ruth Bicknell, were cousins by marriage. James's mother was Grace Shaw, the sister of Mary Shaw, who was the first wife of John Bicknell. After Mary Shaw passed away in March 1658, John Bicknell married Mary Porter, Ruth Bicknell's mother. John had eleven children with his two wives. This situation meant that James was connected by birth or marriage to all of the prominent families in Weymouth, including the Shaws, Porters, Bicknells, and Lovells.

This also accounts for the way James used kinship terms, such as "brother," "sister," "aunt," and "uncle." James referred to twenty-four people using these kinship terms. He always referred to his mother-in-law, Mary Porter, as "Mother Bicknell"

(JRDB, page 1, line 3; page 3, line 28). His wife, Ruth, always appears as "mother" or "my wife" but never by name (JRDB, page 20, line 12; page 83, line 28). His sisters- and brothers-in-law were simply referred to as "sister" and "brother" regardless of their relationship to him (JRDB, page 95, line 3; page 163, line 32; page 224, line 10; page 244, line 28). He did the same with the terms "uncle" and "aunt" (JRDB, page 32, line 1; page 119, line 3).

James's extended family accounted for 70 percent of the transactions recorded in the daybook. Constable John Green became James's most frequent customer and supplier. This may have been because they were neighbors, but it was also a result of family ties. James's transactions with Green began as early as 1694, but they intensified after 1705, when Green's nephew Ebenezer Whitman married James's niece Deborah Richards.

Green purchased commodities ranging from oats and molasses to soap, cheese, tobacco, and salt. He also paid James to make cider, and he hired James's son, Benjamin, to work as a day laborer. In return, James acquired eggs, hay, chickens, and pork from Green. Mostly, however, Green and his two sons, Zachariah and John, exchanged their labor for the commodities James provided them. Green and his boys loaded carts of hay, corn, oats, lumber, and dung and hauled them for James. They also hilled his fields, sheered his sheep, and butchered his hogs and cattle.

Richards likewise did a brisk business with Enoch Lovell. Lovell married James's niece Mary Reed in 1697, and he was the brother of Joseph Lovell, who married James's daughter Ruth about 1705. Again, James did some business with Lovell prior to Lovell's marriage to Reed, but their business picked up considerably after 1697. James sold Enoch commodities ranging from salt and malt to hides and hats. But it seems clear that Lovell was carrying on his own transactions, as many of the items James charged to his account were delivered to other people. A broom he purchased from James was delivered to Hannah Pray. Malt went to Joseph Richards and Joseph Lovell. Candles were delivered to Benjamin Vining and shingles to Lydia Holbrook and a Mr. Brigham. In return, Enoch employed his skills as a cobbler to make and repair shoes for James and his family.

To his brother-in-law Thomas Bicknell, James sold a variety of goods from malt and fish to butter and tobacco, and he charged Thomas for his son Benjamin's labor and for transport to Boston. James purchased barley, oil, eels, and beef from Bicknell, while hiring him to cut and cart hay and salt grass.

James exchanged significant quantities of malt and salt with his brother-in-law John Bicknell, as well as a variety of other items including indigo, molasses, and rum, in exchange for several hundred bushels of barley. He exchanged shingles and lathe for lumber with his uncle John Vinson. He exchanged malt, barley, and other odds and ends, such as candles and barrels, with his brother-in-law Thomas Reed for barley and oats.

The two nonrelatives with whom James did a fairly regular business were Joseph Orcutt and Jonathan Mountford of Boston. James only purchased lumber from Orcutt but sold him a whole range of goods from molasses and brooms to barley and tobacco. James mostly sold Mountford clapboard and shingles but also the occasional bushel of malt, shot, nails, and hats in exchange for cloth, powder, shot, and oil.

We could continue, but the pattern of James's transactions with his relatives and nonrelatives is clear. He constructed social bonds that required him to provide the services and commodities he could produce while making those he could not

FIGURE 10. Map of Boston Harbor, c. 1700

Map produced by Barry Levely

available to himself. He also tended to concentrate those activities with the people with whom he shared the strongest social and familial bonds.

For this reason, the majority of James's transactions took place with residents of Weymouth. He sold goods to neighboring towns such as Braintree, Bridgewater, Nantasket, Taunton, and Easton, which was called North Purchase at the time. He also sold further north to Charlestown, Hull, and Boston and south to Barnstable on Cape Cod. Most of his non-Weymouth sales went to Braintree and Boston.

His sales to Braintree mimicked the variety he sold in Weymouth. But his sales to Boston were mostly lumber materials including clapboard, lathe, and shingles, though he did sell malt, apples, gunpowder, and cloth to Boston customers. He also engaged in shipping goods to and from Boston for residents of Braintree and Weymouth, such as the barrels of beer he shipped from Boston to Braintree for Lamber Desper, stones from Grape Island to a Mr. Hubbard of Boston, and the sails he shipped from Boston to Thomas White, Jr., of Braintree (JRDB, page 54, line 14; page 46, line 3; page 57, line 10). He also used the sloop *The Three Friends* and a smaller boat as his primary method of shipping bulky goods like timber to Boston (JRDB, page 46, line 3; page 53, line 1; page 31, line 13; page 25, lines 17–18; page 135, lines 6–7; page 115, lines 9–10; page 123, lines 25–27; page 82, lines 1–2; page 149, lines 7–8; page 208, lines 31–32). He delivered goods directly to the Boston wharf and once to a sloop in the harbor (JRDB, page 53, line 1; page 211, lines 1–4; page 213, lines 23–25; page 243, lines 31–33).

In return for these services, James received a steady flow of items from Boston and Braintree but on a much smaller scale and in a narrower range of products. From Boston, he tended to acquire expensive cloth and silk thread, and he used his contacts as sources of credit for monetary loans. From Braintree, he received mostly monetary credit and lumber.

James's accounts also reveal the emerging social and ethnic hierarchies of colonial America. One of the most important was the relationship between fathers and sons. In most cases in early Massachusetts, the father controlled the son's labor until well into his adulthood. Fathers "used their son's labor as a tradable asset" to meet debt payments or acquire credit.[84] A true labor market probably did not exist in Massachusetts until after 1750, which meant that farmers had to rely on the labor of their sons or, failing that, of neighbors, friends, servants, and day laborers, which was most urgently needed at busy times of the year, such as harvest.[85]

Fathers did not normally begin to retire from full participation in the farm until their fifties, which meant that most young men did not "acquire taxable land and livestock until their late 20s or early 30s." They were, therefore, often bound to their father's land and farm—and subject to his authority. Young men often delayed marriage until they could acquire sufficient lands to be economically independent in the hopes that their family members would not have to seek employment outside the circle of the family. Consequently, most did not marry until late into their twenties or thirties.[86]

Using the labor of sons was less exploitative than it might appear. The father gained labor, which allowed him to increase the family's productivity at low cost in the labor-short colony. The son gained security of employment and land independence when the father died.[87] So as long as labor remained scarce and land remained available, this practice served both well.

James did not marry until the same year his father died, 1682, and did not inherit the property left to him until about 1692, when he was thirty-four years old, because William Richards had left his estate to James's mother, Grace, until her death. Only then did it revert to James.[88] This expectation of taxable property meant that James could begin his family only after his father's death and he could not offer credit on his own merit until 1692, when his mother died and the land became his. This explains why James's daybook begins in 1692 and not before.[89]

Servants also appear regularly in the daybook on behalf of their masters. At least fifteen of James's customers had male servants referred to as "his man," "your man," or "your servant" (JRDB, page 186, line 8; page 222, line 5). These servants received or made deliveries and sometimes performed manual labor. If anything, the small number of servants appearing in the daybook is surprising. Daniel Vickers's study of rural farmers in early seventeenth-century Essex County, Massachusetts, found that 72 percent of yeomen farmers employed servants. Unfortunately, we do not have enough information on Weymouth to determine how many farmers in Weymouth employed servants. The sample of fifty-nine probates only show that less than 1 percent owned servants or slaves in Weymouth. Younger families with small children and older families whose children had left were most likely to employ servants.[90]

James also distinguished the ethnicity of the servants when they were not European. He referred to a mulatta owned by Widow Mary White in 1706 and a mulatta owned by Zachariah Bicknell in 1705 to whom he delivered goods ordered by their masters (JRDB, page 161, lines 19–21; page 110, lines 15–16). James referred in his daybook to five people, male and female, who owned what he called "negros" or "niggers." He named Richards Agers's slave Frank "Negro" (JRDB, page 203, lines 7–8). These slaves were used to receive or deliver goods ordered by their masters. For example, Samuel Bill of Boston sent his slave to deliver two pairs of gloves to James (JRDB, page 222, lines 1–2). Four of the fifty-nine probates from Weymouth mention slaves. Samuel White apparently owned a family of slaves—Frank, Zipporah, and their two children, Charles and Margaret. James Richards delivered goods to Frank and Zipporah twice on Mary White's behalf after her husband, Samuel, died in 1699 (JRDB, page 115, lines 17–18; page 161, lines 19–21). In White's probate inventory, his slaves are listed with the animals and the Indian corn. But in his will he left his wife two "feather beds and furniture . . . for [the] servants to lye upon."[91]

Toward the end of James' life, as he and Ruth were getting on in years, they began to hire servants to help around the house. On March 15, 1700, Mary Lamb from Braintree entered their service.[92] After his daughter Ruth married in 1705, James began to use servants more regularly. For instance, John Green's daughter Mary worked for one month and three days for the Richardses in March and April 1709 (JRDB, page 238, lines 27–28). Shortly thereafter, James employed Abiall Boutage to work at the house. She began her service in April 1709 and appeared in the daybook as late as September 1710, a few months before James passed away. It is tempting to conclude that Abiall was the "Indian girl" that appears in James's probate inventory. But this is impossible to verify and somewhat unlikely given that Abiall had a last name.[93]

Native Americans only appeared in James's daybook after 1693, and they always appeared as "his Indian" or "the Indian," without any names (JRDB, page 35, lines 23–24; page 228, lines 10–11; page 155, lines 4–6; page 6, lines 5–7; page 45, line 12). John Holbrook also owned an Indian servant named Anthony in 1699.[94] In a society with no "permanent class of agricultural laborers," landowners in colonial Weymouth sought to expand on the labor of sons and daughters by hiring other people's children, acquiring servants, and even purchasing slaves.[95] In Massachusetts, neither Indian nor African slave labor ever became important to the rural economy, but as James's daybook demonstrates, an ethnically mixed labor economy was developing in colonial Massachusetts.

Relationships with women are some of the most difficult ones to find in daybooks created by men. The old simplistic notion that men and women occupied separate and distinct social and economic spheres has been replaced by a more nuanced understanding that women's lives varied from region to region and that they played crucial roles in the formation and maintenance of social and economic norms.[96]

This lack of rigid boundaries between the male and female spheres of production is reflected in James Richards's daybook. Indeed, women assumed a significant presence in his commercial transactions.[97] His daybook reveals women as producers and consumers of goods and products that entangled them in networks of exchange ranging well beyond the "private sphere" and "female economy."

Over the course of the nineteen years recorded in his accounts, James had direct dealings as a buyer or seller with 76 different women, 41 percent of whom were not related to him. If we add to this the 180 deliveries made to women with whom he had no direct transactions, we find that almost 1 percent of all of James's credits and debits included women. This number may seem low and unimportant, but we need to remember that James recorded his credits more frequently than his debits, so these transactions probably misrepresent the real scale of his dealings with women.

When we add to this the hidden female presence in the form of commodities and services that were produced by or for women, we get a very different picture.[98] At least seventy-seven items appear in the daybook that would have been consumed or produced almost exclusively by women.

Products women would have produced as part of their seasonal activities included candles, biscuits, butter, cheese, cider, bacon, lace, cabbages, eggs, chickens, pumpkins, and turnips, among others. These women would have consumed petticoats, bonnets, bodices, needles, buttons, spices, girdles, brooms, and sieves. Taken together and adjusted to avoid double counting transactions, women and the products they produced or consumed account for 23 percent, or more than one fifth, of all of James's commercial dealings.

The real numbers may very well be higher because of the practice of perceiving women as "deputy husbands." Women could and did engage in commercial transactions in their husband's names and on their own accounts. As essential members of the household, their credit was just as important as that of their husbands, and husbands had an obligation to secure and maintain the good name and credit of their wives.[99]

Such transactions, however, often remain invisible in the accounts as Richards would simply record the husband's name.[100] Sometimes, however, James did note his dealings with women. For example, in 1705, Thomas Kingman's wife placed an order for a load of hay (JRDB, page 107, lines 9–11). James also borrowed money directly from women. For example, in 1705, he borrowed pieces of eight from Enoch Lovell's wife, Mary Reed (JRDB, page 108, lines 4–6).

James also gives us occasional glimpses of the relationships he maintained with the women in his life. James purchased barley, rye, cabbages, wood, turnips, and salt from his mother-in-law, Mary Porter Bicknell. Most of these transactions took place in 1692, and the last occurred on June 21, 1693, just prior to her death (JRDB, page 3, lines 27–30). It seems clear that by regularly exchanging credits with his widowed mother-in-law, James was taking care of her, seeing that her needs were met in a way that allowed her a certain amount of independence.[101]

In 1694, James's sister-in-law Elizabeth Bicknell fell ill. James sent riders to Hingham to fetch the doctor seventeen times, which cost him forty-four shillings six pence. Then he paid for the physician to tend to her for six months for a total coast of seven pounds ten shillings. When she passed away, James paid a pound for her funeral (JRDB, page 17, lines 7–11). Three years later, James recorded the birth of his daughter Mary on April 9, 1697, in a quick note in the midst of his other accounts (JRDB, page 89, lines 24). This notation is particularly poignant as Mary appears in the birth records of Weymouth but then disappears from the vital records.[102] James's will only names his daughter Ruth and his son, Benjamin. Clearly, Mary had passed away before March 1710, when James filed his will.

FIGURE 11. Manuscript page from James Richards's daybook

Source: James Richards Daybook

James's wife, Ruth; his daughter; and his sister-in-law Mary Bicknell also appear in the accounts. On several occasions, James purchased shoes for them, including the fashionable French- and wooden-heeled shoes (JRDB, page 20, lines 7–12; page 38, lines 6–9; page 71, lines 25–35; page 164, line 21; page 83, lines 27–28; page 85, lines 35–37; page 89, lines 10–13). James similarly bought French-heeled shoe for himself, which amounted to a public statement of achieved status as they "not only provided higher physical stature, but were also a self-inflicted sign of 'constrained mobility'. Only the members of the upper classes—men and women alike—could wear shoes that clearly symbolized an inability to walk."[103] Here we see a well-to-do maltster/farmer acquiring the little signs of achieved status.

James engaged his nephew Joseph to make a corset for his daughter Ruth in 1706 (JRDB, page 140, lines 19–20). She delivered rum for him to John Pratt, Jr., in 1705 and received a peck of salt from Nathaniel Ford in 1707 (JRDB, page 111, lines 27–28; page 197, lines 10–11). James also recorded some of the purchases and sales that his wife, Ruth, made on her own account. In 1697, James paid John Hunt to repair a pot leg for Ruth (JRDB, page 80, line 5; page 206, line 4). And in 1707, James charged Zachariah Bicknell and Colonel Ephraim Hunt for the salt that Ruth sold to them (JRDB, page 204, lines 9–10; page 212, lines 10–11). James honored a paper bill of credit Ruth received from Hunt for five shillings (JRDB, page 212, lines 12–13) and charged Nichols Whitmarsh for a bushel of malt Ruth delivered to Mary Flood (JRDB, page 90, lines 18–19). And in 1709, James charged John Torey two pence for pipes Ruth delivered to Torey's son (JRDB, page 240, lines 4–5).

James frequently delivered commodities to the wives of the men to whom they were charged. In 1699, he credited Lieutenant Jacob Nash for money he received from Nash's wife (JRDB, page 75, line 28). In 1705, James billed Thomas Kingman for salt his wife had ordered (JRDB, page 107, lines 9–11). James also charged Mary and Lydia Ford for horse passage to Boston (JRDB, page 227, lines 26–27).

Maids and female servants who were clearly engaging in economic transactions on behalf of their masters or mistresses likewise appear in the daybook. As part of the household, their activities formed part of the reputation of credit worthiness of the entire family and so their economic activities mattered. Maids either received or purchased items such as tallow, yarn, fat, mutton, and worsted ribbing (JRDB, page 49, line 15; page 54, lines 4–5; page 69, line 34; page 147, line 29; page 152, lines 7–8).

James's kept a record of all he purchased for his servant Abiall Boutage. He charged her for items he purchased for her, such as girdles, bonnets, various types of cloth, linen, and shoes. But he also purchased what would have been considered finery for a mere serving girl—including lace, hat cases, silk thread, and expensive cloth. He even gave her eighteen shillings in cash (JRDB, page 178, lines 21–32; page 180, lines 17–36; page 241, lines 5, 24–25; page 242, lines 1–2).

James appears to have kept his servant girl well dressed. When James reckoned accounts with Abiall on July 21, 1709, she owed him £2 8s 9d. He never reckoned accounts for 1710, but she owed him £4 17s 7d (JRDB, page 178, lines 21–24; page 180, lines 17–36). It is unclear if Abiall ever had to pay for the things James gave her, or even if she had the capacity to pay. He may have deducted his costs from her pay, but we have no record of it. Still, James kept track of what he spent on her upkeep in a consumer culture in which even servant girls could enjoy a few of the finer things of life. Perhaps James considered a well-dressed servant as yet one more sign of his acquired status.

James Richards's daybook thus reveals the sometimes invisible world, at least in most men's daybooks, of an economy in which women played a significant role. Women in colonial Weymouth enjoyed a degree of independence, regularly produced goods for the local market, sometimes controlled the products of their labor, and influenced the patterns of consumption and exchange in significant ways. They did not occupy some separate sphere of economic activity but were an integral part of the credit economy.[104] A significant portion of the market production and consumption occurring in Weymouth was household production and consumption in which women played the key role.[105]

Finally, James used his involvement in community affairs to construct and maintain personal relationships, to build his reputation and gain influence.[106] After reaching his majority of twenty-five years in 1683, James quickly entered public life. He served the town as a fence viewer (1684–85, 1686–87, 1697–98), a constable (1689–90), and a tithingman (1693–94, 1694–95, 1700–1701, 1701–2). He also served two terms as selectman (1698–99, 1704–5) and several as highway surveyor (1702–3, 1703–4, 1704–5, 1707–8). Sometime in 1701, James was made a sergeant, probably in the town militia, and the town records begin to refer to him as Sergeant Richards.[107] He served on several town committees to find schoolmasters and negotiate the minister's salary.[108] He also collected the minister's rate, the tax imposed on members of the town for the support of the minister (JRDB, page 18, lines 19–34; page 62, lines 6–22; page 81, line 24; page 126, lines 14–28; page 167, line 12; page 169, lines 20, 33; page 173, line 18).

This community involvement created both conflicts and opportunities. James Richards was elected constable on June 24, 1689, with Stephen French. French refused to serve, and Benjamin Ludden was appointed in his stead. The town issued a warrant to fine French five pounds, which Richards collected. French continued to petition the town and finally on April 9, 1692—"after some debate with Stephen French, Senior"—the selectmen decided to let French reclaim the money.[109]

For the nineteen years recorded in the daybook, James spent ten of them in public service.[110] Even though some of his town appointments were not necessarily prestigious positions, they were still a necessary part of the construction of his reputation and status in the community, which in turn gave him access to the relationships that permitted the efficient functioning of his farm.

Conclusion

James Richards's daybook reveals the complex interplay of mixed husbandry, composite farming, and credit relationships that dictated the pace and quality of life in colonial Weymouth.[111] It also reveals the ongoing chains of reciprocity that needed to be remembered and reconciled.[112] In his daybook, the household economy functioned alongside, and embedded within, the larger regional and export-oriented economy. Exotic goods entered this household economy to be consumed for the purposes of fashion, not simple survival, as James sought a comfortable independence for his family.[113]

Indeed, men like James Richards, through their practices of giving and receiving credit, reckoning their accounts, exchanging goods and services locally and regionally, and constructing networks of credit that extended beyond their own kin groups, helped foster "the economic interdependence necessary" for survival and expansion. They created and defined "the ground rules of local economic life." This local trade "fostered the economic and infrastructural stability that launched the region into international markets."[114]

As one of the few extant daybooks from this period, James Richards's daybook provides a rare glimpse of the intricate networks that generated the pulse of life in rural communities. This snapshot of one man's credit relationships confirms much of what is already known about economic relationships in early colonial America, while challenging us to abandon the search for dramatic revolutionary moments of change in American agricultural and economic history in favor of slow evolutionary transformations and continuities.[115]

The James Richards Daybook, 1692–1711

[Page 1][116]

	ll	s	p
James Richards his book to keep his debters in			
and to give Credit			
N Mother Bicknill[117] Credeter, ceeping of sheep			
in 1692 1 of twelve penc a sheep e lamb	00	09	o?
for carting of hay to the barn	00	04	o[?]
for seven bushel and a half of apels	00	03	1[?]
for mooney	00	00	[??]
for one peck of ry	00	00	09
for ayt chabigase	00	01	00
for twenty four bushels of malt	03	00	00
for 6 bushels of turnops			
~~for fife foot of ocke wood~~	~~00~~	~~09~~	~~[??]~~
for 6 bushels of turnops	00	07	o[1]
for 9 feet of cordwood	00	08	00
for fife of walnut wood	00	05	00
for 3 cord e a halef of ocke wood	01	04	00
March the 3: 1693 Joseph hunt credetor for six bushe			
ls e a halef of barly Dll to Joseph hunt foure bushels			
e a halef of malt Dll to Joseph Richards and his debters			
September ye 27 1692 John green creditor for four pigs			
e one fat cow in mony [Ness] [?] [Inus] [as] [as] and R	04	5	00
September ye 27 1692 John green debter for			
money paid in earnist for the above pigs e cow	00	07	00
october ye 28 1692: John Randal debter for 97			
pounds of beef at a 1 peney hapeny per pound	00	12	2[?]
october: 1692: Wido baily debter for paper mony	03	00	[??]
which is to be paid to mee in barly at two shillings per			
bushel e or corant mony of new ingland at nineteen shillings			
for twenty whicks	2	17	[??]
wido smit debter in ~~92~~ october: 92 for 73 pound			
of beef e for quarts of salt: for the which shee is to			
pay mee four bushels of good sound indian corn	06	10	[??]
november: 1692: Zackariah Bicknill debter f[or]			
fife pound of money lent to him by mee			
~~october the 2[5]~~ november the 25: 1692 lent to Zack[?]			
bicknill ~~[twenty] pounds~~ in money for a knife	01	01	[?]
[o]f lard e all to gether			

[Page 2]

Line	ll	s	p
[i]une the 28 recned with Mother Bicknill e there was dwe			
to her from mee: 24: bushels of malt			
[i]une 28 paid to Mother Bicknill in severall peticulars	00	11	08
for a [r]unin bag: e six quarts of lamp oyle	00	04	00
f one dayes work at moing of otes	00	03	00
for solit oyle	00	00	03
September 19: lent in money	03	00	00
September 28 for barels e salt e nails	01	08	08
for ~~muten~~ beef 9 2/1	00	01	02
to mary bicknill[118]	00	01	03
for macrell	00	05	00
[Oct]ober ye 17: for three paper bils[119]	03	00	00
for one peck of salt	00	01	03
~~for 6 bushels of turnops~~	~~00~~	~~07~~	~~06~~
	16	03	
[De]sember the 27: 1692 reconed with Mother Bicknill			
e thare was dwe from hur to mee	11	15	00
[Fe]burary the 28th 1693 for 14 bushels of barly			
for 2 bushels of malt			
for 5 bushels e a halef barly			
for one peck barly			
for three bushels of malt dll to Thomas			
~~[?] [prat] debter for a dayes [moing]~~	~~00~~	~~03~~	~~00~~
[Ec]ebod holbrook debter for a dayes moing	00	03	00
February 1693 Mother Bicknill~~d~~ crediter for 46 bushels			
e a halef of barly e feches: e for money	03	00	00
1693			
Aperel the 26 Joseph Richards debter for one pare			
of trases e hames six bushels of otes to be paide at			
next Chrismas after the date heer of e thirty shillings			
in indian corne good and marchantable e ten shillings in			
otes to be good e merchantable e to be paid at the corant			
price as I can by for mony at the same time insuing after			
the date heere of			
June the 5th 1693 Joseph Richards debter for mony			
dll to himself	09	00	00
July the 2: 1693 Samuell King debter for two			
pound of tobacka at 6 d per pound	00	01	00
for one dayes moing salt grass	00	03	00
[?] a cock to fite	00	00	08
[Aper]el the 26th dll to himself two bushels e a halef of malt			
in [m]oney	00	00	02

[Page 3]

	ll	s	p
iuly th 2 1692 Ebenezar ^{White} debter for money lent	05	00	00
october 27 reseved of Ebenezar Whit 10 bushels			
of barly	01	05	00
for 10 bushels of barly	01	05	00
desember ye 13th 1692 Samuel King cred			
etor for one bushel e a halef of barly			
14th seven bushel e halef a peck of barly			
Jenuary the 3: debter to Samuel King for ten bushels			
barly: more one [3] bushels barly			
march the: 31: 1693: Samuell King debter for thre bushels			
barly for feed			
25 of the 2 [moth] for mony	00	03	00
may the 25th: 1693: Jacob nash debter for two bushels of			
malt dll to his son Thomas nash	00	07	00
dito two bushels malt to Thomas nash	00	07	00
Desember ye 13th Samuel king debter for			
money towards the barly	00	02	04
pheburary 1693: reseved of William hunt twenty bushels			
of barly			
pheburary 1693 dll to William hunt three bushels e a halef			
malt			
march the 23 payde to William hunt in mony	01	04	09
which was for nine bushels of barly			
march ~~the 24~~ for one bushel of malt			
more 4 bushels dll to him selef			
more payd in money and bushel	00	03	00
June the 21th 1693 recned e cleared upon all acounts			
with mother Bicknill e thare was Dwe to mee from			
her two bushels e a peck of malt			
in money	00	07	00
a peck of ground malt			
for one pound of sheeps wool	00	01	00
January the 20th 1693 Samuell King credetor for sixteen			
bushels ~~of~~ e a halef of barly			
Samuel king debtor for money that hee had of cotes[120]	01	00	[??]
iuly the 16th for 9 bushels of indian corn of Samuel [Speer]	00	15	[??]
november the 3 paid to Samuel king to balance	01	02	[??]

[Page 4]

Line	ll	s	p
July th 8 1692 recned with Samuell Speer e			
thare was dwe ffrom him to mee ayt bushe			
ls of indian corn good e marchantable			
e furdermore two cord e a halef of good ocke wood			
at the water side in brantery neck ~~all which is in money~~	01	16	06
[oct]ober 26th 1692 William Reed debter for paper			
money to pay his rate paid to edward bates	04	12	02
which is to be paid to mee in silver mony			
at nineteen shillings for twenty in paper which is	04	04	00
November ye 2 ant: for one hudered e fifty pound of			
pork dll at his hous by my selef at 2 ½ ^{d}			
per pound	01	12	08
1692			
[d]esember the 17th debter to goodman dun for 3 bu			
shels of barly, paid for the same			
two pounds of candels	00	01	00
march 1693 for one pound of candels	00	00	06
may the 25th: 1693: Jacob Nash debter			
for two bushels of malt dll to his son Thomas	00	07	00
29 dll to Thomas nash two bushels malt	00	07	00
iune the 5 dll to him selef ^{24} foure bushels of malt	04	04	00
James Humphrey ~~d~~ credeter for 22 sheeps e eleven			
in the year 1693 the hole payde to him selef	07	03	00
payd for the above said sheep e lames	01	16	00
for halef a barel of salt e a hogsed	00	12	06
october the 2 ^{nt} 1693 Joseph Drake creditor for ffife			
bushels e six quarts of barly			
payd 4 bushels e six quarts in mo^{ney}	00	15	??
more a bushel of malt dll to youre son[121]			
Jenuary the 19th 1694 William pitey creditor for ~~6~~			
six bushels of barly, more reseved—37 bushels e 3 peck			
march the: 16: 1694 dll to william pitey in money	00	10	00
dll to youre son william[122] in money balanced this [?]	00	15	00
Samuell King credetor for 3 bushels e peck of barly			
[i]n Jenuary 1695: March the 30th: 1695 delivered			
Samuel kings son hezekiah two bushels of malt			
~~[?er]~~ october the 3 1696 Maier hunt[123] debter for a quarter ^{muten}	00	02	00
for 25 pound of muten	00	05	02
for 20 [2/] of chees at 3^{d} per pound	00	07	1

[Page 5]

	ll	s	p
October ye 17 1692 Nathanell fford debter for			
two paper bils	01	02	00
for sheep bostoun	00	00	06
for macerel e crickthach	00	01	00
malt	00	13	00
debter to brother fford[124] for weving one pees 15 ^{tee} yards wo^{l}	00	08	09
for 19 yard woolling cloth	00	14	04
~~for one bushel of barly~~	~~00~~	~~03~~	~~06~~
Captaine White debter for a quarter of pork: 34 pound	00	08	06
Liftenant Nash[125] debter for a quarter of pork 34 pound	00	08	06
Jenuary the: 2: 1692 William Pitey debter for [ⱡ] two			
Bushels of malt dll to his sun William			
For 10 bushels of Indian corn,	01	07	06
Aperel the: 3: 1693 Abia Whitman debter for two bushels			
Of malt dll to his son John: n. may the 5th dll			
To John Whitman ~~two bushels of malt~~ the son to Abia			
Whiteman one bushel e a halef of malt			
Jenuary the 22 th: 1694 Abia Whitman credetor for 7			
Bushels e a halef of barly more for 3 bushels e 3 peck of barly			
More ffourteen bushels of barly more 3 bushels e 3 peck, the hole			
[p] is 29 bushels: reseved in money	00	04	00
March the 21: 1693/4 dll to Zacarya Bicknill upon			
Abia Whitmans account by verball order twenty bushels of			
Malt, dll to him two bushels of malt; the same time dll			
To him selef in money	00	02	00
[nils] dll to him selef in money	01	00	00
dll to John Whitman two bushels of malt	00	07	08
October the 14: 1696 Maier Hunt debter for one side			
side of muton 22 pound two penc 2/1 per pound	00	04	07
for 45 pound of muton at 2 2/1 per pound e hed e pluck	00	09	05
for beef 54 pound at 2 2/1 per pound	00	11	03
reseved of Abia Whitman in 1695 ayte bushels of			
of barly, Aperel 95 dll to John Whitman one			
bushel of malt, aperel 27th dll to John Whitman two			
Bushels of malt: for one bushel e a halef of malt dll to John			
Whitman			
July 1696 Mayor Ephraim Hunt debter for one			
hundered wait of chees at 30^{s} per hundered	01	10	00
for twelvef pound of muton at 3^{d} 3^{d} penc per pound	00	03	00
for eleven pound of bacon at 8^{d} per pound	00	07	04
ogaust for 12 pound of veale at 3^{d} per pound	00	03	o[?]
September the 2 dll to youre sun Ephraim Hunt 68 pounds of ^{chees}	01	00	o[?]
September 26 to maier hunt 11 pound muton	00	02	o[?]

[Page 6]

Line		ll	s	p
1	Desember the 26: 1692 John Bicknill Debter			
2	for one bushel e a halef of malt	00	04	06
3	Aperel the: 8: 93 dll foure bushels of malt			
4	Aperel the 27 dll for ten bushels of barly	01	10	00
5	May the 2 nt Zackaryah Bicknill debter for three bushels			
6	of malt: dell to the Indian one bushel of malt			
7	dll to him selef one bushel e a halef of malt			
8	Jenuary the 27th ~~reseved~~ 1692/3 reseved of			
9	John Bicknill sixteen bushels of barly			
10	Wido Pitey debter for three pound of ~~tobac~~ hoges fat			
11	e halef pound of tobacka	00	01	06
12	for one bushel of malt dll to John pitty	00	04	00
13	for one pound of tobacka dll to John pittey	00	00	06
14	for halef a peck of salt	00	00	08
15	for one bushel of salt	00	05	06
16	Wido Pitty credeter for mony: 1693	00	00	08
17	for two bushels e a halef of barly			
18	reseved of John Pitey in money	00	01	00
19	In 93 brother fford credetor for one pees of woolng cloth			
20	31 yards at 7d per yard	00	18	0~~0~~1
21	for 20 yards of shering at 4 per yard	00	06	08
22	for one pare of wimins shoos	00	04	06
23	for a cake at talo 10 pound	00	03	04
24	for money that I had of him	01	10	00
25	March the 13 reved in Barly nine bushels e a peck	01	16	10
26	of barly two 8 yards e ~~d~~ a halef of Shorting	00	02	02
27	for one bushel of otes	00	01	06
28	for halef a peck of indian corn	00	00	05
29	for halef a peck corn e three dayes work	00	06	04
30	November the 22nt 1694 Brother fford debter for two bushels			
31	of malt dll to him selef			
32	Desember the 3rd for foure peck of benes	00	04	00
33	for a stick baskit hold about one bushel e a halef	~~00~~	~~01~~	~~06~~
34	Desember the 19 dll to Brother fford forty bushels			
35	of malt coms to in money	04	03	04
36	Jenuary the 5th for three bushels of barly			
37	dito for six bushels of malt			
38	dito for foure wethers at ayt e three penc a pees	01	13	00
39	March the [?] th dll to brother fford one bushel e a halef barly			

[Page 7]

	ll	s	p
Desember the: 3 1692 Samuel Speer			
Debter for twelve sheep dll Jorge			
Witey[126] ~~twelve~~ twenty bushels e fife bush			
els of Indian corn good e marchant	03	02	06
January 1692/3 debter to James e Nathaniel Hump			
hry twenty seven bushels of barly			
Pheburarey the: 4: ~~9~~ 1693 ~~dll~~ James Humphrey debter			
for [?] two bushels of malt dll to Joseph Pitey			
March the: 25: dll to Nathanell Humphrey four bushels malt			
March 14 dll to James Humphrey 3 bushels of malt			
Brother fford debter in 97 for mony lent	01	10	00
for two bushels of otes	00	03	00
for one bushel of malt	00	04	00
Jenuary the 31 for ten bushels of Indian corn	01	07	00
for a copey of an agreement	00	00	06
March the 13 dll to him selef fife bushels malt	01	00	00
March the: 28: delivered to Jzerel ford in money	00	05	00
Aperel the: 3: dll foure bushels of seed barly	00	16	00
for one bushel of barly	00	04	00
for one pare of huck e hinges	00	01	00
for three dayes work of the beniamins[127]			
May the 31th: for two caleffs e one cow	~~04~~	~~00~~	~~00~~
Balenct accouptents the 21th of november 1694 e thare was done			
To him from mee in money	~~00~~	~~01~~	~~06~~
Dito for fifty six bushels ~~e a halof~~ barly			
Balanced accounpts with Brother Ford in november ~~1694~~ the			
21st 1694 e thare was dwe to him from mee			
in money	00	01	00
dito for barly fifty: ~~e fiv~~ foure ~~bushels~~ e foure bushels			
more reseved fife bushels e a halef e halef a peck			
~~of~~ of barly			
for a pees of wooling carsi cloth: 34: yards at 7 ^{d} per yard	01	00	00
for a pees of shurting at 4^{d} penc per yard 50 yards	00	16	08
March the 3th delivered to Brother fford 3 bushels e a halef of			
seed barly: Aperel the 6th: dll to Brother fford one bushel			
e a halef of barly, dll him—selef two bushels of barly			
for foure of bushels of malt j cared to mill my selef			

	ll	s	p
March the 4: 1693 reseved of Thomas Reed thurty			
bushels e three peck of barly more 7 peck			
March the 28: 1693 dll to Thomas Reed one peck malt			
May 31 for two bushels of mallt dll to Thomas			
July 4 for foure bushels of malt			
for money dll to Mary ^{d} reed 25 bushels	04	07	06
for moing of ~~sal~~ salt grass	00	01	00
for two bushels of malt dll to Thomas ~~the~~			
John Bicknill debter for one bushel of salt	00	05	06
January the 5 1694 for a bushel of malt	00	04	00
for one shilling reseved of youre father sichor money[128]	~~00~~	~~01~~	~~00~~
Aperel the 3 dll to him selef two bushels of barly			
dito: 13: dll to him selef three bushels of malt			
dll to him selef one bushel of malt			
January the 21th 1693/4 John Bicknill credeter for ~~teen~~ ten			
bushels of barly			
1694			
Aperel the: 16th Debter to Thomas Reed snr for ~~thurty~~			
forty fife bushels e a halef of barly			
~~for one bushel of malt dll to him selef~~			
payd to balance with prother reed[129] in money			
to balanc the accounpt for [~~th~~] the above barly	04	13	06
Aperel the furst: 1695 Thomas Bicknill debter for			
three bushels of malt dll to him selef			
dito for three bushels e a halef of seed barly dll him selef			
dito for ~~three bushels~~ two bushels of barly dll to him selef			
dito for two bushels of barly dll to him selef: dll to John			
Gurney two bushels malt			
Reseved of Thomas Bicknill in aperell: 1695			
twenty three bushels e a peck of barly			
John Shaw Jun debter for ~~two acres~~ [?] plowing of two acres			
of hils in the ferey feeld at 4^{s}–6^{d} per acer	00	09	00
dito for soing of otes e plowing e bushing	00	08	06
two pound of tobacka	00	01	0~~9~~0
may the 10th and 29 dll 1695 dll to Thomas Reed Junr two bushels			
of malt: more dll for youre selef three bushels of malt			

	ll	s	p
May the 18th 1693 Samuell Speer debter for sheep			
delivered to him by my selef twenty two bushels of indi			
an corn good e marchantable	02	15	00
May the 19th 1693 Beniaman Sables[130] debter for			
eleven sheep e seven lames deivered to him			
by my selef at brantery at hes one houce	03	15	00
lent March the 21th 1692 to Cornelus Holbrook as			
for loeth,: two bushels & a halef of barly: at the same			
time one bushel of Indian corn: dll Thomas Bayly			
the 27th halef a bushel of barly & a bushel of otes dll to			
thomas bayly,: dito for one bushel of otes dll to Thomas			
bayly			
Thomas Bicknill debter in Desembar the 25: 1963			
for one bushel e a halef of malt			
peburary the 15th 1693/4: reseved of Thomas Bicknill Credetor			
for twelvef bushels of barly: which is beetween Zackarah Bicknill			
e Thomas Bicknill			
Brother Thomas Reed credetor in ~~the~~ phebürary the 25th 1693/4			
for thurty two bushels of barly: more for ffifteen [?] bushels			
of barly			
aperel the ~~2~~ 12th: 1694 recened e cleered with Thomas Reed Snr upon all			
acunpt e thare was dwe to mee from him three			
peck of ~~on~~ barly, e one shilling in money	00	01	00
May the 8th dll to him selef three bushels of malt			
iuly the 16th dll to him selef ~~ther~~ three bushel of malt			
for moing of salt grass	00	01	00
for two pound of candels dll youre wife	00	01	00
for one pound of candles dll to him selef	00	00	06
Phebürary the 28th: 1694/5 reseved of Brother Thomas Reed			
forteen bushels of barly: March the 1 reseved of Thomas			
reed Jun 6 six bushels of barly: March the 16th reseved of			
Thomas Reed Juni twenty ~~thre~~ three bushels of barly			
more reseved 14 ~~tt~~ teen bushels of barly			
paid in Desember 1695 the full of the above barly			
John Shaw June credeter for six bushels of barly braft			
in desember 1695 payd balanced for the barly may			

Line		ll	s	p
1	September 1693 Brther John dyer of bostoun Debter			
2	for twenty foure bushels of apels at 2^{s} per bushell	02	08	00
3	for ffour bushels of malt at 4^{s} per bushel	00	16	00
4	one bushel e a halef of appels	00	03	00
5	Jenuary the 3: 1694 Debter to the wido Bayly for twelef			
6	bushels of barly: more one bushel of barly			
7	wido Bayly Debter for two needles at a peney pees	00	00	02
8	aperel the 14th dll to ebenezer prat three bushels			
9	of ~~otes~~ otes at one Shilling 6^{d} per bushel	00	04	06
10	for one hundered of shoenayeles	00	00	05
11	for one black dog dll to hur	00	00	01
12	for moing of one acer of salt grace	00	03	03
13	november the 16 9 [1]694 Delivered John prat junr	01	04	00
14	dll Ebenezer prat one bushel of mal[t]			
15	march the 13th 1695 brother Joseph Richards Debter			
16	for sixteen yards of damaresh[131] at: 2^{s}–6^{d} per yard	02	00	00
17	dito for foreteen bushels of barly at 3^{s}: per bushel	01	12	00
18	dll to remembr Brigs in money	00	07	00
19	may foure bushels of malt dll to Joseph Green	00	12	00
20	one bushel e a ~~h~~ halef of rye	00	05	00
21	june the 8th dll to brother Joseph[132] in money	00	12	00
22	for the same dll to him selef	01	11	00
23	for ~~nail~~ nailes for the lentwo	01	00	00
24	for one quarter of lam 6 pound a 2 $^{d\ 2/1}$ penc per pound	00	01	00
25	for one pees of ayte	00	06	00
26	for three pound of coton wooll at = 1^{s} 9^{d} per pound	00	05	03
27	july dll to Thomas Randall one bushel of malt upon			
	Joseph Greens acounpt	00	03	00
28	for foure pound of coton wooll at = 01^{s}–9^{d} per pound	00	07	00
29	for a pare of hinges	00	01	04
30	for seven bushels of malt Delivered to Joseph Green	01	01	00
31	for lime: 12 bushels thirteen shillings	10	03	07
32	for 100 e 50 clabords 00 = 06 = 00		13	00
33	This above same debt balanced with my sister[133]	10	16	07
34			6	
35	july 1696 Debter to Maier Ephraim Hunt for	11	02	07
36	one pees of ayt, more for seven peeses of ayt	02	08	00

[Page 11]

	ll	s	p
September 1693 brother John Dyer of Bostoun Credetor for			
foure barels of Salt: at 1^{ll} = 0^{s} = 6^{d} per barel	04	02	00
for one hogsed with one hed	00	01	06
for 5 bushels indian mele	00	15	00
for two barels of salt	01	17	00
Nathanell humphrey Credetor in Jenuary the 12: 1693/4			
for nineteen bushels of barley, ~~for~~ reseved more 22			
bushels of barley in January the: 20:			
phebyrary the 24: 1693/4 James Humphrey debter for one bushel e a			
halef of malt, for six bushels of malt dll to him selef			
march the 25: dll to ~~S~~ Nathanell humphrey two			
bushels e halef of malt			
September 17th 1694 reseved of brother fford thurty one bushel			
e a halef of barly more reseved twenty ayte bushels e a ~~h~~			
halef of barly			
brother ford debter in 1694 for two bushels of barly			
november the 6th for two bushels of barly			
September: 1694: ~~W~~ Maier Ephraim Hunt Debter			
for salt hay dll Brantere side to him selef	01	10	00
for mony lent for his son to him selef	00	01	00
~~for upon cotes acouppts~~ for money upon Thomas cotes[134] acou^{npt}	01	00	00
november the 14th for two hogs dll ~~lb~~ to his wife: 310	03	02	00
reseved of Maier Hunt of the above money	01	07	00
recned with prother Bicknill the 11 of desember			
1694 e there was dwe to him from mee one bushel e a			
peck ~~of~~ e 5 ~~quarts~~ quarts of malt			
desember1694 dll to brother Bicknill one bushel			
e a peck of malt dll to brother Bicknill half of a peck malt			
~~march the 12th 1695 d~~: Cornelias Holbrook debter			
Aperel the: 13th: 1695			
for one bushel of malt at ~~th~~ 3^{s} Shillings ~~e~~ per bus^{hel}	00	03	00
for ~~the tw~~ two bushel of barley dll to him selef	01	06	00
aperel the 30 dll to John vinning three pound buter 6^{d} per po^{und}	00	01	06

Line		ll	s	p
1	phebury the 7th 1694, Thomas Cotes			
2	debter for for beef e candels e tobackah	10	00	00
3	pheburary the: 16: 1693/4 recned e cleered with zacharah bicknill			
	upon all acounts e thare was			
4	dwe to mee from him in money	00	09	06
5	more for three bushels of indian corn	00	09	00
6	for one bushel e a halef of hare	00	01	06
7	for foure bushels of malt dll to Thomas bicknill by order	00	16	00
8	dll to zacaryah bicknill fifteen bushels of malt			
9	march the 27 I lent ~~to~~ in mony to him selef	00	07	00
10	reseved of zackariah bicknill for the above			
11	debt three bushels of indian corn	~~00~~	09	00
12	June the 2th ~~19~~ 1694 John boutage[135] debter for two bushels of			
13	malt dll to his wief	00	02	00
14	Thomas Bicknill credetor for two grates in money	00	00	08
15	for two peeses of ayt in money	00	12	00
16	for rum	00	01	09
17	for two peses of ~~ayt~~ ayt	00	12	00
18		01	06	05
19	the 14 day of november 1694 Samuell King debter for ~~four~~			
20	~~11 bushels of malt~~ one bushel e a halef of malt	00	04	06
21	pheburary the 22^{nt} Brother John Richards debter for seven sheep			
22	at fife Shillings e 3 1/2 penc pr sheep ~~01 10~~	01	17	00
23	for one quarter of mutten	00	01	03
24	reseved for the above said sheep in money one Shilling	00	01	00
25	1695			
26	Insine philips[136] debter for ayte pound of muten	00	01	08
27	more for nine pound of mutene	00	01	10
28	more for three pound of moten	00	00	08
29	for halef a pound of pouder	00	01	06
30	~~for foure pound of coten wool~~	~~00~~	~~07~~	~~00~~
31	for one pound of candeles 7^{d} per pound	00	00	07
32	dll to him selef in money fife Shillings	00	05	00
33	for foure fishes 1^{d} ½ per fishe	00	00	06
34	for money dll to him selef	00	06	00
35	for a qurter of moten 10 pound	00	01	10
36	for one quarter of muten 9 pound e halef	00	01	09
37		1	1	4

[Page 13]

	ll	s	p
pheburary the 16th 1693 Zacheriah Bicknill Credetor For: 19: bushels			
of barly: the same time Thomas Bicknill Credetor for: 23: bushels			
of barly			
pheburary: 16: 1693 Thomas bicknill debter for in mony	00	04	06
dll to Thomas bicknill one bushel of malt			
march the: 28th dll to Izerell Ford by verbal order			
~~one bush dll to thomas bicknill~~			
two bushels e a halef of barly			
~~more of for one bushel of malt~~			
more for six bushels of malt dll to him selef			
aperel the 9th dll to Abraham blancher three bushels of			
malt by a tocon of malt Captain White			
for one bushel~~s~~ e a halef of barly			
Aperel the 27th dll to thomas bicknill six bushels of malt			
pheburary 16th 1693 Thomas Bicknill debtor ~~to~~ in mony	00	04	06
for a bag e a sieth	00	09	06
for a sith e a bridel	00	04	06
for three bushel of indian corn	00	09	00
for one quart of salt e a halef a pound of candels	00	00	05
for 19 teen pound of pork at four penc per pound	00	06	04
for beef e halef a bushel of corn	00	09	09
~~resey~~ reseved the full of this debt	02	04	00
november the 30 1694 Thomas Bicknill debter for			
halef a bedcord three fadam e a halef	00	00	09
Jenearey the 25th 1694/5 peetor ~~harvey~~ harvi			
debter for forty six pound of porck at 3d ½ per pound			
Coms tow	00	13	05
dito for tree pound e a penath of tobacka	00	01	07
Captain Samuel White debter for three peck ~~bushel~~ of malt			
dll to peeter harvi in Jenuary the 25th 1694/5			
more for 5 bushels e 3 peck of malt e a pece of			
Ayt in money the hole is in money	01	04	00
october the 19th 1695 Giden Turell debter for a			
hefer of two yeeres e the vantage olde ~~to~~be			
To be paye to my order the next march	02	01	00

[Page 14]

	ll	s	p
march: 7: 1694 peeter dunbar debter for sheep woooll			
containing a fleec	00	04	00
march the: 5: 1694 wido ~~Cing~~ King debter for			
seven peck of barly at ~~fou a~~ twelve penc			
per peck	00	07	00
Liftenant Nash debter in September 94 for 89 pound of			
beef at 2^{d} penc per pound	00	13	8
~~Io~~ edmon Jakson 93 pound of peef	~~00~~	~~15~~	~~00~~
Thomas White 91 pound e 2 pound [?] c a s halef [?]	~~00~~	~~16~~	~~00~~
John hunt for beef halef a quarter 45	~~00~~	~~07~~	~~06~~
Liftenant White for a quarter of beef 19	~~00~~	~~15~~	~~00~~
Captaine White for a quarter of beef 19	~~00~~	~~15~~	~~00~~
~~Brother Joseph Richards~~			
March the 7^{nth}: 1695 Brother Joseph Richards debter			
For three bushels of barly dll to him selef	00	09	00
March the 18th: 1695 ~~John pratt Junr~~ debter			
For ayt sheep e foure lames at fife e 10^{d} penc per sheep			
e fife e 10^{d} penc per lam comes to	~~02~~	~~18~~	~~00~~
March the 18th: 1695 John Prat Junr debter for			
Ayte sheep e foure lambes at foure Shillings e			
Ten penece per pees ^{both} bot^{h}~~ehe~~ sheep e lambes	02	18	00
reseved of John pratt two pound money, more	0	18	00
Insine phillips debter for two quarters of moten			
In yune 1695 July for one quarter of muten	00	01	08
	00	01	10
July the 10th 1695 John porter ^{junr} debter for			
two bushels of malt deli to ebeneser porter	00	06	00
desember the: 16th: 1695 Ebeneser Cornat White[137] deb			
ter for forteen bushels of barly to bee dll at his one hous			
pheburarey the: 3^{d}: 1695^{6} William Pitey Credetor for eleven			
bushels e a peck of barly D dll to youre wiefe[138]	01	04	00
peburary: 1695/6 William pitey debter for three bushels			
e a peck of barly dll by James humphrey			
Aperel the 21st for salt hay dll to his son	00	08^{2}	00
For one peace of ayt paid by [lt?] way	00	06	00

	ll	s	p
Aperel the: 3: 1694 Joshua Smith debter for ~~foure~~			
three bushels of barly at foure shillings per bushel	00	12	00
July the 2th ant 1694 boroed of James humphrey in money e it			
remaines dwe to him till now	20	00	00
July the 2 ant boroed of brother Thomas Reed in money 1694			
sex pound ~~in~~ which ~~is~~ is dwe to him till ~~now~~			
July the 2 ant 1694 I boroed of Cosen Thomas porter[139] in money			
seven pound e ten shillings e it ~~s~~ is dwe to him till ~~n now~~ paid this sum			
Enoc Lovel debter for one hide in september 1694: september wait 46			
in the same month for one hide wait 56			
For one hide more in octeber te furst wait 53			
Jenuary the 30: 1694/5 reseved John Bicknill fifteen			
bushels of barly			
Feburarey the 27th: 1694/5 delivered to brother John			
bicknell two bushels of malt: Aperel dll one bushel			
of barly: dito for four buchels of barly dll to him selef			
June dll to bushels of malt to him selef			
recned e cleered the hole barly the furst of September 1695			
desember the 18th: 1695 Joshua Smith Credetor for			
foure bushels e a halef of barly			
Joshua Smith debtor for a pare of shoos	00	01	00
March the 26: 1696 for a horce in money	00	12	08
May the 21st: ~~167~~ 1697: Robbord Adcisins[140] debtor for			
54 bushels of malt dll at Bostound at five shillings per			
Bushel which is	13	10	00
reseved for the above malt in money	01	04	00
more I reseved in money	12	06	00

[Page 16]

	ll	s	p
Aperel the 16th 1694 Wido pitey debter for ~~foure~~			
~~bushel~~ one bushel of barly dll to Joseph pitey	00	04	00
the 13th of october 1694 Thomas porter debter for			
two pound of candels e a paire of wimans shoos	00	05	06
october the 31th for one hide wait 57 pound	00	09	06
pheburary the 28th 1694/5 reseved of William pitey a: 11:			
leven bushels of barly: more reseved in barly twelvef			
bushels e six quarts paye the full of this above barly			
July 1695 Thomas porter debter for one ox hide			
waite 66 pound	00	11	00
~~agust the 23~~th october the: 23th: for three yards e three			
quarters of wooling caresi cloth of: 5^{s}: per yard	00	18	09
for one hide 57 pound e for one paire of shoos e candels	00	~~05~~14	06
for one cows hide wait 60 pound	00	10	00
for a hog Dll to him selef	01	05	00
July 1697 John green credetor for the caring			
of 4 cocks of otes out of the fere feeld	00	00	09
for three lodes from the hed of the orchard	00	01	06
for the caring of dyng at wido Humphreys ~~the~~ horce	00	00	06
for the horce caring of two lode to rose hill	00	00	06
for one lode te fere feeld corne e stockes	00	00	06
for carting of corne home lot	00	02	00
for muney paide	00	04	00
october the 12th: 1697 John Green debters for quorter			
of lamb ayt pound e three quorters Dll to John Bicknill	00	01	10
for ~~4~~ making of 4 barels of sider for him selef	00	05	00
for three pound of motten at 3^{d} per pound	00	00	09
for a peck of salt dll Johnathan daese[141]	00	01	03
money pd ~~lld~~ dll to him selef	00	01	00
march the 30th for cuting ~~of~~ out of riding hood	00	00	03
for two quarts of otes e a quarte of indian corne	00	00	03
may the 2^{nt} for two bushels of malt dll to him selef	00	08	00
for a fish dll to Johnath Dase	00	00	03
for one ~~qor~~ quart malases dll hana gren	00	00	06
for an ounce of indego Dll to youre wife	00	00	06
~~for a halef a pint of rum Dll to Johnathon Dase~~	~~00~~	~~00~~	~~03~~
november the: 9: Dll to John Green ~~90~~: 197: pound beef 2^{d} per	01	12	10
paid in mon^{e}y at receving 2^{s} shilling which makes forteen	02	14	05

[Page 17]

	ll	s	p
desember the 1th 1694 william pitey debter for two			
bushels of malt Dll to his son william	00	06	00
Jenuarey the 24 Dll to youre son william	00	06	00
march the 2^{nt} 1694/5 dll to william pitey two			
bushels of malt e six quarts: march the 30 dll to david			
Carver one bushel of barly			
for money led out upon Elizebath bicknills[142] sicknes in 1694			
forty e foure shillings six pence for rideing to the doctors			
seventeen times to hingum; money then layde oute seven			
shillings for halef a yeers tendance e duate	07	10	00
for hur funarall	01	00	00
Aperel the 30th: 1697 recned with John			
Green e cleedd upon all acounpts e thare was			
to him from me in money	00	02	00
Aperel the 30th: 1697: after wee recned John Green debter			
dll one bushel e a halef of malt to him selef			
at fife shilling per bushel	00	07	06
may the 24 for foure pound of tobacco	00	01	o[?]
for the boye[143] 2 dayes	00	03	00
october the 14: 1697 Mr. Torey debter for			
a pound of candels dll to his son Timothy	00	00	09
~~for~~ phebur ary the 11: for 7 pound of candels at 9^{d} per pound	00	05	03
november the 18: 1697 John Green credeter for the			
helpe chilling of fife hoges at 3^{d} per pees	00	04	03
for carting of wood from the water side	00	03	00
for a pees of ayt reseved	00	06	00
for a ~~dag~~ dog	00	00	06
for the lent of youre horce cariing d two lode of otes	00	00	06
for carting of two load of otes out of the feri feeld	00	01	00
for caring of two lode of indian corn out of the fere feeld	00	02	06
for two peeces of ayt	00	12	00
for ~~egs~~ eggs	00	02	08
for one cord of wood e money 3^{s}	00	03	06
for cilling 4 piggs	00	01	06
for one calef	01	00	00
	2	14	05

[Page 18]

	ll	s	p
Pheburarey the 26th: 1694/5 reseved of James Humphry			
forty bushels of barly: dito for 10: bushels of barly			
June Dll two James Humphrey fife bushels e a peck malt			
balanced acounpts for the above barly the 1 of november 1695			
pheburarey 10 1695^{6} John Vining debter for halef a bushel			
of indian corn dll to his wife	00	01	09
~~John boutage~~			
aperell the 16th 1696 John boutage debter			
for one bushel e a halef of malt Dll to his			
wife			
June 1696 Ms. Tyler credetor for 9 yards of blwe lining e			
foure yards of white lining cloth	01	03	00
march the 17th 1696/6 reseved of John bicknill creditor for ayt bushels			
e a peck of barly ~~June~~ more for three peck of barly			
may the 4th 1697 John Bicknill debter for three			
bushels of mallt Dll to him selef			
Dito the 19th Dll to Cornelias Fisher of rentom two bushels			
of malt all paid e clered			
Money Gathered for the ministery in the yeer: 1697			
Zackariah Bicknill paide	00	09	00
Nicolas phillips paide	00	05	10
Samuell Humphrey payde	00	08	10
Wido Humphrey[144] payde	00	01	06
John Torey[145] payde	00	04	08
Mrs Tyler payde	00	08	08
James Smith payde	00	10	05
James Richards payde	00	12	04
John Bicknill payde	00	06	00
Thomas Bicknill paide	00	06	00
John Green paide	00	12	00
Nathnell Ford paid	00	12	00
Nicolas fillips paid	00	04	00
Zackariah Bicknill paid	00	08	00
John Bicknell paid	00	07	04

	ll	s	p
(now all men by these presence that I Remember			
Brigs ~~of waymouth~~ of Tantton in Bristoll carpentor			
dwe one e acnoledg my selef my ayers ^{acitors} e or asines foure pound			
of good e lawful sillver money to the said James Richards ^{malstor}			
or his ~~exsecetors~~ ayers exsecetors or asines baid and aquited e of no ~~for~~ ^{for}			
Jenuary the: 15: 1694/5 Nathanell humphery debter for			
~~tl~~ two bushel of malt: ~~more for two bushels of barly~~			
June the 1 for three bushels of malt			
desember the 30th 1695 Nicolas phillips Credetor for three			
bushels of barly e a peck, aperel Dll to nickolis phillips one			
bushel of barly			
Nathanell ^{humphry} Credetor for ayteen bushels e a peck of barly in phe			
eburary: 1695^{6}			
aperel the: 22^{nt}: 1696 Nanthanell humpherey debter			
for one bushel of barly dll ~~ll~~ to Joshua Smith			
dll to James Humpherey 5 bushels e 3 peck of malt			
July 1696 dll to the wief of nathanell Humphrey:	2	15	0
march the 31: 169~~6~~7 Thomas holbrook debter for fife			
peck e 3^{d} peneworth of barly at 5^{s} per bushel	00	06	06
march the 31: 1697 reseved of Nathanell Humphry ^{credetor}			
fife bushels e a halef of barly, [at] two shilling [f] payd	1	4	
Aperel the 6th: 1697 James Humphrey Credetor for six			
bushels of barly			
Aperel the 15th: 1697: James Humphrey debter for			
one bushel of barly dll to Raffe Tailler by tocan			
of all youre barly to malt that you had to malt			
may 28th dll to him selef six bushels of malt			
May the 11: 1698 Mrs Elizabeth Mumford[146]			
at bostoun debter for ten bushels of malt			
dll to hur selef at hur one l houce	02	00	00
Mr Tyler debtter for 3 barels of appels	00	16	00
for posts e seting of fenc	00	02	00
for one dusen of brumes	00	02	00

[Page 20]

	ll	s	p
march 1695 baniamin e the horce wrought for bro			
ther Ford three dayes	00	06	00
Aperel the furst week three dayes horce e man	00	06	00
dito the thurd week two dayes horce e man	00	04	00
upon Thomas randalls accounpt	00	02	04
Thomas porter Credetor in the ~~in~~ yeer 1695 for a pare of			
shoos ~~my m my~~ my wife, for two pare of shoos for ruth			
for one pare of shoos for marey bicknill, for one pare			
of shoos for my self, for one pare of shoos for beniamin			
for one pare of shoos for ruth: for one pare of			
shoos for mary bicknill, for one pare of shoos for beniam^{in}			
for one pare of shoos for mother[147]			
september the: 4: 1697 Nathanell Blancher debter for			
one quorter of mutten: 10: e halef 2^{d} 1/2 per pound	00	02	02
october 25^{the} for a sede of lamb dll to him selef	00	03	00
november for a pees of ayt e a pare of french held shoos	00	12	00
for thre quarts e a pint of malases at 6 ^{d} 1/2 per quart	00	01	11
for one pound of candeles 9^{d} per pound	00	00	09
Jenuary the furst: 1697^{8} for foure yards e a halef			
carsey cloth dll to him selef at his one houce: 5^{s} per yard	01	02	06
pheburary the: 5: for six quarts of malases	0	03	03
for one pound of candels	0	00	09
september for a quart of malases	0	00	7
march 1698 Nathanell Blancher credetor for weef			
in of 20 yards e 3 quorters ~~of~~ at 4^{d} per yard	00	06	11
september 1698 for: 23: yards of cotten e lining 3 g	00	07	08
the furst weeck in Aperel 1695 I had brother Fords horce			
two dayes to work for my selef	00	02	00
for halef a dayes bushing with youre horce	00	00	06
dito the thurd week horce e man one day	00	03	00
for halef a bushel of otes	00	00	10
for the horce one day to plou amongst corne	00	01	00
Nathanell Blancher for wefeing in 1697 a pes of plaine			
[?] wide 15 yards for a pees of caresi 18 yards	00	19	3
for a pees to of carsey cloth 29 yardes e halef	00	17	2

	ll	s	p
Be it remembred by these presenc that I Nicholas phillips			
of waymouth in the county of Suffolk husband man do owe			
and am indebted unto James Richards of the same waymouth			
the suem of twenty six shillings of lawfull money of new ingland			
all which I do promise to pay to him or his order on the 20th th day			
of June next in testemony whareof I have put my hand and			
seal the: 6: th of desember 1693 ~~Nicholas Phillips~~			
[?] any arh h have[?]			
the mark of Elisabeth Bicknill[148]	[?]	[?]	[?]
May the the 9th 1694 Nicolas phill debter for one peck			
of malt			
iuly the 17th John green debter for halef a bushel of ^{malt} dll to him sell			
lef with ever mesure which comes to	00	02	6
march the 19th: 1695 pasiance Green the wief to John			
Green debter for sixteen yards of damerask 2^{s}–7 2/1^{d} per			
yard coms to in money	02	02	00
march the 19: 1695 pasiance Green the wief to John			
Gren Credetor to four peeses of ayt payd	01	04	00
more reseved in money	00	14	00
pheburary 21st 1695^{6} reseved of Brother Thomas Bick			
nill ten bushels of barly			
march the 9th 1695^{6} dll to Thomas bicknill two bushels			
of barly			
[April 8th to Brother Ford] for halef a pound of tobacka	00	00	03
aperel the 8th dll to brother Ford one bushel of mallt			
aperel the 11 dll two bushels of barly to him selef			
for ~~two~~ ^{one} bushel~~s~~ of otes e a halef dll to him selef			
for loding of his bote for bostound	00	05	00
for two p bushels of indian corne ~~Changed~~ for barly			
for one bushel paid money			
may the 24th: 1697 Betty Coopper debter for ^{one} ~~fife~~			
~~beesl~~ bushe of malt	00	5	00
march the th 30: 1698 mathu pratt Credetor			
for ayt bushels of barly			
dll to Samuell pratt thre bushels mallt			
ougust the: 2^{nt}: paid to Samuell prat a pese of ayt	00	6	0
more in money dll to him sellef	00	9	0

	ll	s	p
September the 6: 1697: John porter Credetor for mony			
reseved of him selef	00	08	04
more reseved in money	00	06	00
Brother Thomas Reed debter for two bushels of			
Mallt dll to Samuel Reed: may ~~the~~ 1698	bele	1	3
	salt	4	0
	Talo	2	6
to two bushels of malt dll to him selef paper		0	6
September the: 5: 1698 recned with brother Thomas			
Reed e cleered uppon all accounts			
~~mo~~ march th: 28: ~~16~~ 1699 brother Thomas Reed			
debtter for three bushells of malt dll ~~d~~ to Samuell			
Reed			
a bushel e a halef of salt to Thomas Reed	00	03	09
~~John both John botage~~ debter for			
desember: the: 16: 1700 John Hupper[149] debter for			
six pounds of sheeps wooll at: 12^{d}: per pound	00	06	00
desember the: 18: 1702 John Greens wife debteer			
for two pound of sheeps wooll at: 9^{d}: per pound	00	01	06
June the: 2^{nt}: 1703 william drack debtter for a ^{boy} hat:	0	00	6
to plouing for weeding	0	03	0
to a bushell of malt	0	03	3
to halef a peck of salt	0	00	6
to a jackit	0	03	0

[Page 23]

	ll	s	p
Aperel the: 20: 1695 Izraell Ford debter for ~~fife~~			
six yards of wooling caresi cloth at fife shillings per			
yarde dll to him selef e halef a pound to tobackah	01	10	09
Maier Hunt debter in ogust 1695 for two cwarters of			
beef 192 pound at 2 pence per pound	01	12	00
october the: 11: th <u>1695</u> Abia whitman Credeter for two			
bushels e a halef of malt: then wee recned e cleered all			
barly e malt acounpt			
Aperel the 23: 1697: ~~Josh~~ John porter deber			
for the best part of a barel of sider	00	06	00
June the 12th dll to John porter two quorters at			
lamb moten wait 13 pound e halef 3^{d} per pound e lamb ^{skin}	00	04	00
ogust dll to your wife a quorter of moten: ~~2~~ 2p	00	02	0~~6~~7
for a side of motten: 17 pound 3 qurter	00	03	08
September the 3 for one quorter of motten $^{of\ tatlurs}$ left	00	02	00
for one ^{quorter} 12 pound dll to youer wife	00	02	06
September the: 8: 98: for a quorter of mutten e hed e pluck:	0	02	05
desember the 23: 1698 recned with John porter Jnr and			
balanced all acounpts and thare wos dwe to mee from him	00	01	07
may the: 23rd: 1703 william drack Credetor for his son James is			
work the first weeck 5 dayes	00	01	08
the secand weeck 6 dayes	00	02	00
the third weeck 2 dayes	00	00	08
the fourth weeck 4 dayes	00	01	04
the fift weeck 6 dayes	00	02	00

[Page 24]

	ll	s	p
may the 13th 1695 recned with Thomas bicknill e thare was dwe to him ten bushells e three peck of malt			
Thomas bicknill deber in 1695 for an earthen pot	00	00	06
for halef a pound of buter	00	00	3
for two dayes e a halefs work of the beniamin	00	02	6
for three ~~d~~ yards of two cloth	00	03	0
for one pound of tobacka 6d per pound	00	00	6
for halef a dayes work of beniamin	00	00	6
for a yarde of coton e linin cloth	00	02	2
for three dayes work of beniamins	00	03	0
for Charges for the land bouft of Joseph Green	00	10	0
for a broom dll d to Experyance Bicknill	00	00	4
for three dayes worck of beniamin plouing for hilling	00	03	0
for one dayes worck of beniamin plouing for hilling	00	01	0
for two bushels of malt dll to him selef			
for two fishes	00	00	~~0~~3
September the: 16: for a pine planck eboute 25 foot	00	02	6
for bringing the bote with hay	00	01	0
~~for moten dll to him selef~~	~~00~~	~~01~~	~~0~~
for moing of salt grace	00	04	6
	1	15	1
balanced with Thomas bicknill the 7 of october 1695			
october: 13th: 1695 Izerell Ford depter for ayte yards of coten e lining cloth at 0 = 02 = 02 per yard	0	17	04
november 1695 Thomas bicknill Credetor for three cord of acke wood	01	09	00
march the 169[6/7] brother Thomas Reed credtor for thurty bushels of barly			
may 1696 brother Thomas Reed debter for three bushels of mallt, July the 1st 1696 dll to marey Reed six pound ayte shillings march the ~~19~~ 9th [I] recned with Brother Thomas Reed balansed upon all accounpts			
march the 9th: 1697/6 reseved of brother Thomas reed eleven bushels of barley, march the 10th for twenty bushels of barly e foure, for six bushels more			

	ll	s	p
may the 13th 1695 Samuel Speer of brantery debter for foure			
calevs dll to his man Jorg. Witey[150] by his order:	02	12	00
for two calefs dll to him selef	01	08	00
June 1695 Thomas bicknill Credetor for one paied			
cortains e valaines	01	18	00
for carting of a lode of hay	00	01	06
for money	01	03	00
for bring of my hay from brantery	00	06	00
	~~01~~	~~06~~	~~06~~
for carting of salt hay	00	02	00
for barly I reseved	01	06	03
	00	12	00
balanced acounpt with Thomas bicknill the	00	0	04
Seventh of october 1695 e thare was dwe to mee	05	09	3
from him in money	07	03	05
~~october the 21st for pound of chees t a~~	~~00~~	~~03~~	~~06~~
october the 24 for loding the bote with wood e			
timber for borstoun	00	10	00
for 6 Cheeses 20 pound at 2d per pound	~~00~~	~~03~~	~~04~~
May the: 13th: 1695 Samuell Speer of brantery debter for			
six calevs dll to ~~him~~ his man Jorge Witey by his order			
~~two~~ foure of the six, the other two dll to him selef, ~~foure~~			
bushels of corne dwe for the six calevs ~~n~~ is fifty e foure			
bushels: with ten sheep which ~~which~~ Samuel Speer had			
after that; this is all done to this day to my selef			
march the 12th 1696/5 balanced acounpt with Samuel Speer			
all cleered e payde of each party			
may the 21: 1696 Sister Hana Bicknill Credetor for			
ten pound of money which I hafe boroed of hur which is			
dwe to hur to this day, memoramdo this money is paid to hur selef			
november 3rd 1696 Simon Garener debter for three pound			
of candels at 8d per pound	00	02	00
desember the 8 for ayt pound e a halef of candes	00	05	08
Aperel the 10th: 1697 Brother Thomas Reed debter for			
three bushels of ~~barly~~ mallt June the 10th: dll to mary			
Reed in money	07	19	00
dll to Samuel Reed two bushels e a halef malt			
to John porter for youre rate	00	02	05

[Page 26]

	ll	s	p
pheburary the: 5th: 1698/7 Mrs Tiler Credetor for fife			
bushels of barly: paid for Mr. Tilers barly	0	15	00
pheburary the: 5th: 1698/7 Nathanell e James Hum			
frey Credetor for thurty bushels of barly			
dll in money to Nathanell Humfry	01	08	08
pheburary the: 19th: 1698/7 William pitty Credetor for			
six bushels of barly e eyles			
March the: 12th: 1698 John bicknill Credetor			
for ~~six bu fife~~ bushels e a halef of barly			
march the: 12th: 1698 John bicknill credetor			
for six bushels of barly			
may the: 6th: 1698 John bicknill debter for foure			
bushels of mallt dll to him selef			
Nathanell Humphry debter for two bushels			
malt dll to him selef			
to a galloone of malases	00	02	02
to James Humphry ~~for~~ six bushels of malt			
to Joseph pitty two bushels of malt upon			
James Humphry acounpt			
to Nathanel Humfry in money	00	01	06
August: 1698: James Humfry debter	00	06	00
September: 29: Icabod Holbroock debter for			
foure quarters of lamb dll to his son	00	06	06
pheburary the: 24: 1699 Nathanell Humfry Credetor			
for twenty bushels of barly			
to three ~~e a halef~~ of barly			
march: 1699: reseved of william pitty twelef			
bushels e a halef of barly			
reseved in: 1699: of Enock lovell fifteen			
bushels of barly			
Aperell the: 3: 1699 brother Thomas reed credetor for: 23: bushels			
barly: more for 24 bushels of otes & barly together			

	ll	s	p
pheburary the 22: 1698/7 Icabood Hollbroock debter for			
wooll dll to him selef thurty six pound	01	14	09
September the: 1st: 1698 for: 4: quarters motten dll to aliser	00	09	00
feburary the: 22: 1698/7 Icabood Hollbroock credetor for money			
paid to my selef	00	13	00
for one cord of ocke wood	00	06	00
for 4 peeses of timber ~~fif~~ six pence per pees	00	02	00
paid and cleered upan all acounpts	01	01	0~~9~~0
march the 30th: 1699 Enock Levell debter for			
three bushels of malt dll to Joseph Lovell			
May the 5th: dll to Joseph Lovell foure bushels of mallt			
for a cavefes scin e foure pound e halef of vele	00	02	2
iuly the: 5th: dll to Joseph lovell three bushels of mallt			
iuly the: 6th: to zecharyah gurny one bushel of malt			
november the 2 [forte?] three bushels of malt dll to him selef			
Aperell the: 5: 1699 Nathanell Humffry ~~Credetor~~			
debter for two bushels of barly & two bushels of malt			
dll to him selef may the: 24: for sixteen bushels of malt			
To James Humfrey three quarts of oyle e a bushel of salt	00	04	00
William pittey debter Aperell the: 28: 1699: for			
foure bushels of malt dll to William pratt son to mathu pratt			
may the 4th: dll to Joseph pittey one bushel of malt			
may the 16 dll to John pittey seven bushels e a halef malt			
in the yeer 1698: reseved of mr ~~peete~~[?] feered 38 bushels			
~~malt~~ barly e otes: dll to him selcf eyght bushels of			
malt: iune the: 16: dll to John Holis eight bushels malt			
paid all			
in the yeer: 1699: brother Thomas Reed debter for			
three bushels of malt dll Samuell Reed			
may the 30 dll to Thomas Reed three bushels e a halef malt			
june the: 16: dll to him selef three bushels e a halef of mallt			
dll to Samuell reed three bushels of malt			

[Page 28]

	ll	s	p
William pitey debter for money in <u>1697</u> which			
Was dwe to me from hizself	01	00	00
for money paid to Johathon torey	00	00	10
march: 98: for three pound of Scraps 4^d per pound:	0	1~~0~~0	00
November the: 14th: 1698 recened with Nathanell			
Blanchard & balanced all acounpts & thare was dwe			
to him from mee	00	04	03
Aperell the 18: 1699 for a pees of tow cloth: 27 yards	00	09	00
To moing of my Swamp	00	03	07
may the 13th ~~Jose~~ 1702 Joseph orcut[?]debter for			
two bushels of barly 3^s–6^d per bushel dll to him selef	00	07	0
the 16 to rafe tailler 11 pound tobacco 6^d per pound	00	5	6
the 18 to two bushels of barly dll to beniamin orcut	00	7	0
to two bushels of barly dll to Josiah riply	00	7	0
june the 4th: to Timothy haccut two bushels barly	00	7	0
to Andru orcut a bushell of barlly	00	03	6
June the: 12 to Josia riply two bushells of barly	00	07	0
the 18 to Andrew orcot a bushel of barly	00	03	6
the first of july to two bushels of barly dll beniamin orcut	00	7	0
July the 4th: Josia Riply two bushels of barly	00	7	0
the 7 to foure pound of tobacke	00	2	0
the 13 to rafe tailler two pound tobacko e halef a bushell salt	00	02	3
to rafe taller in mony at the same time	00	00	6
September the: 4th: to Josia Riply two bushels of barly	00	07	0
may the 1704 brother John Bicknill debter			
[25] to two quarts of butter salt	00	00	04
25 to one pound of hops	00	00	06
[25] to one bushell of salt	00	04	06
July 19: to one pound of hops	00	00	006
August 11: to halef a pound pouder	00	02	00
to halef a pound of shot	00	00	02
to a quart of rum	00	00	11
to halef a bushel of salt	00	02	03
Sept 13 to 6 stadum[?]of rope 8^d per pound 6 ½^{ll}	00	04	04
27 to sister bicknell[151] in mony dll to herself:	0	08	00
to zechery^{ah} bicknill hanckchif	00	03	00
	1	6	06

John[152] during lost time from the 16 of
march: 1705: to the 8 of may seven dayes

[Page 29]

	ll	s	p
July the: 12th: 1698 Thomas Adcisan $^{of\ bostoun}$ debter for			
ninty ayt bushels of malt dll at 3^{s} = 2^{d} per bushel			
at his brow ~~hay~~ hows in bostoun	15	10	4
reseved of Thomas Adcisan of bostoun July the: 12:			
1698 in money	08	10	4
reseved in money ~~f~~ at bostoun 04	04	0	
	2	16	0
dese^{e}mber the: 10 1698 Nathanell Blanchard debtor			
for seven pound of sheeps wool	00	07	08
for 8 pound e halef ~~p~~ motten	00	01	09
for a pare of wimmins shoos at Enock Lovels	0	04	06
July the: 6th: 1699 for one pound of candels	0	00	08
August the 19 for a quorter of lamb	00	01	09
September the 15 for a pound e halef of sheeps wooll	00	01	06
March 1705 wido during ~~debt~~ of brantery			
debter for a pare of shoos french			
heels for hur son John	00	06	00
~~Aperell~~ ^{may} to halef a pees of eight dll hur selef	03	00	
may to ~~me~~ one paire of gloves	00	01	06
[may] 13 to twenty pounds of sheeps wooll: 1^{s}	01	00	00
to foure pound of cotten 1^{s}–6^{d} pound:	00	06	00
to one pound of tobako	00	00	06
July to one paire of shoos to John	00	06	00
to 4 ll of cotten wooll	00	06	00
october: 12: to half a pound cotten e a quort malses	00	01	04
to mony paid to yoore selef	00	09	09
	03	00	01

[Page 30]

Line		ll	s	p
1	reseved of Mr Lambur Desper[153] in money	02	02	00
2	reseved of Thomas Holbroock credit	00	03	06
3	reseved of Increce Bate credit	00	08	04
4	John porter Snr for credit	00	07	00
5	John Harding credit	00	06	00
6	reseved of Increse Bate in money	00	12	00
7	reseved of Increse Bate two bushels of corn:	00	05	00
8	August the: 25: Joseph pratt Snr debter for a quarter of mutten			
9	forteen pound 3 quarters: 3^{d}: per pound	00	03	08
10	for three sheeps ploock: 3^{d}: per pees	00	00	09
11	september the 3rd: dll to youre wife: 15: pound mutten 3^{d} per pound	00	03	09
12	the 8 for a quorter of mutten dll to youre wife a hed e ploock	00	02	07
13	the 15 for a quorter of mutten hed e ploock dll to youre wife	00	02	00
14	the 22 for a quorter of mutten	00	02	03
15	for three quorters of mutten e hed ploock	00	07	00
16	october the 31st: for iar of lamp oyle	00	08	00
17	november the: 1st: for a hole sheepe 42 e hed e ploock	00	09	00
18	the 18th: for three quorters of mutten 41p hed e pluck dll wife	00	08	10
19	the 21 for a hole sheepe e hed e pluck 52	00	11	02
20	the 28 for a bushel of salt dll to youre son John	00	02	06
21	desember the: 15th for 364 pound of mutten $21/2^{d}$: per pound dll to [wi]	03	15	10
22	phebupary the: 10th: for: 28: pound of sheeps wooll 12^{d} per pound			
23	dll to youre selef	01	08	00
24	october the: 20: for a sheep: 2^{d} q	00	06	09
25	iune the 5th 1701 for a chees e baken: 2 ^{ll}: ½	00	02	00
26	July 2^{nt}: 1701 paid to John Bicknell in sheeps wooll	00	06	03
27	the 13th: for a hole sheep ~~e a~~ 43 pound 3^{d} per pound e hed e ploock	00	11	01
28	July the 28th for halef a bushel of salt e two bushels of malt	00	08	00
29	for a sheep ~~hed e p~~ 31	00	07	10
30	August the: 2^{nt}: for a bushel of corne a galloon malases two pound tobacco	00	07	06
31	August the: 9th: 1701 wido Humphry Snr debter for a 11 pound			
32	cotten woull 1^{s} = 10^{d} per pound	01	00	02
33	August the: 9th: ~~wid~~ 1701 wido humphry credit for	00	03	05
34	to buter 2 pound e 1^{s}–6^{d} ays[?] quinses[154]			
35	octobe 1699 reseved of Joseph pratt Snr in money	00	15	00
36	Jenuarey the 4th: reseved of Joseph green for Joseph pratt	01	10	00
37		00	06	00
38	reseved of yower wife: reseved of william Hearse[155]	02	00	00
39	~~3 lase vinting paid in money~~	00	06	0
40	for a cubard	01	00	00
41	for 12000 three hunderd shingels	04	18	05

[Page 31]

Line		ll	s	p
1	Joseph Nash debtter in money	00	01	0[4?]
2	Thomas Holbroock debter for a side of motten	0	03	06
3	John Holis debter for a quorter of motten	00	01	09
4	Josia Riply debter for a quorter of motten e hed e pluck	00	02	07
5	Zeckariah Bicknell deber for a quorter motten e money	00	03	06
6	September the 8: 98: Incres Bate for a side mot^{tn}:	00	04	06
7	for 9 pound of hogs fat dll to his wief	00	04	06
8	Mrs Bedlow[156] for motten hogs fat e two heds e pluc^{k}:	00	03	11
9	~~unceell~~ uncell Shaw[157] for beef	00	02	00
10	Wido eyles for sheeps wooll	00	01	00
11	John Shawe debtor for be^{e}f	00	02	00
12	Wido eyles for a hed & fee	00	02	00
13	Zeckariah Bicknell Debtor for work at bote	00	03	00
14	John Bicknell for: 9: pound of beef 2 ½^{d} per pound	0	01	10
15	mary king for wool e hed e ploock	0	00	06
16	november 1698 Increes Bate for: 29 ½ hoges fat: 6^{d}: per pound	0	14	09
17	Incres Bate for a hole motten 44: pound: 2 ½^{d}: per pound	0	09	02
18	Increes Bate for a pound e a halef sheeps wool 10^{d}	0	01	03
19	november the 30 1699 Lambur Desper 2 ½ motten: 00	0	13	00
20	Lambur Desper for 5 sheep: 180 pound 2 ½^{d} per pound ~~01~~	01	17	06
21	Lambur Desper 3 heds 3 plucks a peck of salt	00	02	00
22	november the: 29: Nicolas Sallter for a side motten	00	03	08
23	Desember the 9th: dll to Lambur Desper: 96: pound motten	01	00	00
24	John Porter Snr for motten	00	10	05
25	John Porter Juner for motten	00	14	00
26	Edward Bate for a motten	00	10	00
27	Thomas White of manetecut for sheeps wooll	00	04	00
28	desember the14th: 1698: Ephram Pray Debtor			
29	for 41 ½ pound motten e a pipe	00	08	08
30	desember the 26th: 1698 Ephraim Pray debter 3 pound wooll	00	03	00
31	desember 26: 98: Nicolas Sallter for one sheep hed pluck wooll for 38 pounds pound	00	09	05
32	Desember 26: 98 Blase vinting for one sheep 42 pound hed 2 pound wooll	00	11	07
33	John Radman desember 26: 98 Debtor for one sheep pound	0	0~~7~~0	08

[Page 32]

	ll	s	p
Jenuary the: 17: 1699/8 Uncle Shawe Credetor for			
twenty one bushels e a halef barly			
Aperel the: 8th: 1699 John Green Debtor for ten			
bushels seed barly: dll him selef	00	06	00
the: 21st: for smelts	00	00	0~~0~~3
for two bushels of Salt 2^{s}–6^{d}: per ~~bushells~~ bushel	00	09	00
for two quarts of lamp oyell dll to his wife 6^{d} per $quar^{t}$	00	01	00
for foure pound e a halef of sope: 2^{d}: per pound	00	0	~~0~~9
July the first Samuell vinson debtter ~~deb~~ for shuger biscake e naiels			
11 dll to him selef	00	06	09
12 the: 2^{nt}: to '80 three pound of sheeps wooll 15^{d} penc per pound	05	04	00
Aperell the 3 1702 John bicknell debtter for one			
bushell and a halef of barlley dll to his son John			
to foure bushels of malt dll to him selef			
may 10 $J^{a}mes$ Humfry foure bushels of malt dll Jonas			
to one bushel of salt to John bicknell			
to one bushe & a halef of salt to John Bicknell			
to halef a hundred of bord nailes			
to a pound of shot			
october to halef a hundred of borde nailes			
desember the: 1st: to two bushels of malt			
desember the: 18: 1702: payd to John bicknell			
1^{ll}–10^{s}: at James Humfries by his order	01	10	00
Jenaury the: 1: 1702 paid to John bicknell mony	01	15	00
May the: 14: 1703 to nailes at Johathan mountford	00	04	09
June 21 to moris Trufant a bushel e halef of malt	00	04	06
July 12th: to two peeses of eyght	00	12	00
to a peck of salt	00	01	00
August to a bushel e a halef of malt	00	04	06
to a bushel e ~~seven~~ three peck salt	00	07	00
desember to halef a bushel of salt	00	02	00
	03	10	09
desember the 21st 1703 ~~paid in mony~~ John Bicknell			
debter to mony paid to him selef	03	00	0
Jenaury: 11th: paid to James Humphrey by an ords to			
Jonathan Mountford	01	10	0
Phebu[ary] to a pound of hops dll to beniamin	00	00	6
to Decon Bates[158] upon youre accounpt	00	06	6
to one hundred shoo nailes	00	00	4
~~paid to John bicknell mony~~		~~5~~	~~7~~
	5	2	11

[Page 33]

	ll	s	p
desember the 28 1698 balanced with John Green upon			
all acounpts ~~nothing dwe upon ethier side~~ dwe to mee	00	02	06
Jenuary the: 23: 1699 Thomas White of Brantery Snr			
debter for one sheep 40 pound: 2^{d} 3^{q}: per pound	00	09	02
for three pound of suit dll to himselef 5^{d} per pound	0	01	03
payde ten Shillings e fife pence			
John Green Credit for carting of barley & otes from fere			
feeld	00	01	06
for thre lode from Tilers[159] barne	00	01	06
for two lode of fresh hay from the lane end	00	01	00
for two lode of salt hay from the lane end	00	01	00
for spining e [th] nine egs	00	01~~0~~	0~~3~~0
october the: 24th: <u>1699</u> uncle Shawe credetor for twelef bushels e a halef of			
barley fife pence dwe in for barley reseved in: 1699/8			
october the 24th 1699 uncle Shawe credetor for twelef busheles e a			
halef of barly: desember the: 4th: ~~sfx~~ for six bushels e a peck			
March the: 9th: Uncle Shawe debter for mony	01	04	00
May the 3 dll to Cornelius Hollbrooke a bushell malt by a			
tocon of waying of mony at John Greens			
may the: 18: 1700: recened with Uncle Shawe e balanced			
accounpts and thare was dwe to him seven bushels e three peck ^{of} malt			
iune the 4th: 1700: richard Devenport a bushel ~~of malt three~~			
e three peck of malt upon Uncle Shawes accounpt			
Jenuary the 7th: 1701/2 John Bicknell creditor for sixteen			
bushels of barly: the 8 reseved four bushels of barly			
the 23 to sixteen bushels of barly: desember: 1702 3 peck barly 6q			
pheburary the 13 Thomas Reed Junr credittor for			
foure bushels e a halef of barly			
pheburary the 20 John bicknell eyght bushels of barly			
~~to a pound of tobacko~~			
desember the: 15th: 1702: recned with John Bicknell			
and ballansed all acounpts and thare was dwe to him ^{in} mony	4	18	00
work by Jo^{h}n _ zeckeryah bicknell	00	1~~3~~4	00
desember the: 10th: 1703 recned with John bicknell and			
balansed acounts and thare was dwe to him in m^{ony}	2	06	3
and in malt twenty bushels	2	16	8
	5	02	11

	ll	s	p
desember the 24: 1698: Thomas holbrouck credetor			
for money payd	00	03	00
desember the: 24: 1698: Thomas holbrouck ~~el~~ Credetor			
for money paid to my self at the delivery of the gun	00	03	00
october: 1699: Samuell king credetor for three bushels			
e a peck e six quarts of barly			
August the 12th: 1701 recned with Joseph pratt for and balanced			
all acounpts and thare was dwe to mee from him in mony	00	04	07
the 12th for seven pound e 3q of chees 4^{d} per pound	00	02	07
the 24 for a side of mutten dll at home by beniamin	00	04	06
September the 3 for one sheep 10 quarts of oyle 3 pound ½ sheeps			
wooll 2 pound hogs fat	00	18	00
for to pound of tobacko			
the 16 to youre dafte Shawe 10 pound sheeps wooll by tocen			
shngels wensday	00	12	06
to youre wife two pound of sheeps wooll three pound coten	00	08	00
for one pound hops dll to John bicknill	00	00	06
the 19 for a sheep 56 pound	00	07	06
for one bushel of salt dll to elder rogers[160]	00	0~~2~~0	00
the 26 to John bicknill a galloun e a halef of oyell	00	03	00
october the 11th to two pound of porck 6^{d}	00	01	00
the 13th to sheep 25 pound	00	05	03
to a barell to brother bicknill	00	03	06
the: 15th: to uncle Shawe a bushell e a halef of sallt	00	03	00
the 16 to uncle Shawe a bushell e a peckof sallt:	0	02	06
the 22th to youre dafter experienc 22 ½ flex 9^{d} per pound			
one broom 2d pipes	00	18	09~~81/2~~
november the 4th to Ephraim burll for caring e order	00	09	04
the 6th to sheep 45 pound hed e plouck	00	09	04
the: 13 to Jon bicknill a bushell e halef of sallt	00	03	0
a broom to John bicknill with oute a hndell	00	00	04
the 22 to two bushels salt	00	04	0
November the 22^{nt}: 1701 recned with Joseph pratt snr and balencd			
all acounpts and thare was dwe to mee from him	02	05	02
aperel the 13th 1702 reseved of Joseph pratt upon zechariah			
Bicknells acounpt in mony	00	12	00
to mony of Steeffen French[161] mony	00	17	00
to mony of Thomas bicknell mony	00	07	06
to two gees	00	03	00
to eyght chikins	00	02	0~~3~~6
to three pigs	00	03	06
to a quorter of vele 11 pound 2^{d} per pound	00	01	10
to mony for hay ~~f~~	01	04	06
to cofe schin	00	01	04
to preacking ground	00	17	00

	ll	s	p
desember the: 24: 1698 Thomas Holbroock of Brantery			
debter for a ~~go~~ gun dll to him selef at lft Nashes dwelling			
houce witnesis Nicholas Salter[162] Isack Hunt[163]	01	04	00
July the 17th: 1699 Samuell king debtter for a bushel e a halef mallt			
march the 19th for a bushelle a halfe of malt: e for some salt			
July the 31: 1701 Zechariah Bicknell debter for goods takup at			
bostoun	04	05	08
for a galloon of malases	00	02	06
for a glas bottell dll to ~~yourell~~ youre selef	00	00	06
August: 17: for a ~~peck~~ $^{\text{halef a bushel}}$ of salt	00	01	00
the 24 for a galloon of mallses	00	02	06
two quorts of mallases to nant bayly[164]	00	01	03
to mony paid to youre selef	01	09	00
to moris truant	00	06	00
the 12 for 6 pound coten wooll e 8 pound of flax	00	17	00
the 26 for seven pound of cotten wooll	00	12	10
for a quart of malases dll to youre wife	00	00	08
payd to Johnathon mumford september the 29	00	11	00
october the 24th: ballanced the account with	08	09	11
zechariah Bicknell upon all aounts	00	00	00
november the 14th to a bushel of sallt dll david	00	02	00
the 28 to josia riply withoute youre note a bushel ^{salt}	00	02	00
march the 23: 1702 zechariah Bicknell debtter for a			
peck of salt dll to his indian	00	00	06
the 28: to: 1500 of salt hay ^{at}: 1^s–6^d per hundered to youre selef	01	02	06
the 27: to: 2000 of salt hay at: 1^s–6^d per hundered $^{\text{to [?]men lovell}}$	01	10	00
aperell the 13 to two pound of hops 6^d per pound	00	01	00
aperell the 13 to hay to Joseph poole	01	15	00
the 18 to Thomas bicknell fife hundered hay	00	07	06
to youre selef three hundered of hay	00	04	06
may the 20: two pushels of malt	00	07	00
to rum e shugar e lickerish	00	02	11
June the 5 to six quorts of malases	00	03	09
to a pound of tobacko	00	00	06
~~to three pigs~~			
to fife pound of tobacko e three yards blwe lining		05	6
to seven pound of shuger 7^d per pound	00	04	01
to a lie e two peeces of eyght	00	13	03
to halef a dayes worck of beniamins	00	01	00
to a peck of salt dll to Josiah riply	00	00	08
August the 12: 1701 Joseph pratt snr Credetor in mony	01	00	00
September the 26 for 7 ^{7000} thousand of shingle	02	16	00
	~~316~~	~~00~~	
august the 15 to zecheriah bicknell two bushels of malt	6	00	

	ll	s	p
Aperel the: 1st: brother bicknell credetor for eight			
bushels & a halef of barly			
for one bushel of pees	00	06	00
July the 31: 1701 Ezra Whit^{e}march credetor for 124 1270 ½			
shingell			
July the 29: 1701 Samuell White credetor for 12000 two hunderd			
of shingles			
Zechariah Gurny credetor for six thousand of shingels	02	08	00
Zechariah Bicknell credit for 2100 of shingall 8^{s} per thousand	8	08	0
Septimber the 22 uncle vinson[165] credetor for 8200 of shingle	3	05	6
[?] october the 22^{nt} uncle vinson ~~ed~~ credetor for 12100	04	04	9
to a halef a thousand of cobbard	04	01	0~~0~~10

[Page 37]

	ll	s	p
may the 5: 1699 brother John bicknell debter for vell	0	01	02
more satisfied brother John Bicknell	0	04	05
for two gallons oyle	0	04	00
paid the ministers rate	0	15	02
for three peck of salt	0	02	0~~2~~1
	1	01	03
July 30th: 1701 dll a grinstone to ezera whitemarch	00	18	00
August the: 19 for two bushels of salt	00	04	00
~~Jul~~ September the 3 uncle yinson debter for a sheep 42 pound:	0	08	09
to john vinson a quarter of motten e a hed e pluck	0	01	07
to September the 12 to John Vinson[166] 12 pound flex 6 quarts oyl	0	12	00
the 12 to uncle vinson: 12: pound flex 6 quarts 4 pound cotten wooll	0	19	04
the 12 to samuell vinson a 4^{ll} of pound ~~flex~~ ^{cotten}1^{s}–4^{d} [?] per pound	0	07	0~~0~~4
the 15 to uncle vinson a lamb 30 e halef a bushel of salt hed ploo^{ck}	0	07	07
the 22 to uncle vinson foure pound of cotten wooll dll to e him	0	07	04
the 25 to samuell vinson nine quarts e a pint of oyle			
e a bushell of salt dll to youre father vinson[167]	0	06	09
the 25 to john vinsons wife a galloon of molases	0	02	06
october the 6th to a drawing knife e a bushel of salt to uncle v[168]	0	04	06
the 11 to Joseph Shawes[169] one bushel e a halef sallt to uncle yinson	0	03	00
the 15 to uncle vinson foure hundered of shoo nailes	0	01	04
the 22^{nt} to wido mash[170] ~~2~~10 gallons molases to bushels salt one			
galloon ^{oyl}	0	11	00
the 22 to Joh vinson a bushel e ½ salt a broom e pipes 4^{d}	0	03	08
the 24 to wido mash 16^{ll} of flex 9^{d} per pound	0	12	00
the 24 uncle vinson a sheep 24^{ll}: 2 1/2 ^{d}	0	09	04
the 29 to uncle vinson in mony e pipes	4	15	04
the 31 to Samuell vinson a galloon $^{e\ quart}$ of oyell a bushel 200			
nails $^{a\ pound\ flx}$	0	07	03
novenber the: 1st: to wido nash a thousand of bord nails	0	10	00
to wido nash 6 barells from bostoun	0	01	6
the 14 to halef a bushel of salt ^{to} ebenezer vinson	0	01	00
desember the 10th to william Trask[171] wido white Samuel vin^{sons}			
account eyght pound of flex 9^{d} per pound eight pound tobacko 5^{d}:	0	09	04
the 18 to peeter nucom[172] a bushel of salt ~~uncle vinson~~	0	02	00
[?] vinson[?] dll to wido white			

[Page 38]

	ll	s	p
July the: 17th: 1699 Samuell king debter for one bushel e a halef of malt. Delivered to hezekah king			
August the 26: 1699 reseved of Enock Lovell one pare of shoos			
for my selef	00	06	0
for a pare of shoos for mary bicknell lether heels	00	04	6
desember 1 for a pare of shoos for ruth	00	04	6
desember: 11th: for a pare of shoos for my wife	00	04	6
for taping of a pare of shoos for my selef	00	01	0
Aperell the: 3: for three pare of shoos: 2: wimmens: 1: my selef	0	15	0
november 6 reseved of ezera whitemarch fif thousand			
of shingels 7^{s} per thousand	01	15	00
Aperell 1705 Johathan mountford dter			
to 1500 shingels at 10^{s}–6^{d}	00	15	9
~~to~~			

	ll	s	p
August the: 19th: 1699 Enock Lovell Debter for a quarter of lamb			
dll to his wief at his one house	00	01	10
the: 25th: for vell dll to his wife	00	03	10
the 22: for a cowe hide: 56: pound	00	09	04
september the: 30: for a cowes hide: 49: pound	00	08	02
the 12 for a cowes hide: 56: pound	00	09	04
november the: 2nt: for a couse hide: 63: pound	00	10	06
the: 7th: for a couse hide 50 pound	00	08	04
for a gallon of oyle	00	02	00
the: 18th: for a bushell e halef salt a quarter ^{pound} peper	00	04	05
July the: 30: Ezera Whitemarch debter for a grinston	00	18	00
August: 19: for two bushels of salt	00	04	00
september the 16 for ten quarts of malases	00	06	03
to mony	00	01	04
october the 29 to Samuell bayly one bushell salt	00	02	00

Line		ll	s	p
1	~~August~~ July: 1699: John Cillbe[173] credetor for one pees damarsk	03	03	00
2	for three yards of blew lining	00	04	00
3	october the: 21: 1700 Joseph pratt jun debter for a sheep e three heds e ~~pl~~			
4	plucks dll to his wife	00	08	04
5	before that for muten e other things	00	07	09
6	november the: 1: for a hole sheep e hed e pluck	00	07	09
7	desember the 13th for foure pound e a halef of wooll	00	03	10 ½
8	the: 19th: for ten pound of sheeps wooll dll to ebenezer hubey[174]	0	10	00
9	the: 20: for two sheep: 88: pound 2^{d} per pound: two heds $^{e\ plucks}$	0	15	08
10	July 28th for a shep dll to hobey sheep 34 38 ½	00	~~0~~19	0~~8~~7
11	for half a bushel of salt e a two bushels of mallt hed e ploock	00	08	04
12	August the 21st for one sheep: 42 pound 2^{d} 3q hed e ploock $^{e\ skin}$:	0	11	01
13	September the 12th for a hole sheep 44 pound 2^{d} 2/1 per pound	0	09	05
14	to oyle two galloones e three quarts	0	05	08
15	the 16 to sheeps wooll e a leven pound of chees dll to wife	0	05	04
16	the 22 to a foure quarters of lamb dll at his house a ^{h}ed ^{hed} ploock	0	06	02
17	october the: 6th: to youre son[175] one sheep 34 pound two heds e plouck [?]			
18	2 quarts of molases	0	09	00
19	the 19 to a sheep e hed e ploock	0	08	03
20	to thurteen pound of flex 9^{d} per pound	0	09	09
21	to a peck of salt to marsey ford dll by beniamin:		00	06
22	november the 4th to a sheepe e hed e ploock	0	08	08
23	the 14th to a bushel of sallt dll to Joseph pratt	0	02	00
24	the: 15: to a bushel of sallt dll to Joseph pratt	0	02	00
25	recned the 25th november 1701 the balance owed to a	7	08	11
26	new boock			
27	aperell the 14 Icobod halbrock debter for two bushels of			
28	barly dll to his son at 3^{s}–6^{d} per bushell	00	07	0
29	the: 16: to stoure bushells of barly	00	14	0
30	the 18 to hay two Shillings	00	02	0
31	to dll two bushells of barlly	00	07	0
32	may to salt	00	00	3

[Page 41]

Line		ll	s	p
1	Mr John kilbee debter: July: 28: 1699: for fifteen b pound of			
2	chees 4 ½^{d} per pound	00	05	07 $^{1/2}$
3	August the: ^{1} sent by william pratt three cheeses: 19:			
	½: 4 ½ ^{d} per pound	00	07	04
4	for foure 4 chabaigs 3^{d} per chabaige	00	01	00
5	for ~~two~~ one buter pott 10^{d} per butter pot thurty four ~~pound~~ butter	00	017	10
6	for twenty foure pound e halef of chees 4 ½ ^{d} per pound	00	09	02
7	for nineteen pound of butter: 6^{d}: per pound	00	09	06
8	for one dosen of chabages	00	02	00
9	paid in m chabbaies the remanider			
10	desember the 7th: Joseph pratt junr credetor for two galloons of rum			
11	october the 28th: 1701 for: 4000 seven hundered e fifty shinels	01	18~~4~~^{8}	0
12		2	06	0

[Page 42]

Line		ll	s	p
1	Nicolas phillips for mony lent	00	02	00
2	for one bushel e a halef of sallt	00	03	09
3	September the: 19th: 1699 Mr Hubard[176] of bostoun debter for			
4	for fraiting of corn and vills[177] e mailes[178]	00	02	06
5	Jenuary the: 15th: 1700/1699 reseved of Mrs Catten Simkins[179] of bostoun in			
6	mony fify two shillings for foure cord of walnut wood which is to be			
7	delivered at bostoun toun dock			
8	Jenuary the: 15th: 1700 mrs mumfurd of B credetor for goods	00	17	00
9	recned with mrs mumford e balansed e cleered all acounts iuly			
10	1700			
11	Jenuary: 1701: Thomas Bicknell debter for wood			
12	sold to him at rose hill	00	10	00
13	phebурary the: 3rd: for a bag of otes	00	08	00
14	march the 5th for ^{two} ~~three~~ hundered of hay	00	03	00
15	mony payd to moses ~~ffeese~~ peneman	00	00	09
16	for feching of corne at ffe^{e}ses[180]	00	01	00
17	may the 19 for fish dll to him selef	00	00	02
18	July the 3 for one bushel e a halef of salt	00	03	00
19	for goods tacken at mr longs[181] at bostoun	01	16	04
20	august the 21th to sixteen ^{flex} pound of flex 9^{d} per pound	0	1~~6~~2	00
21	phebrurary the 18 to knife	00	00	03
22	to a pound of tobacko	00	00	06
23		03	13	00
24	march the 4th: 1702 balanced accounts			
25	with Thomas Bicknell & thare wos dwe to mee	00	08	4
26	the 18th to halef a pound of tobacko	00	00	3
27	to a pint of rum			7
28		00	09	2
29		76		
30		00	16	8
31	August the 15th: balansed acounpts with zechariah Bicknell			
32	and thare was dwe to mee from him in mony	02	16	0

	ll	s	p
september the: 19th: 1699 Mrs willard of branter debtter for bringing			
of a chadern [?] e halef of cole from bostoun	00	09	00
may the: 10: 1700 I dll ~~to~~ Mrs Simkins of bostoun			
one cord of walnut wood	00	13	00
for a cord e halef wood	00	19	06
for a cord e a halef of wood	00	19	06
Thomas bicknell credetor in the yeer: 1701 for winoing barly	00	08	20
for six thousand of shingles: 8s: per thousand	02	08	00
for buter paid	00	02	09
for mony b paid for in sheep	00	08	0
Jenuary 1701/2: to faning of 35 bushels of ots: 1d: a bushel	0	02	11
to two bushels e a halef of barly	3	06	08
october the 25: 1702 zechariah Bicknell credetor			
for a cord e three foot of wood	00	08	03
to turnops	00	03	00
reseved desember the 25 of Joseph pooll mony	00	~~11~~2	00

[Page 44]

Line		ll	s	p
1	desember 1699 reseved of zecheriah Bicknell twelef bus^{h}els			
2	of barly more to zecheriaah bicknell eleven bushell three peck			
3	desember 1699 John Shaw Credetor for six bushels of barley			
4	Jenuary the: 3: 1699 Ephraim Burll credetor for two bushells			
5	e a halef of barley	00	06	03
6	John Bicknell Credetor for foure bushels of ~~malt~~ barly			
7	elder Rogers credetor for two bushels of barly	00	05	00
8	march the 19th: reseved of Thomas Reed: 35: bushels of barlly			
9	john bicknell credetor for three bushells of barly Aperel the: 8:			
10	Aperell the 28 william phese Credetor for sixty bushels of barly			
11	iune the: 7th: recned with zeckariah bicknell and thare			
12	was dwe to him nine bushels e halef malt			
13	iune the: 11: payd to zeckeriah bicknell in mony for nine bushels e a halef ma^{lt}			
14	march the: 7th: 1701 brother b John bicknell boft six bushels barly			
15	James Humfry brot six bushels of barly in jenuary: 1701			
16	James Humfrey foure bushels of barly			
17	march the 22^{nt}: 1701 brother Reed credetor for: 20: bushels of barly			
18	jtm to brother Thomas Reed fife bushels e a halef of barly			
19	november the 28th: 1701 Johnathon Mumford Creditor for			
20	10 yard of baise 2^{s}–4^{d} per yard	01	02	6
21	to 3 dusand butens ~~halef a m~~ quarter of an ounce silk: 9^{d}:	00	03	9
22	to halef a thousand of shingell nailes e a quire of paper	00	03	0
23	Jenuary the 27 to 3 yard filiting 2^{d} per yard an ounc 1^{s}–3^{d} thred tongs	00	02	0
24	to foure pound cotten wooll: 1^{s}–9^{d} per pound	00	07	0
25	pheburary the 18th three pound cotten wooll 1^{s}–9^{d} per poun^{d}:	0	05	3
26	to mony the 18: three peeses of ayt	00	18	0
27	brother Thomas Reed debter in the yeer 1701 for three bushels			
28	malt dll to youre son Thomas Reed two bushels of malt			
29	July the 3: dll to william Reed two bushels of ~~m~~ mallt			
30	the: 23: to john pratt a bushel of malt			
31	paid for the above malt and barly to brother reed october 1701			
32	November the 28: 1701 recened with Johnathon mumford			
33	& balanced acounts and thare was dwe to mee	00	16	9
34	desember the 6 to 106800 shingels 9^{ds} per thousand	03	01	4
35	to two thousand & three hundered of cabbords[182] 2^{ll}10^{s}0^{d}	05	15	0
36	sent by Thomas bicknell six thousand one hundered e fifty:	3	13	6
37	of great shingels e 5000 of small shingels:	2	00	0
38		15	06	5

Line		ll	s	p
1	desember the 22: 1699 dll to zac^{h}hariah bicknell one bushell			
2	of malt: two bushels e a halef more to zackariah bicknell			
3	Jenuary the: 5: 1700 1699 Thomas Reed Debter for two bushels malt dll selef			
4	Jenuary the: 24 John Bicknell Debter for a bushell of malt dll him selef			
5	pheburary the: 10: to zeckariah bicknell one bushell of malt dll him self			
6	to Thomas Bicknell a bushell of malt dll to him selef			
7	march the: 19: to Thomas Reed three bushels e a halef of mallt			
8	march the: 19: Enock Lovell debter for foure bushels of malt dll to Thomas Reed			
9	march the: 19: Sister Richards in mutten lane Debter for a bushel e halef mallt			
10	moris Trufant debter for a bushell of malt			
11	Aperell the: 2: John Bicknell Debter for a bushell e a halef of malt dll son			
12	Aperell the 8 to zeckariah bicknell Indian three bushells of barly			
13	Aperell the 8 to John Shaw Junr two bushells e a halef of malt			
14	Aperell the 9 to John Shaw the remander of malt			
15	Aperell the: 9: John porter Snr debter for foure bushells of malt			
16	dll to ~~Thomas por~~ to his son Thomas $2^{s} = 9^{d}$ per bushell	00	11	00
17	apercll thc: 11: James ^{bostown} freeman ^{bostown} debter for 21 bushell of of mallt			
18	dll at bostown $2^{s} = 5^{d}$ per bush	02	16	00
19	Aperell the: 22^{nt}: John porter Snr of hay e too bushels of otes	00	07	00
20	may: 14th: 1700: to Joseph pratt ^{Junr} two bushels $^{of\ malt}$ of e foure fishoo	06	02	
21	may the: [18] to Joseph Gurny upon zackariah gurnys acount one bushel ^{malt} by Enock			
22	lovells order			
23	may the 29: 3: bushel of malt to enock lovell dll to joseph lovell			
24	may the 29 to enock lovell one galon of ayell by joseph lovell	2	s	0^{d}
25	iune the: 4th: Jo^{h}n Green Debter for one bushel of malt dll to him selef			
26	iune the 4 John Green two bushels of upon David Carvers aconpt			
27	to zeckariah bicknell seven bushel e a peck malt			
28	June the: 18th: Joseph pratt junr for seven bushels malt dll to his son joseph			
29	June the 15 to Thomas Reed three bushels of malt			
30	June the 20 John bicknell 2 bushels of malt			

Line		ll	s	p
31	June the 26 to Joseph lovell three bushels malt			
32	June the 25 to to steeven ffrench six quarts of oyle	00	03	00
33	June the 29 to John Vining two bushels of malt	00	05	06
34	July the 12 to David Carver by James Richards 6 bushels malt			
35	July the 10 joseph ppols wife[183] 2 bushels of malt			
36	July the 12 to william ffeese 4 bushels of malt			
37	August to Joseph lovell foure bushels of maltt			
38	w mr Tilar[184] 2^{s} lent 6^{d} penc john green: 6: cabbaies	00	04	00
39	uncle porter halef a bushel of salt	00	01	00
40	Sister richards mutten lane a bushel of salt a gallion oyll	00	04	00
41	aperell the: 5th: to Joseph lovell three bushels e halef seed barly			
42	may 17th: 1701 dll three bushels of malt to Enock Lovell			
43	may 1701 ll to John bicknell three bushels of malt			
44	may to enock lovell 3 bushels e a halef of malt			
45	July 10 to James humfry 4 bushels of malt			
46	August the 9 to John bicknell two bushels of malt			

[Page 46]

	ll	s	p
January the: 15th: 1699^{700} recned with Thomas white Junr of brantery			
e balanced all acounpts and thare wos due to mee	01	02	01
June 1701 for bringing of the botes sailes from bostoun	00	03	00
hadman fish	00	0~~4~~0	04
Joseph Richards debtter in the yeer 1701 for mony ^{l} paid for			
wood to John Holis	03	16	00
for mony lent at bostoun	00	06	00
for two bushels malt	00	0~~6~~7	00
for mony lent	0~~0~~1	10	00
for thurty e three pound of porck at 6^{d} per pound	00	16	06
for a galloon of malases e a peck of salt	00	03	00
for mony paid at bostoun to wever	01	10	00
for a galloon of oyle	00	02	00
September the 13 for a quorter of motten sent by Joh[n] Hunt:	00	01	09
october the 22 to a penath of pipes	00	00	01
to pato of buter 8^{ll}	00	04	06
to mony of Samuell bagly[185]	00	14	00
november the 28 to three yards & a halef of baise 3^{s}–4^{d} per ^{yard}	00	11	08
	10	02	06
July the 4 Joseph Green Credetor for one 1400 of hay			
at 1^{s}–10^{d} per hundered	01	05	8

	ll	s	p
June the: 25th: 1700 Joseph pratt Junr credetor for mony			
reseved of Colenor Hunt[186]	00	18	00
desember the: 23: 1700: Increse Bate debtter for thurty			
foure pound e a halef of hoggs fatt 4 ½ per pound	00	13	00
for ~~th~~ trancporting the fat to his house	00	01	00
August the: 6th: 1701 Joseph Richards credet mony	01	16	00
November to three thousand of shing 9^{s}–6^{d} per thousand	1	08	06
to three thousand of shingels 7^{s} per thousand	1	01	00
to mony boroed at bostoun of m^{s} barnsdell[187]	1	10	00
	5	15	06
Thomas white Jun of brantery credetor in the year <u>1701</u>			
to mony paid to Ebenezer thare	00	04	10
to a ~~qu~~cord e a quarter of ock wood 6^{s} per cord	00	07	06
July the 4 ~~Jseph~~ Joseph Green debtter for			
a quorter of mutten	00	02	08
to porke	00	04	5
to mony	00	07	4
to mony to youre son[188]	00	10	0

Line		ll	s	p
1	to yore son benjamun[189] one bushel:	00	02	09
2	May the 25th: ~~16~~ 1700 Liftenant Nash debtor for thurty bushels			
3	of malt dll his son James[190] at his whorfe at: 2^{s}—9^{d} per bushel	04	02	06
4	for the frait of the thirty bushels of malt	00	02	00
5	reseved of Lft. Nash the full debt in dsember the 9th 1700			
6	may the 15th 1701 Thomas Porter debtor for goods dll to him selef			
7	one goon one sord e belt 6 broomes one yard e ½ damaresk flints	02	06	04
8	the 16 for 14 pound e halef of flex e a pound of bullets	00	12	04
9	June the: 2: for one bushel of salt	00	02	00
10	the: 15: to foure thousand of shingles dll Mr. Brigam	00	02	04
11	the 30 to a hat e hatbond e a pare of brichis	00	19~~7~~	0~~3~~6
12	july the 3 for forty pound of sheeps wool 1^{s}—3^{d} per pound	02	10	00
13	the 10th for a frait of shingles 10 thousand dll at dochistor	00	07	00
14	march the 3rd 1702: david carver debtor for eyght pound			
15	of scraps dll to Samuell Bates 3d per pound	00	02	0
16	the 4 to Samuell Andruse six pound hops 6^{d} per pound:	00	03	00
17	the Aperell the 16 john randall for frait of four			
18	of hooppules to bostoun 8^{d} per hundred	00	02	08
19	may ~~17~~ 27 to sister wido Richards Junr a scarfe 3 yards:	01	05	6
20	June the 6th Ephraim burll debtor for a gallon of			
21	malasses 2^{s}–6^{d} per galloon e nine pound e halef cotton wooll: 1^{s}–10^{d}			
22	per pound dll to John dracke verball order	00	19	11
23	Joseph Richards for a peck e halef of salt	00	01	02
24	Joseph Richards for eight pound of tobacco dll to James Lovell:	00	04	00
25	to Nicholas Phillips 5 pound e quarter of vele 2^{d} 3/1 per pound	00	01	[?] [?]
26	to John burell a bushel e a halef of mallt 3^{s} per bushel	0	04	06
27	to two quarts of malasses dll to Bimamin Richards[191]	00	01	03
28	reseved of Ephraim Burll e in mony	00	09	00
29	July the 3 to John Shawe six quarts malasses	00	03	09
30	to Mrs. French[192] a quarter of mutten 11 pound 3^{d}	00	02	09
31	to Insine Hunt[193] a quarter of mutten e hed e ploock	00	03	0
32	to pasianc greene a pound of tobacco	00	00	6
33	to Thomas Kingman[194] two bushels of malt	00	06	0
34	to hanah Kingman two pound cotton wool: 3: quarts molasses	00	05	7
35	july 14th to widow burll: 4: pound of cotton wooll	00	03	4
36	to James Humfry six pound cotton wooll e a peck salt	00	11	08
37	to Nicholas Phillips wife[195] for cotton wool	00	01	4
38	July the 23 to Cornelius Holbrook nine pound of tobacco 6d	[?]	4	6
39	to decon dyer[196] a quarter mutten: 12: three quarters	00	3	2

[Page 49]

	ll	s	p
Colanor 1700 Hunt[197] debtor for halef a ~~peck~~ bushel salt dll to his son	00	01	o[?]
for a lamb dll to his son[198]	00	06	00
for ~~a peck~~ halef a bushel of salt dll to his son	00	01	00[2]
may 1701 balanced accounts with Colonor Hunt e thare was			
dwe to mee from him	00	02	00
for two poun of candles dll to Samuell Hunt	00	~~07~~	~~08~~
July the 4 1702 ~~to be~~ to decon dyer a quarter			
of motton 12 pound 3^d per pound	00	03	0
to Decon dyer a quarter of motton13 pound	00	03	3
to Decon dyer a quarter of motton sent by John Hunt 9^{ll} & halef:		0~~1~~2	~~7~~11
August the 24th to Colonall Hunt 3 quarters of lamb 26: 2 ½^d per pound	0	05	05
September the 29th: to moris Truant a quarter of motton 10 p:	0	02	01
the 29th to Colanor Hunt [?] 2 quarters of motten 21 ½	0	04	05
October the 6: to David Carver two pound e halef of cand^{els}	0	01	08
to Samuell Andrues maid six pound talo e a pound of yarn	0	05	06
to david carvers william pittey a pound candles e halef	0	0~~0~~1	0~~0~~8
to david carvers william pittey 9^{ll} e a halef of candels	0	06	04
October the 25th 1704: Beniamin white brantery dter			
two galloons of oyll e a quart 2^s–3^d per galloon			
e halef a bushel of salt	0	06	4
25 to Insine hu^{n}ts wife[199] 4^{ll} of shuger	00	02	0
to mis Torrey[200] 6 quarts of ayll	00	03	4 1/2
28 to john wild[201] two bushels of salt	00	09	0
31 to john Whitman one bushel of salt	00	04	6
31 to Joseph orcut one bushel of salt	00	04	6
31 to Thomas Caplin[202] of brantr 2 bushels			
of salt e 5 quarts of ayll e 3^d penc for [?]	00	12	01
to William coplin[203] of brantery a bushel			
e a halef of salt	00	06	09
novem: to curanall hunt a bushel			
e a halefof salt	00	06	9
to john copling[204] one bushel salt	00	04	6
to john green one bushel of salt	00	04	6
to Joseph green one sheep	00	08	0
3 to Lift. Nash 2 bushel mall^{aco} fesis	00		
to Samuell white halef a bushel salt	00	02	3
to Thomas copling in malasses dll to [?]	00	01	11
July the 10 James Humfry creditor for wefing of 44 yards			
e a halef cotton e lining cloth 4^d per yard	00	14	10

Line		ll	s	p
1	Joseph pittey debter in the yeer: 1699 for a hat	00	10	00
2	for a side of mutten	00	03	00
3	for a sider barell	00	02	03
4	for fife quorts of oyle	00	02	06
5	tallo	00	01	09
6	for a peck of solt	00	00	08
7	may the: 20: 1700: for two peses of ayt	00	12	00
8	for a bushel of salt	00	02	00
9	July the: 14: 1700 James Humfrey debteer for six quorts ^{oyll}	00	03	00
10			01	11
11	September the 20 for one bushel of salt		02	00
12	July the: 11: for a side of lamb dll to colanor hunt son	00	04	00
13	for one pound of candels	00	00	08
14	August the 2^{nt} for a quorter of lamb	00	01	06
15	dito for a quorter of mutten	00	02	03
16	September the 13 for three quarters of mutten dll to John $^{31\ po}$	00	06	06
17	november the 6 to John hunt two bushels sallt	00	04	00
18	the 20 to rafe Tailor a peck of salt dll to youre father:		00	06
19	pheburary the: 25: 1703 William pratt debtter for: 2: bushel malt			
20	march to moris Trewfant three peck mallt	00	02	03
21	Aperell 26 to brother Thomas Reed two bushels of malt			
22	27 to Thomas Reed Ju^{nr} two bushels malt			
23	June: 18: to brother Thomas Reed foure bushels of malt			
24	to brother Thomas Reed a 100 shoonailes	0	00	4
25	July 14 to brother Thomas Reed a bushel of salt	0	03	8
26	desem to two bushels of salt	0	08	0
27	may 2 to two ^{1704} paper biles of cadit	1	02	0
28	5 to three hndered bord nailes	0	03	0
29	to one 1000 clabbord nailes	0	06	0
30	June 28 to one bushell of salt dll to hano[205]	0	04	6
31	July 26 to one thousand bord nailes dll Samuell	0	10	6
32	August 3: to 700 bord nailes	0	08	2
33	to 3000 shingell nailes 4^{s} per thousand	0	12	0
34	to a hat dll to son $Samu^{e}ll$	0	07	0
35	to 3 yards of silk	1	08	6
36	to one pound of logwood	0	00	4
37	desember to mony paid to him selef	0	11	4
38	to John $T^{o}rey$ one six quorts e a pint malases:		06	4
39	Jenuary: 1: to one galloon of oyle	0	02	3
40	pheb 20 to malases dll to youre selef	0	00	8
41	June 1705: to one bushel of salt	0	05	0

[Page 51]

	ll	s	p
pheburary the: 24th: 1699: 1700: mr Samuell Torey[206] debter for			
tooe pound of candels: 8d: per pound dll to his son	00	01	04
August: ~~16~~ 1700: Joseph pratt snr ~~of a~~ for a quorter motten	00	02	00
August Decon Dyer for a quorter of lamb	00	01	11
August James humfry for a quorter of lamb	00	01	11
August the 26th: Samuell porters wife:[207]: 5: pound logwood quort oyle	00	02	06
the 29th: zechariah Bicknell one galloon of oyl	00	02	00
the 31 to Colenor Hunt a lamb: 26: pound	00	06	00
September the: 3: william pratt to joseph pratt halef bushel salt	00	01	00
Jenuary the: 2nt: 1701 ballanced acounpts with william peety			
and thare was dwe to mee from him in mony	00	03	08
phebur the first 1702/3 John Torey[208] credit for six bushels			
of barly			
pheburary the: 24: John Bicknell Creditor for: 20: bushels barly			
march the: 2: 1703 Thomas Reed Snr credit for: 15: bushels barly			
to william pittey six bushels of barly e otes			
to enock lovell three bushels e a peck e seven quorts			
august: 1703: enock lovell credetor for six bushels e a peck			
e a halef of barly			
November: 7th: 1704: Joshua Smith[209] ~~hallf~~ halef a			
bushell of salt	00	02	03
10 to joseph alling Snr[210] of brantery			
a bushell e a halef of salt	00	06	9
16 to Samuell porter a bushell			
e a halef salt e 3 quorts of oull	0	08	0

Line		ll	s	p
1	november the 3 1701 to nickolas whitemarch[211] one busell salt e a halef			
2	the 5 to wido bolter[212] 5000 bordnailes halef bushell salt	0	6	0
3	the 15 to Decon Torey a bushell of salt dll to him selef	0	2	0
4	the 17 to John boutage a bushel e halef of salt dll to son william	0	3	0
5	the 21 to John Shawe a go[u]n dll to him selef with a wormor	1	15	6
6	the 24 to Nicolas Shawe for paper mony over & above the rate	07	07	0
7	to wido Humfry a bushell of salt	0	02	0
8	the 28 to John Randall Snr a bushell	0	02	0
9	to Samuell andreuse ~~a bush~~ two bushels salt	0	04	0
10	desember the 4 to wido eyles 9 heds e ploocks 3d per pees	002	3	
11	the 6 to to mr desperat[?][213] a bushel of salt dll to ater pouell[214]	0	02	0
12	the 6 to ater pouell a bushell of salt	0	02	0
13	the 11 to william Trask[215] a sheep 52 pound 2 ½d per pound 2d: frait:	011	0	
14	the 19 Samuell white manattecut junr[216]	0	00	4
15	the 24 to joseph green a cowe dll to himselef	3	00	0
16	the 24 recened with Increse bates wife[217] e thare was dwe to mee:	0	07	5
17	to wido eyels foure heds e ploocks	0	01	0
18	January the 7: to john pratt jun a bushel of salt	0	02	0
19	the 12 joseph green for a 103 ½ll ~~and three~~ pound e halef porck 3 ½d pound:	1	10	2
20	feburary the 6th to Ephraim pray a sheep 28 pound 2 ½ per pound			
21	and six penc over hed and ploock 4d dll to him selefe	0	06	8
22	the 19 to Samuell french[218] a bushell of salt	0	02	0
23	the 27 a pare of shoos to john holis	0	03	6
24	the 28 to John green mony laid oute at hingham in rum e shuger	0	09	6
25	bordenailes to john green	0	00	2
26	march the 10 to a bushel of salt to John Shawe	0	02	0
27	the 27 a pare of shoos to John hollis	0	03	6
28	Captain french[219] for bringing a bag of cotten wooll	0	01	0
29	Captain french for a ~~pee~~ halef a bushel salt dll bedlo[220]:	0	01	3
30	to Incres bates wife three pound cotten wooll	0	05	6
31	~~july~~ August the: 26: John Tory credetor for sheep	0	15	9
32	1703 Jonathon Torey credit for carting			
33	fifee lode of wood	00	03	09
34	to the bering of 8000 in shingels	00	04	00
35	to one lode of woods carting	00	00	09

	ll	s	p
furst frait with the bote was to bostoun	00	03	00
a frait at bostoun wood fro mrs tilar	00	09	00
a frait of seweed to bostoune	00	07	06
a frait of wod e clabbord at bostoune e mine home e corne	01	02	00
a frait shingle e clabbords to bostoun	00	11	00
2 fraits of wood from Smelbrook[221]	00	07	06
a frait of shingle e clabbord	00	06	00
a frait of wod to bostoun	00	09	00
a frait of wod from Smelbrook	00	05	00
desember the 23 ~~&~~ 1699 Samuell Andrues Credetor for			
two peeses of ayt reseved	00	12	00
more two peeses of ayt	00	12	00
August the: 1: reseved in mony	01	06	1

[Page 54]

	ll	s	p
August the: 19: 1699: recened with Lambur Desper of Bra^{n}terey			
and balanced all acounpts to this day & thare was dwe to mee	00	00	00
A the: 26: ~~Lam~~: 1699: Lambur Desper debter for a quorter of lam	00	02	03
September the: 4th: for a sid of lamb: 17: pound: 3^{d}: per pound hed			
poo$^{ck\ dll\ to\ your\ maid}$	0	04	7
the 8th for a quorter mutten 9 ½ 3^{d}	0	01	11
the 15 for a side of sheep 21 ½ 2: ½	0	04	06
the 22: for a side of a beef: 196 pound: 2^{d}: per pound	1	12	08
for the frait of the beef e foure ounces of peper	0	02	00
the: 30: for a quorter of be^{e}f: 108 pound: 2^{d} per pound	0	18	00
tranceporing of a quorter of beef	0	01	00
october the: 6th: for seven quorters of mutten: 87: pound	0	18	01
the 13 for: 189: pound of beef 2^{d} per pound ~~e frait~~	1	13	02
for bringing two barels of beer from bostoun	0	01	00
for a quorter of mutten dll to youre wife	0	02	07
desember the 8th: for 292 pound mutten 2^{d} per pound	3	00	10
for a bushel of salt & at the same time	0	02	06
desember the: 21: <u>1699</u> recened with Mr Lambur			
Desper and ballansed all acounpts and thare was			
dwe to mee from him in money	07	08	00
pheburary the: 17: for three quorters of mutten dll to him selef:	0	08	00
reseved the hole sum of Lambur Desper all payd in 1700			
desember the 29th: 1699: reseved of lambur desper wife	03	00	00
jenuary the 4th reseved of him of him selef	01	04	00
pheburary the: 17: reseved in mony	00	06	00
aperell the 4 ezera whitemarsh credetor for a pees of ayt	0	6	0

[Page 55]

	ll	s	p
november the: 3: <u>1699</u> David Carver debter for a hundered			
e ten pound of beef dll to James Richards[222]: 2^{d} per ^{pound}	00	18	04
november the: 6th: J~~o~~ohn Rogers[223] a bushel e halef of salt	00	03	09
november the: 3: John Burel for salt e oyell	00	04	03
John boutage a bushel salt seven quorts oyle quorte beef	01	01	00
Samuel White manetecut quorter beef	00	15	10
Thomas White Snr manatecut two bushels salt:	00	05	00
John bouttage for aute feet & a cowes belley	00	01	08
nicolas whitemarch a quarte of oyell	00	00	06
Ephraim burell for a bushell e a hallfe of sallt	00	03	09
the: 16: Thomas white snr six quorts of oyell	00	03	00
Mr hubbard of november: 15: for a frait of eyre ware	00	10	00
Samuell Andrews for a bushell e halef of salt	00	03	09
the 18th to Samuell pittey a quorter of mutten	00	02	08
the 21 for a bushell of salt to zeckeria gurny $^{Ephraim\ burls}$ quart oyl	00	03	00
the 22 to [?] Edward bates one bushell e halef salt	00	03	09
Samuell whitemarch for salt dll to his man John will^{kison}[224]		00	09
decon Torey for a galloon of oyell	00	02	00
Joseph green for one bushell e halef of salt	00	03	09
John Randall two bushels of salt	00	05	00
pasience green tw quorts of oyell	00	01	00
desember the: 16th: 233 $^{2\ ½\ d}$ pound of mutten dll to Samuell			
andreus wief[225] at his one house by my selef	02	08	6
the 18th to Richard devenport 172: pound mutten 2 ½ ^{d} per pound	01	15	10
desember the 20th to John dracke 157 pound mutten two heds ^{ploo}	01	13	00
desember the 20 to beniamin dracke: 111: pound mutten hed ^{ploock}	10	3	03
the 19 to Decon Torey one bushell of salt	0	02	06
the 27th Samuell Andrews: 174: pound mytten 2 ½ ^{d}:	01	10	00
Jenuary the: 4th: gideon turell: 98: pound mutten 2 1/2 ^{d} pound	01	00	05
Joseph richards for cloth	00	03	00
Joseph pratt Junr for fife pound of wooll dll to Johana benson:	00	[9?]	0
pheburary the: 29: Richard devenport debter for: 24: pound of wooll			
dll to his wife[226] 12^{d} per pound	01	04	00
aperell the: 3: Ezra whitemar^{sh} six bushels malt: 2^{s} = 9^{d} per bush^{ell}	0	16	06
aperell the: 10: William Drack debter for hay	00	0~~9~~5	00
aperell the: 10: zechariah bicknell debter for hay	00	18	00
aperell the: 19: John Vinson ^{Snr} debter for hay dll to his son John	00	18	00
william pittey a peck of salt 00 00 08	00	00	08
may the: 2^{nt}: John pratt snr for malt	00	13	00
July nathaniel humfry peck salt	00	00	06
uncle vinson for a bushel e a halef salt	00	03	06
october the: 20: 1700 Samuell Andreus for a lamb	00	05	00
october the: 28: 1700 Thomas White for two bushels of salt	00	04	00

Line		ll	s	p
1	August the: 12th: Incr~~e~~ ees Bate debter quorter muten: 13 pound 3^{d} per ^{pound}	00	03	0~~9~~6
2	Edward Bate for two pound mutten 3^{d} per pound	00	00	06
3	Ezera Whitemarch for: 14: pound mutten 3^{d} per pound	00	05	06
4	mary badlam[227] for two ploocks e one hed	00	00	07
5	August the: 18: 1699: Joshua Smith $^{for\ three\ heds\ pluck}$ dll to Joseph Haiden[228]	00	0	09
6	the: 19: for a quorter of lamb e hed e ploock to Joseph Haiden	00	1	08
7	mary ^{19} badlam for one quorter of lamb dll to hur selef	00	2	00
8	the 21 a chees to Joseph haiden: 5: 1 quor	00	1	11
9	the: 25: to Joshua Smith seven pound vell e quorter	00	01	09
10	August the: 15: John Randall for nine pound e quorter	00	01	11
11	mary badlam for a quorter of mutten: 14: pound: 3^{d}: per p	00	03	6
12	Ezera whitemarch for a quorter of muteron: 6 ½:	00	01	18
13	the 26: Joseph Green 15 pound mutten 3^{d} per pound	00	03	9
14	the 26 Josiah ricply 8 [?] pound mutten[?] 3^{d} per pound	00	02	0
15	September the: 3rd: Josepeh Haiden 2 quorters $^{21\ pound}$ mutten	00	05	0
16	September the 3rd Joshua Smith 10 pound 3^{d} per pound	00	2	6
17	the 3 for a quorter mutten to mar badlam: 14: pound 3^{d} per pound	00	03	6
18	the 3 for a quorter mutten to Icebod Holdroock: 12: pound	00	03	0
19	the 3 for a quorter mutten to John dracke: 12: pound	00	03	0
20	the 4 of September: 1699: dll to william drack wife[229] 13 ^{pound} e quorter			
21	for sheeps wooll	00	14	4
22	the: 9th: for a quorter of mutten Joseph Haiden	00	2	10
23	Samuell Andreus	00	3	2
24	mary badlam	00	03	6
25	September the 8 for a quorter mutten: 10 to Joseph Green	00	02	6
26	September 8 Josiah Ripley for mutten	00	00	8
27	the 12: to Joseph Haiden two pound wooll a peck sallt	00	03	0
28	the 15 a quorter mutten hed e ploock to mary badlo	00	03	2
29	Joseph Pratt Ju^{nr}	00	02	2
30	richard devenport a quorter mutten	00	02	10
31	Samuell Andreus	00	02	4
32	~~Inch~~ Increes bate	00	0~~3~~0	~~9~~5
33	mary badlam	00	02	9
34	the 30 mary bedlo one quorter of motten	00	02	5
35	october the 7 mary badlam	00	02	10
36	Susana Shart[230]	00	01	4
37	Josia riply qu 12 ½	00	02	7
38	Sister richards	00	04	06
39	octo the 13 Joseph allime a quorter of beef^{85} e frait	00	14	02
40	octo the 13 Thomas white for a quorter of beef^{92} e frait	00	15	10
41	the: 15for a bushel e halef of salt for Thomas White dll wi[? Ruh^{or}]		03	09

[Page 56] (*continued*)

Line		ll	s	p
42	Thomas white Ju^{nr} ~~seven~~ ^{six} quorts of oyell dll to Thomas hollbroock		3	00
43	novemebr the: 10: samuell holes[231] a bushell of sallt Thomas White acount 2	06		
44	the: 16: for six quorts of oyll dll to youre wife mare		5	06

	ll	s	p
August the: 19th: John Hunt debter for a quarter of lamb			
dll to his wife at his house	00	01	10
for a gal^{loone}quorts of oyle 6^{d} per quort	00	02	00
for a bushell of salt dll to his son John[232]	00	02	06
desember the 12th 1699 reseved of Increse bate one bushell			
of indian corne by my my sone			
more two bushels of indian corne			
may the: 10: 1700 Mr Hubbard ^{Bostoun} debter for the frait of twenty			
three bars of eyr dll at bostoun to his son	00	02	06
the: 18: for stones brouft from grape iland dll to the farms	0	06	00

[Page 58]

	ll	s	p
July the: 18th: 1699 John portter Snr debter for on			
~~quortertr~~ quorter of muten: 11: pound 2 ½ ^{d} per pound	00	02	3
September the 8 Sargant Whiteman[233] three bushel of salt	00	07	0
Josia ripley one bushell of salt	00	02	4
	00	02	8
Sargant for three galloones of oyll	00	03	0
Sargant whitman ~~six quorts of oyle~~ halef a pound candels	00	030	4
for a quorter of mutten six pound 3^{d} penc per pound	00	01	06
novemebr the: 1st: 1699 John boutage debtter for one bushel of salt			
dll to him selef	00	02	6
Aperell the 10 Mr Long of bostoun debter for foure thousand			
and seven hundered of shingle 9^{s} per thousand			
whareof I have reseved ten shillings in mony for the shingles			

	ll	s	p
Zecheriah Bicknell debter for part of a croscut sawe		01	0
Aperell the 5th 1699 for a quorter of veale 11 pound & halef	0	03	4
Aperell the: 10: dll thhomas Bickmell three bushel of otes	0	04	0
the: 14: dll to thomas Bicknell three bushels of wotes	0	04	0
1/2 15 = 2			
iiiii 1–9			
2 6			
maye the: 1st: 1699 reseved of Zecheriah bicknell	00	12	00
iiii iiiiiii			

[Page 60]

Cnow all men By presence that I phill Reed of Bergwater in the county of plimmouth yeuman do owe and am indebted unto James Richards of Waymouth the sum of ayte shillings ~~mony~~ of lawfull money of new Ingland all which I do promise to pay to him or, or his order on the: 16: of march nex In serving in testimony whareof I have put my hand the fourth of pheburary 1699 phillip Reed [signiture]

	ll	s	p
May the: 4th: 1699 Cornelias ~~Hololbrooock~~ Holbroock			
debter for two ~~hue~~ iron huck for a dore	00	00	05
may the: 15th: for one pound of tobacka dll to Jhon Vining	00	00	06
August the: 25th for a quorter of lamb dll to selef	00	01	09
may the: 14: 1700: Thomas White ^{Snr} of brantery for fish	00	02	00
to Richard Thare[234] of brantery for fish	00	01	00
to Lambur Desper of brantery for fish	00	01	00
to Thomas Reed for fish	00	01	00
to Richard Degurs for fish	00	00	02
the 18 ^{to} Richard Thare for fish	00	01	00
the 18 to Thomas White for fish which John hadman had	00	00	04
the 18 to Joseph Green for fish	00	01	00
the 18 to Colanor hunt for fish	00	01	00
the 18 to Lifenant White for fish	00	00	04
the 18 to Lambur Desper for fish	00	01	04
the 18 to edward darbe[235] for fish	00	00	03
the 23 to Thomas White Sn^{r} for fich	00	01	04
the 23 to blase vinting for fish	00	00	06
wido holbroock[236] for 2 pound wooll	00	02	00
maddam hunt[237] for a peck of salt	00	00	0~~6~~7
ebeneser pratt a bushel of salt	00	02	00
zekeriah bicknell: 77: b pound beef 2^{d}–1q	00	14	05
zekariah bicknell for a galloon of oyell	00	02	00
november the: 3: Samuell Andreus six pound wooll	00	06	00
zekariah bicknell for a bushel of salt	00	02	00
november the 12th: John pratt of Brigwater a bushel ^{salt}	00	02	04
to william pittey halef a bushell of sallt	00	01	02
to william pitty halef a bushell of sallt	00	01	02
may the 27th: 1701 Thomas White ^{Snr} for fish	00	03	00
may the 23th uncell porter for 17 pound tobacka	00	03	00

	ll	s	p
January the: 16: 1699/8			
Theofelus Curtis[238] debter for: 165 pound of mutten			
dll to Blaes Vinting at 2^d 3/1 q per pound	01	17	08
for two heds e ploocks 4^d per pees	00	00	08
this dll by verball order from his one mouth			
I gathered the minister Rate in the yeer 1699			
John bicknell	00	15	2
Nathanell Ford	00	10	0
John Green	00	06	0
Nicolas phillips	00	06	8
William pratt	00	02	10
Josia Ripley	00	00	05
Wido Humfrey	00	03	04
James Richards	00	14	00
Thomas Bicknell	00	06	00
Mord^{e}cai Trewant[239]	00	04	06
Zeckeriah Bicknell	00	10	10
Josia Ripley	00	02	00
Nicolas phillips	00	06	06
Zecheriah bicknell	00	02	00
John Green	00	04	00
William pratt	00	02	10
July the 11th: 1701 paid to beniamin in money	02	~~9~~10	00
desember the 4th 1700brother Thomas Reed debter for two			
bushels of salt dll to William Reed	00	04	00
June: 1700 to two bushels of malt			
July the: 6th to foure pound of cotten wooll	00	07	04
august the 15 to ten pound of cotten wooll	00	18	04
to two bushels of malt dll to him selef	0		
november to 350 shoonailes	00	01	0
to two bushels of sallt	00	08	0
desem: 11 to a bushel of salt e thurty two shillings mony	01	16	0
aperell the 19: 1704: Johnathon mountford debter	4	5	6
for ~~8000~~ 800 clabbords e 6000 of shingells dll to his man	05	06	00
to 2000 in shingels 11^s per thousand dll to his man:	01	02	00
may 10 9000 in shingels 11^s per thousand dll to his man	04	19	00

	ll	s	p
Minster Torey debter for two bushels of sallt	00	05	00
Mr Samuell Torey debter in octeber 1699 for six quorts			
of lamp oyle	00	03	00
for two bushels of whete [?]	00	10	00
for money beef e salt	03	03	00
for thre 4 metse[240] tungs	00	03	00
for a quorter of mutten	00	02	06
for a quorter of mutten 13 pound	00	02	09
for money e wood	01	15	09
	06	00	00
June the: 12th: 1700 recned with Beniamin e thare was dwe to			
him in mony	05	00	05
Desember the: 21st: 1700 recwed with Beniamin Richards			
and balanced all acounpts e hee had then in mony	09	04	00
november the 7th 1701 balanced acounpts with beniamin			
pheburary			
aperell: 1702: brother Thomas Reed ~~er~~ credetor for			
for thirty two bushels of barly at 2^{s}–8 per bushell			
march the 14th: 1704 Johnathon mountford credit for			
two thousand bord nailes: 9^{s}: in	00	18	00
to a quorter of a hundered of shot	00	07	00
to seven pound e a halef of flex	00	07	06
to one pound of powder	00	04	00
aperell: 19th: to one barell of oyell	02	00	00
to halef a quorter of shuger	00	06	00
to a 1000 of shoo nailes	00	03	08
to a pees of scotos clooth[241]	01	03	07
to one pound of pouder	00	04	00
to 4 sives 6^{s} per pees	01	04	00
to one thousand clabbor nailes	00	06	00
to a lock e a one pound of alum	00	02	02

[Page 64]

	ll	s	p
November the: 15: 1698: Joseph pratt Junr deb^{t}er			
for: 49: pound of chees at 2^{d} per pound dll to his wife	00	08	02
march the: 15: 1699: rec^{e}ned with Ezra Whitemarsh			
e balanced all acounpts e thare dwe to ~~him~~ mee from			
him in money reseved in full of his money	01	06	00
march the: 15: 1699: recned with Joseph Richards			
e balanced all acounpts e thare was due to mee from			
him in money ~~reseved in full of his money~~	01	06	00
the of march 1699 reseved the full of Joseph Richards			
in the yeer: 1699: William pratt credetor for moing			
e feching of hay one day	00	03	00
for moing for wido Humfrey fresh grases	00	02	06
for moing at feesey's one day	00	03	00
for two pigs at John Bicknells	00	03	00
for two ~~tue~~ kocks[242] of inglish hay	00	03	00
	00	14	06
desember the: 9th: 1699 [?] William Traske debter for: 113:			
pound of mutten: 2: 2/1d: per pound 6d per last recning	01	04	00
Aperell the 28 William pratt credetor for mony paid	01	0~~9~~0	00
to mony	00	06	00
to mony	00	12	00
to paper mony	01	00	00
	02	18	06
november the ^{1701} 14th balanced acounpts with william pratt			
and thare was dwe to him nor mee nothing	00	00	00
in September: 1702: to a barell of sider grinding e presing	01	[?]	3
november to a peck of salt	00	01	00

[Page 65]

	ll	s	p
August the: 5: 1699: ~~John Hao~~ William prat debter for a side			
of lambe dll to John haydun of brantery: 15: 3 per pound	00	03	09
September the 8: dll to John haidan a quorter of mutten: 12:	00	02	10
the 15 for a side of mutten	00	02	09
to him selef foure bushels of indian corn	00	08	00
to hana youre wife foure pound of sheeps wooll	00	04	08
for fife quorts quorts of oyle	00	02	06
for land at his dare	00	0~~2~~1	00
for a quorter of beef 108 pound: 2d: per pound	00	18	00
for one bushel of salt	00	02	00
	02	06	06
November the 28th: 1699 ballanced acounpts with			
William pratt son to math pratt[243] e thare was dwe			
to mee from him in money	00	07	06
to a beer barell	00	02	06
~~Jun~~ march the: 20: for one bushell malt dll to yoore wife	00	03	00
~~aperel the 3 for two quorts of same~~	~~00~~	~~00~~	~~04~~
~~John~~ to John Haidon in vele	00	01	04
June the 4th for two bushels of malt dll moris	00	06	00
~~June the 19 one shilling lent~~	~~00~~	~~01~~	~~00~~
for a peck a barly e a peck of salt	00	01	02
for a chees	00	00	09
for makeing sider	00	02	00
Jenuary the 10th 1701 for part of a sheep 24 pound:	00	04	00
Decon Bates order[?] for mony	00	03	03
march the: 14th: for a peck of turnups	00	00	04
for a pound of tobackah	00	00	06
for three bushels of indian corn	00	09	06
for two pigs 2s–3d per pees	00	04	06
August the 24 for foull e a sheeps skin	00	02	03
September the 3 for a quorter of lamb	00	01	05
September 3 to goade Green	00	01	00
September 3 for a sheep skin dll to hano[244]	00	01	04
the 13 for a hed e plloock	00	00	03
the 15 for a quorter of lamb e halcf a pound butter	00	01	07
the 16 for one galloon of mallase	00	02	06
the 18 for halef a pound of butter	00	00	~~03~~11
october the 4th: to a quorter of lamb	0	01	10 1/2
	2	18	09
For 19 pound of flex e a bushel e a peck of salt	10	15	09
July the 6th 1703 balanced accounts with ~~la~~ increse bats			
wife and thare was dwe to mee	00	01	09

Line	ll	s	p
September the: 7: <u>1698:</u> recened with Thomas Bicknel			
e cleered all former accounpts & thare was due to mee from			
him in money	02	02	08
Aperell the: 19: <u>1698</u> paid to Thomas White	6	07	
Sn^{r} of brantery for Thomas Bicknell	00	04	06
for ~~one~~ one dayes worck of our boy[245] doune at neck	00	01	06
for one sheepe dll to him selef	00	10	06
Aperell the 30 for one pound of tobacka	00	00	06
for a drawing knife	00	04	06
may the: 8: 1699 for six sheep e six lambes	0~~3~~1	~~0~~13	00
for one bushel of malt	00	02	09
	~~5~~4	~~01960~~	1~~6~~1
Jenuary the: 31th: 1699 Ephraim pray of Brantery			
debtor for foure sheep dll at his one houce to him selef			
waite: 172: pound 2^{d} 3q per pound	01	19	05
for six pound & a quarter of sheeps wooll: 12^{d}: per pound	00	06	03
for foure heds & plucks: 4^{d} per pees	00	01	04
march the: 16th: 1699: paid to Ebenezer Thare[246]			
of Brantery six pounds fifteen shillings in mony for			
the full prise of three hifers to bee delivered the next			
may foloing sound wind e limb the one three yeers olde the other			
two to bee two yeers olde a pees reseved those hiffers			
may the: 13th: 1699 joseph pratt debtor for two bushels malt			
dll to Johane benson	00	05	6
June the: 10: dll to Johane benson three bushels of malt	0	08	3
paide the full of his debt			
July the: 29th: 1699 Collanor Hunt debtor for a quarter			
of lambe dll ~~to~~ at his one house	00	02	00
August the: 5th: for a quarter of lambe	00	02	00
the: 12: for a quarter ~~mutten~~ lambe	00	02	00
the: 16: for forty six pound of ches: 4 ½^{d}: per pound	00	17	03
the 19 for a quarter of lamb	00	02	00
the 19 to Samuell Thare[247] in mutten e hed e ploock	00	01	03
the 21st Samuell Thare in a ches 5 pound 3 quorters	00	02	01
the 25 for a leven pound & halef vell	00	02	08
the: 26: for a quarter of lam: 7 ½: pound 3^{d}	00	01	10
September: the 3rd: for a quor of mutten 17: ½: 3^{d}: per pound	00	03	08
the 3 to Samuell Thare: 10: pound mutten 3^{d} per pound	00	02	06
halef a pound of tobacka to Samuell Thare	00	00	
the 8th for a quarter of mutten 10 ½	00	02	0~~6~~7
the 15 for a quarter of mutten 12 tuppect ½	00	02	06
the 22 for a quarter of mutten 12	00	02	06
the 29 for two cheeses 14 pound 4 ½^{d} per pound	00	05	03

Line		ll	s	p
1	ougust: 1698 Thomas Bicknell credetor for money			
2	reseved of himself	00	18	00
3	for a quorter of beef	00	15	00
4	for worck reseved e a shilling in money	00	02	06
5	Aperell the: 15: for money reseved	00	09	00
6	for money dll to him selef	0~~1~~3	~~0~~12	00
7		~~3~~5	06	06
8	Jenuary the: 30th: 1699 Nicolas Saltter debter for			
9	one sheep 36 pound 2^{d} 3^{q} per pound	00	08	03
10	for three pound of wooll 12^{d} per pound	00	03	00
11	for a pluck	00	00	03
12	this ~~d~~ dll to him selef			
13	pheburary the: 2^{nt}: dll ten pound & a halef sheeps wooll 12^{d}	00	10	06
14	to three pound of candells at 8^{d} per pound	00	02	00
15	september the 18th balanced with Nicolas Salter e thare wos dwe	0	01	06
16	the 15 for a lamb dll to him selef 27 pound	0	06	00
17	Jenuary 1699: reseved of Ephraim pray	00	06	00
18	reseved of Ephraim pray in money	02	01	00
19	Jonuary the: 30: 1699 reseved of Nicolas Sallter one			
20	pare of mens shoos french heels	00	06	00
21	reseved of Thomas porter uppon Nicolas Salters acounpt	00	04	06
22	september 30 for f a quorter of mutten dll at Majors Hunt[248] houce			
23	twelef pound 2 ½^{d} per pound	00	02	06
24	for halef a quorter of beef 53 ½ pound e a halef 2^{d} per pound	00	08	11
25	for halef a pound of candels	00	00	04
26	october the 16 for a frait corn at brantery	00	08	00
27	novemebr the: 9th: for halef a sheep dll to John haidon[249]: 21 ½:	00	0~~7~~6	06
28	the 10th for one pound of tobacka dll to Jo^{h}n haidon	00	00	06
29	the 17 for one quorter of mutten dll to John haidon	00	05	00
30	to Joseph haiden halef a bushell of salt e: 2^{d}:			
	mony e a pound tobacco	00	01	11
31	the: 18th: for a bushell of sallt dll to John Haidon	00	02	06
32	the: 29th: for fifteen pound of pork dll to			
	John Haidon 4^{d} per pound	00	05	00
33	desember the: 1: dll John Haidon two quorts of oyell	00	01	00
34	the 20th to John Haidon for three quorters of lamb	00	04	02
35	to John Haidon for porck desember the 20	00	02	01
36	June the: 25: 1700 reseved of Colonor Hunt three			
	pound foure shillings e seven pence			
37	~~to ballam~~ which wos the balanc of ~~a~~ acounpt between us			

[Page 68]

	ll	s	p
Mrs Catern Simchins Credetor for tweleve pound			
in money which I have boroed of her selef at			
Bostoune which is due to her to this day: June: 1698			
this money is payed ienuarey the 2nd 1699			
July 4th: 1701 Decon Dyer in mutten15 pound 3^{d}	0	03	9
Insine Hunt 6 ½ pound halef	0	01	7
Ms french 6 ½ pound halef	0	01	7
Mr Torey 7 ½ pound halef	0	01	10
John Torey 6 1/3 pound three quarters	0	01	8
the: 15: for a quarter of lamb to Decon Dyer [?] 8P: 3^{d}: pound	0	02	00
the 15 to uncel porter a quarter of lamb: 8 p 3^{d} per pound	0	02	00
the 15 to matthew pratts wife[250] 2 2/1 talo 4^{d} pound e a jynte of lamb	0	~~0~~01	10
the 15 to john porters wife[251] a jynte of lamb	00	01	00
the 15 to Samuell Aandreus wife a ~~bar~~ lambes skin e quarter lamb	0	03	00
August the: 2^{nt}: for a quarter of lambs Ms french	0	01	06
the 2^{nt} to Ms ~~french~~ hunt[252] a quarter of lambe	0	01	06
the 2^{nt}: Coranor Hunt a quarter of lambe	0	01	06
to Decon Dyer 17 pound mutten	0	04	03
to matthew pratt junr	0	01	08
a broom to Ms French	0	00	04
September the 3 to Decon Dyer a side of mutten17 ½	0	03	00
the 15 for a side of lamb 14 ½ to Decon Dyer	0	03	~~6~~7 ½
the 8 to Richard Devenport a galloon of ayell	0	02	00
Captaine ffrench in 1701 for frait 6 thousand of shingels	0	03	06
Captaine ffrench for frait of buls e barels a cask of molases	0	3	00
for a peck of butter salt to mrs french	00	01	00
the 22 to Insine Hunt a galloon of mollases e a peck salt	0	03	00
September the 26 to Decon Torey upon Ebenezer pratts			
acount in sheeps wo^{o}ll e ayle	0	04	09
october the 16th to a peck of salt to m^{s} French	00	01	00
october the 22^{nt} to william pitey a peck of salt a galloon of ayl	0	02	06
october the 24th to Samuell Whitemarch 3: gll e halef ayell	0	07	00
november the 5 to ms french a peck of sallt	0	01	00
the 9th to m^{s} ffrench a peck of sallt	0	01	00
the 14th to william pittey a bushel of salt dll James	0	02	00
the 14 to Thomas Reed junr bushell of sallt	0	02	00
to Captaine ffrench the frait of nine barells	0	01	06
the 24 to Captaine french a bushel salt	0	02	09
the 26 to John Pittey halef a bushel of salt	0	1	06
the 28 to m^{s} french halef a bushel of salt e[?] ^{am}	0	1	04
to william pittey mony	00	09	00
to john pratt for william pittey	00	12	4

	ll	s	p
maye the: 14: 1698 I boroed six pound in money			
of william Toreyes wife[253] and it is dwe to hur to this day			
paid the above sum which I say I boroed in mony			
six pound with my one: hand June: 1698			
desember: 31: 1700 ballanced all accounpts with Cornelyus			
Holbroock e thare was dwe to mee from him in mony	00	03	00
July: the: 25th: 1702 Mr Torey for a quorter mutten			
twelvef pound 3^{d} per pound	00	03	00
Captain french a quarter mutten 12 pound 3^{d} per pound	00	03	00
august the 1st: to a quorter of mutten 11 ½ to Mr Torey	00	02	10
august the 1st to Thomas Holbroock a lamb—	00	06	00
the 8 to Mr Torey a galloon of mallases	00	02	06
to william pratt two bushels of mallt	00	06	00
to capttaine ffrench halef a bushell of salt	00	01	06
the 13th to Joseph pittey to yards of cloth one caresi the other ^{plain}	00	09	0~~3~~6
the 13th to Joseph pittey for shoos dll to him selef	00	04	00
to Mr Torey a quort of salt	00	00	02
the 25 to steeven ffrench jur[254] 3 quarters of mutten a bushel ^{sallt}		08	03
the 26 to forteen pound of sheeps wooll to Samull porters ^{wife}[255]		12	08
the 26 to Mr Torey two bushels e a halef of salt	0	07	06
September the 1st: John Arnall[256] fife pound e halef porck: 5^{d}:			
penc per pound e three pints of beens: 2^{d} per quart	0	02	06
the: 9: to Joseph Nash a quarter of lamb dll to his fathers	0	01	06
the 11 to Capttaine ffrench a quarter of mutten10 pound $^{hed\ plock}$	0	02	04
the 11 to Mr Torey a quarter of mutten 8 pound ½	0	01	09
to Samuell Touer[257] a quarter of mutten 10 $½^{ll}$ e a line 5 ^{ll} pound	0	03	05
rafe tailor	0	02	07
to lft white a quarter mutten 10^{ll} p	0	02	1
to corlonor Hunt a side of mutten 23^{ll}	0	04	9
to Lft Nash a quorter of mutten	0	02	3
to Lft Nash a quorter of mutten	0	02	8
to Joseph Richards a bushel e halef of corn e porck	0	07	0
to Ms Torey halef a pound cotten wooll	0	00	11
to Samuell Andrues maid three pound hogs fatt 6^{d} pound		01	06
to Ms wido white a side of mutten hed e ploock		05	06
to Colanar Hunt foure quarters of mutten 41 pound		08	00
the 22 to wido holbroock a quorter of mutten 10 pound		02	01
to John Hunt a quorter of mutten	0	~~0~~01	~~00~~11
to Joseph pittey candels	0	00	07
to James Humfry two pound off candels	0	01	04

Line		ll	s	p
1	Aperel the 19 1698 Thomas White Snr of brantery			
2	debter for a bushel of seed barly dll to his Thomas White	00	04	06
3	may the: 31: 1698 william Reed Snr			
4	debter for twelvef ~~twilef~~ pound of tobacka 6^{d} per pound	00	06	00
5	in the yeer 1697 e 98 uncle porter debter for motten	00	03	00
6	for a boolluks going at the ester neck	00	02	00
7	for an ancor for thare bote	00	09	00
8	for one quarter of motten	00	02	04
9	marh the 22nd 1699 Samuell Andrues debteter for			
10	two bushels of otes dll to Siman pittey	00	02	08
11			2	09
12	September 1699 Enock Lovell Credeter for twenty three busels			
13	e three peck of barly			
14	may the 29th 1700 then I recened with Enock Lovell e balanc			
15	ed: all accounpts and thare^{was} due to him eytteen bushels and halef malt			
16	october 1701 for ~~hale~~ three thousand of ^{shingles} Wido holbroock upon			
17	Enock Lovellels accounpt 8^{s} per thousand	01	04	00
18	november the 4th to three thousand of shingles of iohn vinson			
19	e a [?] nine hundered 8^{s} per thousand	01	11	02
20	to mony reseved of zechariah bicknell	01	10	00
21	november 1701 one pare of shoos for my selef e toping $^{a\ pare}$	00	07	00
22	desember the 31st 1701 reconed with Enock Lovell and			
23	balanced all accounpts and thare was due ~~the~~			
24	to him nor mee	00	00	00
25	Jenuary the 1st 1702$^{2/1}$ dll to Enock Lovell a cake			
26	of talo thirty two pound and ~~a~~ 6^{d} per pound	00	16	00
27	may 1702 to salt half a bushel	00	01	03
28	to black grape 10 yards 1^{s}—9^{d} per yard e triming	00	19	00
29	June to a besom dll to Joseph 30 Lovell	00	00	04
30	to ~~wido e a~~ halfe a hide 25^{ll} e a halef	00	04	03
31	to a hole hide 50^{ll}	00	08	04
32	desember the 31st 1702: reconed with Enock Lovell			
33	and ballansed all acounts and thare was due to mee	00	07	04
34	march 1703: to six broomes 4^{d} per pees	00	02	00
35	June to a peck of salt	00	00	11
36	to halef a pound of powder	00	01	04
37	to the frait of six barels e a hogbut	00	03	06
38	to clabbord nailes 3000 4^{s} per thousand	00	12	00
39	desemberto ~~two~~ two bushels of sallt dll to Joseph	00	08	00

Line		ll	s	p
1	March the: 11th: 1698 Samuell Speer debter for			
2	money payde too him selef by my one hand	04	10	00
3	which was for ~~corne~~ indian corne at 3^{s} per bushel			
4	reseved of this corne from him selef twluf bushels			
5	recened with Samuell Speer November the 8th 1698			
6	and balanced all accounpts and tha^{e}re was due to mee	00	04	06
7	paid at the recening twowards fifty two bushels of indian			
8	corn which I was to have for six ~~pound ayt shilling~~			
9	pound thurteen shilling money in the yeer 1699	00	08	06
10	Enock Lovell debter for halef a bushell of ground malt forgot in the			
11	balance which was boroed			
12	in the yeer 1700 for a hefers hyde 53: ½ pound	00	08	11
13	for a cavfe hyde 56 pounds	00	09	04
14	~~in~~ June the 11th 1701 to a frait of shingles 12 thousand brigam	00	07	00
15	the 12 to a frait of shingels 12 thousand dll Mr Brigam[258]	00	07	00
16	the 15 to a six thousand of shingel dll to Mr Brigam	00	03	06
17	the 18 to a ten thousand of shingle dll to Mr wintorth[259]	00	05	10
18	August the 28 for a bushel e a halef of sallt	00	03	00
19	october the 1st to thurty ~~br~~ pound of flax e halef a peck salt	01	03	00
20	to mony lent	04	00	00
21	to a galoon of oyell	00	02	00
22	to twenty pound pound of flex to Joseph Lovell	0	15	00
23	november to a galloon of oyell	0	02	00
24	to a hide 52: pound	0	08	08
25	pheburary the 6th $170^{1/2}$ Enock Lovell Credeter			
26	to toping of a pare of shoos for benjamin	00	01	05
27	the 19 to toping a pare of shoos for ruth	00	01	05
28	to six bushels of barlly reseved			
29	march the 7: to two pare of mens shoos	00	12	00
30	may to toping of a pare of shoos	00	01	0
31	to a pare of shoos for my wife	00	04	3
32	to a pare of shoos for ruth	00	04	3
33	September to a pare of shoos for my self	00	06	0
34	to toping of a pare of shooses for benjamin	00	01	0
35	to a pare of shoose ruth e a pare for benjamin	00	10	3
36	in 1703 Enock Lovell credit for a pare of men shoos			
37	to a pare of ~~menes~~ wimings shoos			
38	to a pare of mens shoos			

	ll	s	p
March the: 10th: 1698 Isack Hunt credeter for plating			
of a slice e two seters e fife stapeles	00	03	08
in money reseved	00	01	00
for seting of a pare of horce shoos	00	00	08
for two ~~nw~~ nwe shoos for my horce	00	01	04
for two ~~nwe~~ new shoos for my horce	00	01	04
for a brod howe	00	03	00
for money	00	02	00
for money at another time	00	04	00
for a brode howe	00	03	00
	~~01~~	~~00~~	~~00~~
for money reseved in a cowe	00	14	11 ½
August the 4th 1699 Thomas Bicknell credeter for ~~fife~~ seven peck			
of mallt & one days work for benjamin at the ester neck	00	06	06
for a ele 7 pound 2 ½^{d}	00	01	06
for a cafes bag	00	01	06
for six quarts of lamp oyle 6^{d} per quart	00	03	00
~~for a quarter of mutten~~ for a butter pott	00	00	~~09~~10
for a bushel e a halef of salt	00	03	09
for a nounce of peper	00	00	03
for two quarts of oyle	00	01	00
Aprell the 26th for two bushells e a peck of dll to him selef	00	06	03
may the 17 for halef a fishing line	00	00	11
october the: 19: 1700 recned with Thomas bicknell e balanced all			
accounpts	00	00	00
october the 28: 1700 Thomas Bicknell debter for two quarts of			
oyl e a peck of salt dll to marsey secole[260]	00	00	06
~~in~~ Aperell 1701 brother John Bicknell credeter for mony			
lent e two calefs	06	18	0
for plumes	00	00	6
for a pot of buter e two hoops	00	09	3
	07	08	0
	7	07	9
october the 31 1701 wido Holbroock debter for twenty ~~pound~~			
eight pound of flex 9^{d} per pound	01	01	00
to six pound of cotten wooll 1^{s} = 10^{d} per pound e a broom	00	11	05
to two galloons of malases	00	05	00
the 14 to John burll a bushell e a halef of sallt	00	03	00
aperell ~~the~~ 1702 to a bushell of mallt	00	03	06
may to salt	00	00	03

	ll	s	p
September 12: 1697 Charles Clarcke debter for a side			
of mutten: 24: pound 2 1/2^{d} per pound e frait:	00	05	02
September: 1697: Charles Clarcke debter for mutten	00	01	03
october for a side of mutten dll to his wife 21 pound e hed ^{ploock}	00	04	10
march the 5th: 1698 ~~Isack~~ Iseeck Hunt debter for seven			
teen pound of porck at 5^{d} pence per pond	00	07	01
dito for twenty ~~to~~ two pound of beef at 3^{d} per pound	00	05	07 2/1
dito for thirteen ^{pound} of moten ~~at~~ 3^{d} per pound	00	03	03
for foure pound of motten dll before this acound	00	01	00
dito for six pound of beef e motten scraps at 4^{d} per pound	00	02	00
desember the 13th ½: for a hole sheepe: 43 pound 2 ½^{d} pound	00	09	00
Itm for foure pound of sheePs wooll: 1^{s}–2^{d} per pound:	00	04	08
for a pound of candeles	00	00	07
for seven pound of mutten scraps: 3^{d}: per pound:	00	01	09
	01	14	11 1/2
may 170~~0~~1 brother john bicknell debtter for one bushel of			
salt e thirty eyght pound of sheeps wooll	01	09	02
for a bottle of rum	00	01	02
	00	2	00
for a cock pin	00	01	00
for two pound of pigin shott	00	00	08
for one ounce of indego	00	00	06
~~Aug~~ August the 9th: for one bottle of rum	00	01	00
for a galloon of malases	00	02	06
for halef a hundered of bordnailles	00	00	06
August the 27 for a botell of rum	00	01	03
copperas rum	00	01	00
	01	09	06
october th: 1: payd in mony	05	16	00
wido holbroock ^{credit} in desember for six thousand of shingell			
at seven shillings per thousand	02	02	00

[Page 74]

	ll	s	p
September the 4th: 1697: john wilde depter for a quarter of			
mutten wait 10 pound e halef at 2^{d} ½^{d} per pound	00	02	02
for a quorter of mutten dll at Eward darbeys by order	00	01	11
for a quorter of mutten dll to edward darbees	00	01	11
for a quorter of mutten dll to edward darbees	00	01	08
to thre quarters of mutten	00	05	08
october for a quorter of mutten	00	02	00
for a quorter of mutten	00	01	09
for a quorter of mutten	00	02	01
for a quorter of mutten	00	02	01
john wild credetor for money	01	01	3
m^{r} Danell Willard[261] debter for four sheep: 148: pound at			
2 ½ per pound ~~th~~ dll at ~~S~~ his dwelling house in brantery the			
sixt of desember: 1698	01	11	03
Itm for: ~~16~~: 116 pound of mutten 2^{d} ½ per pound	01	04	02
Nickolas Sallter note to mee ~~fr~~ from yow	00	03	08
	02	19	01
Jenuary the: 23: 1699 edward Bate debtter for a leven			
pound of sheeps wooll dll to his wife at 12^{d} per pound	00	11	00
m^{r} Danell Willard Credetor for: 225: pound of			
eyrn dll two Joseph Richards 1^{ll} 6^{s} 0^{d} per hund^{ered}	2	18	6
march the: 12: 1702 uncell Shawe debtter for mony			
dll to him selef	01	00	0
aperell the 4th: paide in mony	00	06	0
june the: 2^{nt}: 1702 hana kingman debtter for			
~~the pound of~~ cotten wooll e a pound of tobacko	00	02	0

Line		ll	s	p
1	September the 4th: 1697 Samuell briant[262] dbter for a quorter			
2	of motten ~~9~~ 8 pound 3 quorters 2 ½^{d} per pound	00	01	10
3	october the 15^{he} 1697 Thomas white Junr debter for a			
4	quorter of mutten 8 pound 2 ½d per pound	00	01	08
5	desember the 28th: 1697 Samuel Bagly Junr debter for			
6	mutten dll to him selef at my houce	00	02	6
7	dito for fife heds e six plucks of sheep	00	01	6
8	Jenuary the 29 for six quorters of mutten e 2 plucks e one hed	00	07	0
9	June the 3: thrd 1698 for a hat e a one pound of tobac^{kah}:	00	01	0
10	one pees of ayt reseved of majer hunt upon samuell bagleyes			
11	desember: 1698: ~~Joseph clarck~~ Liftenant Nash debter			
12	debter for one sheep: 38: pound 2 ½^{d} per pound dll to Joseph			
13	Clarck of Brantery	00	07	11
14	dito dll to John dyer one sheep: 4: 2 ½^{d} per pound	00	08	06
15	dito dll to youre son Thomas Nash 35 pound talo 5^{d} 3^{s} per pound	00	16	09
16	for motten: 24: ~~d~~ 2 ½^{d} per pound	00	05	00
17	desember the 21 paidd to John pratt of birgwater by consent	01	05	00
18	pheburary the: 28th: 1699/8: receved with Lift Nash and			
19	balanced all accounpts and thare was dwe to mee	02	02	02
20	~~[Aperell the [?]dll one bushell to send barly to youre~~			
21	~~son Beniamin Nash]~~	~~00~~	~~05~~	~~00~~
22	Aperell the 7th dll to alce Nash[263] 23 two bushels of malt	0	06	00
23	may the: 2: dll to James Nash two bushels of malt	0	06	00
24	may the: 12: for two bushels of malt dll Thomas Nash	0	06	00
25	may thc: 25: for ~~th~~ two bushels of malt dll to beniamin	0	06	00
26	iune the: 9: for thre^{e} bushel of mallt dll to beniamin	0	09	00
27	iune the: 17: for three bushels of malt dll to beniamin	0	09	00
28	Lift Nash Credetor for money reseved of his wife	00	18	00
29	Aperell the 10th 1699 Liftenant Nash credetor for			
	mony reseved of him	01	10	~~0~~1
30	may the 30th reseved in money	00	12	0
31	may the 30th reseved in money uppon mary Bicknells accoun^{pt}:	01	10	0
32	yr ~~march the 12~~			
33	iune the: 27: dll to Thomas Nash two bushells malt	00	6	0
34	iuly the: 1st: dll to beniamin Nash three bushels of malt	00	9	0
35	July the 23 dll to beniamin Nash two bushels & a halef malt	00	7	6
36	August the th dll to beniamin Nash two bushels & a halef malt	00	7	6
37	the 25: dll to beniamin Nash two bushels of malt	00	6	0
38	September the: 8: to beniamin Nash ~~th~~ two bushels of malt	00	6	0

[Page 76]

Line		ll	s	p
1	ougust the: 26th: 1697 Thomas kingman ^{Snr} debter ^{for} money			
2	dll to Johnnathan Torey constable by verbal order	00	13	10
3	July the: 8th: 1698: Zackarah debter for four			
4	pound of tobackah at 6^{d} per pound dll him selef	00	02	00
5	July the: 8th: 1698: James Lowell Juner[264] debter for			
6	two pound of e a halef of salt porck at 7^{d} per pound $^{dll\ to\ his}$ wife	0	1	4 ½
7	& to two pound of tobacka: 6^{d}: per pound	0	1	0
8	ougust the: 5th: for fife pound of tobacka: 6^{d}: per pound:	0	2	6
9	Jenuary the: 21: 1699: John Wilde $^{of\ brantery}$ debter for two ^{hundered}			
10	fifty three pound of ~~p~~ mutten at 2^{d} 3q per pound dll to his wife			
11	at his one houce by his one order	02	17	11
12	for three heds e plucks: 4^{d} per pees	00	01	00
13	for ten pound of sheeps wooll: 1^{s}: per pound a penath ^{more}	00	~~1~~09	0~~0~~1
14	iune theth: 29: dll to Mrs Willard of brantery: 14: pound motten			
15	3^{d}: per pound	00	03	06
16	Jenuary the: 17: to three pound of sheeps wooll	00	03	00
17	September the 21 1700 for a 175 pound beef 2^{d} = 9q fruit	0~~0~~1	13	09
18	for two bushells of salt	00	04	00
19	pheburary the: 21: 1701: recned with John wild $^{of\ brantery}$ and balansed all			
20	acounpts and thare wos dwe to me from him in mony	00	13	00
21	liftenant nash in 1699 for candels seven pound e three quorters			
22	november the 13th recened with Ephraim pratt and			
23	balanced all acounpts and thare was dwe to me in mony	0	3	6
24	the 14th to a bushel e a halef salt	0	3	0
25	the ~~2~~19 to a pare of bodis 3^{ll} quord sheeps wooll 6 pound tobacko e			
26	a pound three quorters of logwood	0	11	10
27	desember the 3 to three sheep 113: 2 ½ ^{d} per pound dll to his wife	1	03	03
28	may the 2: to halef a pound of tobacko e two bushels $^{and\ halef}$ to barley	0	09	0~~3~~0
29	may the 12: 1705 Enock Lowell debter			
30	to one bushel of salt dll to his wife	00	04	6
31	26 to Sarah Richards goods in	03	19	8
32	26 to Sister Reed[265] goods in	00	18	10
33	June 8 to Elisebath Lowell[266]: 15^{ll} cotten 1^{s}–6^{d} pound:	00	15	00
34	to six pounds of shuger at 6^{d} per pound	00	03	00
35	to 4 four pounds of tobacko	00	02	00

Line		li	s	p
1	ougust the 18th: 1697 James lovel[267] credetor for 10 foot of ocke			
2	wood at 9^{s} per cord	00	11	03
3	reseved of widow Humfry uppon youre accounpt	01	0~~0~~1	0~~0~~7
4	Captaine ~~deb~~ White debter for a quorter of lombe ^{1697}	0	1	8
5	June the: 2^{nt}: 1698 Sara Richards Sner debter for			
6	two bushels e a halef of indian corn	00	08	6
7	for two quarts of malses	00	01	0
8	for halef a bushel of malt dll to Jno Richards[268]	00	02	0
9	pheburary the: 17: 1699: Samuell Bagly debter for foure			
10	quorters of mutten e a hed e pluck delivered to his			
	wief at his dwelling			
11	houce: 36 pound of mutten 3 ½^{d} per pound	00	09	01
12	e the hed e pluck 4^{d}	00	00	04
13	November ^{the}: 25th: 1699 recened with Samuell Bagley ^{brantery} e cleer			
14	ed upon all accounpts e thare was dwe to mee from him:	00	03	05
15	pheburary the: 12: for ^{1700} nine peneworth of salt e a pound of wooll	00	01	09
16	for a bushel of salt e a pound of tobacka	00	02	6
17	march the: 10th: 1701 for a sarg cote redey made e completly finish^{ed}	00	15	00
18	desember the: 7th: 1703 then recened with Enock Lovell and			
19	balansed all accounpts e thare was dwe to mee	00	15	07
20	~~six bushels~~ e ~~a pecke a halefof barlyexcepted~~			
21	June the: 19: 1704 to halef a bushell of salt	00	02	06
22	to two g^{a}lloones of oyell	00	04	00
23	July 1 to two brass cittels	01	11	00
24	August to three pound of logwood	00	01	00
25	Novem: to one hide 59 pounds	00	09	10
26	24 to two bushels of salt	00	08	00
27	to Iz fford halef a bushel of salt	00	02	03
28	pheburary the: 12th: 1705: then reconed			
29	With Enock Lovell and thare wos dwe to him	02	08	3
30	William copling paid in goods	0~~0~~7	03	03
31	may for: 12 250 of shingels = 8^{s}	04	16	00
32	12 to 650 clabords e 4000 shingels 8^{p}	02	18	00

[Page 78]

Line		ll	s	p
1	ougust the 7th: 1697 Maier Hunt for one			
2	quorter of muten wait 2 ½ at 3^{d} per pound	00	03	01 ½
3	for one quorter of mouton 10 pound at 3^{d} per pound	00	02	06
4	for one quorter of motten 11 pound at 3^{d} per pound	00	02	09
5	for one quorter of lambe 7 pound 3q 2 ½^{d} per pound	00	01	07
6	September the 4 for a quorter of lamb 8 pound	00	01	08
7	october for a quorter of mutten	00	02	00
8	october for a hole lamb 31 pound 2 ½^{d} per pound	00	06	06
9	november the 10th for a side of mutten 22 pound ~~½~~ 2^{d} ½	00	04	07
10	September the: 9^{the}: 1698 Mager hunt debter for one			
11	hundered wait of chees ~~halef new m~~ three quorters $^{new\ milk}$	01	15	00
12	for a sheep: 31: pound: 3^{d}: per pound	00	07	09
13	for one pees of ayt payd to Samuell baglly	00	06	00
14	November for a side of: 19 ½: at 2^{d} ½ per pound	00	04	00
15	for money delivered at the same time to youre Son John	01	04	00
16	Jenuary the: 11th: 1699/8 Lambur Desper debter for			
17	373 pound of motten at: 2^{d}–3q per pound	04	05	06
18	to six pound of ^{sheps} wooll 12^{d} per pound	00	06	00
19	to a peck e a halef of otes 4^{d} per peck	00	00	06
20	this dll at his house in Brantery by the eyr works			
21	iune the: 29th: 1699 ~~dll~~ to 68 pound of moten dll to Lamber			
22	despers wife: 3^{d}: per pound	00	17	00
23	July the 29th for a quorter of lambe e pluck	00	02	04
24	August the: 12: for a side of ~~lam~~ lambe e a skin	00	05	04
25	Aperell the: 25: John J porter[269] debter for a ~~po~~ quorter of motten / twolfe			
26	pound 3 quorters dll to Thomas porter his brother	00	03	04
27	September the 12th ~~Ebenezer~~ ^{Eephraim} pratt depter for a sheep 40 pou			
28	nd 2 ½^{d} per pound	00	08	04
29	the 26th to Decon Torey[270] in oyle e sheeps wooll	00	04	09
30	october the 10: to one bushel of corn one galoon pint ma^{las}	0	05	10
31	to eight pound sheeps wooll: 11^{d}: two pound cotten wooll	00	11	00
32	to six pound porck one peck salt	00	03	06
33	the 13th to a sheep 26 pound	00	05	05
34	the 15th to Samuell king a bushell of sallt	00	02	00
35	the 23 to three pound of sheeps wooll e a peck of salt e a broom	00	03	08
36	the 24 to a sheep 4^{ll} 2 ½ ^{d} per pound	00	0~~4~~ 8	0~~8~~4
37	the 29 to Richard danford one bushell of sallt	00	02	00
38	to Ephraim burell for corting the shingell	00	06	00
39	october the 9th Ephraim pratt Credetor for 7000 thousand of shingles			
40	dll at Smelbroock	02	16	00
41	to ten young chickins	00	02	04

Line	ll	s	p
ogust the 6th: 1697 William Turell debter for a quorter			
of muten wait ten pound at 2 ½^{d} per pound dll to him	00	02	01
for one hed e ploock dll to him selef	00	00	04
itm for a quorter of lambe e two heds e ploocks	00	02	00
recned with William Turel ougust the 18th: 1697			
~~ad~~ and cleered upon all acounpts from the begining of the			
world to this day e thare was dwe to mee from him	02	00	00
august the 18th: 1697 James lovell debter for two acers of salt			
march grace e the mowing of the two acars	01	08	00
for fecing of the hay over the water	00	02	06
for a quorter of moten 9 pound e a halef at 3^{d} per pound	00	02	04
ougust the 29th: 1697: Samuell Bagly debter for two			
quorters of mutten e a hed e ploock 20 pound 2 ½^{d} per pound	00	04	07
for a quorter of motten 11 ½	00	02	06
desember the 8th: 1697: James Humphry debter for money			
paide to Johnathan Torey for his rate	00	13	00
January the 12th: for foure yards e a halef of carsy cloth			
at fife shillins per yard dll to Joseph pittey by my one hand	01	02	06
for a pound of candels	00	00	06
reseved of Mrs Tyler uppon Samuell ^{baglys} acounpt	00	02	06
more reseved in money of him selef	00	03	01
desember the 8th: 1697 Nathanell Humphrey debter for			
money paide to Johnathon Torey for his rate	00	07	00
desember the 8th: 1697: Johnathon Torrey debter for a note			
~~re~~ reseved by mee from the Tresurer	00	7	4
~~desember~~ november ~~29~~ 30: 1697 William [n?]esie[271] debter for			
a barell of sider dll to him selef	00	08	0
Jenueary the: 31: 1697/8 James Humfry Credeter for two			
bushels of indian corne 3^{s}–6^{d} per bushel	00	07	00
November the: 6th: 1698 reseved of Majer Hunt			
a quorter of beef	00	18	00
of the same time reseved of money	00	17	00
Aperell the: 10th: 1697 reseved of Lambur Desper wife	1	15	00
the 15 reseved of Lambur desper in money	0	11	00
June the: 1: reseved of in money	02	02	00
		18	
June the: 28th: 1699 reseved in money	00	12	00
July the 19th reseved in money	01	10	00

[Page 80]

	ll	s	p
July the: 26: 1697 Insine John Hunt Credetor for shoo			
ing of my horce befor	00	01	04
more reseved in money	00	12	00
for two bushels of indian corn at 3^{s}–6^{d} per bushel	00	07	00
for puting a pot leg for mother	00	01	06
for grace at Brantri side	00	03	00
	01	04	10
desember: 1698: balanced all acounpts with John Hunt			
July the: 8th Ebenezer pratt debtter for caring part of a frait			
of shingels to Camebrige dll Solomon prentis	00	07	00
the 15: for two pound of candels	00	01	04
for a galloon of oyle e a hed e ploock	00	02	03
for a peck of salt	00	00	06
for mony payd	01	05	00
Aperell the 22: 1702: John mountford bostyn debtter			
for 2500 of clabbord at 2 ll = 10^{s} = 0^{d} per thousand	06	05	0
~~mr. gellile~~			
Aperell the 24: 1702: mr. gellile bostoun debtter for			
~~an~~ 1900 clabbords: 3 ll = 15^{s} = 0^{d} e: 6000 of shingell 8^{s} per thous	06	13	0
the 30 to one thousand clobbord 2^{ll} = 10^{s} per thousand	02	10	0
to 2450 shingell 8^{s} per thousand	00	19	6
to 5000 of shingels deliver to him selef at 8^{s} per thousand	02	00	0
June 1702 Robburd Lash of bostoun debtter for 2100 of shingels			
at: 12^{s}: per housand	01	05	0

	ll	s	p
desember the 18th 1696 Edward Bates debter for twenty ayt			
pound of sheeps wool dll to him selef by my one hand	01	04	00
this money is payd over hed			
Aperel the 7^{nth}: 1697 Joseph Green debter for two bushels			
of otes at: 2^{s} = 4^{d}: per bushel	00	04	08
Jm dll to Samuel fford one bushel of otes	00	02	04
July the 23rd: 1697 Insine John Hunt debter for one			
quorter of moten 8 pound at 3^{d} penc per pound	00	02	00
for one hed e pluck	00	00	04
dito for two quorter of lamb at 13 pound 3^{d} per pound	00	03	03
for a sids of moten 20 pound e halef 3^{d} per pound	00	05	01
for a quorter of moten 9 pound e halef	00	02	04
for a quorter of motten 9 pound e 3 quorters 3^{d} per pound	00	02	05
for a quorter of motten 12 pound 3^{d} per pound	00	03	09
september the ~~3~~29$^{th\ the}$ for a quorter of mutten 10 1/2	00	02	02
october for a quorter of mutten	00	01	10
for a quorter of mutten e hed e ploock	00	02	04
Jenuary the 7th: 1698/7 for fife yards of carsi cloth 5^{s} per yaid	01	05	00
September the: 23: ~~1689~~ 1698 for one			
lamb: 32 ^{pound}: 2 ½^{d} per pound dll to youre son John	00	06	08
dito for two pound of candeles dll to youre son John	00	01	04
october the: 1: for: 2 $^{of\ yards}$: e a halef carsey cloth 5^{s} per yard	00	12	06
for 4 quorters of motten $^{44\ pound}$ at 2 ½^{d} per pound	00	09	02
for money payd to the minister the rate	00	1~~4~~3	06
November the: 9: for a quorter of beef: 97 ½: pound: 2^{d} per pound:	0	16	03
for thurty pound of beef tallo at 4^{d} per pound	00	10	00
	05	19	02
may the: 10th Ezera Whitemarch debter for fife bushels dll			
to william Richards[272]	00	13	09
Ezra Whitemarch credit for a pare of horce shoos	00	01	03
August: 1701 Ebenezer pratt credetor for eyght sheep e lam^{bs}			
boft of him	02	07	00

[Page 82]

Line		ll	s	p
1	1696 I sent to saee by mr Tylar	01	10	00
2	november 1696 I sen^{t} to saee with mrs Tylar by			
3	the halef of ^{to} barels of beef which coms to	02	02	02
4	Joseph dyer one quorter of moten 7 pound	00	01	9
5	~~of~~ for a hed e ploock	00	00	~~4~~3
6	for a quorter of moten wait ~~9~~ 101/2 pound	00	02	7~~3~~
7	for a qurtr of lamb 7 pound	00	01	9
8	desember the 13th 1696 Jacob Nash credetor for a pees of ayt	0	6	0
9	Jenuary the 16th for a pees of ayt reseved of youre son Thomas	0	6	0
10	phebrurarey the 2^{nt} for one pees of ayt of youre selef	0	6	0
11	phebrurarey the 12th for one pees of ayt of youre son Thomas	0	6	0
12	reseved in money	2	16	5
13	July the 13 1697 Ezera Whitmarch debter for ~~two~~			
14	moten dll to him selef	00	6	6
15	agust the: 4: 1697 Liftenant Nash debter a side of moten			
16	dll to his wife[273] at his one houce	00	05	06
17	dito for a quorter of moten a 11 pound at 3^{d} per pound	00	02	09
18	for one qurter of moten 9 pound e a halef at 3^{d} per ^{pound}	00	02	04½
19	for one quorter of mutten 9 pound ~~6~~ ^{d} 3^{d} per pound	00	02	07
20	ougust the 22^{nt} for a quorter of of moten: 11:			
	pound dll nickolas salter[274]	0	02	09
21	ougust the 25th for ^{two} quorters of mutten: 18: pound: 2^{d} ½: per pound	0	03	09
22	dito to liftenant nash a qurter of moten for salter	0	02	02
23	dito for a sid of lamb wait 18 pound at 2 ½^{d} per pound	0	03	09
24	september the 4th for a quorter of mutten 10 pound for salter	00	02	08
25	a side of mutten dll to his wife: 22: at 2 ½^{d} per pound	00	04	07
26	for a quorter of mutten for ~~satler~~ salter dll to youre wife	00	02	00
27	for a quorter of motten for hadman[275] dll to youre wife	00	02	02
28	for a side of mutten dll at his one house 20 pound 2 ½^{d} per pound	00	04	02
29	for a quorter of mutten to salter	00	02	00
30	for a quorter John Hadman	00	02	00
31	for a side of mutten e a hed e ploock	00	03	10
32	for a quorter of mutten to hadman	00	01	11
33	for a quorter of mutten to salter	00	02	04
34	for a quorter of mutten to youre selef	00	01	09
35	for a side of mutten for youre selef	00	04	01
36	~~for a~~ october for a quorter of mutten to salter	00	02	00
37	for a quorter mutten to hadman	00	02	00
38	for a quorter of mutten to Samuel willes[276]	00	02	02
39	for 2 heds e ploock	00	00	08
40	~~for~~ november he 15th for a 100 e 9 42 pound a halef candels 8^{d} 3^{d} [fe?]	04	00	00
41	balanced all			

Line		ll	s	p
1	desember the 13th 1696 Jacob Nash debter for twelvef			
2	pound of candels dll to his sun Thomas 8^{d} penc per pound	00	08	00
3	Jenuary the 16th dll twelvef pound candels			
	8^{d} per pound youre son Thomas	00	08	00
4	pheburary the 12th dll to youre son Thomash Nash 10 e halef pound	00	07	08
5	march the 16th dll to youre son Thomas narsh 8 pound candels	00	05	10
6	may the: 6th for ayttee pound of buter at dll			
7	to youre son Thomas at 7^{d} penc per pound	00	10	06
8	for 50 seven pound of candels e a halef	02	00	01
9	July 23: 1697 John Gurny of bergwater debter for one			
10	quorter of moten 9 pound at 3^{d} penc per pound	00	02	03
11	minitor Torey[277] debter for a quorter of moten wait 10			
12	pound at 2^{d} ½ per pound dll in ougust the 4th 1697	00	02	6
13	ougust the 6th 1697 John porter snr debter for a side			
14	moten dll at his houce wait 25 pound at 2 $½^{d}$ per pound	00	05	2½
15	for a side of moten: 24 ½ at 2 $½^{d}$ per pound	00	05	2½
16	ougust the 29th 1697 recned e cleered with with John porter			
17	Snr e clered all but nine pence dwe to mee in money	00	00	09
18	september for a side of motten: 21: pound	00	04	04
19	for a sid of mutten 23 ½	00	04	10
20	paide			
21	october the 25th: 1697: reconed with david Carver			
22	~~e cleered w~~ e thare was dwe to mee from him	00	14	10
23	october the 25th for a side of lamb 4 pound e halef2 $½^{d}$ per pound	00	03	00
24	november the 17 for 22 pound of woll dll to him selef	01	03	06
25	october the: 15: 1698 ballanced all acounpts			
26	with David e thare was dwe to him	00	00	o[?]
27	desember 1697 david Carver credeter for two pare			
28	of shoos one pare for my selef one pare for my wife	00	10	6
29	mrs Tilar debter for: 168: pound of porck 3 $½^{d}$ per pound			
30	amounds to in money	2	09	00
31	mrs Simcines debter for: 159: pound of	2	06	03
32	porck 3 $½^{d}$ per pound			
33	a pig 40 pound 3^{d} per pound	0	10	00
34	for eggs dll all to ~~all~~ pillgrim Simicins in 1698	0	04	06

[Page 84]

	ll	s	p
july 1696 Mager Hunt credeter for one pes of ayt	00	06	00
for seven peeses of ayte reseved at bastoun	02	02	00
this i as free from debt as the other side e as truely ~~b~~ paide			
ogust the fifth 1697 Zackeriah Bicknill debter for			
moten dll to him selef	00	00	6
dito for moing at salt grass ~~and~~ one day for mier Hunt brantery	00	03	0
Minster Torey debter in ogust the 5: 1697 for a			
quorter of moten wait 9: pound at 3^{d} per pound	00	02	03
ogust the 4: 1697 Mary Nash debter for a pare of			
wimins shoos wooden heels	00	04	03
ougust the 6th: 1697 Edward Darby debter for a side of			
moten dll at Lifttenant Nashes house by his order 22 pound			
at 3^{d}: pence per pound	00	05	06
Hen for one quorter dll ~~to~~ at his one houce: 10 po^{und}	00	02	06
september the 4 for a quarter of lamb	00	01	10
for a quorter of moutten dll to youre wife[278]	00	02	02
for a quorter of mutten	00	01	09
for a quorter of mutten e a hed e ploock	00	02	02
october for quorter of mutten	00	02	04
desember the: 29: 1698 to a jacket redey made	01	04	00
november the 25: 1701 recened with John green & bala			
nced all acounpts& ther was dwe to meein many	0	0~~1~~2	0~~0~~1
moris Truant debter in the yeer: 1702: for the rent of			
a paster at rose hill mony	01	05	0
to two pound of cotten wooll ^{at}: $1^{s} = 10^{d}$ per pound	00	03	8
to eyght pound of sheeps wooll at 10 per pound	00	06	08
to a bushel and a halef of malt	00	04	6
in september 1697 edward darbey credeter to two peeses of ayt	00	12	0
Aperel the: 19: 1698 Thomas Bicknell debter for a			
brode how dll to him selef	00	01	09
July for one quart of malases	00	00	07
July the 10 to two bushels of indian corne	00	07	00

	ll	s	p
iuly: 1696 Mager Ephraim Hunt debter one 100 wait of			
chees at 1^{ll}–10^{s}–0^{d} per hundered	01	10	00
for twelvef pound of lambe muten at 3^{d} per pound	00	03	00
for ~~elve o~~ eleven pound of bacen at 8^{d} per pound	00	07	04
ougust for twelvef pound of vele at 3^{d} per pound	00	03	00
for 68 pound of chees	01	00	06
september for eleven pound of muten at 2 $2/1^{d}$ per pound	00	0~~2~~3	03
for one qurter of muten ten pound at 2 $2/1^{d}$ per pound	00	02	01
for 25 pound of muten at 2 $2/1^{d}$ per pound	00	05	02
october for 28 pound e halef of chees at 3^{d} per pound	00	07	01
for a side of muten 22 pound at 2 $2/1^{d}$ per pound	00	04	07
for two sides of muten 45 pound at 2 $2/1^{d}$ per pound	00	~~0~~19	0~~2~~4
for one hed e pluck	00	00	04
for 54 pound of beef at 2 $2/1^{d}$ per pound	00	11	03
november the 2^{nt} for thirty $^{seven\ e\ 2/1}$ wait of chees at 2 $2/1^{d}$ per pound	00	07	09
for ayteen pound of chees at 2 $2/1^{d}$ per pound	00	03	09
desember the 9th for fife sheep 214 pound at 2 per			
pound e 1^{s}–8^{d} over e and a bove	01	17	04
all this above mentioned debt is cleered e payde	07	14	9
~~pheber~~ pheburarey the 3^{d} 1695/6 Captaine white[279] debtor for			
one quorter of motten twelvef pounds 2 $2/1^{d}$ per pound	00	02	06
Aperel the 22^{nt}: 1697 Captain Ephraim Hunt debter			
for one bushel of barly dll to his son John[280]	00	05	00
dito dll to youre son John ayt ~~p~~ pounds of buter			
at ~~8~~7^{d} penc per pound	00	04	08
june 1697 maior Hunt[281] Credetor	00	09	08
Captaine white debter for one quorter of moten dll to his wife			
in ougust the 6th: 1697: wait 11 ½ at 3^{d} per pound	00	02	10 ½
ougust the 14th: 1697 John Shaw debter for a side of			
lambe wait 12 pound e a half dll to him selef: ~~12~~ ½ ^{pound}	00	03	00
ougust the 22^{nt}: 1697 Captaine whit debter for a quorter of			
motten: 10 pound at 3^{d} per pound	00	02	06
poud dll			
~~david~~ david Carver credetor for shos in 1697			
for one pare of shoos for my wife wood heels	00	04	6
for one pare for mary bicknill wod heel	00	04	6
for one pare my selef	00	06	0

[Page 86]

Line		ll	s	p
1	november 1696 Thomas Bicknill credetor for one dayes carting			
2	a from seader swamp	00	07	06
3	itm more for wood at lane end	00	06	00
4	resevd of Johnathan Torey in money	00	00	06
5	for plouing ground	01	02	06
6		01	16	06
7		01	04	00
8		03	00	6
9	July 1697 david Carver debter for one side of			
10	lamb wait 13 pound e a halef at 2^{d} ^{29} 11/3 per pound	00	02	10
11	Itm for 9 pound per ^{muten} e a hed e pluck sent by our Beniam^{in}[282]	00	02	03
12	dito for two quorters of lamb 2 ½^{d} per pound: 16 pound	00	03	04
13	for one pound of condels	00	00	09
14	ougust the 22 for a side of lambe	~~14~~00	02	11
15	for four pound of sheeps wooll dll to his wife	00	04	08
16	september the 3^{thd}: for a side of lamb 16 pound	00	03	04
17	for a side of mutten 21 ½ pound	00	04	05
18	september the 25th for a pound candels dll to John pittey	00	00	09
19	october for a quorter of 10 ½	00	02	02
20	for three pound of canddels dll James Richards	00	02	03
21	for a quoter of mutten	00	01	11
	[upside down in the text at the bottom of the page]			
22	Know all men by these presenc that I Remember Brigs			
23	his eyers, or asines or administer for the county of bristoll			
24	of the toun of Tanton carpentor doe owe & am justly [indebted?]			
25	unto James Richards of the toune of waumouth in new england mal[st?]^{er}			
26	the full sum of ffoure pounds of lawfull money of new england to be			
27	payd to the s^{d} James Richards his execetors lawfull Atorney Adm^{rs}			
28	or asines on or before the tenth day of aperell which shall be in the			
29	year 16935 to the [11?] trwe perfromanc I set myne one			
30	hand the twenty ayth of iune 1693			
31	Joseph Richards Remember Briggs			
32	november the 12 1696 Incres bate debter for three pound			
33	of ~~haugs~~ hogs ffat at 6^{d} per pound	00	01	06
34	october the ~~12~~ 20th 1696 Enuc Lovell debter for a cowes hide			
35	wait 57 pounds at 2^{d} per pound	00	09	06
36	ogust 1697 Beniamin Lincorne[283] debter for one			
37	quorter of motten 9 pound e halef 3 ^{d} per pound	00	02	4 ½
38	ougust the 5th 1697 Zackariah Bicknill debter to two			
39	pound of motten: e moing of salt grass for maier Hunt	00	03	6
40	for one quorter of muten 7 pound e a qurter	00	01	6

[Page 87]

Line		ll	s	p
1	Uncle porter debter for beef	00	05	02
2	Ezera whitemarch debter for 100 pound of p beef	01	01	00
3	october 1696 John hunt ~~cred~~ credetor for on pes of aut	00	06	0
4	more for fife peses of ayt reseved	01	10	0
5	Edw[a]rd bates debter in october 1696			
	for ~~a~~ fife e a halef pound of wooll	00	05	00
6	for three yards ~~of~~ e three quarters of carsey cloth woolling	00	15	00
7	october 1696 wido bayly[284] debter for two pound of candels	00	01	04
8	november 1696 Thomas Bicknill debter for: 900:			
9	e 24 fwoot of bord	01	09	00
10	novmber for money lent to hiym by my one hand	01	00	00
11	desember the 14th for money lent to him selef	00	18	00
12	for part of a fishing line	00	01	00
13	for Timber solde	00	01	00
14	~~for [?] the [?] for a halef of shee~~	~~00~~	~~09~~	~~00~~
15	for tobackah	00	030	01
16	aperel the 2nt: 1697 for one barel of sider	00	09	00
17	for a toun rate paid to brantry constable[285] in aperel the 5	00	01	o[?]
18		04	02	[??]
19	May the 6th: 1697: recned e cleered with Thomas			
20	Bicknill uf all acounts e thare was dwe to mee from			
21	him ~~[?]~~	01	01	o[?]
22	may the 17tnth: for two pound of tobacka	00	01	o[8]
23	for feching of the connon from bostoune	00	02	08
24	for two dayes work of beiamins at hilling	00	03	00
25	July for a quarter of lamb 7 pound e a halef 3d per pound	00	01	10
26	agost the 2 dll to his wife a pound of wooll	00	01	00
27	for two pigs at 2s–6d a pees	00	05	00
28	for mutten dll to John Tayler snr	00	01	08
29	for the lent of my iudg twise	00	02	00
30	for the of my iudg againe the thyrd timee	00	01	00
31	for moing for John ~~hurt~~ Hunt at brantery shed pint	00	03	06
32	for the lent of my iudg	00	01	00
33	for the lent of my iudg	00	00	o[8]
34	for the lent of my iudg	00	01	00
35	for the lent of my iudg	00	01	00
36	for three acers of salt grass e a quorter	01	12	06
37	october for two pound of sheeps wooll dll to his wife	00	01	08
38	jenuary the 10th for rates paid for me do at brantry	01	01	06
39	aperll the 13 for one peck of sallt	00	01	03

Line		ll	s	p
1	november the: 11^{nth}: 1695 phillip Reed $^{\text{snr of bridgwater}}$ debter for			
2	one pare of shoos at the 12	00	03	00
3	for money lent to him selef	00	00	06
4	for a ~~ba~~ foure bushel bag dll to him selef	00	05	00
5	november 11th: 1695: John Green debter for fife lambe at 3^{s} = 10^{d}			
6	per la^{m}be to be paid in may 1696	00	19	00
7	~~July James 8~~ July 1696 James Smith debter for one sith			
8	e [o] e a rake	00	05	03
9	Joseph pooll debter for one pare of tramels for his horce	00	04	06
10	Thomas bicknill debter for thurteen pound of chees	00	04	00
11	Johathan Torey debter for one rake	00	01	03
12	ogust 12 Thomas Bicknill debter for foure pound toba^{cko}	00	02	00
13	J ogust the 20 1696 John hunt debter for			
14	23 pound of muten at: 2^{d} 2/1: per pound	00	04	09
15	John Burll debter for muten	00	01	00
16	Joseph dyer debter for 8 pound of muten 2^{d} 2/1 per pound	00	01	08
17	[Jul]y the 13 m^{rs} badlam[286] debter for 8 pound muton	00	01	08
18	for 21 pound muten to John Hunt	00	04	04
19	september ^{the} 6 for 53 pound of muten to			
	John Hunt at 2^{d} 2/1 $_{per}$ ^{pound}	00	11	00
20	~~ag~~ ougust 16 for mine pound of candels dll to the minister torey	00	06	06
21	september the 9th: 1696 Icabod Holbroock depter for four quorters }			
22	of muten dll to his wife	00	09	00
23	John Shaw snr[287] debter for moing f of salt gras at rund medo	00	11	00
24	william Torey debter for moing of salt gras at round march	00	11	00
25	for two pound of tobacka e a pees of shilworck[288] twelve foot	00	02	00
26	september 10 Izera whitmarch debter for 28 pound moten	00	05	10
27	september 10 John porter snr debter for 28 pound moten	00	05	10
28	september 10 John porter jun^{r} debter for ~~28~~ ^{13} pound of moten	00	02	09
29	september 12 wiliam Turel debter for two acers salt graces	01	07	03
30	william Turell for 6 pound of ~~mo^{t}en~~ muten	00	03	06
31	~~the~~ september the 26 to John hunt 22 2/1 muten e a hed e plu^{k}	00	04	10
32	september the 26 to Captain holbrook 10 2/1 muten	00	02	02
33	Ezera whitmarch for one quorter of muten	00	02	00
34	Icabod holbroock debter for muten	00	06	00
35	october for one quorter of muten dll to his wife portor	00	02	02
36	october 5 1696 John Arnall debter for a camllat cote	00	16	00
37	october 10 John Hunt 24 pound of muten	00	05	02
38	John porter debter for muten	00	04	00

Line					ll	s	p
1	David carver debter for muten in 1696				00	01	[?]
2	september the 10 for 28 pound of muten				00	05	[10]
3	october for halef a muton 24 dll to him selef				00	05	[?]
4	for two pound of candels 8 penc per pound				00	01	[?]
5	for 23 pound of muten to him selef				00	04	[?]
6	for one hed e pluck				00	00	0[?]
7	for nine pound e a quarter of candels at 8^{d} per pound				00	06	02
8	march 23 for two calves cins				00	02	00
9					01	1~~3~~1~~3~~	0
10	september the 18–1696 David Carver credetor for one pare of						
11	shoos for my self french heels				00	06	00
12	for one pare of shoos for my wife french heels				00	04	09
13	for ~~one~~ two pare shoos for mary bicknill				00	09	06
14					01	00	03
15	desember the 7th 1697 Enock Lovell debter for						
16	twelvef pound of candels dll to beniamin ~~dracke~~ vining				00	9	6
17	march the 9th: 1698 for two bushels of barley at 4^{s} ^{6d} per bushel				00	9	0
18	novemeber the: 9: for two cowes sides one:						
	66: pound for other: 54: pound				00	19	6
19	octeber for 4 quarters of muten to John Hunt dll to Joseph Richards				00	08	[??]
20	novemebr 1696 for foure sheep wait 189 pound of						
21	2 ^{d} per pound e 4^{d} per sheep over which is				01	12	[?]
22	all the this above mentioned cleerd e payde				00	04	[?]
23					00	04	[?]
24	my dafter mary Richards born ~~Jm~~ Jn				00	11	[?]
25					00	04	01
26	Aperel the: 9th: 1697				10	05	02
27	ogust the 10 Thomas Bicknill credetor to				~~03~~	~~03~~	~~00~~
28	a pees of ayt in money	00	06	0	03	11	0
29	for a corde of wood at smellbroock	00	06	6	2	17	00
30	for caring for haye from the warter side	0	00	8	4	15	01
31	reseved Abia whiteman	0	12	00	4	0	
32	for faning of otes e barly	0	01	08	4	19	[?]
33					2	1~~3~~7	[?]
34	for youre man Timothy H [?] dayes e s halefo2 06				2	02	8
35	for a hifer calef				0	16	00
36	for one pees of ayt				0	06	00
37	for carting of four lode [?] of hays				0	0~~4~~ 2	00
38	Enock Lovel Cred[?] [?] 1697 for t two[?]						
39	[?] pare of sh [?]						
40	[?] pare of sh[?] thes[?]						
41	[?] th [?]						

[Page 90]

Line			ll	s	p
1	[?] uary the 4 1694 brother Joseph Richards debter				
2	[?] mony lent ~~lent~~ to him [?] [?]		03	00	00
3	[?] rch the 3rd 1694 Joseph Richards debter for two				
4	[?]shels of malt dll dll to his sun James Richards		00	08	00
5	[?] ~~rch the 13: lent to brother Joseph in money~~				
	~~reseved three shallings~~		~~00~~	~~00~~	~~00~~
6	Edward[289] debter in may the 31th: 1694 remaines debter				
7	for twelef shillings in money for two wethers e six yews e [?] six				
8	lames to be delivered the next fall after the date hereof the remainer				
9	for the shepe is in money for thees sheep is three pound to be paid at				
10	the deliver of the same				
11	June the 16th 1694: Mr Joseph Colse[290] of waymouth				
	debter for two bushels				
12	of malt at 4^{s} per bushel		00	08	00
13	at the same time dll aytteen poand of pork at 4^{d} per pound		00	06	00
14	dito for seven pound e a halef of beef at 2^{d} 2/1 penc per pound		00	01	06
15	dito for ~~shre pound~~ three pound of candels at 6^{d} per pound		00	01	06
16	dito for six pound of buter at 6^{d} per pound		00	03	00
17	Jully the 23rd 1694: nicolas Whitemarch Snr debter				
18	for one bushel of malt dll to mary flood[291] by my				
	wife foure shillings money				
19	[?] reseved two shillings of the above said malt				
20	[?] nsine phillips[292] debter for beef in 1694		00	06	00
21	[?] or candels 4 pound e one peck of malt		00	02	09
22	[?] march the: 12th: 1695 Thomas Randall debter for				
23	[?] 40 pound of beef at 2^{d} hapeney per pound		00	07	9
24	[?] for halef a pound of candeles		00	00	3
25	march the 12 th 1695 Thomas Randall deter for				
26	3 40 pound of beef at 2 hapeney per pound		00	07	9
27	for halef a pound of candeles		00	00	03
28	march the 12th th 1695 Edward Darby debter for				
29	53 pound of porck at 3^{d} hapeney per pound		00	15	6
30	for six pound of beef at the same time at 2^{d} per pound hapen		00	01	3
31	march the 12th 1695 Thomas kingman snr debter for thre				
32	bushels of lime 1^{s}–6^{d} per bushel		00	04	6
33	Aperell the 5th 1695 John [?] [?]bter[293] for one bushel				
34	of seed barly delivered to ~~fo~~ Sa [?] es		00	03	00
35	Aperell the 8th Thomas k[?] [?][?]er[294] for foure yards				
36	[?] cloth e a halef at	[?]	01	02	[?]
37	[?] peck [?] pound	[?]	00	[?]	[?]

Will Pratt Codin to 6: = 4 = 5
8 bushel of molt:
and 4^{s} money

[Page 92]

Line		ll	s	p		ll	s	p
1	<u>July 26 1702 saint porter 12: 8^{d}</u>				will pittey 10 ^{bus} barley			
2					Cred{ John Torrey 13 ½			
3					Enoc Lovell 19: 3 ^{peck} & 3 quorts			
4	Dept							
5	Sept 1709 Nicholas Phillips					00	00	08~~(con)~~
6	Sept 1709 Ben White B	00	08	00				
7	Sept 1709 Nick Phillips	~~00~~	4	0~~4~~ 2	3 Oct. 6 1709			
8	Sept 1709 Capt Hunt	00	07	00	Dept			
9	Oct 1709 Joseph Pittey	00	00	04	~~Josep Joseph Nash~~	~~01~~	~~18~~	~~00~~
10	Novem 1709 Incres Bate	00	07	10	September 1710			
11	Novem 1709 Joseph Pittey	00	00	04	Ebenezer Clow	0~~0~~3	12	00
12	~~Joseph~~ 1709 Joseph Torrey	00	02	11	Abia Whiteman	00	03	10
13	Nov 1709 Henry Kingman					00	12	06
14	Apr 1710 John Torrey	00	01	09	Capt Hunt	00	08	00
15	Apr 1710 Joseph Pitty	00	02	01				
16	May 1710 Capt french	00	03	00	Ebenezer Clow	04	10	00
17	May 1710 Richard Egers	00	03	00	October			
18	May 1710 Ebenzer Clow	01	04	09	Ebenezer Clow	05	14	09
19	May 1710 Thomas Reed	00	07	04	Nicolas Phillips	03	14	00
20	May 1710 Sam^{ll} Vinson	00	00	02	Joseph Richards	00	00	09
21	June 1710 Ebenezer Pratt	01	02	00	Nicolas Phillips	00	01	04
22	June 1710 Nicolas Phillips	00	10	00	Decon Bate	00	05	06
23					Nicolas Phillips	00	01	06
24	June 1710 Nicolas Phillips	00	10	00	Joseph Nash	00	08	00
25	June 1710 Ebene Pratt	00	15	00	Abraham Shaw	00	00	05
26	June 1710 Left Nash $^{2\ mole}$	00	06	00	Nicolas Phillips	00	10	06
27	June 1710 Ebenezer Pratt	01	06	00				
28	Novem							
29	July 1710 Witt Pittey snr	00	01	04	John Torrey	00	08	03
30	July 1710 John king	01	07	03	John Torrey	00	08	03
31	July 1710 Ebenezer Pratt	00	01	03	Joseph Lovell	15	13	07
32	July1710 Capt french	01	12	05	Capt french	00	13	09
33	July 1710 Ebenezer pratt	00	05	08	James Humphery	00	05	06
34	July 1710 Joseph Pittey	00	02	03	Mr. holey	01	07	06
35	July 1710 William Pittey	00	00	05	John Bicknell ^{senr}	00	00	06
36	July 1710 Ebenezer Pratt	00	60	00	John Torrey	00	01	03
37	oug 1710 Ebenezer Clow	02	14	00	John Bicknell	00	09	04
38	oug 1710 Ebenezer Clow	01	07	00	Mr. Needham	03	00	02
39	oug 1710 Mr. Jacson	02	14	0[?]	Enock Lovevell	03	09	11
40	oug 1710 Capt french	00	00	06	John Vinson Junr	06	11	09
41	oug 1710 Joseph Pittey	00	02	0[?]	John Vinson Snr	02	00	02
42	oug 1710 Joseph Richard	00	02	09	Sam^{ll} Vinson	04	12	00
43	oug 1710 Nicolas Phillips	05	15	05	EbnzVinson	00	11	04

[Page 92] (*continued*)

Line		ll	s	p		ll	s	p
44	oug 1710 Joseph Pittey	00	05	05	Ben Dyer	00	18	08
45	Sept 1710 Mr Jonson	03	12	0[?]	~~Joseph P~~			
46	Sept 1710 Ebenezer Clow					01	09	02
47	Sept 1710 Sergt Whiteman					00	07	03
48	Sept 1710							
49	Sept 1710 Abiah Whitman					00	00	06
50	Sept 1710 Sa^{ml}l bill					00	00	08

	ll	s	p		ll	s	p	
Dept	Crd							
June [?]th 1703 Will Drake	00	10	03	May 1703 Will Drake	00	07	07	
June 6 1702 Ephr Burl Dept	00	~~01~~	10	Credit				
Febr 6 1701 Ephr Pray Dept	00	06	08	1704 Tho. White	01	11	03	
27 1701 poush John holis dept	00	03	06	1704 Tho. White	01	16	00	
July 6 1703 Incres Bate Dept	00	01	09	1704 Joseph Green	00	01	00	
				1705 Joseph Drake	00	00	03	
Sept 1702 Rafe Tailar Dept	00	02	07	1705 Joseph Green	00	10	00	
Sept 1702 Jose Richards Dept	00	07	08	1705 Capt French	00	03	09	Bal
Sept 1702 Sath Andruse Dept	00	01	06	1706 Increse Bate	00	10	00	
				1706 John Pratt	00	00	07	
Sept 1702 John hunt Dept	00	01	11	1707 Samll White	00	06	04 ½	
Oct 6 1703 Tho White Dept	00	06	00	1709 Joseph Allen	00	08	00	
Nove 1703 Tho. White Dept	01	02	00	1709 Nic Phillips	06	07	06	
Decem 1703 Tho White Dept	00	03	02	1709 Joseph Nash	01	18	00	
Janr 1703 Tho. White Dept	00	00	06	1709 With Manley	00	09	06	
Janr 1703 Will Richards Dept	00	00	06	1709 Joseph Nash se[?]	01	06	00	
Jan 1703 Tho White Dept	00	10	00	1710 Ebenezer pratt	00	01	04	
Pheb 1704 Tho White Dept	00	11	00	1710 Mary Philips	00	13	03	
Pheb 1704 Tho. White Dept	00	05	00	1710 Ebenezer Pratt	00	12	06	
Mar 1704 Josep Green Dept	00	01	00	1710 Nick Phillips	00	05	00	
Mar 1704 Tho White Dept	00	10	00	1710 Eben Pratt	01	00	00	
Apr 1704 Tho White Dept	00	08	09	1710 Eben Pratt	00	03	09	
apr 1704 Samll White Dept Junr	00	17	06	1710 Eben Pratt	00	01	00	
apr 1704 Tho White Dept	00	03	00	~~1710 White~~				
June 1704 Capt hunt Dept	00	01	02	1710 Abiah Whitman	00	02	06	
Oug 1704 Ben Ludden Dept	00	00	09	1710 Eben Clow	12	00	00	
Nov 1704 Joseph Green Dept	00	13	06					
Jan 1705 Gideon Turrel Dept	00	02	05	1710 Nicolas Phillips	03	10	00	
Jun 1705 Joseph Pittey Dept	00	00	08	Capt french	02	00	00	
Aug 1705 Joseph Pratt Dept	00	01	03					
octo 1705 Joseph Pittey Dept	00	00	04	Capt french	00	08	00	
nov 1705 Mr. Mortemore Dept	00	06	00	Mr. Needham	03	14	06	
Janu 1705 John Pratt Dept	00	08	08	1709 Enoch Lovel	03	19	11	
~~capt~~ 1705 Capt french Dept	00	08	06					
Sept 1706 Jacob Turner Dept	01	04	00	John Vinson Junr	08	08	07	
octob 1706 Jacob Turner Dept	00	00	09	John Vinson Senr	00	11	07	
octob 1706 Jacob Turner Dept	01	08	00	Samll Vinson	05	00	01	
Nove 1706 Nath ford Dept	00	01	06	Ebner Vinson	01	05	10	
Nove 1706 Jacob Turner Dept	00	05	00					
Nov 1706 Lidea Thomas Dept	00	04	00	Joseph Pittey	00	00	03	
Dec 1706 John Pratt Dept	00	05	00					
July 1707 John Shaw Dept	00	01	03	Joseph Lovel	00	06	11	
Octo 1707 John Pratt Dept	00	00	04					
Octp 1707 Joseph allen Dept	00	07	06					
Janu 1707 Doc Bate Dept	00	03	03					

[Page 93] (*continued*)

Line		ll	s	p	ll	s	p
47	Apri 1708 Tho. holbrock Dept	00	0~~6~~2	06			
48	June 1708 Joseph Nash Dept	00	07	11			
49	July 1708 Zech Bicknell Dept	00	00	09			
50	Sept 1708 Ben orcut Dept	00	05	00			
51	octo 1708 Zec Bicknell Dept	00	01	00			
52	Nov 1708 Zec Bicknell Dept	00	03	06			
53	Nov 1708 Mrs Barnsdil Dept	01	15	06			
54	Dec 1708 Will Pratt Boe Dept	00	05	00			
55	Apr 1709 Steven french Dept	00	17	04			
56	June 1709 Tho Manley Dept	00	04	00			
57	June 1709 Tho Holbrock Dept	00	00	08			
58	July 1709 Will Manley Dept	00	13	06			
59	Oug 1709 Jospeh Nash Dept	00	02	11			
60	Aug 1709 Tho. holbrock dept	00	05	00			

[Page 94]

Line				ll	s	p
1	Desemb 13: 1706 Josesph Aallen[295] too cords of ocke wood					
2	Dr tow cords of oak wood		July 19th 1710			
3	oct 1707: Dept	00: 07: 6	Left Nash Dept to: 4 bushels			
4			of mault dll to his Indian			
5			boy	00	14	00
6			June 2 bushels of moult			
7	1709 Joseph Aallen Cred			00	00	08

Line		ll	s	p
1	desember the: 1st: 1701 recened with Joseph Richards,[296] and balanced acounpts			
2	and thare was dwe to mee from him in mony	04	0~~4~~3	03
3	to mony of sister Richards[297]	00	04	06
4	pheburary the 27 balanced acounpts with Joseph Richards			
5	and cleered ~~all~~ from the beginning of the world to this day			
6	his credit was	04	07	09
7	desember the: 11th: 1701 Ebenezer hobbe debter for			
8	143 pound mutten 2 d ½ per pound dll at Joseph pratts Jnr. hous	01	09	06
9	the 17 to halef a bushell of salt dll to Joseph pratt	00	01	00
10	jenuary the 30 to foure bushels & a peck of otes	00	08	0
11	June the: 15: to a bushell of ~~cornt~~ corn e a bushell of malt fife pound cottenwool	00	15	02
12	desember the12th 1701 recened with Joseph green 8 &			
13	ballansed acounpts and thare was dwe to mee	01	11	04
14	June 1702: ballanced the above acounpts e all paid			
15	desember the 12th: 1701 Samuell Bayly debter for			
16	eyght pound of flex 9d per pound	00	6	00
17	the 17th to a jacote	00	04	6
18	pheburary the 19 to a b pound of sheeps wool	00	06	06
19	march the 16th to two pound and quorter of toback	00	01	[00?]
20	November the first 1703 ballansed acounpts with Samuall Bayly and thare			
21	dwe to mee in money from him	00	04	10
22	the balanc was in: 1703			

[Page 96]

	ll	s	p
November the 22^{nt}: <u>1701</u> ballansed 2 ^{all} acounpts with Joseph ~~pr~~			
pratt snr and thare was dwe to mee from him	02	01	02
to two bushels of sallt 2^{s} per bushel	00	04	00
to thurty pound of ches and wine 3^{d} per pound 3^{d} batted upon			
the hole	00	09	06
to Enock Lowell for carting of shingell from swamp	00	06	00
to a hundered of bord nailes	00	01	00
to one bedcord dll this which is above to him selef	00	01	09
desember the 4th for seven sheep wait 270 pound dll at his one houce			
price 2^{d} ½ per pound	02	15	3
to John bicknell halef a hundered bord nailes pipes 1^{d} 4^{d} lent	00	00	11
Jenuary the: 21st: to a pound of butter	00	00	07
~~Jenuary~~ the 10: 1704 for malases dll to Ephram pratt	00	00	7
march to malases dll to yoruer daftter Hana pratt[298] ~~5 q~~	00	03	2
to carting of 8000 in shingels 3^{d} per: in	00	02	01
to a coster hat	01	00	0
29 to porck 27 pound dll to him selef	00	11	0
to seven quorts of malases dll to him selef	00	04	5
march the: 29: 1704: balanced acounts with Joseph pratt			
senr and thare was dwe to mee ^{in} money	00	17	4
aperell 25 to two bushels & a halef barly 3^{s} per bushell	00	07	6
october 16 then ^{1704} recened with Joseph pratt snr			
and thare was dwe to mee in mony	00	07	04
november: 2^{nt}: to halef a bushell of salt	00	02	3
to three cheses: 17: ½: 2^{d} ½ per pound	00	03	7
to salt dll him selef 3 peck 7^{d} peneth	00	04	1
21 to 8 pound of porck at 5^{d} per pound	00	03	0
march 7 to one peck of sallt	00	02	2
October the 3: 1710			
Mr Needum of bostoun[299]			
credit to one pees of scots			
cloth 21 yards at 3^{s} 6^{d} per yard	03	13	6
to mending a goos neck	00	01	0

[Page 97]

	ll	s	p
June: 1702 Joseph pratt snr credetor for: 900: of clobberd			
foure shillings per hundered	01	16	00
itm more 800 of clabbords 4^{s} per hundered	01	16	00
to mony receved a Joseph green	01	00	00
ienuary: 1704 for 8000 of shingells: 9^{s}: per thousand	03	12	00
June the 6th 1704 Joseph pratt snr creditor			
to thre thousand of shingels	01	07	00
		2	02
november: 21: 1704 to mony reseved of			
Joseph pratt snr	00	02	03
october the 3: 1710			
Mr Needum debt to money			
upon the balance of acounpts	01	02	06
to a parsell of appels	00	01	09
to 31 ll cheese at 3^{d} per ll e 5 ll			
of butter at 10^{d} ll	00	11	11
31 to 8 bushels e a hallef of appells	00	17	00
31 to 28 ll of chees at 3^{d} per ll	00	07	00

[Page 98]

	ll	s	p
November the 25 recened 1704 balansed acounpts with Joseph			
pratt jnr and thare was dwe to mee from him	05	02	11
the 28 to thurty pound of tobacko 5^{d}	00	12	06
the 29 to two sheep 80 pound 2^{d} ½ per pound two heds e plooks	00	17	04
desember the 8th to twenty one pound of sheeps wooll 12^{d} per [?]	01	01	00
the 13 to thurteen pound of sheeps wooll 12^{d} per pound	00	13	00
the 13 to foure pound and a halef of hops 6^{d} per pound	00	02	03
Jenuary the 19 to de^{c}en Torey a pound of tobacko	00	00	06
may to a peck of salt	00	00~~71/2~~	08
to butter	00	00	02
July the: 2^{nt}: to ten pound of cotten wooll dll marse fford[300]	00	18	04
September: 15: to a sheep 44 ^{ll} at 2^{d} ½ per pound	00	09	02
to mony taken up at wintworth of bostoun by david carver	00	08	00
September the 23 Enock Lowell debt to one			
bushell of salt dll to him se^{l}f	00	04	00
23 to foure yards galick scolun[301] at 3s 4d y	00	13	04
october: 14: to six ll of tobacko at 8d	00	04	00
november: 13: to two busheles of malt	00	08	00
desember the: 13: 1708 then balanced			
acounpts with Enock Lovell there was			
dwe from him to mee mony	01	01	06
march the 29: to one yard e halef of damarsk	00	04	06
Aperell: the 26: 1709 to three ll tobacko	00	01	09
August the 5: 1709 Enock Lovell			
debt to shot dll to him selef shoonailes	01	01	
29 to fife yards of scots cloth at 3s yard	00	15	10
September			
the 20 to: 9: quorts oull almost	00	05	03
october to two bushels of sallt	00	14	00
1710 to: 11: ll of cotten at 1^{s}–8^{d} per ll	00	18	04
ougust the 18 dll to yoore wife	00	09	00
october to one bushel of salt e two quorts salt buter	00	06	02
to two bushels of salt dll to selef	00	11	00
	03	19	10

Line

Febrewary 26th 1707 James Humphery credit to eight bushels & a halfe of barly

---

march the: 9th: brother pratt debt to two bushels malt
12 brother John bicknell credit to teen bushels of barly

Enock Lovell credit to sixteen bushels of barly

---

26 Mrs White[302] wido debt to two bushels e a halef of malt

James humfrey debt to foure bushels of malt dll to him selef

April
21 Mrs White Dept to one bushell of molt dll to Tho Dyer:

---

may 5 brother fford dept to two bushels of malt

---

may 13 Thomas Reed Junr debt to two bushels of malt dll to him selef

---

16 brother John Bicknell debt to foure bushels of malt e a hafe

---

19 Will pitty Dept to one bushell and a half of malt dll to Nathanell pitty
23 Tho- Reed senr Dept to too bushels of molt dll to him self

---

June the: 27: Tho- Reed senr Dept to too bushels of molt dll to his son Will Reed[303] = II = II

---

28 William pittey debt to one bushell e a halef of malt dll to thanell pittey
July 10 James Humffrey to: 4: bushels e a malt dll to him selef

---

August 6: Thomas Reed snr debt to two bushels malt
brother pratt debt to one bushel of malt

---

september 23 Joseph Lovell cred to one bushel barly

[Page 100]

Line	ll	s	p
November the 29: 1707 John Randell Snr cred to 10 bushels of bar^{ll}y			
29 John Randell debt to one bushel salt	00	05	00
January the 2th: 1708/7			
Enock Lovel credit to figh^{ive}teen bushels of Barly and halfe a peck			
20 John Vinson cred to two bushels barly			
Ferew 7th: 1708/7 John Bicknelle cred to twenty foure bushels of barley			
18 William Pratt cred to seven bushels a halfe ^{to} barly			
18 Nicholas Phillips cred to twelve bushels of barly			
26 John Bicknell cred to ten bushels of barly			
27 Tho: Reed senr cred to sixteen bushels of barley			
28 Will Pitty senr cred to six bushels of barley			
29 Will Pitty senr Dept to one bushell of molt			
mar 10 James Humfrey cred to six bushels barly			
13 Micajah Torey credit to two bushels barly			
13 Micajah Torey debt [~~18~~] halef a bushell malt			
John bicknell debt to one bushel malt			
23 Thomas Reed Snr debt to two bushels malt dll him selef			
27 John Torey cred to: 20: bushels of barly			
8 Micaj torey cred to 4 bushels e part			
of a peck of barly			
8 Micaiah Torey debt to 2 bushels of malt			
12 Joseph Lowell Dept to one bushe of malt dll to him selfe			
13 Nicolas phillips debt to two bushels of malt dll to John phiilips			
Aper 16: John Torey ~~dll~~ debt to seven bushels of malt dll to selef			
brother ffbrd cred to foure e a halef of barly			
19 Will pittey debt to one bushell e halef malt dll to nat			

	ll	s	p
May the: 3 1708 Enock Lovll debt to six bushels of malt dll to him selef			
5 John Torey cred to foure bushels barly			
14 John Torrey Dept to three bushels of molt 15 Nathaniell ford Dept to three bushels & halfe of molt dll to sone 15 Nathaniell ford Dept to one bushel of molt			
John torrey Dept three bushels of molt			
John Torrey Dept to five bushels of molt dll to 22 Benjamin tower by order of John Pratt			
22 Widdow White Dept to one bushel of molt dll to the Dyer			
25 Thomas Reed senr Dept to too bushels of molt dll to him			
29 James Humphery Dept to foure bushels of molt dll to ~~him~~ Zecariah bicknell			
31 Micajah Torrey Dept to three bushels and three peck of molt dll to him selfe			
June Ms White Wido reseved all her malt for the time past of dealing			
~~John~~ une John Bicknell Dept to foure bushels of molt dll to His son benjamin July 2 William pittey debt three bushels e a halef of malt dll to Nathanell 6 Tho Reed senr Dept to too bushels of molt dll to him self			
August 26 Tho Reed senr Dept to too bushels of molt dll to wiff			
26 Zecariah Bicknell Dept to one bushell malt dll to his son zecariah			
september Zecarah Bicknell cred to 5 bushels e halef barly 18 John Randol senr cred to five bushels of barly			
october 1 John randel senr Cred to too bushels of barly ~~SR~~ 30			
11th Zecariah Bicknell Dept to one bushe and a halfe of molt dll to his son ze			
desem^{b} 3 balland acounpts thomas Reed senr and thare was dew to him from mee in money	00	00	02
16 Joseph Lovell Cred to ten bushels of barley (10)			

Line				ll	s	p
1	2	122	elder blossomes good for any grenere [?]or [greeling]			
			~~beete n~~ butter fresh			
2	4	124	beete to gether in an earthen pott put in bileing water			
3	4 6	128	over ers then straine it out then tack rosom e bees			
4	6 8	130	wax e turpentim white e incorparate it together			
5	8 10	132	over a saft pire till it be well mixt: then ad to it			
6	12	134	red led e ~~black led~~ e white led of each cwontety till			
7	14	136	its of the culer led work it all to gether then clapt			
8	16	138	into cold water			
9	18	140				
10	20	142				
11	22	144				
12	24	146				
13	26	148				
14	28	150				
15	30	152				
16	32	154[304]				
17	34	156				
18	36	158				
19	38	160				
20	40	162				
21	42	164	Joseph Prout at bostoun debter			
22	44	166				
23	46	168				
24	48	170	to 1400 of clabbords			
25	50	172	at 5^s–6^d per hundred	03	17	00
26	52	174	to 4 bushels of malt			
27	54	176				
28	56	178	to Joseph Prout	00	12	00
29	58	180	to 4000 of shingles to			
30	60	182				
31	62	184	Joseph Prout at 12^s	02	08	00
32	64	186				
33	66	188	shingels to [?] Mr prout credit to			
34	68	190	[?] paper mony	03	00	00
35	70	192	Joseph prout debter			
36	72	194	foure thousands shingels at ~~3~~ 2^s: 1000	02	08	00
37	74	196	Joseph prout credit to mony	02	05	00
38	76	198	Joseph prout credit to mony			
39	78	<u>200</u>	paid to my selef	1	0	00

		ll	s	p
80 ~~5220~~	mr shipery of bostoun dll			
82 6320	to twoo fraits of hay dll into his			
84 2320	barn 3400 at 2^{s} = 6^{d} per hundered	04	05	00
86 8640	Sara Richards spinning 1705			
88	cotten 50 schains			
90	3 ll ½ wooll: [a] 119: scaines woostid			
92	John Whiteman: 2 dusen of biskeake			
94	4 ^{ll} shuger 6^{d} cloves			
96	6^{d} of sinemen 6^{d} [mase]			
98	~~ag~~ quar of an ounc nutmag			
100				
102				
104				
106				
108				
110				
112				
114				
116				
118				
120				
2320				

[Page 103]

	ll	s	p
November 16: 1704 [?] [?]			
to capt ffrench one bushell salt	00	04	6
to John bicknell one bushel salt	00	04	6
to Joseph green one bushel salt	00	04	6
to James hersy 2 bushel salt upon			
Joseph greens acounpt	00	09	0
Joseph green paid mony	00	01	00
to Enock lovell a hid 59 ll	00	09	10
to John bicknell two bushels salt	00	09	00
to a bridell to Joh bicknell a bridell	00	07	00
25 to Willam Richards halef a bushell salt:	00	02	03
30 to Nicolas phillips one bushel salt	00	04	06
30 to William pitty halef a bushel salt	00	02	03
desem: to Ebenezer pratt: 3p: salt	00	03	05
: 1st: to John Torey one bushell of salt	00	04	06
to Lit nash 4 bushels of malt			
1 to Joseph orcut at mountfords	00	10	00
4 to Lit nash four bushels of malt			
to mcaiah Torey halef a bushel salt:	00	02	03
to michaiah Torey 50 bord nailes	00	00	06
15 recened with Thomas holbroock			
& thare was dwe to mee	00	02	06
16 then ballanced acounpts with Incres			
Bate wife e thare was dwe to mee			
in mony for hogs fatt	00	17	10
wido Eyels det to lamp oull	00	01	05
19 to curanall Hunt[305] one			
bushels of salt dll John	00	04	04
23 Samuell Junr White of brantery			
debtter for one hog 73 ll			
2 d = ½ per pound	00	15	02 1/2
27 Joseph pitty debt to one gallen			
of lamp oyll	00	02	3

	ll	s	p
desember 1704			
Joseph orcut debt ^{by} a norder to wido			
Eyles at mr mountford	00	13	0
desember 27 nicolas Salter debt to			
a parsell of sheeps wooll bouft			
by the lump dll to him selef:	00	02	0
28 receoed with John Greens wife			
and theire was dwe to mee for ~~s~~			
six ~~f~~ pound of shuger 6^{d} per pound	00	03	00
and one garllon oyll dll	00	02	03
29 Zeckeriah bicknell det for			
halef a bushell of salt	00	02	3
Jenuary: Johnathon Torey detr to one			
the 1st galloon of oull dll his wife	00	02	3
9 Ebenezer pratt debtr to			
shuger and pipes	00	00	6
16 John pratt debt for to two			
pound of shuger	00	01	0
15 recned with moris Trufant			
about the run of the sloope			
in the yer 1703 which was dwe			
to mee in that yeere and [?] shall			
in mony to mee	00	04	4
John Torey dtr to halef a hund			
ered of bord nailes	00	00	6
26th Joseph orcut dt to an order			
at Johathon mountfords with foure			
shilings hee had before	01	14	0
recned with coronall thare was dwe to mee	00	00	8

[Page 105]

	ll	s	p
Jenuary the: 26: 1705			
29 brother fford det for a galloon of oyll	00	02	03
29 Abya whitman det for one galloon of ayll	00	02	03
30 Insine Hunt det for one peck of salt dll to danell	00	01	02
31 Abya whiteman det for one halef a bushell of salt	00	02	03
pheb:1: John Bicknell detr for one galloon of malases	00	02	00
decon bates detr for 200^{m}: this mony dwe altho crosed 1 of bard nailes e: 6^{d}: in salt	00	02	06
5 william pittey cordwinder detr for one galloon of oull	00	02	03
5 william pittey wever detr for two quorts of oyll	00	01	02
7 John Bicknell debt for ~~three~~ foure pounds of shuger	00	02	00
8 brother fford detr for ~~three~~ six pounds of shuger 6^{d} per pound dll to ruth fford	00	03	00
9 John Bicknell deter for a broom dll by biniamin	00	00	05
15 Zeckerah Bicknell deter to two pounds of shuger	00	01	00

	ll	s	p
Feburay the 17: 1705			
Samuell pratt deter to part of			
a paire of shoos	00	02	4
19 John porter debter to one			
galloon of oyll e a peck of salt			
e one pound of shuger	00	03	11
22 Ezera whitemarsh deter for			
three quart of oull 7^d	00	01	09
27 John frathingham[306] debtter			
to sixteen pound of butter			
at 7^d per pound with a pot at: 6^d:			
and two bushels of corn: 2^s–9^d:			
per bushel	00	15	4
Joseph Richards detter for			
beens dll to him selef	00	00	06
march: 2: william reed snr debter			
for one bushell of indian corn	00	02	09
6 ~~Beth~~ Elizebath Simes[307] debtter			
for shuger	00	00	04
6 Gideon Turell debr for halef			
a bushell of sallt	00	02	~~6~~3
7 John vining debter for two			
bushels of barley	00	06	00
7 Gedian Turell debt for three			
pipes dll to his son	00	00	02
Zeckeriah bicknell debter			
to halef a hundered of bord nailes		00	06
15 to william Reed debtter three			
peck of corn dll to his son			

[Page 107]

	ll	s	p
march the 15 1705			
John vining debtter for one			
bushell e a halfe of corn	00	04	2
1~~5~~6 Joseph orcut debtter for			
two pound of shuger	00	01	0
16 Joseph orcut debtter for			
25 ½^{ll} e a halef of beef at			
2^{d} per pound dll to himselef	00	04	3
19 dll to Thomas Kingman one			
thousand of salt hay ~~for~~ from			
an order by his wife	01	00	00
19 John Torey debter to one galloon			
e halef a pint of ayll	00	02	05
20 Capt ffrench debter for halef			
a busell of salt dll to Joseph green	00	02	03
21 brother fford deter for ten			
bushels of malt dll him selef			
22 John porter debter for two			
pound of shuger	00	01	00
22 John Torey debtter for one			
pound of shuger	00	00	06
23 Joseph Aalling[308] debtter for two			
bushels of malt	00	06	00
23 mrs Torey[309] debtter for biskit	00	01	00
24 Lft nash debtter for two bushels			
of malt dll to simeon nash	00	06	00

	ll	s	p
march the 26th: 1705: then baroed of brother John bicknell in mony wait	05	00	00
26 then baroed Enock Lowells wife in peeses of eight e halef peeses of eight silver mony	07	00	00
28 John pratt jur deter for 800 Hund salt hay dll to william negro	00	16	00
John Torey debter for three pipes dll Joseph Torey	00	00	02
28 Thomas Holbrowck debter for two pound of shuger	00	01	00
28 John pratt debtter for: 400: of hay dll to Thomas Holbroo ck of brantery	00	08	00
28 John Torey debtter for for two pound of shuger e to biscakes	00	01	02
29 John bicknell debtter for two pound of shuger dll sarah	00	01	00
30 John pratt junr debter for 2000 of hay dell to william reed junr by order	2	00	00
31 Thomas Holbroock debtter for two bushels e halef seed barly	0	06	9

	ll	s	p
Aperell the: 2^{nt}: 1705 John pratt debter for 1000 of salt hay dll Thomas Kingman	01	00	00
6 Thomas holboock debter for one 105 pound of hay	00	03	08
6 ~~Tholbo~~ Thomas holbroock debter for two bushels of malt	00	06	00
6 Joseph Richards debtter for one pound of shuger	00	00	06
7 John Torey debter for two pound of shuger	00	01	00
John Randall debter for one peck of salt	00	0~~2~~1	0~~0~~2
9 John pratt debtter for 800: hund of hay dll John Randall	00	16	00
10 Left nash debtter for salt dll to Simeon nash	00	00	3
10 brother fford debtter for one quart of malases dll to lidea	00	00	06
11 John Torey credit for one quorter of vell 9^{ll} 1/2 2^{d}: 1/5 per pound	01	11	3/1
14 michaiah Torey debt to two pound dll to his garl	00	01	00
moris Truffant debter for one shilings worth of egges	00	01	00
17 John Kingman debter for four malt dll to him selef	00	12	[?]

[Page 110]

	ll	s	p
Aperell 17 1705			
then recened with Joseph Richards			
and ballansed all accounpts and			
thare was dwe to mee in money	00	0~~3~~1	0~~4~~ 2
17 Joseph Richards debtter for			
100 bushels of indian corn and			
at 3^s and one peck salt: 1^s–2^d	00	07	02
18 mosis peneman of brantery debt			
for ~~mony~~ ten shillings in many			
paid him at Lft Nashes for the			
which hee is to pay mee ten pound			
of good well washed sheeps wooll	00	10	0
21 brother fford debter for three			
pounds of shugar dll lidia	00	01	6
26 Zechariah bicknell debtter			
for one peck of salt dll to malata[310]	00	01	02
27 decon bates debtter for 100 3/1 qu			
arters of clabord nailes	0	01	02
27 decon bates debtter for halef			
a bushell of salt dll to him selef	02	03	
28 beniamin Luding[311] debter for			
halef a bushels of salt e fife			
peck of indian corn	00	06	00
28 beniamin Luding Credit for			
for many reseved of him	00	12	00
may: 1: Johnathon bill of bostown debter			
for ~~20~~ 225 spora gras e one			
shees 6 ll 5 ^{d} per pound	00	04	04
3 Joseph orcut debter for one			
bushel e a halef of malt	00	04	6
4 Samuell bill of bostoun debter			
for spara[312] e chees	00	05	3

[Page 111]

	ll	s	p
may the 5: 1705			
Mrs White Senr[313] credit for two bushels of barly	00		
Mrs White Senr debter for one bushel of salt	00	04	6
5 John pratt Jur debtter for one peck of salt	00	01	2
7 then ballansed acounpts with with John Torey e thear was dwe to mee in mony	00	01	05
7 John Torey credit upon ~~to~~ the acounpt of John Vinson	00	13	06
8 Elder Neales[314] of brantery debt for six quorts of oyll	00	03	04
23 John pratt debter for halef a hundered of bord nailes	00	00	07
24 beniamin Luding debtter for one bushell e a halef of corn	00	04	06
26 Thomas Holbroock debter for one galloon of oyall	00	02	00
28 Lft Nash debter for two bushels of malt dll to Simeon nash	00	06	00
June: 1: brother pratt debter for halef a hundered of bord nailes	00	00	4
1 moses peneman crediter for twenty one bushels of corn			
4 John pratt Junr credit for one quort of rum reseved of ruth			
6 Joseph orcut debter for two bushels of malt dll to him selef	00	06	00

	ll	s	p
June the: 9th: 1705 Joseph Drack debter			
for corne e tobacka: 1 ll	00	01	02
11 Ebenezer pratt debter for halef			
a bushel of salt	00	02	06
Ebenezer pratt debter for a			
[1?] paper bill	00	10	00
12 James Humfry debter to foure			
yards of blew lining: 1^s–4^d per yard	00	05	04
14 Joseph pittey debter for one			
pound of ~~to~~ candels	00	00	8
16 hana yles debt for 4 quorters			
of vels caring to bostown			
to beniamin Luding debter for			
one pound of pouder	00	03	06
22 Coranall Hunt debt for one pound			
of pouder dll to John hunt	00	03	06
22 brother fford debt for a peck of			
salt ~~e two shillings worth of eggs~~	00	051	303
22 brother fford credit to eggs	00	02	00
22 Mrs Torey debt to biskeak	00	01	00
22 John Torey debt to caring: 4: quorter			
of yell to bostoune	00	00	06
John Torey det 2 pipes	00	00	201
25 Jacob Holbroock[315] dter for foure			
pound of cotten wooll at 1^s–6^d pound	00	06	00
26 beniamin Luding debter to 12 flints			
e bulits	00	00	09
mosis peneman credit to: 21 bushels			
of indian corn			

[Page 113]

	ll	s	p
June the 27 1705 then ballanced acounpts			
with beninmin Luding E thare wos dwe			
to mee in mony	00	03	00
to one bushel of indian corn	00	03	04
28 Joseph orcut debt to two bushels of			
barly dll to william pratt	00	06	00
29 Joseph orcut debter to fife			
pound e a quorter of tobacko	00	02	08
29 Sister Richards Junr debt for			
one peck of salt dll mary	00	01	03
29 william pittey credit for vell	00	01	04
July 6 brother vining[316] credit to mony	00	11	00
10 zeckariah bicknell debt to			
one nutmeg	00	00	03
11 Jcebod Holbroock debtter to			
5 q garlick holun 2^s 3^d E a caleco			
aporn 3^s $4^{d:}$ e specled caleco 4^s	01	03	03
11 Jcebod Hollbroock debtter to 3 y^d			
of colominko 5^s per yard dll wife	00	15	00
13 Zeckeriah bicknell debter to			
two dayes worck at hilling at neck	00	04	00
17 to captain ffrench one peck			
of salt dll bedlo[317]	00	01	03
17 ~~to~~ Enock Lovells wife debtter			
to goods reseved at bostoune	01	03	10
Lift Nash debt to two bushels			
of malt dll to simeon nash	00	05	08
18 John bicknell debt to one			
quort of rum	00	01	00
12 Joseph orcut debter to one			
bushel of barly dll to william			
pratt son to Joseph pratt	00	03	03

	ll	s	p
July the 21 1705 Joseph orcut credit to			
six thousand of shingles 8^{s}	02	08	00
21 to John bicknell one peck salt	00	01	03
24 80 Insine Hunt one peck of	00	01	03
Salt Dll to his son John			
Joseph orcut debter to fife bushels			
of barly which was forgot in the			
time of the run e the month	00	15	0
26 Petter Newcumb Deptter			
for one peck of Salt	00	01	3
27 to beniamin Luding goods dll			
at bostoune with 3^{s}–6^{d} in mony	00	19	00
27 beniamin Luding debter to six			
quorts of rum e one bushell of			
indian corn e one bushel of barly	00	12	10
27 beniamin $^{\text{luding lu}}$ cred to 5000 of sh			
ingels at 8^{s} per thousand	02	00	00
Ougust: 2 John Kingman Deptter	00	05	10
for one bushel of corn: & ½ bushel salt	~~00~~	~~04~~	~~09~~
2 Joseph orcut Deptter for			
too bushels of barly	00	06	08
3 Mrs Shipery debt to 12^{ll} of porck			
at [?] 6^{d} per pound	00	06	00
4 Thomas barnut of bostown debt			
to 3000 of shingels at 12^{s} m	01	16	00
6 Ebeneser pratt debter to 300			
of bord nailes a 1^{s}–2^{d} per hundered	00	03	~~6~~06
6 Zechariah bicknell debt to two			
peeses of eight dll to Joshua[318]	00	12	00

[Page 115]

	ll	s	p
August: 7th: 1705 John Shawe debter to malases e plysh brickes[319]	00	11	00
6 to Enock Lovell six pound of shot 4^{d} per pound	00	02	00
8 Jcebod Holbroock debt by one peck of salt	00	01	03
9 Zeckariah bicknell debt to halef a peck of salt	00	00	08
10 William pratt credit to mony paide for the run of the bote	01	00	00
10 Lft Nash debt to two bushels of malt dll to simeon nash	00	06	00
Joseph allin$^{n\ sener}$ Deptter for too Bushels of malt Dll to his wife	00	06	00
Morris trufant Deptter for one peck of salt ~~Dell~~ to his wife	00	01	0~~4~~3
Mrs Mary White Deptter for one ^{one} Bushel of Salt Dll to franck	00	05	00
11 Lft Nash debt to two bushels malt	00	06	00
11 brother fford debt to halef a hundered of dubell[320] to mee	00	01	10
Enock Lovell debt to 2 yards osenbrogs	00	01	08
12 to William pittey one peck of Salt dll nathanell	00	01	03
12 John Randall debt to one bushel of salt dll to him selef	00	05	00
to John Randall debt to six pound and halef of porck at 5^{d} per pound	00	02	05

	ll	s	p
~~Aperell~~ the 12 1705			
August Zecariah bicknell debt to			
one sife dll to Jsack pool[321]	00	06	6
13 decon bates debt to 4^{ll} shot			
4^{d} per pound e one peck of salt	00	02	07
to James Humphery debt to			
200 bord nailes	00	02	04
to Ebenezer pratt debt to			
turning of a grinstone	00	00	02
to Joseph orcut two s bushels			
of barly dll to him selef	00	006	00
Joseph orcut debt to a			
pees of a rope 3 fodam	00	01	00
24 to James Humfry debter to			
500 e ~~bor~~ shingell nailes	00	02	00
to Mr vesey[322] debt to one bushel			
of malt dll by benigmin			
James Humfrey cred for his			
e carts caring hay of cowes	00	01	00
Ebenezer pra^{a}tt debt to			
2500 shingel nailes	00	10	00
Enock lovell debt to 1: y: hofe			
quorter of caleco	00	03	04
24 Joseph orcut debt to one			
peck salt dll his wife[323]	00	01	03
zechriah bicknell debt to			
two quorts of malases dll orcut	00	0~~2~~1	02
25 John Bicknell Dcptter for onc			
~~peck of l Salt~~	00	01	02
hondred of bord nailes			

	ll	s	p
August the: 25 1705			
Enock lovell debt to museling	00	05	11
25 to zeckeriah Bicknell dbt to			
a peney payd for a tancur	00	00	01
29 Capt. french Deptter for			
one peck of Salt dll to Badlo	00	01	03
29 Joseph pratt Deptter for one			
peck of salt dll to him selfe	00	o[j]	o[9]
nicolis phillips debt to			
three yards of silk 9^{s} per yard	01	07	00
Sep^{te} Caleb litell feeld of brantery			
debter to one peck of salt	00	01	03
6 John vinson Dept for			
halfe a bushel of salt	00	03	00
& for six pence dll John Whitm^{an}	00	00	00
mosis peneman debt to one bottel rum	01	00	
6 John Whitman Depter for			
salt del to himselfe	00	02	o[o]
6 Joseph orcut Deptter for			
one bushell of barly dll to him selfe	00	03	00
6 Morris Trufant Deptter for one			
quart of malases & halfe a pound			
of pouder & halfe a pound of shot	00	02	06
7 Joseph orcut debter for 300			
bordnailes e one pound of tabacko	00	04	00
8 Jcebod Holbroock debt to one			
peck of salt	~~00~~00	01	03
10 Samuell pratt debt to halef a			
dayes mowing salt grass	00	o[?]	[?]^{6}

	ll	s	p
September 10 1705 Samuell pratt debter upon a balanc of acounpt when wee recened	00	05	4
11 Joseph orcut debt to two bushels of malt	00	0~~4~~6	0
12 Joseph orcut debt for eleven quorts of malases	00	06	0
Joseph orcut debt for ~~to~~ loding two lod of hay	00	01	6
13 Sister Richards Junr debtor to sheeps wooll dll to hr selef		07	00
14 baanced acounpts with Joseph ^{o}rcut and thare was dwe to mee from him ~~to mee~~	03	1~~9~~3	05
Joseph orcut debt to mony paid to him selef	01	08	0
14 Enock Lovell debt for six pound of cotton wooll 1^{s}–8^{d} ll	00	10	00
Enock Lovell debt to waits to way money complement 13:	00	0~~4~~5	00
16 Joseph orcut cred to six thousand of shingels 8^{s}	02	08	0
19 James Humfrey credit to 34 of yard wide clat wefing[324]			
21 beniamin Luding debt to one bushel of barly	00	03	0
22 William pratt cred for many paid twards the bates rum	00	04	6

	ll	s	p
September the 23 1705			
Ebenezer pratt debtter to			
goods dll to Ant bayly upon the			
acount of Sara^{h} bayly by a verbal order			
from him selef	01	10	00
Ebenezer pratt debt to 200 bordnailes		~~02~~	~~4~~
dll to ante bayly	00	2	4
24 John bicknell debter for			
halef a peck of salt	00	00	8
25 James Humfrey cred for his			
horce e cart halef a day	00	01	00
26 Lft Nash debt to foure bushels			
of malt dll to Sime Nash	0	11	04
29 Ms Torey debt to a rope	00	05	03
29 Joseph orcut credit to six			
thousand of shingels at 8/	2	08	00
october 1 Joseph orcut debt to mony			
paid to him selef	1	10	00
1 John bicknell debt by two			
quarts of malases	0	01	0~~2~~1
2 Epraim burell debt by			
200 bubel tenes e 500 bordnailes		09	02
10 John Shawe cred for 750			
at 10^{s} ~~m s~~	0	07	06
11 recned with brother ford and			
thare was dwe to him seven			
bushels of malt			
11 Willm pratt Deptter for three bushels			
of malt dll to him selfe	00	09	00
12 to John blancher in 5 ll cotten			
upon Ephraim burells accounpt	00	08	04

	ll	s	p
october the 12: 1705: brother ford debt to frating of appels to bostoun	00	04	00
13 decon wales[325] debt to 2 iares of lamp oyll	00	07	00
13 to John blanchar one galloon malases upon Ephraim busls co:		02	2
15 James Humfrey debt for 20 ^{ll}: ½ talo at 6^{d} per pound	0	10	3
Joseph pittey debt to one pound of shot dll beniamin pittey	0	00	4
19 beniamin Luding debt to one bushel of barly	0	03	00
John Randall cred for three bush Els of appels e one bushel quinses:	0	03	09
Lft nash cred to mony paid	1	06	06
3~~3~~1 zecariah bicknell debter to one hundered bordnailes	0	01	02
3~~30~~1 Nicolas phillips debt to halef a pound pouder e one pound e halef shot:	0	02	03
3~~31~~0 William pratt debt to two bushels of indian corne 3^{s}	0	06	00
30 John pratt debter to fife bushels of Turnups dll yoor son	0	06	00
novem: 1: Joseph orcut debt to: 12: of cotten at 1^{s}–8^{d} per pound dll micaiaTorey:	1	00	00
1 Joseph orcut debt to eight pound of cotten dll John Torey	0	13	04
2 Joseph orcut debt to one bushel of turoupse a gallneoon of malases	0	03	05

[Page 121]

	ll	s	p
November the: 3: 1705			
Samuell Andres debt to: 8: bushels of turnups e 8 dusen of cabges	00	17	6
3 John Torey debt to one dusen cab^{age}	00	01	6
5 John pratt junr debt to two bushels of indian corn	00	06	00
6 decon bates debt to 8 bushels Tur^{nups} e a quorter of hundered of punpings	00	11	03
6 Izera whitmarch debt to 4 bushels of Turnops dll decon bates	00	05	00
7 John Green debt to two bushels of turnips dll his son	00	02	06
9 John whiteman ju^{n} debt to one bushell of salt dll to Insine Hunt	00	05	00
John whiteman ju^{n} credit 850: of clabbords at 4^{s} per hundered	01	14	00
9 James humfrey debt to one paire of belis e a bushel e halef salt	00	11	06
mr mortemore[326] of bostoun det to one hundered of clabbords	00	06	00
James freeman of bostoun debt to appels dll to his wife	00	04	00
James Humfrey credit to one pot butter: 13 dll 6^{d} per pound	00	08	06
9 Abia whiteman debt to two bushels of salt 5^{s}	00	10	00
John Torey debt to three dayes work of mans Johns	00	04	06
John whiteman debt to 500 bord nailes e swon shot 4^{li} 1/2	00	07	00

[Page 122]

	ll	s	p
November the 12: 1705 Mr Torey: debt to 28 ll shooger: 5^d: pound	00	11	08
John whiteman debt to two pound of pouder dll to him selef	00	06	08
12 William pratt cred to mony paid:	01	10	00
12 Lft nash debt to: 4: bushels of malt dll Simean nash	00	11	04
13 Ephraim burell debt to one bushel e a halef salt 5^s per bushel:	00	07	06
13 Joseph drack credit to mony paid by beniamin pooll	00	00	03
13 Joseph orcut credit by forty ~~b~~peesees of seder 2^d ½ pees:	00	08	04
14 James Humfrey debter for one bushel e halef salt	00	07	06
James Humferey credit for his horce work	00	03	00
15 Joseph Aling snr debt to halef a bushell of salt	00	02	06
brother fford debt to 3 bushels of malt dll to butler[327] bostoun: 16 Joseph orcut debt to 3 b of turnups at 1^s = 3^d per bushell	00	03	09
17 brother fford debt to pipes dll to Sarah ford	00	00	02
Joseph Aling cred one cord e three foot off ocke wood at: 6^s:	00	08	03
Enock Lowell debt to two pound wool		0	08
Enock ~~f~~ Lovell a hide: 68	0	11	04

Line	ll	s	p
desember: 1: 1705 Thomas white debt to 3 yards silk 9^s per yard	01	07	00
Jseph Aling cred to mony	00	12	00
1 Joseph richards debt to ~~2~~ two quorts of mallases	00	0~~2~~1	02
3 Joseph Richards cred by: an order from John whiteman junr	00	04	00
5 Joseph Richards cred by John vinsons ^{order}	00	00	09
6 Joseph Richards debt to ~~two~~ one bushels of turnops	00	0~~3~~1	03
6 Joseph orcut debt to ten quorts of malases 2^s 4^d per galloon	00	05	10
6 Joseph orcut debt to an order at mounfford at bostoun bring part of the order	01	00	00
6 Joseph orcut debt to forteen pound of cotten wooll ^{a} and $^{1s\ 5d}$ three pound of sheeps ^{10d} woll	o[8?]	05	10
7 then ballanced acounpts with Joseph orcut and thar was dwe to mee from him	05	19	03
8 Jcabod Holbroock debt to six pounds cotten 1^s = 6^d per pound	00	09	o[?]
12 ~~Jo~~ William pratt credit to mony payd for the run of the bote	05	00	o[?]

	ll	s	p
desember the 12 1705			
Joseph Richards ~~er~~ debt			
to seven quorts malases 7^{d}			
per quort	00	04	01
13 Joseph or^{c}ut Deptter for			
one Bushel of malt dll to him selfe	00	03	00
19 Ebenezer pratt debt to three			
bushels of malt dll Jacob Turner	0	04	06
19 Jacob Turner debt to a bill of			
credit e one neckcloth the bill			
being one pound	01	02	09
19 Jacob Turner debt to two pound log^{wood}	0	00	06
28 Joseph Richards debt to			
two pound e halef of candels	0	01	08
28 Joseph Richards debt to			
six pound of chees at 5^{d} pound:	0	02	06
Jenewa![328]: Joseph ^{Joseph} orcut credit for			
2 a paper reseved	01	~~0~~10	00
9 Jseph orcut debt to six pound			
of cotten wooll at 1^{s}–5^{d} per pound		00^{10}	00
10 John pratt debt to 14 ll			
of butter e a pot 6^{d} dll son	0	08	08
10 Joseph green debt to beef			
180 ll 2^{d} per pound dll to his sones:	01	10	00
Joseph green cred mony paid			
by an order to william peety	00	10	00

[Page 125]

	ll	s	p
January 14 <u>1705/6</u>			
Thomas Reed Deptter			
for three pounds of shoot	00	[01?]	00
18 Thomas Reed Sn^{r} deptter			
for 100 Bushels of malt	00	06	00
20 Capt ffrench debt to three			
bushels of malt dll to bedlo	00	08	06
21 Joeseph orcut debt to an			
order gaven to micaih Torey	00	18	00
ballanced acoupts with Capt			
franch e thare dwe to him			
my Toune rate being paid one			
bushel of malt e a 11^{d} pence	00	03	09
21 Capt ffrench debt to three			
bushels of malt	00	08	6
pheb: ~~10~~6: Joseph richards debt to			
halef a bushel of tunops	00	07	0½
7 Joseph orcut debt to six			
ll of tobacko e one bushel of malt		06	0
7 John bicknell debt to goods			
upon a recening upon boock e all			
bock depts cleered ex^{e}tping			
malt e barly acounpts f~~o~~rom			
the beginning of the world to			
this day dwe to mee	00	10	07

	ll	s	p
phebuary the 12 1705/6 Joseph orcut debt to writing of a bill	00	00	06
13 Joseph Richards credit to mony reseved of him selef	00	10	10
15 Joseph Richards debt to 67 ½ ll beef dll to him self	00	12	02
19 ~~Will~~ pitty credit for foure mnisters rat bushels of barly: Rcd m 07 10	2	4	5
John Whiteman junr debt to money payd to him selef	00	05	09½
~~January the 15th 1707/8~~ November the first ~~one [?] orcut pafters[sic?] m^{r}~~ 1707 mr thach[er][329] ~~Thacher salery began in~~ rate to mee:	1	01	0
November the first 1707 one reverant mr Thachers salery begane: paide to the ffirst quorte January the 18th 1708/7	00	05	02 $^{2}/_{1}$
may the: 2: the secand quorter	00	07	00
July the: 18: the third quarter	00	03	00 2/1
august the 15: the fourth quorter	00	07	00
feburary: 5th: 1708 the fift quorer to micaja Torey cunstable mony	00	10	2
may 3 the sixt quorter to micaja Torey	00	10	00
July the 26: the seventh quorter to micaja Torey	10	00	
november the 3 the 4 quoter	00	06	10
jenuary: 30: $170^{10}/_{9}$ the first $qu^{ort}er$	00	10	00
may the 2nd the secand quorter	1	12	00
august the 15 the third quoter to James Humfry	0	12	00

[Page 127]

	ll	s	p
June the 22: 1703 John Whitman creditor for six thous			
of shingles: 9^{s}: per thousand e 300 of the same	052	~~0~~16	0[3]
Desember the 20th: 1703			
to Samuell Bagly a bushel of malt upon			
Thomas bicknells acount	00	03	[?][?]
the 21 to Joseph orcut a bag 5^{s} 6^{d}: to $800^{1s–2d\ 100}$ bord nails			
and to two 250 shngell nails at: 4^{s}: per 1000	00	16	1[?]
the 21 to Thomas Bicknell: 2: galloons malases dll wife	00	05	[?]
to Thomas Bicknell a botell	00	01	0[?]
the 22 to Samuell ffrench halef a bushell salt	00	02	2[?]
Jenuary 10 to moris Trewant[330] one broom	00	00	[?]
the 14 recned with william pratt and moris			
Trufant about the sloop named the three			
frinds and thare was dwe to mee from			
them	03	01	[?]
reconed with Johnathan mountford of			
Bostoune and thare was dwe to mee			
from him	04	[?]	[?]
Johnathen mountford in bifes reseved	00	07	[?]
to Thomas bicknell a bushell and halef of malt	00	04	[?]
21th to Ebenezer pratt a galloon of malases	00	02	[?]
24 to william pitty 2000^{m} borde nailes dll to james pitty	07	00	[?]
to Thomas White for the writing of a pill	00	00	[?]
27 to william richards for writing of a bond	00	00	[?]
27 the thomas white forer cheeses sold at a lump	00	10	00
28 to John greens son zechariah a broom	00	[?][?]	[?]
28 reseved of william pratt a pare of shoes	00	[?][?]	[?]
28 to samuel $Andrews^{chees\ 42\ ll\ 5\ d}$ per pound	00	1[?]	[?]
pheber: 1: 1704 to Thomas White by an order			
from Josef Green paid to joseph in $che^{e}s$	00	[?][?]	[?]
10 to Thomas White of Bantery junr bag	00	05	[?]
to pasienc green flex	00	00	[?]
to John Green wife a quort of maleses	00	00	[?]
28 to Michaja Torey a bushel of salt	00	04	[?]
march 1 to Joseph orcut two pounds of tobacko	00	01	00
3 to Joseph greens dll to his son a peck salt	1	0[?]	[?]
to Thomas Bicknell upon Samuel Baglys account			
to micajah Torey a bushel of malt	3	0[?]	[?]

Line	ll	s	p
march the 8 1707 [?] Joseph orcot debter			
for two bushels of malt	00	06	00
[th]e 10th to Thomas White of b[r]anttery foure			
galloons of malases 2s–6d per galloon dll to			
Johnathan Clarck[331]	00	10	00
11 to Johnathan Torey two quarts malases	00	01	03
14 to ms barnsdill Bostoun: 3: bushels of mallt	00	09	00
14 to m[s] Jorg Robbeson of Bostoun 3 bushels of malt	00	09	00
21 to Joseph richeds wife[332] a broom	00	00	06
23 to mrs Torey two broomes	00	00	10
23 balanced acounpts with Thomas Bicknell			
and thare wos dwe to him fife bushels			
of mallt			
25 to moris Turfant: 800: salt hay 1s–3d per			
hundered	00	10	00
to will pratt: 412: at 1s–3d per pound	00	05	02
31 to Johathan Torey two quarts malases	00	01	03
[A]perell 3 to samuell andreuse a galloon of malases			
and six buskits dll to his man siman pitty	00	03	00
the: 7: to micajah Torey 500m bord nailes	00	05	00
7 to micajah Torey a paire of shoose	00	06	00
11 to Thomas white of brantery 3 pecks of salt:	00	03	09
[?]21 to peeter Nucum of brantery two galloons			
of malases upon the account of Thomas white:	00	05	00
15 to moris Trufant halef a peck of salt	00	00	06
10 to micajach Torey 300 shoo nailes	00	01	00
to micajah Torey 200 shoo nailes	00	00	08
[2]2 to micajah Torey two bushels seed barly	00	06	00
[2]5 to joseph pratt snr: 2: bushels e a halef			
of barly: 3s: per bushel	00	07	06
[?] Thomas white credit for: 6: cords e quarter wood:	01	1~~0~~1	03
[?] Samuell white credit for: 5: cords e three quarters wood	01	08	09
28 to joseph orcut 35ll ¾ at 5d per pound pork			
with a sum tobacko	00	15	00
[t]o Samuell white of brantery junr in salt			
hay e inglish hay	00	17	06
to Thomas White of brantery a bushel malt			
dll two samuell white	00	03	00

	ll	s	p
aperell 1704 Thomas white of brantery credit for 800 h			
of clabbords 3^{s}–3^{d} per hundered	01	06	00
Thomas white credit for 60 posts: 3^{d}: per pees	00	10	00
May 14 to joseph orcut two pound of tobacko	00	01	00
to joseph orcut in indian corn	00	0~~0~~3	00
20 to john $green^{n}$ cunstable for moris trufant			
for his cuntery ratte	00	13	04
27 to beniamin Luden in mony	00	04	00
to wido Eyels: [6]: quorts of oyell	00	0~~0~~3	06
to moris Trufant a peck salt e a galloon oyel	00	03	00
to mr landgdun[333] two lambes 6^{s}–6^{d} per pees	00	13	00
June: 1st: to mr landgdun 3 [l]ambs e 3 wethers prise	02	03	06
To mr h^{o}ucheson[334] 5500 ^{shinges} 11^{s} per thousand	03	00	06
to mr houcheson 1000 clabbords 2^{ll}–10^{s} per thousand	2	10	00
Mr houcheson credit for: 13 hh salt: 1^{ll}–4^{s} per hh	15	12	00
7 to mathy pratt snr[335] halef a bushel salt	00	02	06
To beniamin Ludings rate payd to john green	00	05	00
william pratt cred for a paper pill	01	00	00
to hana bicknell halef a peck salt	00	00	06
to wido vining halef a peck salt	00	00	06
to beniamin Luding a yard e halef silk 8^{s}	00	~~0~~12	00
to william Torey a sife dll to his son John	00	06	06
to James Humfrye a peck butter salt:	00	00	o[4]
to Johnathan toreys wife a galoon of ayell	00	02	00
to ebenezner pratt two pound of shuger	00	01	00
17 to wido phillips a broom e half peck salt ½ ho[ps]		01	02
to moris Trufant halef a bushell of corne	00	0~~2~~1	03
22 to moris Trufant for a hundred of nails	00	01	02
to Colanal Hunt a peck of salt dll to Jo^{h}: $hu^{n}t$:		01	0~~0~~2
to Jnsine hunt a peck of salt dll to his son John:		01	0~~0~~2
to wido smith[336] one 1000: pines e two brooms	00	03	01
to one hat a pound of shuger e a peck of salt $^{to\ joseph\ orcut}$	01	01	08
to john green a penath of shingell nails to mony:	0	00	01
27 dwe to goode green[337]	00	00	~~0~~15
To John Torey one pound of shuger	00	00	06
Jun 30 to mrs Torey twenty seven pound shuger			
at 5^{d} ½ per pound	00	12	41/2
July: 1: to Joseph orcut a yard e halef of silk e a hatt	01	18	00
to ~~a~~ Joseph orcut one bushel of corne	00	02	06
1 to amy ^{Phillips}~~dracke~~ a silk hood upon ben ludings	0	12	00
6 to Joseph orcut a bushel e halef corn dll Epraim pratt	0	00	o[?]
to mrs. Torey one pound of shuger	0	00	06
to joseph pittey in salt	0	00	08
12 to mr houchison a cord e three foot of ocke wood	0	12	04
to mrs Torey in a hat	0	02	00

Line		ll	s	p
1	July 13 1704 to: Joseph pittey a broom	00	00	04
2	18 to mrs Torey for a proom e part of a hat	00	01	02
3	to beniamin Luding a hatt	01	00	00
4	to samuell vinson: 2: yards of damarash			
5	e one hundered of shoonails	00	06	04
6	to biniamin Luding a hundered of shoo nails	00	00	04
7	19 to beniamin Luding: 1000: bord bar nailes dll			
8	to gideon Turells Soon by an order	00	10	00
9	to John Torey a peneth hops	00	00	01
10	ougust: 2: to Johnathon Torey wife: 3: pound shuger	00	0~~3~~1	6
11	ougust 3 to Thomas Reed 7 hundred bord nails:	00	08	2
12	to John Torey ten quarts of oyle	00	05	0
13	to John Torey a grinstone	00	08	6
14	william pratt credit to 6 quorts of rum	00	04	6
15	to capt ffranch halef a bushell of salt	00	02	3
16	to Thomas Reed 500 bord nail ^{nails} e 4^{s} 6^{d} dwe			
17	upon a recening before the nailes	00	10	4
18	to benianin luding 6 yards of sarg	01	04	0
19	to benianin luding triming for the sarge	00	14	0
20	to John copelin in oyell	00	01	4
21	17 to zecheriah bicknell halef a peck of salt	00	00	6
22	19 to John Torey in mony	01	14	0
23	19 to Samuell Aaling[338]: 9: yrds bedlick oyl $^{\text{e iar}}$ e salt	01	06	9
24	to Samuell Aaling creditor to 1000 clabbords ^{shnges} 300:	02	02	0
25	to Samuell Aling one pound of shuger	00	00	6
26	to James Humfrey a pound of hops	00	00	6
27	to a blue caleco aporn e tope to joseph orcut	00	02	10
28	to Thomas Reed in shingell nailes	00	03	05
29	to Joseph orcut one bushell of malt	00	03	0
30	to beniamin luding the ministers rate to deon: torey	00	04	6
31	to James Humfry a peck of salt	00	01	2
32	Solomon Tounsend[339] debter for 800 clabbords			
33	which is now living bostoun	02	00	0
34	to samuell Aling 6 pound of flex e 2 pound hop	00	06	0
35	25 coranall houchson[340] dt to 500 hndered clabborde	01	05	0
36	to Joseph pittey 5 pound of flex 10^{d} per pound	0	04	2
37	to Joseph pittey 200 bordnailes	00	02	4
38	Septem: 2: to Thomas holbroock in porck e tobacko	00	01	2
39	to samuell Aling one bushell of malte a 100 bord ^{nailes}	00	04	0
40	to zechariah bick^{n}ell half a hundered bord nailes	00	00	7
41	to beniamin luding [?] at bostoun at mountfords	00	08	0
42	13 to [???nall] [Huchason] 12[?] cord e three quorts wood	04	16	9

[Page 131]

Entry	ll	s	p
May 24th 1706			
Joseph orcut debt to 4 ll of cotten wooll e a: [1]: ^{ll} 3/2 of sheeps wooll dll beniamin orcut	00	07	06
27 Joseph Nash debt to three bushels of malt dll to his boy: Canterbery[341]:	00	09	00
27 Josep Lowell dept: to: 100 Bushels of malt dll to him selfe	00	06	00
27 Joseph orcut debt to 100 brooms: dll to his wife[342]	00	00	10
John mountfford debt to a chees	00	00	09
27 Robbard Hayward debt to ~~two~~ 8000 of shingles at 10s	07	00	00
29 Ebebezer prattt debt to 800 of of bord nailes at $1–3^{d}$	00	10	00
John green debt to 100 cabbig plants:	0	00	06
29 Jonh vinson snr debt to two bushels of indian corn	00	06	00
30 Lft Nash debt to three bushels malt	00	08	06
June 3 brother fford debter to 1/3 q of shoonailes	00	00	03
5 then recened with Jcebod Holfroock wife[343] ɟ what shee had in the yeere 7005 which amoynted to	03	16	09
wido white junr debt to one pound hops	00	06	
5 John greens wife debter to a pot	00	00	06
Nickolas phillips credit to chees	00	01	08
7 John Burl Dep to too bushels of malt dll to him selfe			
Nicolas phillips cred for eggs	00	00	10

	ll	s	p
June ~~may~~ the: 11: 1706 Lidea Thomas[344] debt for bringing of a chist from bostoun	00	03	00
12 capt french debt to [two] bushels of malt dll to william bedlo	00	06	00
15 John venson snr debt to two bushels of indian corn	00	06	00
15 John gree debt to two bushels of malt dll to him selef	00	06	00
15 moris Trufant debt to sheps wooll	00	00	07
17 moris Trufant debt to one quarter of lam	00	01	03
william pratt debt to sheps wooll	00	15	06
Joseph Ricahards debt to a quarter of lamb e 4 ll pork		03	03
Joseph orcut credit to 4000 of shingels at 8s	01	12	00
19 Joseph orcut dept to six pounds of cotten wooll dll to his wife at 1^s: 6^d p poudr:	00	09	00
20 William pratt dpt to: too Bushels of molt dll to him selfe	00	06	00
brother John bicknell debt to 29 ll of sheeps wooll at 1^s2^dll e som of all woll dll to his wife[345]	0~~0~~1	17	00
James Humfry debt to a grinstone	00	07	00
John Torey debt to a quorter of lamb about 7 ll	00	01	06
Joseph Richards debt to one quorter of lamb 8^{ll} quarter e hed e pluck	00	02	00

	ll	s	p
June the: 25: 1706			
25 william pittey debt to one			
yard e a quorter of tickin at 5^s y	00	06	03
26 John green debt to 3 pipes			
dll to ~~s~~ his wife	00	00	02
27 then recened with Joseph orcut			
and ballansed all acounpts and			
thire was dwe to mee	05	10	10
27 Joseph orcut debt to an			
order to marah turell[346] dll to			
him selef	02	00	00
29 John Torey debt to halef ll hops	00	00	03
dll to william[347]			
John burll debt to money lent	00	00	06
July 1 Thomas Nash debt to			
one peck of salt dll drack[348]	00	01	06
Nicolas phillips debt to biskacke	00	00	06
Nickolas phillips credit to 8 he[nes]			
at 8^d per pees	00	05	04
Nicolas phillips debt to a quort			
of rum	00	00	11
wido white ^{snr} debt to 200 bord nailes			
e one sithe	00	08	06
9 John green debt one peck			
of salt dll to his wife	00	01	06
James Humprey dept to seven poushels			
of molt dll to John holbrock			
John Nash dept to 25^a: ½ porck 6^d p pound			
dll to Simme Nash:	00	12	09
John Torey credit to mowing of			
barly in the orchard	00	01	09

Line		ll	s	p
	July 7th beniamin Luding debt			
	to mony paid to Enock Lowell	00	17	10
	Beniamin Luding debt to one			
	bushel e halef of indian corn	00	07	06
	beniamin luding debt to one			
	bushel of malt	00	03	00
	beniamin luding credit to: 5750			
	shngels at 9s m	02	14	09
	11 brother moris debt to salt			
	dll to Abia whitemans son	00	03	04
	12 deecon bates debt to: 6: ll cotton e			
	a quorter of turnup seed dll selef	00	09	06
	13 John Torey credit for the			
	horses e: cart to carey wood	00	00	06
	13 ebenezer pratt debt 10 ~~6~~ ll			
	cotton at 1s–6d per pound p pes pot	00	06	02
	19 John Vinson snr Dpt for 400 bushels			
	of corn—3 p bushel~~s~~	00	06	00
	John green debt to one quart malases	00	07	
	william pittey debt to one peck			
	salt	00	01	06
	John Torey credit to 250 shingels	00	02	06
	balanced acounpts with william			
	pittey cordwinder e thare was dwe to mee	00	00	02
	moris Trufant debt to one galloon of			
	malases e a quarter of lamb	00	03	04
	Joseph Richards debt to one pound			
	of candels e a quarter of lamb	00	01	09

Line	ll	s	p
July the: 24th: 1706 then recened with Lift Nash e balanced all acou^{n}pts e there wos dwe to mee in mony	00	08	08
26 Joseph orcut debt to one bushel of malt dll to Joshua Phillips	00	03	00
John Torey credit to cart e horce to care wood out of the bote	00	00	06
28 John vinson snr debt to two bushels of malt dll to him selef	00	06	00
Capt ffranch debt to two bushels of malt dll to bedlo	00	06	00
John Torey credit to his e cart to care hay at roos hill	00	00	~~0~~06
John Torey debt to one galloon of malases	00	02	04
ougust: 2: beniamin Luding debt to mony dll to John burll by order	00	12	00
beniamin Luding credit to 1000 s clabbords at 4^{s}–6^{d}	02	05	00
mr white senr[349] debt for porck dll to franck[350]	00	01	02
brother Trufant to one ll talo e a pound candels	00	01	02
Joseph Richards debter to one bag dll to him selef	00	00	06
Ebenezer pratt credit to butter e chees	00	02	09

[Page 136]

	ll	s	p
August the: 5th: 1706			
John Torey debt to lamp oyle	00	01	02
5 Joseph Richards debt to			
one galloon of malases e ll hops	00	02	10
5 balansed with Joseph Richards			
wife e thare dwe to mee	00	08	03
7 John green debt to one bushel			
e a pack of salt at 5s per bushel		06	03
7 John Torey debt to one bushel e			
a halef of salt at 5s shill bushels	00	07	06
Joseph Richards debt to halef			
a pound of candels			
10 beniamin luding debt to 6 quorts			
of malases e halef a bushell salt	00	06	06
12 John Torey cred to carting			
of hay the first time	00	00	06
John Torey credit to mony	00	02	04
Ebenezer pratt debt to 9 pipes	00	00	05
Joh Torey credit to his horce			
carting of hay the 2 time	00	00	06
Joseph Richards credit to macking			
of one paire of stees	00	05	0~~0~~6
Joseph orcut credit to 6000 shingels			
at 9s peer thousand	02	14	00
Ebenezer pratt credit to eggs	00	02	06
John Torey credit to cart e horce wood		00	06
John green debt to one quort			
of malases dll wife		00	07

[Page 137]

	ll	s	p
August the 21 1706 brother ford debt to the frait of two bags of appels e other ware e hide as pashage	00	01[?]	00
13 Coranell Hart debt to halef ~~a busell of~~ a peck of salt	00	1	3
Joh Torey cred the 3 frait e horce	00	03	06
John green debt to one quort of malases dll to mary green	00	00	06
John green debt to two bushels of malt	00	06	00
beniamin Luding debt to two galloons e a peneworth of malases dll to Thomas kingman by order	00	04	07
29 Joseph orcut debt to two galloons of malases e one poun of tobacko	00	05	02
Joseph Richards debt to malases dll to his wife	00	00	06
John green debt to cotten wooll	00	01	02
decon Bate debt to two ll of hogs fat dll to Samuell bate	00	01	00
John Torey debt to fife dayes moing	00	15	00
Lft nash debt to fife bushels of malt dll simeon nash	00	14	02
4th William pittey debt to one September: peck of dll to John	00	01	03
4 John green debt to three pounds of cotten at 1s: 6d ll	00	04	06
Sarjant Whitman debt to one peck of salt	00	01	03

[Page 138]

	ll	s	p
September the: 24th: beniamin luding			
debt ~~th~~ to 500 of shinges wont of talle[351]	00	04	06
24 William pratt debt a sid of lamb			
e two bushels of corne	00	08	00

[Page 139]

	ll	s	p
September the: 8: 1706			
Ebinezer pratt debter to a pees of of a rope	00	00	03
12 John Torey credit to his horce caring of crick	00	01	00
John Torey debt to feching of a lode of hay	00	02	00
John Bicknell Dept to a hundred of bord nailes	00	01	03
12 I William pittey debt to one pound of tobacke	00	00	06
14 Lft nash debt to two bushels of malt dll to simeon nash	00	05	08
John Torey cred to his horce e cart for topt stockes	00	00	06
John pratt Snr debt to: 500 of bord nailes	00	0~~5~~6	0~~0~~3
John Torey debt to a quorter of Lamb	00	01	02
Moris Trufan debter to malases		00	06
Johnathon Torey debt to foure ll of shuger	00	01	06
23 Jacob Turner debt to cotten wooll sundery goods	01	04	00
Johnathan Torey debt to one pound of resons of the son	00	01	04
brother pratt debt to met e corne	00	08	00

[Page 140]

	ll	s	p
September the 24: 1706			
ebenezer pratt ~~debt~~ credit			
to a parsel of eggs	00	00	11
beniamin luding debt 500			
of shingels last at bostoune	00	04	06
24 Samuell Whitemarch debt			
to two busels of salt dll to son	00	10	00
Moris Trufant debt to bord nailes	00	00	05
25 John Torey debt to one quorter			
of lamb	00	01	02
25 Moris Trufant debt to one			
quorter of lamb	00	01	02
25 Joseph Richards debt to			
one pare of shoos to his wife	00	04	3
John Torey credit for cart e			
horce carting corne e stockes			
7 lode at fere feeld	00	01	09
brother pratt debt to a side of lamb		02	00
30 Joseph Richards credit to macking			
of ruths stees	00	05	00
Joseph lovell debt to one peck			
of salt	00	01	0~~0~~3
John green debt to two ll cotten	00	02	8
October: 6: John pratt Snr debt to 500 bord			
Nailes	00	06	00
12 balansed accounpts with John			
green upon all accounpt from			
the beging of the world to this day	00	00	00

[Page 141]

	ll	s	p
october the 12 1706 Jacob Turner debt to one pound e a halef of tobacco	00	00	09
12 Samuell King debt to one bushell of salt	00	05	00
John Torey debt to one quorter of lamb	00	01	00
John Torey credit to his horce 7 lode at rose hill	00	o[o]	09
John Torey credit to his horce at Tilers 3 lodes	00	00	08
18 John green debt to three pounds of cotton dll to marah[352]:	0	04	00
21 Zecheriah Bicknell debt to halef a hundered of nailes	00	00	08
32 Thomas white glasier debt to one bushel of salt	00	05	00
mr pretter of bostoune debt to foure cheeses			
mr wadsworth[353] debt to ~~foure~~ six cheeses waits 50 ll 2^{d} ½	00	04	02
25 James beniamin Luding debt to a paper bill one hat e ruling	03	02	00
Joseph Lowell debt to one neckcloth e one dusen of pipes	0	05	00
John burell credit to 6000 shngels			
Joseph Lowell credit 6000 of shingells at 9 ll	02	14	00

	ll	s	p
october the 28: 17006 Joseph Lovell debt to macking a necaloth	00	00	02
25 beniamin Luding debt to 300 bordnailes e one bushel of salt	00	09	00
28 Zeckeriah Bicknell debtr to halef a peck of salt	00	00	08
28 Jacob Turner debt one grinston	00	13	00
29 Capt ffrench debt to one peck of salt	00	01	03
29 william pratt debt to one bushel of corne	00	03	00
29 Jacob Turner debt to: 4: bushels of turnops	00	04	00
30 Jacob Turner debt to one bushel of turnops e two bushels salt	00	11	00
30 william pratt the son to Joseph pratt debt to one bushel e ½ turnips	00	01	06
30 Jacob Turner debt to two bushels of turnops	00	02	00
30 Insine Hunt debt to one pound of pouder e a pound e halef shot	00	04	00
Novem^{r} 1 Collinell hunt deptter to one bushel and a half of salt dll his son:[354]		07	06
1 Joseph Lovell d^{e}pt to one bushel of salt dll to his brother Enock Lovell	00	05	00
1 Samuell Vinson dept to one bushell of salt dll to him selfe	00	05	00
2 James Humfry debt to a hat dll John Holbroock	00	10	02
Bother fford debt to coring of apeles to bostoun	00	01	06

[Page 143]

	ll	s	p
November the 4: 1706 ~~Sameuell~~ Samuel whitmarch debt to foure buselels of turnops	00	04	00
6 Joseph Lovell debt to 4 ll of cotten at 1^{s}–4^{d}	00	05	4
11 Joseph lovell debt to 5 y of halef thick cloth e 5 y of ~~blue~~ red cloth e two dusen of butten at 5s e woostted mohaire 2^{s} 5^{d}	02	05	09
12 brother John Bicknell debt to ~~two~~ one bushel of salt dll zeckeriah	0	05	00
beniamin Luding debt to 500 of bordnailes	00	06	06
william pratt debt to two bushels of turnops	00	02	00
John Torey debt to one quorter of motton 9 ll ½	00	01	07
moris Trufant debt to halef a bushel of salt	00	02	06
16 moris Trufant debt to one bushell of salt dll beniamin Aalling[355] of brantery	00	05	00
17 william pratt debt to ~~halef~~ 6^{d} of pine dll to Johno	00	00	[?]6
17 william pratt debt to one bushel of malt d jahano[356]	00	03	00
18 beniamin Luding debter to one bushell e a halef salt	00	07	06

[Page 144]

	ll	s	p
Nuember the: 18: 1706 moris Trufant debt to mony paid to mosis peneman	01	00	00
18 moris Trufant debt to ½ a busell salt		02	06
19 Jsak pooll debt to: 5: yards of home made cloth at 6^{s} s y	01	10	00
19 J^{a}cob Turner debt to one busell of salt ~~e halef a thousand~~ ~~of bord nailes~~	00	05	00
19 william pratt debt two pipes	00	00	2
19 moris Trfant debt to fife pound of ~~cotten~~ sheeps woll	00	04	02
20 Lidea Thomas debt to one bushel of malt dll to her negro dwe to mee:	00	01	00
20 mris Trufant debt to 4 ½ of sheeps wool at 10^{d} per pound	00	0~~6~~3	06
21 william pratt debt to 20 ^{ll} of cotten dll to Samuell vinson wife	01	10	02
21 william pratt debt to 3 pipes dll to his wife	00	00	02
John br^{u}llell credit to 6000^{m} e 250 shingell	02	16	00
John burell debt to mony paid to him selef e ½ bushel salt	01	10	02
Sattisfied John burll for his shingels the holle			
22 Joseph Richards debt to one pound of candles dll wife	00	00	08
William pratt debt to mony paid to John nash	00	07	00

[Page 145]

	ll	s	p
November the: 22: 1706			
~~william~~ p			
brother pratt credit to 9^{d}	00	00	09
23 Thomas white of brantery debt			
to one bushell of salt dll to selef		05	00
23 Thomas white debt to one sheep			
e a lamb ded or a life wheare hee			
can find them out of my posesion	00	07	00
23 Samuell ~~jan~~ whit debt to			
~~the~~ one bushel of salt	00	05	00
26 Capt ff^{r}anch debt to one bushel			
of salt dll to William badlowe	00	05	00
26 Joseph Torey debt to porck			
delivered to him selef	00	09	11
John green credit to cilling of hogs	00	01	00
26 Colanor Hunt debt to two			
bushels of salt dll his son	00	10	00
27 John green debt to 50 bord			
nailes	00	00	08
31 Joseph Aling Junr ~~de~~ of bantery			
debt to one caster hat	00	18	00
31 then paid to John green upon the			
acounpt of of Jsack pooll for			
three yearlings bouft of Jsack			
pool mony	04	00	00
desem Nicolas Phillips debt to one			
the 2 bushell of salt dll to son	00	05	00
5 brother Bicknell debt to one:			
bushe of salt:	00	05	00
7 Samuell white the the white dll			
to one ~~bushel to one~~ bushel of mall	00	03	00

[Page 146]

	ll	s	p
desember the: 2: 1706 John pratt jnr debt to one bushell of salt dll to Joseph white by a toke of chang	00	05	0
John pratt credit for the chang	00	00	07
9 Joseph Lovell debt to one peck of salt e one pipe	00	01	04
Ebeneser pratt credit to mony paid to my selef	01	00	00
13 ~~Joseph Aling~~			
13 December then ballanced acounpts with Joseph Alling snr and theire was dwe to mee from him two cords of good ocke wood to be dll at ~~a~~ the laning plase in brantery handey to [blotched out]			
16 Joseph Lovell dpt to halfe a bushel of salt dll to Ben orcut	00	02	06
16 then ballanced acounpts with william pratt the son to Joseph pratt e theire was dwe to mee	00	05	06
17 John Torey debt for nine bushels e a halef of Indian corn foor foure sheep dll to him selef			
Joseph lovell debt to halef a bushell of salt e 3 ll of cotten dll to beniamin orcut	00	07	00
18 Zechariah Bicknell debt to one bushell of salt dll to him selef	00	05	00
18 mr william Torey debt to a pipe	00	00	01
23 Ebenezer Whitmach debt to foure bush and halfe of corn dll to his son Eben	00	13	05

[Page 147]

	ll	s	p
d desember the 23: 1706 ballanced acounpts			
with Colanor Hunt dwe to mee	00	00	05
23 then ballanced acounpts with			
lft Nash theire wos dwe to him	00	08	06
23 then reseved of John blancher			
upon samuell Andreus acounpt	00	05	06
24 william pittey credit to pouder			
of steel	00	00	06
25 Lft Nash debt to three bushels			
of malt dll to simeon nash	00	08	06
28 Joseph orcut credit Sum peeses			
of seder	00	04	00
31 Samuell white of branterey jun			
debt to halef a bushell of salt			
dll to his man	00	02	06
Jenuarey 4: 1707 Samuell white cred			
1707 to halef a bushell of barly ~~dll~~			
reseved of Joseph white	00	01	06
Joseph orcut cred to 70~~0~~50 shing			
at 8^{s} s	02	08	08
8 then recened with brother			
Thomas Reed and ballanced all			
acounpts dwe to nether party	00	00	00
10 John green debt to 3^{ll} e ½ of sheps			
wooll dll to his wife	00	02	11
10 wido green debt to ½ a pond sheps			
e two ounces	00	00	06
10 Joseph Richards debt to one yard			
of wosted ribing dll to his maid	00	00	03

	ll	s	p
Januarey the 20: 1707 James Humffrey cred to: 35: yards of 3/2 cloth weefing at 4^{d} per yards	00	11	08
James Humffrey debt to mony paid to Jhnas Humffrey[357] a paper bill	00	10	00
21 Johnathon Torey debt to halef a bushell of salt dll to Joshua[358]	00	02	06
25 John pratt junr debt to two paper billes of credit at 10^{s} per pees	01	00	00
29 Jsack pooll ^{snr} debt to: 12: of indian corne e one bushell of salt	02	00	00
30 then ballansed acounpts with John Torey e theire was dwe to mee mony	00	06	06
pheburarey 3^{d} Joseph Richards debt to two plow sheer molds e the bar of eyre between them[359]	00	12	00
4 Joseph Richards cred upon the acounpt of Joseph orcut e william pratt e yower wife	00	05	0~~9~~0
11 mr Lendall[360] cred. to one bolt of duck	07	00	00
13 Joseph richards debt to one bushel of corne e five ll of eyre	00	05	00
beniamin Luding debt to one bushell of turnips	00	01	00
17 Joseph Lovell cred to a pees of paper	00	06	00
Joseph Lovell credit to a paire of shoos for my selef	00	06	00
18 Thomas white debt to halef a bushell of salt	00	02	06
19 John ffrench[361] debt to mony paid to him selef	00	18	01^{29}

	ll	s	p
May 14: Left Nash Dept to five Bushels of [of] malt Dll Simeon	00	15	00
14th William pratt Dptter to five quorts of Corn	00	00	07½
14 witt pitty Debt to halef a bushell of Corn Dll to James	00	02	00
14 John Torrey Deptter to halfe a bushel of corn Dll to him selfe	00	02	00
Joseph orcut debt to a pees of eight:	0	06	0
16 Joseph orcut debt to two bushels of malt at 3s	00	06	00
18 brother Bicknell debt to one pound of powder	00	03	04
19 Enock Lovel Debt to one pound of powdor ^{fei} Dll to John Reed			
19 John Reed Dept to too pou^{n}ds of powder and flints & pound of boolits	00	07	10
19 John Bate[364] Dep to too pound & halfe of powder	00	08	09
19 David Carver Dept to halfe a pou^{n}d of pouder Dll Joh Bate	00	01	09
19 micajah Torey debt to halef poud poud^{or}	00	01	09
william Torey debt to corne and shot e frait a barell sider	00	02	05
Ebenezer pratt credit to mony resever of william pratt	00	01	04
John Vinson snr cred to mony	00	09	09
John Vinson ^{snr} debt to two bushels of corne	00	06	00

[Page 152]

	ll	s	p
May 31 1710 Samull Vinson debt ~~John vison~~ to pipes	00	00	02
31 Joseph Lovell debt to money reseved by him selef	03	19	10
June: 1st: Enock Lovell cred to money boroed of his wife mary lovell[365]	06	00	00
2 Mr Thacher Debt to a quarter of lamb Dll to his maid Experience	00	01	06
3 Joseph Lovell debt to a pare of cordes 2 comes: 6: quarts of oyll	00	11	07
ebineser pratt cred to 54 eggs	00	001	04
5 Ebenezer pratt debt one worm- -ing pan 17^{s}: 6^{d} to one remnant of Scots cloth 2^{s}: 1^{d}: to 3 quors mallases	01	02	01
6 Nicolas Phillips debt to two ll of tobacko dll to son	00	01	00
7 mary Phillips cred to to lase	00	13	03
7 Ebeneser pratt cred to butter	00	12	06
7 Nickolas phillips cred to 24 ll chees [?] 2^{d}: 2/1 per ll	00	05	00
Nickolas phillips debt to money dll to mary Phillips	00	~~0~~10	00
9 John green debt one quart of salt dll to saree green[366] 12 Joseph Lovell debt to money dll to yoore servant ~~by a make~~	01	00	00
12 John green debt one ll shuge^{r}	0	00	6
John green debt to two bushel malt	00	07	00
John green cred to 12 eggs	00	00	04
John green debt to bushel of malt the same day a dll to son John[367]			

[Page 153]

	ll	s	p
Aperill the 11: 1710			
John green debt to two bushels of barly dll by John Torey	00	07	00
22 John Torey debt to a quarter of wooll	0	01	09
22 Joseph pittey debt to a quarter of wooll o	02	~~001~~	
may 4 John green debt one quart of malases	0	00	10
5 Joseph Louel debt to 3 ll of toback	00	01	03
12 Joseph pittey debt to 18 ll tobacko at 6^d per ll	00	09	0
13 Capt ffrench debt to halef a bushel of salt dll to steeuen	00	03	0
15 John green debt to one ll shuger	00	00	6
15 John green cred to: 8: eggs			
16 Richard Degerr debt to one bushel of malt dll to Salter			
17 Ebenezer pratt debt to tobacko e som other thing	00	07	00
17 Joseph Lovell cred to 4 lambes	01	02	0
17 John green cred to 4 henes e 21 eggs	00	03	11
17 John green debt to one pare of cards e a stocken needell: 1^d:	00	5	01
21 Abraham shawe debt to one bushel e halef of malt 3^s 8 bushel e 8ll of tobacko at: 6^d e 4 pipes	00	09	8
25 Ebeneser Clow of bostoun debt to: 2750: laths at 9s	01	04	09
Thomas Reed ^{junr} debt to two bushels of malt	00	07	4
Moris Trufant cred to two pigs	00	04	00
Joseph Louell cred to 4 lambs	o[1]	02	00
Joseph Lovell debt to 25 ll shuger	o[page torn]		

[Page 154]

July the 6 1710
6 david Carver debt to 6^s–4^d mon for 2 bushel of malt e one bushel e halef of malt dll to Thomas dyer

11 Richard Egor[368] dept to too bushels of molt Dll to his son[369]

19 Joseph pitey debt to two bushels malt

25 Tho Reed senr to too bushels of malt Dll to him selfe

ougut 8 Will pette Dept to too bushel and halef of molt Dll to Nathanell

22 William pittey debt to two bushels of malt dll to mathy pratt seniar by

septem brother fford cred to 13 bushes of barly e otes

Thomas Reed debt Snr for two bushes of malt dll william

[?]ber 25 James humfry debt to 4 bushels malt

jenuary the 20 Enock lovell cred to 19 ~~bus~~ bushel e a ~~halef~~ 3 peck e 3 quarts of barly

20 John Torey cred to 13 bushels e a halef of barly

phebuary 3 William pitty credit to: 10: bushels barly

[Page 155]

Aperell the 24: 1710

24 John Torey debt to four bushels dll to him selef

---

28 Morris Truant dept to too bushels of molt Dll Left Nashes Indian by the same token that he brought barley heare

---

may

5 Moris Trufant debt to two bushels of dll to him self

John Randall Snr debt to two bushels malt

John Randall Snr dept to one bushel of molt

---

16 Moris Trfant debt to one bushel and halef of malt dll to John Nash by order

---

18 Colonel Hunt Dept to one bushel of molt Dll to Thomas Kingman: Tocon of fellhing bech pees[370]: PA N[?]

---

19 Brother pratt debt to: 6: bushels of malt dll hana pratt

---

19 Ballanced acounpts with Moris Trfant thare wos dwe to him two bush[page torn]

June Will pitty Dept to too bushels & halfe of molt Dll to [Nat]

---

12 beniamin dyer debt to mony: ~~12 fwith~~ e two bushels of ~~6~~ malt: 6: bushels of

---

12 brother Reed debt to two bushels malt

20 ballaned acounpts with William pittey dwe to him seven bushels of malt

---

22 John Torey debt to 8 bushels of malt

---

22 ballanced acouptnts with John Torey theire was dwe to him one bushel malt

---

26 Moris Trfant debt to two bushels malt

July. 3 James Humfry debt money for barly: 27: bushels dwe to him in malt 8 bushels

	ll	s	p
Aperell the: 24: 1707 Joseph Louell debt to one bushellof corne	00	03	6
25: John coreser[371] of Bostoune debt to 6000^{m} of shingles at 12^{s}	03	12	00
25 Joseph Louell debt to one dusen of wooden heeles	00	01	00
28 Abraham Shawe debt to mony paide to him selef a bill of credit	02	00	00
29 John Gooding cred to seven galloones e a halef of malases at 2^{s}: 6^{d}	00	18	09
29 John Gooding debt to 900 ^{m} of clabbords at 2^{ll} = 10^{s} ~~of~~ per thousand	02	05	00
29 Abraham Shawe debt to an order at Johnathon mountffords	04	00	00
29 Abraham Shawe debt to an order to Mr waldoes[372] of bostoune	04	16	00
Wido Eyles debt to for corne	00	00	06
May the 2 John Green debt to a hatt	00	08	00
2 Abraham Shawe debt to a quorter of a pound of pouder	00	01	00
2 Abra^{h}m Shawe credto mony paide upon Joseph Louelle accounpt	00	04	00
2 Joseph Louell debt to mony paide to Abraham Shaw	00	04	00
2 recened with John Green and ballansed all accounpts there was dwe to mee	00	19	00
2 John Torey debt to halef a bushel of seed corne	00	02	[page torn]
2 [page torn]			

	ll	s	p
September the 23: 1707			
Abraham Shaw debt mony			
paid to Joseph Nash	02	12	00
23 ballansed acounpts with Abramha			
Shaw there wos dwe to mee	03	08	01
23 Joseph Louell debt to mony			
paid to Joseph Nash	00	08	00
23 John Torey cred for his			
horce carting	00	00	06

[Page 158]

	ll	s	p
November the: 25: 1709 Joseph Louell debt to 8 y^{s} of cotton e billing cloth	00	16	00
26 Joseph Louell upon the ballanc of accounpt wos debt to money to mee	13	05	09
Joseph pittey debt to ~~2~~3 pipes	00	00	02
Baallanced acounpts with Capt ffrench theire was dwe to him	00	02	10
Dcem^{b} 6th Edword Richards credit to five pounds In bills of cred Rocd	05	00	00
11 Moris Trufant Credto a quorter of ^{ll} cotten			
14 John Green debt to 20 bordnailes	00	00	03
Increes Bates debt to 16 ½ hogs Fatt at 5^{d} per ll fraitı: ^{s}	00	07	10
19 then balanced accounpts with John Shaw Snr there wos Dwe to mee from him money	01	09	07
29 Jospeh pittey Dept to: 7: pipes	00	00	04
31 Joseph pittey debet to a sheep e lamp oyll	00	07	02
Jenuary: the 9 1709 ^{10} John phillips debt to money dll to him selef	01	12	05
9 ballanced acoupts with John phillips e cleared all aco^{u}pts from the beginning of the world to this day			
9 Lft Nash debt upon a balance of Acounpts between us	[?]	[oo]	[page torn]
[page torn]			

[Page 159]

	ll	s	p
Jenuary the 15 1709 ^{10}			
Solomon Toonen[373] cred to money			
paid to my son Beniamin	00	14	00
William pittey Junr debt to			
14 pipes	00	o[?]	8
pheb the 19 Jacob Lovell debt to			
money reseyed of [b] myselef			
eight ll 3~~d~~ s by his one hand			
Jacob Lovell			
March the: 2: ^{nt} 1710: Then ballanced acoun^{pts}			
with Joseph pittey e theire wos			
dwe to him goods	00	05	00
march			
1710: 9 Abraham Shawe debt to halef			
a ll of pouder dll to him selef			
13 Joseph Lovell debt to hay			
dll with wait	01	00	00
14 Johnathan moundford debt to			
10 bushels of malt dll John pittey			
18 Joseph pittey debt to: 6: ll of toback			
at: 7: ^{d} per ll dll to him selef			
20 William pittey debt to: 6: pipes	00	00	4
20 Henery Cingman[374] debt 2 bushels			
of malt dll to him selef	00	07	8
23 Henery Kingman debt to one			
bushell e a peck of malt dll to man oo			
28 John green debt to too bushels of			
malt del to son John			
[Enock] Lovell cred to 25 sheep			
[page torn]			

[Page 160]

	ll	s	p
march 1706 first william pittey credit to eighteen bushels of barly			
6 ballanced accounpts with John Torey there wos dwe to mee	00	03	10
8 Joseph orcut debt to ^{hay} to him by the lump ^{sold}	00	13	04
Joseph orcut debt to one bushel and a halef of barley	00	04	06
John Torey credit for his horce at plouing	00	02	00
15 to William Torey's wife three pounds cottenr^{s}–8^{d} per pound	00	05	00
Joseph Richards debt to two bushels of malt e one quort mal^{ases}	00	06	07
25 balanced accounpts with Ebenezer pratt e thare wos dwe to mee	01	00	00
27 then balanced acounpts with beniamin Luding and thare wos dwe to mee	00	09	04
27 beniamin Luding debt to one bushel of malt	00	03	00
Joseph richards debt to one pound of butter e one pound of candels	00	01	02
John Green debt to halef a bushel of turnops	00	00	08
John [bowdig][375] debt to turnops	00	01	00

[Page 161]

	ll	s	p
march the: 28: 1706			
Thomas Kingman debt for three bushels of malt	00	09	00
Capt ffrench credit to one dayes carting of dung	00	08	00
Aperell ~~01~~ Joseph Richards debt to two bushels of indian corn	00	06	00
John Torey credit to two dayes plouing for his horce	00	02	00
6 John green debt to one peck of turnops dll to mary	00	00	04
6 Thomas white of brantery debt to two bushels e hafe otes	00	03	09
Inchrees bate credit to mony:		10	00
John green debt to one peck of turnops	00	00	0~~8~~4
8 Joseph orcut credit by 1000 s of shingels 8^s m	04	00	00
wido white Snr debt to two bushels of malt dll to hur malata[376]	00	06	00
16 Nicolas Shawe debt to a parsell of salt hay sold to him by the lump at a venter	02	00	00
22 Lft Nash debt to 48 pound of porck at 5^d per pound dll to Edmond Jackson of litell	01	00	00
Joseph Richards Debt to porck	00	07	
24 John green debt to two bushels ~~and a haf~~ of indian corn dll Joseph green		06	00

[Page 162]

	ll	s	p
Joseph pratt junr credetor for a: 1 1000: of clabbord in: 1702			
of two pound per thousand	02	00	00
to two thousand foure hundred e halef shingles			
to 7150 shinels: 8 s: per thousand	02	17	00
to 1000 of clobbords	02	10	00
may the 25: 1709: Enock Lovell			
cred to mony rseved of william			
Richards living in brantery	01	05	00
reseved mony yoore selef	00	02	09
1709 Enock Lovell cred to			
6000 s at 8s	02	1~~0~~84	00
may 24 to mony reseved of yoor selef	00	00	06
25 to: 4: henes	00	03	08
to 21 ll e halef of chees Sem milk	00	05	03
Janur 26th Enock Lovel cred to money Recd	00	16	06
	03	19	11

[Page 163]

Line		ll	s	p
1	Nvember the 26th: 1701 Ebenezer pratt debter for			
2	sixteen pound & a halef of sheeps woll at a: 11^{d}: per pound	00	15	00
3	to a barel of sider frait to bostoun	00	00	08
4	to a brode [?] how	00	03	00
5	November the 13th: 1701 reconed with Ephraim pratt			
6	and balanced all formor accounpts and thare was dwe to mee	00	03	06
7	the £ 14 to a bushel and a halef of salt	00	03	00
8	the 29 to a paire of bodise 3 ll sheeps wooll 6 ll tobacko			
9	and a pound and three quarters of logwood	00	11	10
10	desember the 3 to three sheep: 113 ll: 2^{d}: ½ per pound dll to ^{h}s wife	01	03	03
11	may the 2^{nt}: 1702 to halef a pound tobacco e two bushels e half ~~barly~~ ^{baly}	00	09	00
12	Aperell the: 8: 1707			
13	Enock Lovell debt to: 5: bushels of malt			
14	May 23: 1707 Enock Lovell Dept to one bushel of salt			
15	Dll to his father Reed	00	05	00
16	July the 25: to 5 bushels of malt dll to him selef			
17	Novem 19 to two cows hides: 101 ll	00	16	10
18	27 paide to John Torey money	00	06	11
19	may the 3 paid to him selef paper mony	02	00	00
20	3 to three bushels of otes dll to him selef	00	04	06
21	8 to cords bouft at bostoune	00	03	00
22	8 to a line	00	01	09
23	8 to two seith at: 7^{s}: per pees besed^{frait}	00	17	00
24	to one bushel of otes	00	01	06
25	may: 11: balanced accounts with Enock			
26	Lovell [?] dwe to mee	00	06	08
27	to six bushels of malt dll to selef			
28	24 to eight yards of garllick holan at 3s 9d	01	02	00
29	to 10 ll flex at 9^{d}	00	07	06
30	26 to one yard calico at 3s 6d	00	03	06
31	to one bushel and half of molt dll megoon[377] oo			
32	to a calefebag dll to sister Reed	00	01	00
33	July 5 to 8 ll 2/1 of to backo	00	04	~~04~~ 8
34	to 7: ll 2/1 of Tolo at 6d	00	03	09
35	to pipes 19 teen	00	01	00
36	august: 7: to two hats for boise	00	09	00
37	to three bushels of malt dll Jacob			
38	Septem to fife ll cotton at 1^{s}–8^{d} [?] ll	00	08	0~~8~~4
39	23 to 12 ll cotton at 1^{s}–8^{d} ll	01	00	00

	ll	s	p
Ebenezer pratt credeterfor paid	00	07	00
to corne e other things	00	11	08
June: 1702 Ephraim pratt credeter for: 7000 of shingels			
at seven shillings per thousand	02	09	00
~~Jen~~ desember the 23: 1706			
then ballansed all acounpts between			
both parties there was dwe to him			
from mee three bushels e a halef of mallt			
desember 27: 1706 then ballansed			
all acounptswith Enock Lovell and thire			
was dwe to him from me three bushels and a halef of malt			
1707 to 16 ½ bushels of barly			
Novem 28 yoore cred Samuell vinson	00	12	00
Aper 27: 1708 cred upon the acoupt of John Torey			
by order from him self	00	03	06
two pare of shoos	00	09	6
to taping of two pare of shoses	00	02	4
may 11 dew to to Enock Lovell fifteen			
bushels e a halef a peck of malt			
to 12000 thousand shingles at 7s	04	04	00
July 5 to a pare of shoos for Ruth	00	04	06

[Page 165]

Line		ll	s	p
1	november the 27th: 1701 Gideon Turell debter for			
2	fife sheep: 196 ll dll at his one houce at 2^{d} ½ per pound	02	00	10
3	more for 98 pound of mutten2^{d} ½ per pound	01	00	05
4	September the 30 ^{1702} balansed accounts with Gideon Turell thares due to mee:	0	16	03
5	november the 18 to a bushel of salt bt butter dll to his man bensen[378]	00	05	00
6	jenuary the 9th to foure pound of sheeps wooll 9^{d} per pound	00	03	00
7	desember the 30: 1701 Joseph orcut debter for a			
8	role of tobacco twenty foure pound e halef: 5^{d} t per pound	00	10	021/2
9	Jenuary 22 to 32 ll and halef porck: 4^{d} ½ per pound	00	11	11
10	to a note at Joseph Greens for twenty bushels of corn	03	00	00
11	pheburary the 13 too foure bushels e a peck of ates d ben^{ok}	00	08	00
12	to the 21 to beniamin orcut dll foure bushels e a peck otes	00	08	00
13	march the 14 to seventeen pound of chees 4^{d} per pound	00	05	08
14	may the first to fife pound e a halef of tobacco 6^{d} per pound	00	02	09
15	the 4 to josiah riply three bushels of barly by a token of tobacco	00	10	06
16	Jenuary the 9th 1701/2 Joshua Smith debter for twenty			
17	pound of flex: 9^{d}: per pound & six pound 3/1 q talo: 6^{d}: per pound &			
18	drugs of oyle: 8^{d}:	00	19	00
19	pheburary the: 11th: to two pound of tobacco 6^{d} per pound	00	01	00
20	to a bag boroed a yard e halef woolling cloth in it	00	02	06
21	to 12 pound cotton wooll 1s–8d per pound	01	00	00
22	to two hundered of salt hay	00	03	00
23	to two bushels of malt	00	07	00
24	to one yard o quarter bluw caleco: 2^{s} 6^{d}: per yard	00	03	08
25	to [a] peck of corne e six penc mony	00	01	0~~8~~4
26	to two pound tobacko	00	01	00
27	to a pound of toba e other things	00	01	06
28	August the 22: 1709			
29	22 John Vinsen debt to ~~seven[?]ll~~ of			
30	~~half tobacco~~	00	00	00
31	27 to: 5: ~~galloons~~^{quorts} of lamp oyll dll son John	00	02	11
32	octb to one bushel of salt	00	07	00
33	to two paper bills dll to him selef	03	00	00
34	Aper^{ell}: 19: 1710 to two bushels of malt dll to			
35	Ebebezer vinsen[379]	00	07	04
36	to paid at mountffords	00	14	06
37	sept to money bills cred	02	00	00
38		06	11	09

	ll	s	p
June 1702 Gideon Turell credeter for a thousand clabbords			
three e sixpenc per thousand	02	00	00
reseved of John Torey	00	05	00
reseved of William Torey mony	00	12	00
march the 14: 1702 Joseph orcut credeter for			
mony payd by my selef	01	10	00
pheburary the 20 to: 1500 clabbords: 2^{ll} = 0^{s} = 0^{d} per thousand	03	00	00
to mony ~~paid~~ reseved	00	05	08
may to 5002 shingels	0~~2~~1	16~~1~~	06
Aperell the 24: 1702: Joshua Smith credeter for			
one thousand fife hundered of clabbords: 2^{ll} 0^{s} = 0^{d} per thousand	03	00	00
John vinson junr cred to 7000 S at: 11^{s}:	03	17	00
to money reseved of Abrham Shawe	00	07	00
to mony reseved of Abraham Shawe	00	01	00
to 325 of lathes at 7^{s} 6^{d} e 2000 s			
shingels at 10s	02	04	04
to 2000 of shingles at 10	01	00	00
to 2750 lathes at 7s	00	19	03
	8	08	07

	ll	s	p
desember the 30: 1701: recenedand balansed			
with john vinsen Snr and thare was dwe to mee	01	13	01
desember the: 25: 1702 to foure pounds of sheeps wooll: 9^{d} po^{und}	00	03	00
may the: 21: 1703 to a bushel of salt dll to him selef	00	03	06
october: 14th: to two hundered of bordnailes	00	01	08
the 15th to a hogsed dll at smelbroock river	00	04	00
november 4th to a bushel e a halef of salt to your selef	00	06	00
may the 27: 1704 to four pound of shuger dll ebin[380]	00	02	00
august 5 to a yard and halefof silk 8^{s} per yard	00	12	00
13 to yore wife: 1500 clabbord nailes 6^{s}	00	09	00
and pound porck 6^{d} per pound e a chees: 1^{s} 9^{d}	00	16	09
in mony payd for the ministers ratte	00	08	07
25 paid to cunstabell Green in mony for the cuntery ratte	00	12	06
Septem to one galloone~~-e~~ to oull e 2 bushels malt	00	08	00
to twelvef pound of flex	00	10	00
21 to a peck of salt	00	01	02
to three wethers	01	00	00
novem 8 to one peck of salt	00	01	02
13 to one bushel of salt dll to his son Eben	00	04	06
Jenuary the: 9th: 1705/4 then recened with John			
vinsen Snr and ballnced all acounpts			
and thare was dwe to mee from him	02	04	10
Jun^{21th} 1705: John vinsen det to a bushel barly			
e one of indian corn	00	06	08
16 to one pound of tobacco dll to Samuell	00	00	06
July 5 to one one bushel barlye a bushell			
of indian corn	00	06	08
10 to mony payd to him selef	03	00	00
to one bushel of barly e one bushel corn	00	06	08
october 24: to mary bayly Thomas bailys wido			
two pound of cotton wooll 1^{s}–8^{d} per pound		03	04
november: 19: $_{1705}$ to Ephraim burll by verbal order	01	10	00
Jenuary 25 to mary pittey the wife to Joseph pittey	01	00	08
to fife pounds of cotten1^{s} 8^{d} per pound	01	08	04
to two bushels of corne	00	06	00
to two bushels of corne	00	06	00
~~1706~~ to two bushels of corne	00	06	00
June 16 $_{1706}$ to two bushels of salt dll to Ebinene^{zer}	00	12	00
July 11th to two bushels of corne	00	06	00
to two bushels of corne	00	06	00

[Page 168]

	ll	s	p
June the: 5th: 1703 John vinson ^{snr} credit for foure			
thousand of shingels: 9^{s}–0^{d} per thousand	01	16	00
october to to one thousand of shingles	00	09	00
august: 1st: to 4000 m of shingles 8^{s} per thousand	01	12	00
to 3000 m of shingels e 500 clabbords	02	04	00
may 1705 reseved of John vison snr			
2500 of shingels 8^{s} per thousand	01	00	00
June 16 to 7000^{m} of shingells at 8^{s} thousand	01	12	00
24 to 4000 ^{m} of shingels at 9^{s} per thousand	01	16	00
July 10 to 4000 ^{m} of shingels at 9^{s} per thousand	01	16	00
June 1706: to one thosand of clabbords	02	05	00
to: 4500 of shingels at 8s	01	16	00
money paid for indian corne	00	09	06.9
	10	14	6

	ll	s	p
Jenuary the 6th: 1702/1 reconed with Samuell vinson			
and ballansed all acounpts and thare was dwe to mee	02	09	01
october 1703 to 10^{ll} cotten wooll: 1^{s}–8^{d} per pound	00	16	08
to a leven hundered bordnailes	00	09	08
to one hundered e three quarters bordnailes	00	01	09
may 20 to a cuntery rate payd to cunstable green	00	11	04
to a hat a pound of hops e a three pound shuger	00	09	00
June 7: to a county rate payd to John green	00	00	05
June ~~8~~9: to ~~8broo~~ pounds of suger 6^{d} p pound $^{dll\ to\ Sara\ white}$	00	03	00
17 to: 1000 bordnailes e 100 dubell tens dll Enock ^{Lovell}	00	12	08
to two sifes $^{dll\ to}$ Enock lovell 6^{s}–6^{d} per pesse	00	13	00
to 14^{s} money paid to him selef	00	16	00
to two pound of shuger	00	01	00
to one pound of whalebone	00	02	00
July 18 to two yards of damaras e a hundered shoonails	00	06	04
august: 4 to mony paid to youre mother	00	16	10
to 9 pound of flex 10^{d} per pound	00	07	06
to 5 quorts of oyle	00	02	06
novem to: 500: m clabbord nails	00	03	03
to ministers Rate	00	08	04
to a galloon of oyll	00	02	03
	09	1~~7~~6	09
Jenuary the 6th: 1702/1 reco^{n}ed with John Vinson Junr			
and ballansed all acounpts and thare was dwe to mee	01	00	09
may the 4th: 1702 to a c^{a}lef	00	09	00
the 5 to six pound tobacco 5^{d} per pound	00	02	06
July the 1st to a galloon malasese a pound tobacco	00	03	00
to six pound of cotton wooll e a gallo^{o}n of malases	00	13	06
July the 12th: 1703 to a bushel of malt 3^{s}–3^{d} per bushell	00	03	0~~3~~0
to a pettecote e a bushel of malt	00	16	00
Septem7th: to a hefer of three [yeres?] e a the pastering 6 weex	02	12	6
octob: 29: to cunstable green for a cuntre rate of youres	00	13	07
novem first to the ministers rate	00	09	09
to one bushel of salt	00	04	00
Jenuary18th to two thousand of bord nailes 11^{s} = 6^{d} per thousand	01	03	00
to one payre of shoos french heels	00	06	00
Septem to 6 quorts of oyll	00	03	00
to a: 11^{ll}: po of flex	00	09	02
to 5 dusen 3 quorters of pipes	00	01	06
octob 31 to one bag e one bushel of salt	00	10	00
Novem 1704 to John vinson: 50: dubell tens nails	00	00	0~~0~~5
pheb22: to lamp oyll e a bushel of malt	00	07	04
may 7: 1705 to ~~one~~ paper biles paid to him selef:	1	00	00
pide to John Torey upon youre acounpt	00	13	06

	ll	s	p
aperell 1702 Samuell vinson credeter for one thousand			
of clabbords	02	00	00
~~october 1703 to eleven hundered of bordnailes~~	~~00~~	~~09~~	~~08~~
~~to 10^{ll}of cotton wooll at 1^{s} 8^{d} per pound~~	~~00~~	~~16~~	~~08~~
~~to 100 e 2/3 [qu?] bordnailes~~	~~00~~	~~01~~	~~09~~
october 1703 Samuell vinson credit for foure			
thousand of shingells reseved of his father			
at bostoune	01	19	00
aperell 1704 ~~00~~: to six 6000 of shingells 8^{s} per thousand	0~~6~~2	08	00
may 20th ~~to euntery ratt~~ pay to the cunstable Green	00	~~17~~	~~04~~
to 5000 m of shingles 8^{s} per thousand	02	00	00
august: 1st: to 4000 m of shingles at 8^{s} per thousand	01	12	00
septem ~~to 1000 of clabbords~~			
~~28 to fife quorts of ayle 300 bordenailes~~	~~00~~	~~06~~	~~00~~
	0~~7~~9	19	00
reseved of John vinson ^{inr} in shinges e in			
sheep	02	08	09
october 1703: to a thousand of clbbords	02	00	00
to 4500 shingels	02	00	06
may 1704 to: 4000 m of shingles	01	16	00
sept17th to 4000 e a halef of shingles e clabbord	02	00	00
novm 7th to one bag	00	05	06
november: 7th: 1704 then recned e balan^{e}d acounpts			
with John vinson ^{junr}e thare was dwe to him	00	09	06

[Page 171]

	ll	s	p
July the 20: 1705 John vinson junr debt			
to mony paid to him selef	0	06	00
August 4 to mony paid to him selef	01	10	00
sept 29 to goods dll to youre wife[381] a bostoune	00	11	08
with a dish	00	00	06
a pare of cards dll yore wife	00	05	06
october: 9: to mony paid to him selef	02	06	00
30 to: 9: ll of cotton e a halef at 1s–8d ll	00	15	10
to a parsel of turnips sold by the lump	00	03	00
Novem 14 to halef a pound of pouder	00	01	09
19 to John Blanchard ~~by an order~~	00	04	00
desem: 5 to halef a bushel of salt e to Jospeh Richards	00	03	03
6 to Joseph orcut by an order	01	10	00
to salt dll to youre selefe John Richards	00	03~~0~~	00
1705/6 whiteman forgot in the time of it	00	03	00
Jenuary 13 payd to Samuell ffrench constable	01	08	04
Pheburar 28: to John phillips by an order	00	04	03
march: 14th: to two bushels of malt	00	06	00
1706: to Gideon Turell by an order	00	12	00
march the: 25: 1706 then balaned			
all acounpts with John vinson Junr			
and thare was dwe to mee	06	02	06
to one peney spent	00	00	01
august: 9: to two biles of of: 20s: per pes	02	00	00
September to money to hano cingman[382]	00	01	05
to bils of credit paid to yore self	03	00	00
21 to Enock Lovell	00	15	00
John Vinson Dept to one peck of salt	00	01	03
Dll to Joshuah Phillips	00	01	03
Desember the 4th 1706 then recened and ballansed acounts			
with John vinson Junr and there	00	4	00
was dwe to mee	00	09	00
4 to halef a steer sale at a lumpt	01	15	00
to one hole steere	03	06	00
march the 289th to John vinson halef a lode of hay	00	10	00
Aperell 23 to 12 ll of cotton to 1 = 4 per pound	00	16	00

[Page 172]

	ll	s	p
May the: 13th: 1702 Joseph orcut debtter for two bushels of			
barly 3^{s}–6^{d} per bushel dll to him selef	00	07	00
the: 16: to Rafe Tailer a: 11^{ll}: pound of tobacco at: 6^{d}: per pound	00	05	06
the: 18: to two bushels of barly dll to beniamin orcut 3^{s}–6^{d} per bus^{hell}	00	07	00
to two bushels of barly dll to Josia riply 3^{s}–6^{d} per bushel	00	07	00
June the 4th to Timothy haccut two bushels of barly	00	07	00
to Andrew orcot a bushel of barly	00	03	06
J the 12 to Josia riply two bushels of barly dll to sis son	00	07	00
the 18 to Andru orcot a bushel of barly	00	03	06
July the 1st: to two bushels barly dll to beniamon orcot	00	07	00
the: 4th: to Josia riply to bushels of barly dll to his son	00	07	00
the 7 to foure pound of tobacko	00	02	00
the 13 to rafe Tailler two pound of tobacco and halef a bushel salt	00	02	03
to rafe Tailler in mony at the same time	00	00	06
August the: 7th: to two bushels of barly dll to him selef	00	07	00
march the: 1st: 1703: paid to yow from Rafe Tailer mony	00	02	07
Novem12th: to halef a bushel of salt	00	02	00
August: 1 st 1705: John vinson ^{junr}credit to			
4000 of shingles at 9^{s} per thousand	01	16	00
october: 9: to: 1200 of clabbords	02	14	00
May: 8th: 1706 John vinson ^{Junr} credit			
to one thousand of clabbords	02	00	
august 2 to: 6000 s shingelsat 9^{s} s	02	14	00
September to 1500 clabbords e a 1000 of lots	03	14	06
to 4000 shingles 3000 s lats 100 clabbord	03	01	06
Jeanuarey the: 29: 1707 then reseved of			
John vinson by the hand of Jsack pooll	01	00	00
march the 28th to six hundered of clabbord at 4^{s}–6^{d} per hunderes	01	07	00
to 5500 lathes at ~~7~~^{s} 6s per thousand	01	1~~3~~5	0~~0~~9
June 16 to one thousand of clabbords	02	05	00
Sept 3 to one thousand of clabbords	02	05	00

	ll	s	p
desember the 7th: 1704 then			
recened with Samuell vinson and			
balanced all accounts e thare were dwe to mee	00	12	05
June 14 to mony paid to Joseph pittey	02	00	00
to a hat for yower selef	00	07	00
to one pound of tobacco	00	00	06
to: 3: paper biles e a pees of eight	01	03	00
16 to one pound of tobacko ~~to~~	00	00	06
July 10 to one pound of tobacco	00	00	06
10 to mony paid to him selef	02	00	00
August 6 to ten pound coten e a pound shot	00	13~~5~~5	04
6 to mony paid to yoore selef	00	06	00
septber: 14: to 500 shoonailes e 200 late nailes	00	02	04
29 to goods dll to yore wife at bostoun	00	11	02
to a paire of cards dll to yore wife[383]	00	05	06
Jenu^{ary} 3 1705/6 to Samuell ffrench a cuntery e			
a county rate upon yowre acounpt	01	05	06
1706 to the ministers rate	00	08	08
phebur 21 to one pound of hops	00	00	06
march 19 to decon bates paid in mone	00	06	00
September 5 to decon bates in money	00	09	00
6 to money pade to yore selef	03	00	07
November: 1706			
Samuell vinson debt to			
one bushel of salt	00	05	00
8 to money payd at in bils of credit	03	00	00
november the 21 1706 samuell vinson			
debt to cotton wooll	00	00	04
desember 18 to one bushel of malt e 2 biskcakes	00	03	0~~2~~0
Jenuary the 12: paid to Joseph orcut in mony	00	06	00
1717 to 300 bordsnailes	00	0~~4~~3	00
october 18 to two paper bils e a parel of wooll	03	07	03
15 to 17 ll shuger a 4^{d} per pound	00	05	08

Line		ll	s	p
1	June the 21 1705 Samell vinso credit for			
2	one 1100 of clabbord 4ˢ the hundered	02	04	0
3	July 18 to one 1000 of clabbord 4ˢ the hundered	02	00	00
4	August 1 to 4000 m of shingels at 9ˢ per thousand	01	16	00
5	to one calef scin	00	00	10
6	septem to 1200 clabbords at 4ˢ per hunderd	02	08	00
7	may the 8: 1706: to one thousand of clabbords	02	00	00
8	august 5 to 500 of clabbords at 4ˢ 6ᵈ	01	02	06
9	to 4500 of shingels at 9ˢ thousand	02	00	06
10	September the 6th 1706 then			
11	recened with Samuell vinson			
12	and ballansed all acounpt and there			
13	wos dwe to him from mee	00	01	05
14	october 23: to: 1500 of clabbord at 2ll 5ˢ per thousand	03	07	06
15	to one thousand of lates	00	06	06
16	November the 19 1706 then reconed with			
17	Samuell Vinson e balanced acounpts			
18	e thare was dwe to him	00	1~~3~~0	~~0~~1~~0~~5
19	July 1707: to 1000 clabbords 4ˢ–2ᵈ	02	02	00
20	Sept 6: to: 600 clabbord at 4ˢ–6ᵈ	01	07	00
21	to 2~~0~~500 lathes	00	16	08
22	6000	02	05	00

	ll	s	p
october 1704 Johnathon			
Montford credit to 3y e ½ silk			
at 8^s per yard	01	08	00
Novem 1st to ½ an ounc of thred	00	00	09
1 & yards of silk at 9^s per yard 100 shoo nals	02	14	04
to Joseph orcut ~~tuck up in goods~~	00	10	00
July 10 1705 recened with Johnathon mountford			
and ballansed all acounpts e thare			
was dwe to him	01	12	11
18 one yard of esenbrigs 1^s–4^d per yard	00	01	04
to six yards of silk	02	14	00
to one 1000 bordnailes	00	11	00
to six yards e a quorter of centin	00	07	00
27 to severall perticulares beniamin Luding			
reseved oute of the shop	00	14	00
to 50 pound of shot e a wooden dish	00	16	04
August: 10: to one bage of cotten at 72 ll pound			
at 1^s–4^d per pound	04	16	00
to 500 shoo nailes e ½ a hundered dubeltens	00	02	06
to one dusen of sifes	03	10	00
to one pees of eight	00	06	00
to 3000 of shingel mailes	00	12	00
25 to halef a yard e halef a quorter musling	00	05	11
to one quires of paper	00	01	02
to two pound of starch	00	01	04
Sept 18 to halef a bag of cotten wooll: 1^s–6^d			
per pound	06	16	00
29 to goods to the yinsones[384] e dish	01	02	10
to 2 ounses of thred 200 dubeltens			
e one yard e halef quorter caleco	00	11	04
Novem 7 to: 8: bushels e halef sot 4^s	01	14	00
to halef a hundered of shot	00	16	04
to shoonailes 1500 2^s: 10^d f	00	04	03
to 500 bordnailes	00	05	06
to 2 ounses e a halef of silk	00	07	00
to one pare of beles	00	04	00

[Page 176]

	ll	s	p
July: Waymouth the 19 1705 Johnathan mountfford			
debt to 3750 shingels forgoten when balanced			
at 01^{s}–6^{d} per hundered	01	19	041/2
July 18 to 4000 of shingels at 10^{s}–6^{d}	02	02	00
to 3000 of shingels	01	11	06
27 to nine bushels of malt at 3^{s} per bushel	01	07	00
august 3 to 5000 m ^{shingels} at 10^{s}–6^{d}	02	12	06
to three bushels of malt at 3^{s} bushel	00	09	00
to 9950 shingels at a 11^{s}	05	04	06
to: 8: Siphes at: 6s: per pees	02	05	00
septem: 18: to [1]0500 shingels at 10^{s}–6^{d}	05	1~~5~~0	0~~0~~3
29 ~~to goods to the Vinsons~~	~~01~~	~~02~~	~~10~~
to ~~3~~6000 of shingels 1^{s}–6^{d}	03	03	00
October to 3000 of shingles 1–6	01	11	06
to 6000 of shingels dll Capt beries mate	03	03	00
Novem: 8: to 850 clabbords—of 5^{s}–6^{d} hundered	2	06	09
June 26: 1707: John green cred to two ~~dayen~~			
one dayes worck of his two boyes hilling			
at tilers	00	01	04
to one dayes worck of his two boise hilling			
at home	00	01	04
to one daye for Zechariah[385] hilling at home	00	00	10
to one daye worck for the two boyes the one			
August: at brantery macking hay thether[386] at home	00	01	04

	ll	s	p
June the 5th 1705 then recened with			
John Vinson Junr and ballansed			
all accounpts and thare was dwe to mee	1	13	05
14 to one hat dll to your selef	00	06	06
to mony paid to him selef	00	06	06
August: 4: to mony paid to him selef	01	10	00
Jenuary the: 3^{rdt}: 1705/6 then recened with Enock			
Lovell and ballanced all acounts exept			
malt acounpts and nothing dwe upon balanc			
Jen 16 to twelef pound of cotten at: 1^{s}: 8^{d} pound	01	00	00
to one pare of shoo strings for youre wife	00	00	03
to one neck cloth for yoore selef	00	02	09
22 to one paire of shoo strings dll Sarah Rich^{ards}	00	00	03
pheb 5 to one hide: 64: ll 2^{d} per pound	00	10	08
to a hefars hide 25^{ll} 2^{d} per pound	00	04	02
to 14 ^{ll} e a quorter of cotten 1^{s}: 8^{d} per pound	1	03	09
to one paire of mens shoos	00	06	00
to halef a pound of sheeps wooll	00	00	06
Aprl 11 to two bushels of otes dll John Reed	00	03	00
may 3 to two quorts of salt dll to him selef	00	00	04
13 to goods dll to Jacob Lovell by order	04	17	02
19 to one pound of poder	00	03	06
to flints dll John reed	00	00	04
29 to one yard of cotton e lining cloth e			
a neck cloth to Jacob Lovell	00	06	10
June 3 to one bushell of of salt	00	05	00
to one ounce of peper	00	00	04
4 to one hat dll John Bicknell	00	08	00
July 10 to one barell of malases	02	15	00
August to thre pound of piging shot	00	01	00
Septem to one bushel of salt	00	05	00
to one hat	00	16	00
octaber 13 to a pees of baper[387]	00	01	00
novim to one hide 49 ll	00	08	02

[Page 178]

	ll	s	p
June the to 21th 1705 John Vinson debt to 1000			
of clabbord at 4^{s} per hundred	02	00	00
July 30 to 4000 m of shingels at 9[s]	01	16	00
Jenuary te 3^{dt} 17–5/6 then recened with			
Enock Lovell dwe to him since			
that for to pare of menes shoos	00	12	00
to one pare of wimings shoos	00	04	06
20 Enock Lovell credit for deviding sheep	00	00	10
Aperell 1 to three dayes plowing	01	04	00
to one barell of sider	00	08	04
may 3 mony paid for me to Tho white	02	10	00
13 ~~to goods dll to Jacob Lovell by order~~	00	00	00
18 to 4000s of shingels at [8]s	01	12	00
to 8000s of shingels at 8s	03	04	00
July 10th to mony reseved of benianmin Luding	00	12	00
1706 to 1250s shingels at 10s	00	12	06
September reseved of Samuell Vinson	02	05	00
reseved of John Vinson	00	15	
to 12000 of shingels	05	08	00
to 1750s Cb at 3^{s}: 6^{d} the hundered	03	01	03
Abiall Boutage e and my selef			
rekned the: 21: of July 1709 theer			
wos dwe to mee mony	02	08	09
may 3 to two m lases. dll to hir selef	00	00	03
septe 6 to mony payd to Nathell wales[388]			
dll to myca pratt[389]	00	15	00
october to pines e hat case e ~~asenb~~ osenbrigs	00	01	07 ½
to 3y e ½ e ½ quorter of 2^{s}: 2^{d} per y	00	07	07
Novm to: 1: y ½ blwe linning e ½ ll flex	00	02	05
phebu to one pare of shoos	00	04	06
march to one pare of single soles shoos	00	04	06
to deyget 4y ½: e halef a quarter	00	19	09
	05	04	04

[Page 179]

	ll	s	p
Aperell 8–1706 balansed aconpts			
with Johathon mountfford of			
Bosttoune e thare wos dwe to mee	01	08	00
may 9 to seven rumall neck cloths 2^{s}–6^{d} per pees	00	17	06
17 to 1650 ^{clabbords} at 5^{s} 6^{d}	04	17	09
to 4000 shingels at: 10s	02	00	00
June 7 to 5500 of shingles at 10s	02	1[9]	0~~0~~4
July 30 to two thousand of shingels	0~~0~~1	04	00
August to 500 clabbords at 6s m	01	10	00
to [1]2000 of shingels a 11^{s}–6^{d}	06	18	00
September: to one thousand of clabbords	03	00	00
to twelvef thousand shingels	06	12	00
to one thousand of clabbords at 6^{s}	02	10	00
to 10000 of shingels at a 11s	05	10	00
to 3000 of lates e a 100 clabbords	01	13	00
October balanced acounpts ~~aeoun~~ with			
the 21 Johnathan mountford duwe to him	02	18	
October $_{\text{the 25}}$ Johnathan mountfford debt			
to 11000 of shingels at a: 11s	06	00	00
to 4250 shinge of a 11s	02	06	09
to 1000 of lots at 9^{s}: s	00	09	00
to 1500 of clabbords at 3^{ll} 1000	04	10	00
8 to 1600 of clabords at 6s	04	16	00
to 3000 of shingels at 11s	01	13	00
march the 21: 1707 Johathon mountford			
debt to 1000 of shingels at 10^{s}–6^{d}	05	05	06
Aperel 22 to 7000 of shingels at a $10^{s:}$ 6^{d}	03	13	06

	ll	s	p
Conterary Credit Aperell 8th 1706			
to 4000 of bardnailes at 11^{s} m	02	04	00
to three yards ½ of garlick holloone	00	08	00
to one pound of pouder	00	03	00
may 9 to one thousand of clabbord nailes	00	06	06
13 to one pound of pouder e a dusen e halef but^{ens}	00	03	10
to: 12 ll pouder 3s 4^{d}	02	00	00
19 to one pees dameres at 3 ll 5s	03	08	00
to two hats at fornums ~~s~~ per hat	00	15	00
to a yard e halef of cotton e lining cloth	00	03	00
28 to buttens two yards e quorter of ozen brigs			
halef an ounc woostid hare	00	06	03
June 1 to 4000 of bordnailes	02	04	00
to 1 yard e haalf quorter of striped lin^{ings}[390]	00	04	01½
october $_{to\ 21}$ balansed acunpts with Johathon mount^{ford}			
of bostound e there was dwe to him	02	18	00
Aperell the 10: 1710: Abiall Bouta^{ge}			
began hir secand yeeres servis with mee			
at the beegining of hir yeer dwe to mee	00	09	00
to blwe lingng	0	02	00
to black grape a 11 y 2^{s}: 3^{d} per y	01	14	09
to garlick holan 3 y ½ at 2^{s}: 3^{d} yard	00	07	10
to a girdell	00	02	04
to tope sillk thred e needels	00	01	10
to lase of mary phillip	00	04	03
to one filit 1: y 2/1	00	04	04
to mony e mackig of a goune	00	04	11
to mony of gwinops[391]	00	02	04
to one thred lase	00	00	02
to one bonat	00	01	8
to 3 yards e a halef of cotton e lining	00	07	00
septe to one pare of shoos	00	04	06
to 2 peneworth of hatcase e 2/1 a ll starch	00	00	07
to 1 yard e halef of cats cloth 3^{s}–6^{d} y	00	05	03
to money paid for lace	00	03	09
to toping of a pare of shoos	00	00	1

	ll	s	p
Jenuary the: 13th: 1707			
then recened with John Vnson Snr			
e ballanced all acounpts dwe to mee	01	17	02
13 to halef a steer	01	15	00
June 16 to one peck of salt	00	01	03
July the 24: paide to ebeneser vinson for			
12000s of lathes in money	04	00	00
~~to ebeneser vinson money~~			
sept: 1: paide to John Vinson money for Ebeneser:	02	10	00
10 to Ebeneser in paper biles	01	09	06
to mony pade to ebing	01	10	00
Novem the: 29: 1707 John Vinson Snr debt to			
93 ll porck at 2^d 1/3 per ll 3^d 1/3 paid	01	01	0~~3~~0
Aperel the: 17: 1708: John Vinson Snr debt to ~~one~~			
two bushels e a peck of of seed barly	00	07	0~~6~~3
to ~~foure~~ three bushels of otes dll selef	00	04	06
June 14 to sheeps wooll dll to him selef	00	07	05
	02	00	02

	ll	s	p
June 1707 John vinson Snr cred			
to: 1000 of clabords	02	05	00
July 1 ~~to 6000 of cathes~~ to: 6000 of laths	02	00	00
19 to 6000s of lathes at ^{s}6–8^{d}	02	00	00
August 7 to 500 of clabbords at 4^{s}–6^{d}	01	02	06
27 to: 6000 of laths	02	00	00
Sept 6: to 6250 lather	02	01	08
to shingles	00	01	00
to 3000 of shingles at 10^{s}	01	[1]0	00
march 25: John vinson Snr cred to mony			
paid by william prall e moris	00	11	06
to mony reseved of him selef	00	00	01

	ll	s	p
october the: 28: 1707			
John vinson debt to mony paid to him selef:	0	17	09
29 to six ll of shuger at 4d per pound	00	02	00
navem: 4: to mony paid to youre selef	04	01	07½
12 to one bushel of salt dll to selef	00	05	00
Des 22 to halef a bushel of salt	00	02	03
march the 5: 170 8/7 paid to yooreselef at mountfords a	01	00	00
bond of Joseph orcut	05	00	00
March the: 5: 1707^8 then ballansed acounpts with			
John vinson Junr dwe to mee mony	02	02	07½
Aperell 12 1708 to one peck of salt dll to his son	00	01	03
to six ll of shuger	00	02	00
June 12 John vinson Dept to six pounds of			
cotton wool 1^s–9^d	00	10	06
to monyey paid to him selef	00	00	06
July 8 to mony paid to him selef	03	00	00
to James Humfry money	00	08	00
August 16 John vinson Dept to one peck of salt Dll to his son	00	01	03
Novemb 4 John vinson Dept to five peck of salt Dll to him self	00	05	00
14 to money paid to yoor selef	03	14	02
17 John vinson Dept to twe[?]^{15} pounds			
of Cotton wooll Dll to his son	01	05	00
Dec^{br} Jno Vinson Dept to six pounds of sheeps			
at 10^d p ll Dll to him selef	00	05	00
April 11 Jno vinson Dept to one bushell molt Dll to selfe	00	04	00
to two bushels of otes to him selef	00	04	00
19 to two bushels of ote to his son John	00	04	00
may 5 $_{1709}$ to fife ll e a quarter of toback at 7^d	00	03	01
June the 4th 1709 then ballanst			
Acunpts with John vinson Junr			
There was dwe mee in mony	02	09	071/2
27 to a bill of credit to yoos selef	0-42	00	00
30 to mony dll to cornelias holbrcock	13	05	
by order	00	12	00
July 8 to two ll tobacco e 10s pill	00	11	04
To one ll of gut dwe to ben pooll[392]	00	00	05
to nricrite[393] torey	02	00	0

	ll	s	p
october the 26: 1707 then ballanced			
acounpts with John vinson Junr			
theire was dwe to him	00	17	06
27 to 6000 shingles e 500 clabbore e 3500 lathes	04	08	00
march the 5 1708/7 to 5000 of s	01	16	00
to 1000 clabbord	02	05	00
march the 5: 1708/7 then ballanced acounpts			
with John vinson Junior dwe to mee	02	02	01½
June: 4th: 1708: John vinson Junr cred			
1100 of clabbords: 4s 6 per hunerd	02	09	06
July 1 John vinson cred to 4000s at 10^{s}	02	00	00
to 600 clabbords at 4s 6d per hundered	01	07	00
oct 27 to 4000 s at 10^{s}	02	00	00
to 2000 s at 10^{s}	01	00	00
to 8000 s at 9^{s}–6^{d}	03	14	00
June the: 23: 1709 John vinson Junr			
cred to 1000 s clabbords	02	05	00
to 6000 s at shingell	02	014	00
to 13 of clabbordes at 5 s 0: 500: lathes	03	08	06

	ll	s	p
November the 4 1707			
Samuell vinson debt to one bushel salt			
Dll to him selef	00	05	00
20 to ^{mony} paid by william pratt boteman	03	00	00
28 to Enock Lovell	00	12	00
to mony paid to him se^{lf} e a sithe	04	08	00
September $_{8}$ to a bushel of malt dll to him selef	00	03	06
to province bills Dll to him Selfe	01	00	00
octber 1 to yoore wife at mountford bostoun	02	04	04
to tobacco dll to him selef 5 ll	00	03	09
~~22 Capt Hunt Dept to one peck of salt~~			
oc 16 to silver paper	02	12	00
Nov^{em} the 14 Samuel vinson Dept to five peck of salt Dll to him se^{lfe}	00	05	00
~~de~~^{m}~~ber~~ 30 to Six ll of cotton at 1^{s}: 8^{d} ll	00	10	00
November the: 30: 1708 then ballanced			
Acounptes with Samuell Vinson and			
August $_{20}$ theire was dwe to mee from him	01	12	07
to 4 ll e ½ toback at 9^{d}	00	03	4½
to 3 ounses of lase thered at 1^{s}–6^{d}	00	04	06
to money reseved the balance	00	00	07
desember the: 10: 1709			
Samuell Vinson debt to: 12: ll			
of cotton at 1^{s}–5^{d} per ll	01	13	4
10 at the same time reseved in			
money by him selef	02	08	00
to aboute 3 fadam of rope	00	00	02
phebu 20 to 7 pipes dll to him selef	00	00	03
20 to two bushels of malt	00	037	06
may5: 1710 to shuger dll to him selef	00	01	06
July 7 to Samuell pater by an order mitler	00		
of cloth	00	09	00

[Page 186]

Line		ll	s	p
1	June the: 3: 1706			
2	Wido white Junr debt to one ll hops	00	00	06
3	July to 200 bord nailes e a sith	00	08	06
4	october ^{23} to Thomas white glasuer one bush salt	00	05	00
5	Aperell: 1707: ^{to} thomas white 6 ll of cotten	00	08	00
6	to a barel e tar e 3 ll of ocom	00	05	03
7	November the: 6: 1707 Joseph Nash			
8	debt to six ll of cotton dll to your man	00	10	06
9	June the 28 to two bushels of malt e a pek salt	00	07	11
10	to 5 quorts of oyll	00	02	11
11	to salt grass	01	11	00
12		02	11	10
13	Joseph Nash credto mony [?]			
14	dwe from Abraham Shawe	01	18	00
15	dwe from Joseph louell	00	16	[page torn]

[Page 187]

Line

[page torn]

[willia]m pittey debt to two bushels e halef of malt dll to nathanell[394]

28 Coronall Hunt cred to 18 2/1 of barly

brother Reed Reed cred to 10 bushels of barly

Aperell the: 3: Beniamin dyer debt to two bushels ~~ea halef~~ of of malt dll to him selef

11 John Torey cred to two bushels of Barly dll to John Green

17 Brother Thomas Reed debt to two bushels of malt dll to Samuell

19 Colanal Hunt cred to 3 bshels of barley

21 John Torey cred to: 14: bushels of barly

24 Brother pratt credto: 10: bushels of barly

24 Enock Louell debt to: 7: bushels of malt dll to Joshua Louell

[Page 188]

4 william pittey debt to one busels e a halef of malt

John Vinson Junr cred to two bushels of malt

Beniamin dyer cred to 17 bushels of barly

20 Joseph pittey credit to: 4: bushels of barly

20 Joseph pittey debt to two bushels of malt dll to him selef

20 Moris Trffant debt to one bushel of malt dll to Samuell Bagly

22 Moris Trufant cred to 6 bushells of otes e barly

28 William pratt debt to two s bushel malt

Moris Trufant debt to two bushels of malt dll to Joseph Nashes boy

	ll	s	p
November to 20th 1707			
Samuell Vinsan cred to 1000 clabbords	02	05	00
to 4000 of shingles [8?]	01	12	00
August the 5 ^{1708} to 24000 of clobbards at	05	12	00
oc 16 to 8000 s of shing at 9^{s}: 9^{d}	03	17	00
desember the 15: 1708 Enock Louell			
cred to ten bushels e a peck barly			
July the 5 Samuell Vinson cred to 1000 clabbords	02	10	00
pheburary: 20: 1709/10 Samuell Vinson cred			
to 6000 shingels e: 11: of clabbords	05	00	00
~~July 7: 1710 paid to Samuell [bate] by an order~~	~~00~~	~~09~~	~~00~~

	ll	s	p
october the 16 1710			
Jacob Lovell of [basebell] in new england			
do owe: him selef to be Justly indebted			
to James Richards of waymouth malster			
the just sum of two pounds e two shillings			
which hee doth promise to pay by the			
next march insueing after the date hereof			
Jacob Lovell			
September the: 1st: 1710 Ebenezer Vinson			
Cred to shingels goods	01	05	10
[page torn]			

[Page 191]

	ll	s	p
September the 24th: 1710			
Ebenezer Vinson debt to 2/1 ll pouder ll shot	02	1	
to 2/1 a bushel of salt e a galloon rum	00	06	09
to a pot pan e siue	00	02	06

[Page 194[395]]

	ll	s	p
Aperell the 27: 1710 then			
ballansed acounpts with Johnathon			
mountfort theire was owed to mee	03	14	11
to: 100: clabbords neglected to get down	00	06	00
28 to 9000: of shingels at: 12 S	05	08	00
11 to 600 of at 68 yor hundred	01	16	00
to 1500 S clabbords a 3 ll thousand	04	10	00
to 6000 S shingells at 12 thousand	03	12	00
to 1500 clabbords at 3 ll thousand	04	10	00
to 1400 clabbords at 3 ll thousand	04	04	00
to 2000 clabbords at 3 ll thousand	06	00	00
to 1000 clabbords at 3 s ll	03	00	00
October the 20 1710 recened with Johnathon mountfford			
and ballance all accounpts and their			
was dwe from him to mee money	11	07	03
to 1000 of shingels	~~00~~	~~11~~	00[396]

[Page 195]

	ll	s	p
July the 12: 1709			
Johathon Mountfford debt to			
6000 at 12^{s} per thousand	03	12	00
$Septem_{ber}$ to 1700 of clabbords a 6 S per 100	05	02	00
October to 7000 ~~feh~~ shingels at 14 S 1000	04	04	00
to 3000 S at 12 S per: 1000:	01	16	00
to 6000 shingols at 12 S	03	12	00
to 1000 of clabbords a 6 per hundred	03	00	00
November the 3: 1709 there ballonced acounpts with			
Johnathon Mountfford theire was			
dwe to mee mony e goods	10	06	04
8 to 2650 clabord at 6S	07	19	00
Aperell 27 Johnothon mountford cred to			
three quorters and foure ll shuger	01	08	00
to 300 bord nailes of 1^{s}: 3^{d} the hundered	00	03	09
to 2 yards e halef a quorter caleco 4^{s}: 6^{d}	00	09	07
to 4 yds and halef of rusell at 5p	01	02	06
to 4 yds of tapde 4^{d}: of silk	00	00	10
to money to John mountfort e myself	01	00	00
to one y fustin 1 ounc fine thred	00	05	00
to 1 hamer 2 dusens of buttons	00	02	06
to a 11 y of black grape a $2/3^{d}$ y	01	04	09
to 3 y of garlick e halef at 2s 3y	00	08	071/2
to money e a girdle 3	02	02	04
to money	01	10	00[397]

[Page 196]

Line

November the 18th: 1704 | James Humpfry Credit to twenty three bushels of barly 20 James Humfry cred for twenty seven bushels of barly

---

Desmber 4 William pratt cred for 4 bushels barly

---

9 John bicknell cred for 14: bushels barly

Jenuary 9th Ebenezer pratt cred to fifteen boos hels of barly

---

Nathanial fford credit for forty bushels of barly

Johnathon Torey credit for twenty foure bushels of barly ~~e a peck~~

---

26 James Humfry credit for fifteen bushel of barly

---

31 Abya Whiteman credit for eleven bushels e three peck e a halef of barly

---

pheb 1 James Humfry cred for fife bushels of barly

---

17 Samuel pratt credit for four bushels e three peck e six quorts of barly

---

20 moris Trufant credit to two bushels e three peck of barly

---

21 Enock Lovell credit to ninteen bushels of barly e a halef

---

27 William pratt credit for Sixteen bushels of barly

---

27 Thomas Reed credit for foure bushels of barly

March 2 John bicknell credit for eight bushels of barly

---

7 James Humfry credit for six bushels of barly

---

9 Johnathan Torey credit for sixteen bushels of barly

[Page 197]

	ll	s	p
Desember the 2: 1707 Thomas Reed Junr debtter for two bushels of malt			
Jenuary: 5: Joshuamith detr to one bushell of malt dll to Joseph orcut			
10 William pittey deter for two bushels of malt			
18 recened with moris Trufant and to^{hare} was owed to mee for two bushels of malt			
19 Nathanell fford dt for one peck of Salt dll to ruth	00	01	02
24 William pratt dtr for two bushels of malt dll to him selef			
phebur: 2: John bicknell detr for two bushels of malt			
5 Samuell pratt detr for three bushels of malt			
6 Joshua Smith debt for three bushels of malt dll Joseph orcut			
17 Samuell pratt credit for four bushels three peck e six quarts of barly			
march 14 William Pratt debtor for two bushels of malt			
19 John Torey debter to fife bushels of malt dll to him selef			
John bicknell credit for twenty Six bushels of barly			
brother fford debter for ten bushels of malt to dll him Selef			
21 moris Trufant debter for two [b]ushels of malt			

[Page 198]

march the 21: 1705 26 moris Truffant debtter for two bushels ~~of~~ e a halef of malt

Aperell: 2: William pittey debtter for three bushels of malt dll to John

6 John bicknell credit for foure bushels of barly

135 brother fford debter for two malt bushels dll to his Son

135 brother fford debtter for one bushell e a halef of malt dll Jsrall ford

brother Thomas Reed credit for two bushels of barly

may 3 William pittey creditor for eight bushels of barly

4 Mrs. White Snr credit for foure bushels of barly

14 Samuel pratt credit for three bushels of barly

14 Samual pratt debtter for two bushels e a halef of malt
14 brother Reed debtter for two bushels e of malt

15 John Bicknell deptter for foure Bushels of molt 11 = 11 = 11 = 11

28 Ebenezer pratt debter for one bushell e a halef of malt dll to margarit vining

June 4 Thomas Reed debtter for two bushels of malt dll to him selfe

June 8 William Pratt deptter for too bushels of malt Dll to him selfe

[Page 199]

	ll	s	p
June the 15th: 1705			
Thomas Reed Deptter for three			
of molt Dll to his son William Reed			
18 William pitty Depter for three Bushels	00	00	00
of molt Dll to his Son John pitty	00	00	00
18 Benjamin Ludden Deptter for too			
Bushels of molt Dll to him selfe	00	06	00
18 Enock Luell Deptter for foure			
Bushels of molt Dll to him sefe = 11 = 1			
brother fford debt to two bushels of malt			
dll at bostoun to bushel frait	00	00	04
23 James Humfry debt to fifty bushels			
bushels ~~bushels~~ of malt dll to			
Joshua Smith			
23 Joshua Smith credit to forty six			
bushels of barly			
23 Joshua Smith debt to many upon			
a recening beetween us	00	03	06
July 10: moris Truant debt to two bushel of			
malt dll to Zeckeriah bicknill			
16 brother fford debter to one bushell and			
halef of malt dll to Jserell fford			
18 James humffrey debter to Six bushel of malt			
25 Samuell pratt det to three sushels			
of malt dll to benjamin Richards			
26 brother fford debter to two bushels			
of malt dll John Shaw			
31 brother Reed debter to two bushels			
of malt dll to for Thomas			

	ll	s	p
October the 6th 1705 Ebenezer pratt debt to two bushel of malt			
14 Johnathon Torey debter to mony paid to him selef for 40 bushels barly:	05	00	00
13 James Humfrey debtter to mony paid to him selef	03	15	00
novem 5 Elder pratt[398] debt to many paid to him selef for 4 bushels of barly	00	10	04
7 Sergent Whitman debt to mony paid to Ezra whitemarch to the cuntery rate	00	10	06
14 ~~apawhiteman~~ Abiah Whiteman debt to mony paid for: 11^{b}: 3 peck e half barly	01	10	00
Jenu 4th: 1705/6 brother fford debt to one bushel malt dll to gurny[399]			
10 John pratt Snr debt to Six bushels of malt at 2^{s}: 10^{d} per bushell			
John Torey debt to ^{two} bushels of malt	00	17	00
22 William pitty ^{debt} two bushels of malt			
pheb 7 John bicknell debt to two bushels of malt dll to zeckeriah			
7 William pratt debt to two bushels of malt dll to him selef			
^{21} 1705/6: Enock Lowell credit forteen bushels of of barly			
March the first 1706 reseved barly of William pittey William pitte credit for eighteen bushels of barly			
18 John Torey credit to seven bushels of barly			
18 William pittey debt to two bushels of mallt			
21 John biknell credit for nine bushels e a peck barley			

[Page 201]

	ll	s	p
march the 21st 1706 brother fford credit for two bushels of barly			
21 brother fford debt to foure bushels of malt			
22 brother Reed credit for eight bushels of barly			
25 William pittey debt to three bushels e a halef of malt dll to Ebenezer pratt by a tocon of 18 bushels of brou ft heer to malt			
brother biknell debt to foure bushels of malt			
pheru 10 brother Reed debt to two bushels malt dll to John Reed			
Aperell 15 Enock Lovell debt to four bushels of malt John biknell			
16 John Torey debt to fife bushels malt			
20 brother John bicknell debter to mony paid to him selef for forty bushels of malt 20 then recened with brother john Bicknell upon all malt and barly acounpts and those was dwe to him for nine bushels and a peck of barly	05	00	00
may 3 William pittey debt to three bushels of malt to John			
14 brother John bicknell debt to one bushell of malt dll mary gurny			
June 14 brother reed debt to two bushels malt dll to william			
July 10 Enock Lovell debt to three bushels of malt dll to him selef			

[Page 202]

	ll	s	p
July 9th 1706: William pitty debt to two bushels of malt dll to James Humfrey	00		
14 William pittey debt to two bushels of malt dll to nathanell			
25 brother Thomas Reed debt to two bushels of malt dll william Reed			
august 10 brother fford debt to: 4: bushels of malt			
September $_4$ William pittey debt to two busells of malt			
october: 6: Thomas Reed Jun debt to two bushels of malt			
Desember 13 brother pratt debt to two bushels of malt			
January the 2^{nt} 1707 Thomas Reed ^{Jnr} cred to eight bushels of barly e otes			
3 micaia Torey cred to foure bushels e a halef of barley			
4 Joseph white cred to one bushel e a halef of barly			
22 ballansed all acounnts with brother John Bicknell upon all barley e malt nothing dwe of noone side			
22 then ballanced with william pittey and [?] theire was owed to mee	00	03	00
upon his part dwe to the said william pittey one bushell e a halef of malt			
31 Mrs white credit to ten bushels of otes with som barly amongst it			
17 William pittey credit to three bushells of barly e a halef			
19 Enock Lovel credit to foure bushels e & a halfe of barly brought by jacob love			

	ll	s	p
May the 5 1707			
5 Beniamin Richards debt to 7^{ll} of cotten dll to Sariant whiteman	00	10	06
9 Moses peneman debt to: 7: y of garlick holan dll at Johnathon mountford of bostoune	01	03	02
11 Mr Egeres debt to one bushel of indian corn dll to franck negrowe[400]	00	03	06
13 zechariah Bicknell debt to two quarts of Salt	00	00	04
16 brother John bicknell debt to a macker line dll to beniamin	00	03	06
17 decon Bate debt to one peck of salt Samuell	00	01	03
19 John Green Cred to eges	00	00	04
19 Joseph Shawe debt to ^{6000} 6 of shingell nailes at 5^s: 6^d	01	13	00
19 Joseph Shawe debt to 2000 of clabbord nailes a: 5^s:	00	16	00
19 Joseph Shawe debt to 3000 of borde nailes at 12^s	01	16~~14~~	00
19 Joseph Shawe debt to the fraite of the nailes ffrom bostoune	00	01	06
19 John green credit ^{shering} of: 35: sheep	00	02	05
John Green cred to egges	00	00	04
19 James Humffey cred to 7 quarters of vele	00	13	02
21 Abraham Shawe debt to a paper bill of 40 ~~shilling~~ shillings	02	00	00
21 Joseph Lovell debt to seven peck of corne at 3^s–6^d bushell	00	06	041/2

	ll	s	p
May the 24: 1707 Capt french Dept to halfe a bushel of salt Dll to S^{t}p^{h}n Badlow[401]	00	02	06
24 Mrs. Baset cred to money	00	01	04
27 Coll Hunt debt to halef a bushell of Salt dll to youre Sone	00	02	06
Zeckeriah Bicknell credit to mony	00	00	08
30 Zeckeriah Bicknell debter to one peck of Salt by my wife	00	01	03
John Gibson cred to mony paid	03	10	00
June 2 micaia Torey debt to: 3: pints of malasos e one peck of Salt	00	02	04
5 James Humffey debt to a gun dll to him selef	01	04	00
7 brother fford debt to rum in a iugg	0	00	08
Richard Eguers debt to two bushels of corne dll by beniamin	0	07	00
11 Joseph Lowell cred to 6000 of Shingels at 10^{s} m	03	00	00
11 Joseph Lovell debt to mony paid to him selef	03	09	06
Joseph Lovell debt to mony paid to Joseph Nash for carting	00	03	00
11 Salamon Halle debt to 4000 m Shingel e a thousand of clabbords	05	08	00
11 pharwume[402] of bostoune debt to shingeles	00	09	00

[Page 205]

	ll	s	p
June the 12 1707			
12 Joseph Lowell cred to six thousand of shingels at 10^{s}	03	00	00
16 John Vinson: Senr Dept to one peck of salt Dll to him selfe	00	01	03
~~Joseph Nash debt to do~~			
Joseph Lovell debt to a sithe and a bushel e a halef of corne deliverd Joseph nash	0	13	09
17 ~~Jos~~ Abraham Shawe debt 10^{s} paper e 10^{s} mony	01	00	00
17 Abraham Shawe cred to 6000 of Shingels at 10s	03	00	00
17 John Green debt to 4 ll shuger at: 5^{d}: ll and biskake: 1^{s}: e a quart of rum	00	03	08
17 Joseph willis of Bostoune debt to 6000 shingels e 1000 clabbords	06	12	00
17 Joseph willis of bostoune cred	05	00	00
John Torey cred to horse e cart : 1: lode from Tilers inglish hay	00	00	03
John Green debt to six biskcakes dll to mother green[403]	00	00	06
27 Joseph Lowell debt to halef a pound of Turnops seede	00	01	00
John green cred to 12 eggs 5 rotten			
July 1 Elisha web of Bostoune debt to six thousand of lathes 8^{s} s m	02	08	00
1 Mr ffarnum debt to 1500 of shingles dll upon his one wharfe	00	18	00
1 Joseph Shane cred to 5500 at [?] s of shingles at 10^{s}	02	15	00

	ll	s	p
Jully the 3–1707			
Joseph Lovell debt to one bushel ½ ~~to two bushels~~ of indian corne	00	0~~7~~5	0~~0~~3
3 John Green debt to malases dll to mother[404]	00	00	02
7 Abraham Shaw debt to one bushel corne		03	06
7 Joseph willis of Bostoune debt 1000 of Clabbords at 3ll m	03	00	00
8 reconed with beniamin Richards and ballansed all acounnts there was dew to him	02	01	010
9 Zechariah Bicknell debt to mony lent to him selef	01	00	00
9 ~~Zebt Z~~echariah bicknell debt to money paid to him sellef upon the account of brother fford	02	00	00
9 John Torey cred to the horce e cart barly at silers[405]	00	00	04
9 Joseph Shaw debt to a peer of Sithe dll to him selef	00	01	06
9 Abraham Shawe debt to one galloon of rum dll Joseph Shawe	00	04	00
9 brother moris debt to wool dll to yoore wife	00	09	01
9 Abraham Shawe debt to 24 ½ ll porck at six penc per pound	00	12	03
Beniamin Richards debt to goods reseved of James Humfry	00	07	06
John Torey cred to his horse e carte carting wood	00	00	06
15 Joseph nash debt to two bushels of corne dll to his boye	00	07	00
16 John green cred to 33 eggs	00	00	09

[Page 207]

	ll	s	p
July the 18: 1707			
18 John Torey credit for his horce e cart			
carting wood from the water side	00	00	06
19 Abraham Shawe cred to 6000 s			
of shingels	02	17	10
21 John green cred to 23 eggs			
reseved of John green	00	00	06
21 Ereza Whitemarch debt to two paper			
of ten shilling a pees dll John Randall Snr	01	00	00
21 John Shawe debt to one peck of			
beens dll to his Son John	00	01	3
24 Abraham S^{h}awe debt to money paide			
to him selef	00	10	00
24 Joseph Lovell debt to 3 paper biles			
10^{s} per pees dll to him selef	01	10	00
24 Abraham Shawe debt to one pound			
of pouder dll to him selef	00	04	00
26 Beinamin Richards debt to mony reseved			
of his sister whiteman	00	02	09
29 Enock Lovell debt to mony paide			
to Smith woodword of wontam	02	00	00
29 Samuell bill of Bostoune debt to			
a parsel of lambes	02	13	06
aug: 2 John Torey debt to one quorter			
of lambe	00	00	09
4 Abraham Shawe debt to mony			
paid to him selef	01	00	00
John gooding cred to 7 1/2 malases			
at $2^{s} = 4^{d}$ per galloone	00	17	06
5 Abia whiteman debt to: 250: shoonales	00	01	02
John green debt to 4 biskeakes	00	00	04
John green cred to: 45: eggs	00		

	ll	s	p
Ougust the 7th 1707			
Daniel Hunt dept to h^{a}lfe a pound of pwder Dell to him selfe	00	02	02
8 John vinson Junr debt to halef a pound of powder dll to decon bates for Samuell[406]	00	02	00
8 John Torey cred to horce e cart: 2: turnes at rose hill	00	00	04
9 John bicknell cred to one day worck of beniamines at brantery rockin hay	00	01	00
11 wido phillips debt to halef a peck salt dll to Joshua philips	00	00	08
13 Samuell pooll debt to 2 bushels of indian corn dll to pratt	00	07	04
13 Mrs white debt to one bushel of malt dll to beniamin dyer			
13 John Green debt to one quort of malases	00	00	08
13 John green cred to 17 egges			
14 John Torey cred to a tract of hay e horce to cart the hay	00	03	6
16 Samuell whitemarch debt to halef a bushell of salt dll to his son	00	02	06
17 John Torey cred to his horce e cart wood from the water side	00	00	06
19 Capt ffancch debt to to one bushel of salt dll to bedlowe	00	05	00
19 Samuell white cred to one cord e a halef of a foot of wood at 6^{s}	00	06	41/2
19 Tho white cred to two cord of wood at 6^{s} s	00	12	00
19 John Geen cred to helping loding the bote	00	00	06

[Page 209]

	ll	s	p
August the: 20: 1707 John Torey cred to his horce e carte carting wood	00	00	06
20 Zecharah bicknell debt to halef a peck of salt	00	00	008
21 John green debt to great delle of water side for his moor	00	00	04
23 Richard degers debt to: 12: ll wooll	00	12	00
23 Richard debgers credit money	00	08	071/2
23 Thomas halbroock of brantery debt to two bushels of corne	00	07	00
23 mr butler debt to 8000: of shingels 2000 at: 12^{s}: 6000 at: 10^{s}:	04	04	00
23 Mr butler cred to a rope e two bushels of corne	01	04	08
23 John green debt to halef a peck of sallt	00	00	08
24 Joseph pratt debt to hat e 6 ll porcke e one ll tobacko dll to Samuell pratt	00	11	06
28 Abraham Shawe Dept to one gallon of rum & one pound of powder and five pounds of sheeps wooll Dll to him selfe	00	13	06
29 Serg^{nt} Whitman Dept to halfe a pound of powder Dll to his son abiah	00	02	00
29 Joseph Lovell debt to: 4 pipes e	01	00	00
two barells	00	07	04
29 beniamin Luden debt to goods reseved at bostoun of mr willard[407]	03	05	00
29 Mr Willard of Bostoun shopceeper debt	06	15	00
29 beniamin Luden debt to mony paid bassels	00	00	05
29 beniamin Luden debt to: 100 shoe nailes	00	00	05
29 John Torey debt to one ounce of indego	00	00	10

	ll	s	p
August the 30–1707 John green cred to horce e cart	00	00	07
Spetember: John green cred to 19 egges			
: 1: John Greene debt to one pint of malases	00	00	04
2 Joseph pratt debt to halef a bushel of salt e 1^{s}: 4^{d}: money	00	03	10
3 John green cred to: 4: chikins 3 [?] per pees	00	01	02
Abraham Shawe debt to seven ll of sheeps wooll at: 12^{d}: per ll	00	07	00
John Torey debt to 12 ^{d} biskcake	00	01	00
John Torey cred to: 12^{d}: of eggs	00	01	00
3 Abraham Shawe cred to 18000 of shingels reseved of Joshua phillips	07	04	00
5 Cajin of charlstowne Jyner living near the brigg debt to: 650 clabbords dll t his father capeing	01	19	00
5 Joseph pratt debt to two bushel of indian corne dll to him selef	00	07	06
5 Joseph orcut debt to three quorts of salt dll to mary riply[408]	00	00	06
5 Samuell pooll debt to two bushels of indian corne	00	07	04
5 Beniamin Luding debt to one galon of rum dll to beniam	00	04	00
John Torey cred to one chikin	00	00	04
John green credit to foure chikin	00	01	02

Line	ll	s	p
September the 8–1707			
8 Joseph Willis of miltaick[409] debt to: 8750 lathes at 8^{s} per thousand dll to him selef upon his one whoref at Bostowne	03	10	00
8 left at the same time with Joseph willisis for 600 of clabbords	01	16	00
9 James Humfry debt to 26 ll talo at 6^{d} per pound	00	13	00
9 John green debt to one hogsed dll to him selef	00	02	00
10 Beniamin Richards debt to a neckcloth butens e mohare	00	04	01
12 Joseph pratt debt to 4^{s} mony e 4: ll sheeps wooll e one ll 1/2 hoges fat dll hana pratt youre daf^{ter}	00	08	09
12 John vinson Junr debt to 1 ½ of silk dll to his son	00	15	00
15 John green cred to to a pees of timber	00	10	06
15 John green debt to mony paid	00	00	08
16 beniamin Luding debt to two rummales dll James Luding	00	04	08
16 beniamin Luding debt to an order dll to James Luding	04	00	00
16 Joseph Nash debt to mony dll by biniamin reseved by him selef	03	00	00
19 Zechariah Bicknell debt to halef a peck dll to hana	00	00	08
20 Joshua phillips debt to halef a peck of salt	00	00	08
22 Biniamin Luden debt to two pounds dll to James Luden by an order	02	00	00

	ll	s	p
September the 23–1707 Abraham shawe debt to mony paid to Joseph Nash	02	12	00
23 Abraham Shawe upon the ballance acounpts was indebted	03	08	01
23 Joseph Lovell debt to mony paid to Joseph Nash	00	~~0~~08	00
23 John Torey cred to his horce caring of crick	00	00	06
25 Colonor Hunt debt to halef a bushel of salt dll by my wife	00	02	06
25 Colonor Hunt credit to a paper bill of credit reseved by my wife	00	05	00
26 John Torey cred to his horce caring crick	00	00	00
27 Samuell whitemarch cred to 6000 S at 10^{s} m	03	00	00
27 Abraham Shane cred to 4000 S at 10^{s} m	02	00	00
27 Sarjant Whiteman debt to to one peck Salt dll to the negur	00	01	03
30 Abraham shawe debt to goods reseved at mr willards of bostoune	03	11	02
e to hat ~~hat~~ e two barels e two ll shot: 12: ll cotten e a bill of 20^{s} a 11^{d}: penc at baseets	02	16	11
30 William pratt cred for 38 ll of cotten reseved of mr grant of bostoune	03	03	04

	ll	s	p
October: 1st: 1707			
Decon Bate Dept to halfe a pound of powder and halfe a bushel of salt Dll: to his son: Sam^{ll}	00	04	06
3 mr hayward of bostoune debt to 10 s shinges dll at mr combes[410] whoref	06	00	00
3 Joseph Lovell cred to 6000 of shingels at 10^{s}	03	00	00
6 John pratt debt to a grat lent	00	00	04
7 Joseph Lovell debt to two paper biles of credit	02	00	00
7 beniamin Richards debt to two pounds of shot	00	01	00
8 Samuell Whitemarch credit to 6000 s shingles at 10^{s}	03	00	00
8 Jcebod halbroock cred. upon the acunpt of beniamin Luden	00	08	06
8 Jcabod halbroock debt to 26 ll of cotton at 1^{s}–9^{d} per ll	02	05	06
to goods at bostoune at mr willards reseved by his wife	01	06	00
11 John darell debt to 1000^{m} clabbord dll at beniamin galaps whorfe to him selef at bostoune	02	16	00
Abraham Shawe debt to one bushel of corne	00	03	06
13 Decon bates cred to 1000^{m} of shingels at 10^{s}	05	00	00
13 Samuell pratt cred to 1000^{m} of clabbords–2^{ll} = 5^{s}	02	05	00
13 John brick debt to 1000^{m} clabbords	2	17	00

[Page 214]

	ll	s	p
October the 13: 1707 13 Mr hayward of bostoun debt to 7350 shingels			
13 ric^{h}ards of bostoune Jyner debt to 2700 of shingels	01	12	02
13 Joseph Lovell debt to 6 barels at 3^{s}–6^{d} per pees	01	02	00
13 William pratt cred to: 12: ll cotten reseved of grant of bostoun	01	00	00
13 John Green debt to 20 bord nailes	00	00	03
17 John Whitman of north purchas debt to 1 ½ pouder at: 4^{s}: e 4 ll shot at 6^{d} per: pound e one peney ppes	00	08	01
18 Joseph pratt debt to 6 ll cotton at 1^{s}–9^{d} per pound	00	10	6
18 Joseph pooll cred to 6000 s at 8 ^{s}: 6^{d}	02	12	06
10 Joseph pooll debt to a paper bill dll to Samuell Vinson by order	02	00	00
12 John Torrey Dept to a quarter of Lamb Dll to him selfe: six pound and three quarters 15 Ben: Ludden Dept to Eight pound of suger Dll to James Ludden 4^{d} p pound	00	02	08
25 John darell debt: a: 1150 clabbords at 3^{ll} thousand	03	09	00
25 John Shawe debt to Stockes	00	06	00
25 Beniamin orcut debt to fife peck of Salt at 5^{s} per bushel	00	06	03
25 John green debt to a peck of salt dll to John green	00	01	02

[Page 215]

	ll	s	p
October the 26: 1707 John green debter mony paid to ginnys[411]	00	03	03
John green credit to 6 foules 4 per pees e in mony 1^{s}–10^{d}	00	04	10
John green cred to 8 ll ½ porck $2^{d\ ll}$ farthing	00	01	07
Abia Whiteman debt to bringing of salt from bostoune	00	00	04
26 ballansed aconpts with Samuell Whitemarch upon all acounpts due to ^{him} two bushels of salt			
Joseph Lovell debt to one barell	00	03	08
Thomas Reed debt to one barell	00	03	08
28 Colanor Hunt debt to halef a bushell of salt dll to clarcks son of brantery[412] be an order	00	02	06
28 Zechariah Gurny debt to one bushel e a halef of salt	00	07	06
28 recened e ballansed all acounpts with beniamin luden from the begining of the world to this day e theire was dwe of nether side	00	00	00
29 Zechariah gurney cred to thrashing of otes: 18: bushels	00	03	00
30 Tho: Reed Dept to P five peck of salt Dll to him selfe	00	06	03
30 James Humfry debt th halef a pound of pouder Dll to him seleff	00	02	00
31 Decon Bate Dept to halfe a bushel of salt and one broome	00	03	00
31 Joseph Aallen Senr Dept: to one bushell and a halfe of salt Dll to him selfe	00	07	06
31 Brother fford debt to halef a bushel of salt	00	02	06

	ll	s	p
November the 1: 1707 John brick debt to goods	3	[?]	00
Novem: 3: balansed acounpts with Joseph Lovell dwe to him	00	11	10
4 William Richards debt to: 2: ll of poudell e one bushel of corne dll to James Luden	00	07	06
to halef a bushel salt dll to selef	00	02	06
6 Joseph Nash debt to six pound of cotton dll to youre man	00	10	06
8 brother Bicknell det to a broom dll to him self	00	00	05
8 Johnathon Torey debt to one peck salt	00	01	03
8 John Torey credit to horce e cart carting wood	00	00	06
9 Joseph Lovell debt to one bushel of salt dll to selef	00	05	00
10 Colenol Hunt Dept to one bushell of salt Dll to James Ludden: upon tocon N^{or} Cleb^{ords}	00	05	00
10 Samuell White of brantery Ju^{r} debt to halef a bushel salt dll man	00	02	06
10 Joseph Green cred to: 4: ll e a quorter of pork at 2 1/3^{d} per pound	00	00	11½
11 Captn ffranch debt to two bushels of salt dll to william bedlo	00	10	00
11 John Torey debt to 14^{ll} motten	00	02	06
12 Ebenezer white debt to part of a bushel of salt	00	02	01

[Page 217]

	ll	s	p
Novmber the 15: 1707 Abrham Shawe debt to halef A bushell of salt dll to him selef	00	02	00
18 John Torey cred to a peck of lime of his wife	00	00	03
18 John Torey debt 4 quorters of beef and a hed beef: 339: ll hed 6d	02	17	00
19 Elder Rogers[413] debt to halef a bushel of salt dll to him selef	00	02	06
19 Ben: Dyer Dep to one bushell of salt dll to him self	00	05	00
20 Capt ffrench Dept to halfe a bushell of salt dll to steven Budlo[414]	00	02	06
Joseph Lovel cred for taping of a pair of shooe for my self:	00	01	00
21 balanced acounpts [accounts] with John Green theire [there] was due to him	00	04	10
John Green debt a peck of Salt	0	01	03
28 Decon Bate Dept to one bushell of salt Dll to his Son Ebenezer	00	05	00
Decem 1 Ben: Ludden for salt one peny	00	00	01
3 Lft Nash debt to two bushels of malt dll to Simeon nash	00	07	06
3 paid to Jcabod holbrooks wife mony e goods	00	08	06
14 Joseph Lovell Dept to ~~one~~ halfe a bushel of salt Dll to him selfe	00	02	06
18 John Burl Dept to halfe a bushell of salt Dll to him selfe	00	02	06
John green debt to halef a ll pound of shuger	0	00	2

[Page 218]

	ll	s	p
desember the 22 1707			
Joseph Torey debter to 100 ll porck			
at 3^{d} per ll	01	05	00
24 John Green Dept to halfe a bushell			
of Salt Dll to his sone zecariah	00	02	06
27 ballanced acounpts with			
Thomas Holbroock of Bran^{tery}			
theire wast dwe to mee mony	00	03	09
Jenuary ^{16} Balansed acounpts with			
Abraham Shawe dwe to mee	01	07	06
20 Dec^{c}on bates debt to three			
pecks of Salt dll to Samuell	00	03	09
28 then ballanced acounpts with			
Brother John bicknell dwe			
to hime mony	00	14	07
Zechariah Bicknell cred			
to fanning of otes	00	06	00
Feren 4th 1708/7 Abraham Shaw Dept to too			
pounds of candels 8^{d} per pound	00	01	04
Abraham Shaw Dept to te~~m~~^{n} shillings			
for got in Recconing	00	10	00
11 Sam^{ell} Reed Dept to: too bushels			
of otes Dll to him selfe	00	03	00
Thomas Kingmam Dept to three			
bushels of otes Dll to him selfe	00	04	06
March the 3 paid to brother John Bicknell			
the ballance ~~due to me~~	00	14	06
8 Ballanced acounpts with			
Sariant Whitman due to him	00	02	08
12 then ballanced with John Torey			
due to him	00	05	01
13 John Bicknell Dept to one			
peck of salt Dll to Zecariah	00	01	03

	ll	s	p
march the 17th <u>1708</u> John V^{i}nson Deptt to: too bushels of malt: and six pounds of sugar Dll to his Eldest son[415]			
17 Capt French dept one bushel of Salt Dll to Smll Badlow	00	05	00
19 Abraham Shaw debt to one bushe of malt	00	03	04
22 John green debt to three quorts of sider dll to mare green[416]	00	09	06
29 John Green D^{e}pt to three bushels of molt Dll to his son Zecariah 29 William Pratt Dept to too Bushels of malt			
31 John Randall cred to: 46: posts 3^{d} per pees	0	11	06
31 John Ranall Snr debt to money paid to him selef	00	07	00
John Kingman[417] debt to: 1000^{m} of salt haye at 1^{s}–6^{d} per: 100:	00	15	00
31 John Kingman debt to foure bushels of otes dll to hener Kingman[418]	00	06	00
Aperell Steefen ffrench debt to: 2: bushels of otes dll to his son Steefen	00	03	00
8 Thomes Kingman debt to three bushels of otes dll to haiden[419]		04	06
8 Samuell Bill of bostoune debt to 33 ~~e three~~ la^{mb}es	05	18	3
8 Samuell Bill of Bostoune ^{cred} for one pound reseved for the lambes sold	1	000	00
8 Thomas Holbrock debt to halef a bushel e of salt dll son	02	06	
12 Joseph Lovel Dept to one bushe of barley Dll to him selfe			
13 Steeven ffrench Jun 2 debt to one bushel of malt one hay	1	0~~6~~3	00

	ll	s	p
Aperell the 17th: 1708 Joseph Lowell debt to two bushels of barly dll to selef	00	06	00
16 John Green debt to one bushel of barly dll to his son zeckeriah	00	03	03
16 Abraham Shawe debt to one bushel of Indian corne dll to him selef	00	02	09
16 Joseph Lovell debt to three bushels of otes dll to him selef	00	04	06
2~~2~~0 John Randal[420] debt to one pound of candels dll to him selef	00	08	00
20 Moris Truant debt to one bushel e a halfe of malt dll to William Trassk by order of a tocen of rate	00	04	00
Capt ffrench debt to three bushels of otes dll bedlowe	00	04	6
27 John Randall Snr debt thay e strawe dll to him selef	00	10	00
27 John Shawe debt to three bushels of otes dll to him selef	00	04	06
27 John Shawe debt to two bushels of otes dll to him selef	00	01	06
27 John Torey debt to three shilings e six pence paid to Enock Lovell	00	03	06
19 Samell whitemarch debt to seven bushels of otes e a peck of selt	00	11	09
30 Samuell whitemarch debt to seven bushels of otes dll to Samuell	00	10	06
30 Miciah Torey cred to mony payde to beniamen	00	00	03

	ll	s	p
Aperell th: 30: 7108 [1708] Samuell bill			
30: ~~Sahthon~~ Semuell Bill of bostoune debt to			
one wether: 10^{s}: returning the scin e wooll		10	00
and 4000s p 10^{d} pe ham e seven ll buter at 6^{d}		707	10
30 Samuell bill cred to two paper bils paid	00	15	00
May the: 1: moris Truffant debt to seed			
barly e plowing e a peney	01	03	06
3 John Green debt to one ll shuger			
dll to his selef	00	00	04
4 John green cred to 12 eggs for shuger	00	00	03
John green debt to the horce opening			
ground for himselef	00	00	10
Thomas Reed Junr cred to			
8000s shingels at 8^{s}–6^{d} per thousand	03	08	00
11 John Green Dept to one quort of benes	00	00	02
brother John bicknell debt			
to rum	00	03	09
19 Sarjant Whitman Dept to one peck of salt	00	01	03
20 Epraim pray debt brantery			
a cote red madie for him selef	00	11	06
to mony paid to youre selef	00	14	00
to mony paid to ms baset of			
bostoune e biskcake	00	06	02
20 balansed acounpts with Eprhraim pray			
of Brantery dwe to him in mony	00	06	10
20 after baance of acounnts with			
Eaphraim pray of brantery			
the debt wose paid in mony to			
him selef	00	06	00
20 John Green Dept to three pips	00	00	02
Mr. Cumbe[421] of bostoune debt			
to 1000s of shingels at: 10^{s}–3^{d}	05	02	6

[Page 222]

	ll	s	p
May ~~Sammy~~ Samuell bill credit to two pairs of gloves from his niber	00	08	02
20 Mr. Clowe of Bostoune mason debt to 3000s ^{shingles} e a parsell of clabb dll two him selef e his man	01	03	09
21 John Torey debt to halef a pound shuger dll for William	00	00	02
22 Mr huslis of bostowne debt to 6000 S shingel at 12 s	03	12	00
25 John Kingman debt to mallt	00	05	00
25 Abraham Shawe cred to two thousand quorter shingell at 8s	00	10	09
25 Joseph Lovell cred to 1200s shingles at 10^{s} e 1000 of lathes o 6^{s} 6^{d}	06	06	06
25 Thomas Reed Senr Dept to halfe a bushel of salt Dll to him selfe	00	02	00
John green debt to a cafes bag	00	01	00
John green cred to 3^{ll} 1/2 ll butter	00	01	09
27 John green debt to a line	00	02	06
27 John green cred [4] eggs	00	00	09
27 John green cred to sheep sher^{ing}	00	02	06
27 John Greene debt to one yard e halef of cot[s] cloth at 4^{s} s per yard	00	06	00
28 morris Trufant Dept to one peck of salt Dll to his wife	00	01	03

	ll	s	p
May the: 28: 1708			
Mr pemertin of bostoun bruer			
debt to fifty bushels of malt at: 3s	07	12	00
28 Mr Robard hayward of bostoun			
debt 6000 of shingels at: 12s ll Salley:	03	12	00
30 Joseph Lovell debt to a ~~fass~~ sithe			
dll to him selef	00	07	6
31 Joseph Lovell debt to mony paid to			
Samuel whitemarch by order	00	15	00
31 John Green ~~dept~~ cred to fife pound			
of buter at 6d ps	00	02	06
June the John Green debt a mony			
2 1708 about a peney payd at skiners	00	00	01
2 Mr hayward of bostoune cred			
to money lent	00	10	00
2 Mr hayward of bostoune debt			
to 2250 shingels at 12s	01	07	00
2 Mr Cumbee cred to mony	02	00	00
John Green cred to sheering			
to sheering of shepe	00	02	11
3 to [sind? runte?] e a 1/ll of shuger			
moris Trufant 00			
5 balans a-~~a~~ count [nut] micia torey			
dwe upen nether a sid	00	00	0
5 Nicolas phillips debt to 4 yards of			
garlick holam at 2s 9y	00	17	00
7 John Knigman debt to two			
bushels of malt dll to his man	00	06	00

[Page 224]

	ll	s	p
June the 7: 1708			
7 Thomas Reed debt to money Youre ^{to} sister phillips[422]	00	07	00
Joseph Lovell cred to a calef	00	13	0[?]
John Torey credit to horce e cart caring hooppoles	00	00	06
11 Mr hayward debt to 6000s at: 12 ^{s}	03	12	0[?]
11 Abraham Shawe cred to 6000s at 9^{s}–6^{d}	02	17	00
11 Brother bicknell debt to a broome dll to marah[423]	00	00	03
Samuell whitemarshe cre to 1000s at 10^{s}	00	10	0[?]
14 Then ballanced acounpts with Capt ffrench dwe to mee	00	07	03
Capt ffrench cred to 12000s of shingles at 9s	05	08	00
Capt ffrench cred to a calef	00	07	00
John Greene debt to indego and alum	00	0~~9~~0	07
Joseph Shawe cret to 6000s shingels at 10^{s}:	03	00	00
16 John Randall debt to mony paid to him selef	00	07	00
Mr penerun[424] dbt to malt e sparagras	01	12	00

	ll	s	p
June the 19 1708			
Abraham Shawe debt to stakes			
e ~~h~~ money dll to him selef	00	06	00
19 Joseph Lovell debt to money			
paid to him selef	10	00	0
19 ~~Joseph Lowell debt to money~~			
Joseph Shawe debt to money			
to Abraham Shaw	00	14	00
19 Joseph Lovell debt to two			
sickels dll to him selef	00	04	04
Joseph Lovell cred: 2~~3~~3000 of s			
at 10s and 500 clabbords	07	12	6
John Randall cred to a calef	00	12	00
26 Jhon ^{cred} Bicknell upon the balanc			
of acounpt dwe to him money	00	09	6
26 John Randall debt to mony	01	00	00
28 Joseph Nash Dept to too bushels of malt			
and a peck of salt Dll to Canterbery	00	07	11
28 John pratt Snr debt to two sickels			
at 2s 3d per pees	00	04	6
John Green debt to two quorts salt	00	00	4
July 2 then ballansed with John Green			
dwe to mee besides the boyes work	00	12	11
2 James Humfry debt to some rum			
dll to his dafter silance[425]	00	00	07
Micajah Torey cred to 6000s at 8^{s}: 6^{d}	2	11	00
Mycajah Torey debt to a petecote stuf			
and 4: yards of galick halan at 2s 9d	01	09	00

[Page 226]

	ll	s	p
July the 3 1708 William pittey debt to a peck of salt	00	o[1]	[6]
William pittey cred to a peaper bill	00	02	00
3 Will pratt debt to: 14 1/2 ^{ll} lam at: 2^{d} 1/2^{ll}	00	3	00
5 Abia whiteman debt to two ll 2/1 of cotten at 2s 1s 9^{d} per ll dll to Sara fford	00	03	o
8 then balansed acounpts with Joseph Lovell dwe to him	00	12	[1]
8 Abia whiteman debt to two ll of powder the prise two bushels of barly $^{e\ halef}$ to be dll at my house			
78 Capt ffranch debt to mony paid at bostoune at guinups	01	00	[?][?]
8 Capt ffrench debt to: 92ll e 1/2 porck at 5^{d} per pound	01	18	[?][?]
9 John green debt to a quorter of a pound of powder	00	001	[?][?]
John Bu^{r}lle debt to a quorter of a ll of powder	00	[?][?]	10
13 Capt Hunt Dept to one pound of powder Dll to Dannell	00	03	8[?]
13 Micajah Torey debt to goods dll at mountffords to his wife	01	13	00
13 John Green debt to one peck salt dll to John Green	00	01	o[?]
13 Joseph Lovell cred to money forgot m reckening upon ballanc	[?][?]	1[?]	[?][?]

	ll	s	p
July the: 7: 1708 John Shawe debt to mony lent to him selef dll to his dafter mary John S Shaw	04	00	0
16 Richard Deguers debt to a quorter of lambe dll to him selef 5ll 3/1: 2 2/1^d	00	01	21/2
16 William pratt debt to a quorter of lambe dll to hana pratt	00	01	02
16 William pratt debt to fife bushels e a halef of malt dll to hana[426] 00			
19 John Randall debt to 9 ll scraps at 3^d e 2^{ll} 1/2 of fat at 6:^{d}	00	0~~6~~3	06
19 balanced ~~aco^{u}pt~~ counpts with John Randall Sand Snr dwe to him	00	03	5
19 Enock Lovell Dept to one broom Dll to hannah pray[427]	00	00	6
John Torry Dept to one brom Dll to his son William	00	00	6
21 John Green Dept to too bushels of molt Dll to Zecariah	00	06	8
John Green cred to horce e [secef]	00	00	8
John green debt to rum e a pint of malases	00	01	2
William pratt debt mony lent to him selef at bostoune	00	10	10
Mary fford e Lidia fford[428] debt to horce pasage to bostoun	01	00	
24 Moris Trufant debt to a quorter of lambe 6ll 2/1	0	01	4
26 Zechariah Bicknell debt a peck of salt Joshua[429]: 6^d paid	0	00	9

	ll	s	p
July the: 26: 1708			
26 Mjcajah Torey debt to 6: ll of cotten at: 1: s 9^{d} per ll e a shilling	00	11	06
27 John green debt to a pint of malases	00	00	4
27 Moris Trufant debt to one ll of shuger	00	00	04
29 Joseph Lovell debt to a horce which hee bouft of mee dll to him selef Joseph Lovell	06	00	00
August 2 Joseph Lovel Dept to one pipe	00	00	01
2 Left Nash Dept to too bushels of molt Dll to his Indian	00	07	00
4 John phillips of the North purchase debt to 33: ll of cotton at 1^{s}–9 per ll dll to Joshua phillips e a bushell of malt dll to the same person Joshua phillips 3^{s}–6^{d} pr bus^{ill}	3	01	3
4 John phillips cred to money reseved of Joshua phillips	00	14	6
4 Mr Gredwood[430] of bostoune debt to: 1200: of clabbords at 16^{s} per hund[431]	03	12	0
4 Mr Richard[432] of Bostoun Jyner debt to 1000 of clabbords at 6^{s} per hundred dll to him selef	03	00	0
4 Capt ffranch debt to halef a bushel of salt dll Steeven bedlo	00	02	03
4 John Torey debt to one ll e halef of ocum dll to him selef	00	00	05
4 John phillips cred to seven ll of cotten at 1^{s}–9^{d} per ll	00	12	3

[Page 229]

	ll	s	p
August the: 4: 1708: then ballanced 4 acounpts with Abraham Shawe there was dwe to him	00	05	5
4 Moris Truefante debt to a quarter of lambe sent home	00	01	05
John Torey cred to horce cart otes two lodes at home	00	02	04
4 John Torey debt to one galloon of tar	00	01	00
William pratt debt to a quorter of lambe	01	04	
Micajah Torey cred to: 6 ll of butter	0	02	09
10 John Torey debt to 3 ll of cotton	0	05	3
12 Mr. Clowe of bostoune debt to one hundred ~~hundered~~ e a halef of clabbords	09	00	
12 Mrs basset of bostoune debt one Barell of vinegar	0	16	0
Thomas Reed Junr to a peck salt	0	01	03
12 Mr. Varne[433] of Bostoune debt to one thousand of clabbords	03	00	00
12 Mr beniamin browne of bostoune debt to 1050 clabbords at 6s per 1000	03	03	00
12 Abraham Shawe debt to two ll of shot dll to beniamin shawe	0	01	2
Micajah Torey debt to mony paid to Mrs amey of Bostoune	00	00	6
16 John Green debt to moing Salt grase at the neck	00	03	00
John Randall Snr debt to two bushels of malt dll to him selef	00	07	00
18 Deckon Bate Dept to halfe a bushel of salt Dll to his son Samuell	00	02	06

	ll	s	p
August the 19: 1708			
19 Mr greenwood of Bostoune credit to a hhog 3/1 salt at 2^{s} per ll	01	16	00
19 Mr Richards of Bostoune cred one hlg 2/1 fall at 20^{s} per hlag[434]	01	10	00
19 mr Needum upon the balanc of acounpts wee recconed dwe to mee	01	00	10
19 Zeckeriah Bicknell debt to wifes pasage e mackerell	00	00	08
20 Samuell whitemarch debt to one peck of salt dll to son	00	01	00
Nicolas phillips cred to two dusens of pigings e 6d egs	00	01	6
29 John Green to mony paid to Nicholas phillips by his wifes order	00	05	00
John Green cred to a lambe	00	04	06
Sep 8: William Richards debt to money dll to him selef	01	00	00
8: Joseph Lovell Dept to one peck of salt Dll to him selef	00	01	00
9 Joseph Lovell ballansed with my selef theire was dwe to me	00	06	4
Moris Trffant debt to 5^{d} e 6 ll shuger	00	02	5
John Torey debt to two ll shuger	00	00	08
John Green cred to cilling a s^{t}eer	0	01	00
14 Joseph Torey debt to 75 ll beef at 2d per ll e of suit at 4^{d}	0	12	10
14 Joseph Torey cred to a bill	0	10	00

	ll	s	p
September the: 14: 1708			
14 John green debt to money paid to			
him selef	00	04	06
14 Capt ffrench debt to a quorter			
of beef dll to william bedlowe	00	12	06
14 Capt Hunt debt to beef dll to him selef	00	07	05
14 Colenor Hunt debt to: 48: ll of beef	00	08	00
Joseph Lov^{e}ll debt to bord nailes			
dll to John Reed: 108 which is	00	01	10
Beniamin Orcut debt to mony lent	00	05	00
22 Mr Richards of Bostoune Jyneer			
debt to: 4000 s at 12^{s} per thousand	02	08	00
23 William Rich[435] debt to halef a			
bushel of salt e a twenty shilling bill	01	02	00
27 James Humfry debt to money lent			
to him selef by my one hand	05	00	00
Ebenezer pratt debt to a broom			
dll to Ebenezer whitemarch	00	00	06
October Abraham Shaw debt to goods			
1st e mony at Bostoune e at home	01	10	071/2
4 Beniamin orcut debt to six			
ll of cotten dll to him selef			
at 1^{s}–8^{d} per ll	00	10	00
6 Decon Bates debt to halef a			
bushell of salt dll son ben			
11th Zecariah bicknell Dept to one of			
of salt Dll to zec	00	01	00
11 Abram Shaw Dept to: a shep molt and salt			
Dll to him selfe	00	14	00
Abrham Shawe cred to 6000s at 8^{s}–6^{d}	2	08	00
Joseph Shawe cred to 6000s at: 8^{s}: 6^{d}	2	08	00

	ll	s	p
October ther 12: 1708 Joseph Lowell cred to: 6000s	3	00	00
William Richards cred to 7000 s at 10^{s}	03	10	00
14 Joseph Lowell debt to mony paid to Samuell bagly	00	04	10
14 Capt ffrench dept to halef a bushel of salt	00	02	00
14 John green cred to catting of stockes	00	01	00
15 Bother fford debt to one of salt dll to his son	00	04	00
19 Joseph Lovell debt to halef a bushel of salt dll to Samuel whitemarch son	0	02	00
19 Abraham Shawe debt to 4 ll of cotten wooll dll to him selef	00	06	08
21 William Richards debt to one bushel of salt dll to Joseph white	00	0[?]	00
22 Capt Hunt Dept to one peck of salt	00	09	00
25 Joseph Lovell Dept to too pounds of tobackoo Dll to him selfe	00	01	6
27 Mr Hayward of bostoune debter to: 1800 of shingels dll to him selef	10	16	0
Joseph Lovell cred to 6000s at 9^{s}	02	14	0
Joseph Shawe cred to 6000 s at 8^{s}–6^{d}	02	11	00
Joseph Shawe debt to steer	03	00	00

[Page 233]

	ll	s	p
October the 28: 1708			
28 John Green debt to a peck of salt	00	01	00
29 William Richards debt to money	01	04	00
e a mutten: two ll of powder	00	12	04
29 wido Eyles debt to a sheepskin	0	01	06
30 Joseph Lovell cred to 6000s at 10	03	00	00
30 Beniamin orcut debt to a sheep			
e fife peck of salt e one pound e			
a halef of candalls	00	13	06
Novem 1 Joseph Lovell Debt to halfe			
a bushel of salt Dll to him selfe	00	02	00
1 Joseph Lovell Debt to two pips: 3:	00	00	02
2 Zechariah Bicknell Dept to halfe a peck of			
salt Dll to his Daughter hanah[436]	00	00	06
2 William Richards debt to one bushel of			
salt and six pounds of cotton wool Dll to			
Ephraim Arnal[437] by a tocon that he had a sheep	00	14	00
sheare the Last tirdsday Night & that ye shinds: Down			
3 Capt Hunt Dept to one bushel of salt			
Dll to him selfe	00	04	00
4 William Richards Debt to Seven pounds			
of cotten woolle & too bushes of salt dll to himselfe	00	19	08
4 Zecariah Bicknell Dept to three pecks of			
salt Dll to Joseph Pratt by a tocon that you			
met me at mical Toreyes twise in one Day	00	03	00
4 Mr Hayward of Bostoun debt			
to 6000 of s at 12s	03	12	00
6 John Bicknell Dept to one bushell			
of salt Dll to him selfe	00	04	00
8 ~~Benjamin Tharesal~~			
William Richards Debt to one bushel of salt Dll to	00	04	00
Benjamin Thare			
10 Capt french Dept to too Bushels of salt Dll to			
William bedlow	00	08	00

[Page 234]

	ll	s	p
November the 10–1708			
10 Nic^{o}las phillips dept to one bushel of salt dll to his son[438] at 4s	00	04	00
Mr Hayward of bostoune det to 10500 of shingels at 12s	06	06	00
William Richards cred to 5000 of s at 10^{s}	02	10	00
10 Coranall Hunt debt to one bushel of salt dll to son John	00	04	00
10 John green debt to halef a bushel of salt dll Joseph Pratt	00	02	00
10 Joseph Lovell debt to two bushel of salt dll Samuell Whitemarses son	00	08	00
10 William Richards debt to one bushell and a halef of sallt	00	06	00
11 John Phillips debt to 21 ll 1/2 cotton at 1s 8^{d} per ll	01	15	10
11 Will manely ^{Snr} debt to 4 ll cotton at 1s 8d per ll	00	06	08
11 Jcabods wife[439] debt to 6 ll of cotton at 1^{s} 8d per ll	00	10	00
11 Wido Eyles debt to halef a bushel of salt e two ll of cotton	00	05	04
11 Wido Eyles cred to 7 ½ ll of butter e 6d peneworth of egges	00	04	031/2
11 John bicknell debt to one bushell of salt dll to son Joseph	00	04	00
Necolall Phillips[440] cred to truck	00	00	8
13 John green Dept to one peck of sat Dll to his son John	00	01	00

	ll	s	p
November 13th–1708 John Wild Dept to 168ll ½ pork at 2d–3q pr pound Dll to him selfe	01	18	07
13 William Richards debt to one pound of cotton dll to his wife	00	01	08
14 Mr Barndill of Bostoune debt to 171 ll of pork dll to his wife at 3d per ll	01	15	06
14 Mr holsey debt of Bostoune debt to butter e chees e edger dll to his wife	00	18	08
15 Mr Hayward of Boston Ballancd Acoupnts and thare was dewe to mee from him in money	20	00	00
15 Joseph Lovell Dept to sondry goods Dll to him selfe at Boston	08	09	10
15 James Richards Dept to mr. Barber[441] of Boston to sondry goods Dll to him selfe	05	04	00
15 John Roberts of Boston Dept to money	04	01	00
17 Mrs Torrey Dept to one bushel of salt Dll to her selfe	00	04	00
17 Icabod Holbrock Dept to one bushel of salt Dll to his son John	00	04	00
17 Icabod Holbrock cred to money by his son	00	03	01
17 John Pratt cred to money payd by his selfe	00	00	06
17 John green Dept to one quarter of scotch cloth Dll to his wife	00	01	00
17 John green debt to a peck of salt	00	01	00
John green credit to cilling a cowe e six hoggs		02	06
18 Joseph Shawe debt to mony paide to John Randall Snr	00	08	0

[Page 236]

	ll	s	p
November the 19th 1708			
18 Joseph Shawe cred to: 5000s at 10^{s} s	02	10	00
18 John Randall ^{senr} Dept to five pounds cotton wool Dll to him selfe e 20^{d} ll pod	00	08	04
18 John green debt to one peck of salt dll to zechariah green	00	01	00
18 wido Eyles cred to two ll butter	00	01	02
18 wido Eyeles debt to rum	00	00	11
18 Recd and ballanst acounpts with John green for the boys work and all ^{acounpts} besides and ther was dew from mee to him	00	05	07½
20 Increes Bat dbt to 37 ll of hogs ffat a to 4^{d} ½ e frait of the fat	00	14	10 2/1
20 Joseph Shawe credit upon balance of acounpts dwe to him to pay to John nash constble	00	15	00
20 Peter Weeb[442] of Branthree Debt one bushel and halfe of salt t	00	06	00
20 Peter We^{e}b of branther cred to: too shillings and six pence	00	02	06
23 Joseph Lovell debt to an order from William pratt goods	02	00	00
23 Joseph Torey debt to one bushel e a halef of salt at 4s	00	06	00
24 John green debt one pound of tobacko dll son John	00	00	09
24 John Torey debt to one pound of shuger dll son John	00	00	04
29 William Richards debt to mony paid to the constable Randall	00	12	7

[Page 237]

	ll	s	p
Desm^{b} 2th 1708 Nicolas Phillips Dept to one pound and halfe of cotton	00	02	06
2 Joseph Lovell dept to a 50 ll hide reseved of William pratt the son to Joseph pratt	00	08	0~~6~~4
3 Joseph pittey debt to 3 sheep dll to him selef of a 120 ll 2^{d} p ^{ll}	01	00	00
6 William pratt sone to Joseph pratt debt to 4 sheepe skines with the wooll e 2 ^{ll} e 1/3 qu of pinions	00	05	00
14 John green Debt too pounds of cotten Wool Dll to him selfe 20^{d} p ll	00	3	04
17 Ben^{i} Orcutt Dept to one pound of cotton wool Dll to h[im] selfe	00	01	08
Mr Hayward of bostoun crd to mony reseved of him selef at Bostoune	05	00	00
18 ballanced acounpts with John Bicknell e cleer upon bothe parte^{e}ys	0	00	00
20 John Torrey Dept to too pipes Dll to his son Will	00	00	02
John green debt to one ounc of peper	00	00	03
20 Cpt Hunt debt to one broom	00	00	05
21 Thomas Nash deb to som indian corne dll to Simeon Nash	00	01	08
27 Will Richards Dept to three pounds of cotton wool & too pounds of sheeps woll dll to him selfe	00	06	08
John green debt one ll cotten	00	01	08
Jan 8 Beniamin orcut debt to 8 pipes e 6 ll e a halef candalls at 8 ll	00	04	06
12 ~~colla ? with abram shawe~~ one ~~pound three s 8s two pences~~	00		

[Page 238]

	ll	s	p
January the 12 1708: 9 Abraham Shaw ball ands acounps and there was dew to him from mee one pound three Shillings & too pence	01	03	02
12 abraham shaw Debt to one pound of candes dll to him selfe 8 p	00	00	08
20 John Gold of hull Dept to 10^{ll} of chees 6^{d} p pound & too pound ½ of of butter p 7^{d} p pound	00	06	05
27 Capt french Dept to too pounds tobak 9^{d} p ll Dll Samll French	00	01	06
27 John Randell debt to two ll of tobacko at 9^{d} ll	00	01	06
pheb Capt ffrench debt to foure ll e halef tobacco at 9^{d} p ll	00	03	05
7 Joseph Shawe debt to him selef to pay his cuntery rate	00	15	02
John Bicknell debt to a broom	00	00	05
John green debt to: 2: ^{ll} of tobacco	00	00	09
19 Abraham Shawe debt to two bushels of otes dll to selef	00	04	00
John Randel cred to money	00	00	07
$March^{h}$: 1: John green debt to one yard of garlick holan ^{at} 3s per y: and halef a y: and halef a quorter muzeling: at 10^{s} per yard	00	04	06~~9~~
John green cred to his dafter mary serves one month e three dayes[443]	00	04	06
3 William pitty debt to one pound of sheep wooll dll to his wife	00	00	10
4 John Torey debt to four pipes	00	00	02

	ll	s	p
March the: 8: 1708/9			
William pratt son to Joseph pratt debt to			
a lumpt of tobacko dll to his son	00	02	00
9 Abrham Shawe debt to two bushels of			
otes dll to him selef	00	04	00
9 John Randall debt to halef a pound of			
powder to simeon pittey	00	01	08
14 John Randall Snr debt to a pig			
sold e baft by the said randall			
by the lump	00	07	00
14 John randall Snr debt to money	00	01	00
16 Left Nash Dept to three bushels of			
molt Dll to simeon			
17 John vining junr debt to two bushels			
otes dll to himselef	00	04	00
18 John Randall debt to one thousand			
of hay dll to him selef	0~~0~~1	00	00
18 Joseph Lovell debt to hay dll			
to him sellef prise agred	01	05	00
25 John pratt Snr debt to seven			
bushels of malt dll to him selef	01	08	00
29 Johnathan Mountford debt to			
2000 of clabbords at 3 ll per thousand	6	00	00
e nine bushels of malt at 4s bushels	1	16	00
Biall debt to one pare of shoos Jos Lovell	04	06	
to money reseved at Bostoune with goods	03	04	1/2
reseved of Mr Hayward of Bostoune			
in ballanc of acounpt of all debts			
between him and my selef	15	00	00
Aperil 4th the John green debt to three quorters			
of a ll of cotten e one ounce	00	01	05
6 John Bicknell debt to rum e			
shuger coming from Bostoune	00	00	04
6 John tor[444] debt to three quorts of rum			
at bostoune e a grate coming home	00	02	07

	ll	s	p
Aperell the 6 1709			
6 John Randall Snr debt to a bill dll			
to him selef at Bostoune			
John Torey debt to pipes ll to his			
son ~~by~~ by my wife	00	00	02
7 Steeffen ffrench debt to	~~705~~	~~50~~	750
waite of salt hay a two shill per h	00	15	00
7 Steefen ffrench debt to two cheses			
wait 8 ^{ll} or tharabout at 3^{d} 1/2 per ll	00	02	04
7 david carver debt to two ll of candels	0	01	04
7 david carver debt to one ll e 3 quorters			
of candels	0	01	02
9 Thomas Hollbroock debt to three bushels			
of barely at 3^{s}–10^{d} per bushel	00	11	06
to three bushes of otes $^{at\ 2s}$ dll to him			
selef all at the same time	00	06	00
12 John phillips cred to money reseved			
of William mandley sen^{r} of the north			
purchas	00	02	00
12 William Ma^{n}dly Junr e Thomas mandls[445]			
debt to three pounds dll to there			
father mandly by Tocon when that			
I had sold ^{the} ~~them~~ ^{clabores} would pay them	03	00	00
20 John green debt to three bushels			
of malt dll to zeckeriah green	00	11	06
23 John Shawe debt to two ll			
of tobacko dll to selef	00	01	02
23 Nathenell fford two ll toback	00	01	02
23 John Torrey Debt to two ll of tobaco			
Dll to his son John 7d pr ll	00	01	02
25 John Bicknell Snr debt to four			
ll of tobacko at 7d per ll	00	02	04
25 John green debt to halef a ll of tobacko	0	00	04

	ll	s	p
Aperell the 25 1709			
25 John green debt to one ll of cotten dll to Sara green	00	01	07
26 Abraham Shawe debt to halef a ll powder	0	01	06
26 Abiall Bouttage debt to one lase hat case	0	00	02
26 mr Tor^r^ey[446] wido debt to tobacko	00	01	00
26 Abraham Shawe debt to one ll of tobacko e halef a pound of candels	00	00	11
John green cred to 31 eggs at: 7: 2d	00	00	09
28 John green debt to halef a bushel of seed corne dll to him selef	00	02	00
30 then balanced acounpts with John Ranall Snr theire was dwe to mee in money	00	1~~5~~0	00
30 capt french debt to foure ll of tobacko dll to son samuell	00	02	04
30 Joseph Lovell debt to eleven ll of tobacko at 7d per ll	00	06	05
30 John green debt to one peck of seed corn	00	01	00
May 3 John green Debt to too pounds of cotten wool Dll to youre wife	00	03	02
~~3~~5 John green debt to two ll of tobacko at 7^d ll dll to him selef	0	01	02
~~3~~5 Biall boutage debt to 1 y e ½ bluwinin[447] at 1s–4d per yard	0	02	04
5 John green cred to sheering two sheep	0	00	03
Joseph Lovell debt to goods at montfford of Bostoune dll to a tailer o	06	06	1/2
9 William Richards debt to halef a bushel of corne dll selef	00	1	04
9 wido white of Brantery debt to two ll of cotten	00	03	02
12 Left Nash Debt to too bushels & halfe of malt Dll to simeon Nash			
12 Mr ~~Ban~~ Beniamin Brinsdill of Bostoun debt to six thousand shingels at 12s e 1200 h clabbor at 6s	07	04	0

	ll	s	p
May the 16: 1709			
16 Abiall Bouttage debt to mony	0	18	00
17 Mr Burnall[448] debt to 250 Shingels	03	00	
17 Mr Gee[449] debt to 4000s e 300 ^{h} clabbor			
dll mr broune[450] a Jyneer	03	06	00
18 reseved of mr gee mononey	01	00	00
mr gee debt to 3000 clabbords at 6s			
per 100: and 4000 of shingles at 12s			
1000s dll to broune a Jyneer	03	00	00
mr gee cred to mony reseved	01	00	00
mr burnall Junr debt to 250	00	02	00
mr grant shipwriter debt 1000s at 12s	00	12	00
19~~2~~ Decon Bates debt to 5 ll of tobacko			
dll to him selef	00	02	11
25 then balanced acounptes with			
william Richards living in brantery			
cleered all ~~aceounp~~ debts of each side	00	00	0
27 John green Cred to sheering			
of Sheep 32 coms to	00	02	08
Simon Tounfin of bostoun debt			
to too thousand of shingels at 12 ^{d} s	01	04	00
30 Decon Bates cred to mony	00	05	00
John green debt to six ll of			
cotton dll to son Jon at 1^{S} = 7$^{d\ ll}$	00	09	06
31 John Burll debt to one bushell			
of malt to him selef	00	04	00
Ju~~ne~~ly the 2^{nt}: John Bicknell debt to one			
ll of tobacko dll son Joseph	0	00	07
3 Ebenezer pratt debt to tobacko			
dll to him selef	00	01	03
3 Moris Tr^{u}fant debt to two			
bushels of malt dll to selef	00	08	00

[Page 243]

	ll	s	p
June the: 3: 1709			
3 Joseph pittey debt to 12 ll porck at 5 d per ll	00	05	00
3 Joseph pittey debt [?] qurter of a pound of tobacko	00	00	02
4 then balanced acounptes with micjah Torey dwe to mee mony	00	14	05
13 Joseph orcut debt to two ll of tobacko e two peneworth of pipipes	00	01	06
13 Mrs Torey debt to porck dll to Selef	00	06	01
Mr Gee debt to six thousand of clabbords of at six shilling per 100	01	16	00
13 Joseph orcut debt to an olde sadell prise 12s dll to him selef	00	12	00
John Green cred to carting of wood from the water side	00	01	00
20 William mandly Junr of [?] Birgwater debt to mony dll to John burls	01	15	00
20 Then ballance all acoupts with John Green ~~upon all~~ a theire was dwe to mee	00	12	00
William madly cred to 1350 clabbords			
24 Lift narch[451] debt to three bushels of malt dll Simeon Nach	00	11	03
25 Thomas Mandly Dept to one bushell of malt Dll to him selef	00	04	00
26 Joseph Louell cred to 6000 of Shingells at: 10s	03	00	00
26 Edward Richards debt to 6000s of shingles dll onbord a sloope at mr grinwoods[452] dock in Bostoune	03	12	02

[Page 244]

	ll	s	p
June to 25–1709			
Solomon Tounsin credit to mending of an ancer	00	04	0
27 William mandly debt to mony dll to John buril	01	01	0
29 Joseph Pitty Dept to three pips Dll to him selfe	00	00	02
30 John Green debt to one ll tobacco	00	00	08
July th 2: John Randall Snr debt to foure ll of cotten at 1^{S}–7^{d} per ll e a one ^{ll} $tobac^{o}$	0	07	00
4 John biecknell Snr debt to: 100 bord nailes	0	01	06
5 Edward Richards debt to: 2300 of clabbords dll to him selef upon mrs Grimwood[453] whorfe at three ll per thousand	06	18	00
11 Lft Nash Dept to three bushels of Molt dll to Simeon: 3 ^{S} and 9^{d} p bushel	00	11	03
Joseph Lovell debt to one peck salt	00	01	04
11 John Whitmach Dept to six pounds of tobackco Dll to him selfe at 8^{d} p pound	00	04	00
John S Shawe debt to money e goods paid at bostoune	02	13	00
John Shawe cred to 6000 s at 9s	02	17	00
1-~~4~~ 3 balanced acouptents with Joseph Lovell dwe to him	00	09	09
13 Thomal holbroock debt one ll of tobacco	00	00	8
moris Trufant debt to one bushel of corne dll brother fford	00	05	03
John Green debt to a hat	00	7	8
20 John green debt to one ll shuger	00	00	05
21 Abraham Shawe debt to 12 ll of cotten at: 1 ^{s}–7^{d} per ll	00	19	00

	ll	s	p
July the 22: 1709 Brother bicknell debt to 21 ½ ^{ll} of sheeps wooll at 1^s–2^d per ll	01	05	01
Abraham Shawe debt one ll toback:	0	00	06
Brother moris debt to two bushels of malt dll to him selef	00	08	00
25 John Shawe Jnr debt one ll tobac^k:	01	00	
25 Decon Bates debt to three ll of tobacko a 8 ^{d} per e ll	00	02	0
25 Decon bates cred to mony resed of his for Samuell	00	00	6 ½ g
26 Joseph pittey debt to two bushells of malt dll to him selef	00	08	00
27 Abraham S[454] debt to $^{a\ one}$ ~~two~~ bushe	00	04	00
29 Joseph Lovell debt to ^{mony} lent e dll to him selelef	08	00	00
Joseph Lovell debt to cloth for brichis	00	04	08
29 Mr Holsey Dept to ten bushels of molt Dll to him selfe 4 s p bushel	02	00	00
August 3 Mrs Holsey debt to a ches	00	02	05
3 John Torey dll to two ll shot	00	00	9
John green debt to halef a ll of tobacco	00	00	4
3 Joseph lovell debt two ll shott e halef a ll pouder	00	02	3
4 Abia [W]hiteman debt to one ll ½ tobac^{ko}	0	01	00
7 John green debt one yard e halef			
e halef a quarter scots cloth	00	07	12
8 William pittey debt to one ll shot e halef a ll of pouder	00	01	02

	ll	s	p
July the: 8: 1709 8 Abraham Shawe debt to one ll of shot	00	00	09
9 Abraham Shawe debt to: 5: quarts of lamp oyll	00	02	11~~7~~
11 John Bicknill debt to halef a hundred of borde nailles	00	00	09
12 Moris Truffant debt to two bushels of corne dll nicolas phillips	07	00	
12 Moris Truffant debt for one bushell e a halef of corne forgot	0	05	03
12 John Torey debt to two ll of tobacco	00	01	04
12 John Green credit to 24 eggs	0	01	00
12 Mr hustis of Bostaun debt to 350 clabbords at 6 pe 100	001	01	00
12 Mr hol~~sol~~sey debt to 3500 shingels at 12	02	02	00
12 Left Nash deb to 10 bushels e halef of m malt at 3^s 9^d	01	19	[012]
13 William mandly Senr of the north purchas debt to ll of cotton at 1^s = 7^d per ll	00	09	06
e one bushel bushel malt	00	04	00
13 Joseph orcut debt to: 3 ll of tobacco dll to Josia ripley	00	02	00
13 Beniamin Richards debt to 6 ll cotten e halef a ll tobacco	00	09	10
Nathanell Ford Depet to one ll tobacco	00	00	08
15 Joh bolentine debt to ~~27~~ 2850 shingels at 12s	01	14	00
15 husttis debt to 200 clabbord	00	12	00

[Page 247]

	ll	s	p
August the 15 1709			
15 John Cilbee debt to 2500 of lalhes at 8^s s 6^d per ~~hundred~~ s	01	01	03
Lft Nash cred to 3000 s a	01	10	00
Lft Nash debt to nine bushels of indian corne at 3^s–6^d per bushel	00	11	06
16 John Bicknell Sn^r debt to two ll of Shot dll to him selef	00	00	09
17 Wido green cred to to one pare of stockins	00	03	00
18 Joseph Nash Dept to five quarts Lamp oil	00	02	11
22 Abraham Shaw Dept to too pounds of shot Dll his father[455]	00	00	09
22 Mr. holsey of bostoune debt to 9: henes e 3: ll of butter e plumes	00	13	06
Josep Lovell debt a galloon of rum e a rundlat e 1^{ll}–0 = 0 John Torey	01	07	00
Abraham Shawe debt pouder one dll to his brother beniamin	00	00	05
27 Thomey Holbroock debt to: 1~~5~~0 ll of porck at 6^d per ^{ll}	00	05	0
27 John green debt to two ll of sheps wooll dll to his wife	01	8	
2~~8~~9 Abraham Shawe Cred to clabbords e lathes	0~~2~~0	0~~2~~0	~~2~~0
28 Abraham Shawe debt to mony paid to him selef	00	15	00
29 Abraham Shawe cred to: [?]: 675: clabbords at: 4^s = 3^d ½ per 100: to a 1250 ~~1500~~ lathes at 7^s	 01 01	 12 08	 04 09
31 John green debt to 4 ll 2: ounses of sheeps wooll at 8^d per ll	00	02	09

[Page 248]

	ll	s	p
September the: 2: 1709			
2 Joseph pittey debt 31 ll e hafe			
of mutten at 2^{d} ½ ll e hed e pluck			
a galloon of lam oyll e hale a ll toba^{ck}	00	09	8
Joseph pittey cred to a dayes worck			
at cricking[456] at brantery	00	02	0
Joseph pittey debt to 3 pipes	00	00	02
6 Joseph Alring of br^{a}ntery cred			
to money paid by brother fford	00	08	00
11 Moris Truffant debt to one			
ll of sheeps wooll	00	00	10
11 Solomon Tounesin cred to money			
paid to my selef	00	06	00
John Kingman Dept to one pound			
of shot Dll to him selfe	00	00	08
Nicolas Phillips Dept to one pound of			
Tobaco dll to his sone	00	00	08
John Torrey Dept to one pound of			
Tobaco Dll to Ruth ford[457]	00	00	08
Abraham Shawe debt to one			
galloon of oylle dll beniamin shawe	00	02	04
17 Benjamin White of Brantery Dept to			
too bushells of molt Dll his sone James	00	08	00
19 John green cred to: 85: egges at: 5: 2 ^{d}	00	02	10
John green debt to paid at the same time	00	04	
19 Moris Truffant debt to one Bushell			
e a halef of corne	00	05	05
Nicolas phillips cred to: 8500: s e: 950:			
clabbords	06	07	6
Nicolas phillips debt to moni paid to			
him selef	04	00	00
to youre son Nicolas 6 ll shot q	00	02	3

Line		ll	s	p
1	September the 20: 1709			
2	20 John phillips cred to: 1500 of clabbords			
3	at 4 s 6^{d} per hundred	03	07	06
4	20 Wido green debt to lamp oylle dll to			
5	Zeckery gurneys wife[458]	00	03	00
6	24 Abrham Shawe debt to a			
7	quarter of a hundred of shot	0	08	6
8	to one ll of pouder o	02	4~~6~~	
9	to 7 peck of rye e a halef	00	07	6
10	oc^{t} John green Dept to pips	00	00	01
11	John gren Dept to bord nails	00	00	04
12	4 Thomas Mandley debt of the			
13	North purchas debt 4 ll cotten			
14	at 1^{s}–8^{d} per ll e 3 ll shot e 5 pipe	00	08	00
15	4 John green debt to 2 quarts of oyll	0	01	2
16	Anah Richards[459] Dept to oile	00	00	06
17	6 Joseph Lovell debt to: 2: ll	00	06	6
18	John Torey debt to one bushel of			
19	salt dll to him selef	00	06	10
20	7 John bicknell debt to to frait			
21	of a barell of apell to Gwimips	00	00	8
22	brother fford debt to 2 of apels e			
23	a parell of perey[460] dll to butler			
24	e two bages of apels	00	02	8
25	12 Capt Hunt debt to two bushels of			
26	indian corne dll to his son	00	07	0
27	14 Capt ffrench Dept to one bushell of salt dll			
28	Samll Budlo	00	07	00
29	14 Joseph Lovell debt to a cowe hide			
30	42 ll e peck of salt	00	08	7
31	17 Edward Richards of bostoun Cr			
32	to money which I reseved	04	00	00

	ll	s	p
October the 15 1709			
15 then ballanced acounpts with moris Truffant theire was dwe to mee	0	01	06
15 Joseph Nash credit to mony reseved of Abraham Shawe	01	18	00
15 then ballanced acoupts with Abraham Shawe theire was to him	0	03	[?]
15 John green debt one pek salt dll John	0	01	09
John Shawe Sn[r] debt to money lent to him sellf by my hand	03	00	00
16 Nicolas phillips debt one pound of pouder ll to him selef	00	02	00
Joseph Shawe cred to 675 clabbords e a 1250 lathes	02	01	01
18 John Torey debt to money reseved of Thomas Kingman	00	18	3
18 Abraham Shawe debt to money paid to John Vinson	00	01	00
18 John green e I reckened e ballanced acounpts Dwe to him a peck of salt	00	01	09
19 then ballanced acounpts with John Bicknell theire was dwe to him from mee two bushel malt			
Brother fford debt to frait 2 barels of sider e a bag of apels	00	01	07
11 Moris Truffant debt to 5 peck of Salt e one galloon of oyll	00	11	03
21 John Shawe cred to 3 bushels of turnips	00	04	06
21 Joseph Lovell cred to one shilling Recd of ~~of~~ Tho Kingman	00	01	06
Thomas mandly cred to 1000 clabbord [?] oo	02	09	00

	ll	s	p
October the 21 1709 Abraham Shawe cred to 6000s 3			
23 Joseph Shawe debt to one bushel of salt e one ll pouder	00	09	6
23 William mandly cred to money reseved of his son william	00	09	6
25 Thomas mandly debt to halef a bushell of salt dll nathanell	0	03	6
25 Abraham Shawe debt to a bill of credit e one ll pouder e 3 pipes	02	02	8
26 Joseph Lovell debt to one hide 48 ll	00	08	0
26 John green debt to one galloon e a pint of oyll with three peck salt	00	08	01
3~~0~~1 Morris Trufant cred ~~Reed~~ to thirty shillings in money Recd of himself	01	10	00
31 Joseph Pitty Dept to six pips	00	00	04
Joseph lovell debt to rum e wine	00	06	6
Novem 17 John phillips debt to too bushells of salt dll to yoore son John phillips	00	14	00
John phillips debt mony paid to 17 hoore son John phillips	00	04	0
25 Joseph Lovell debt to money paid to Joseph Nash	00	16	0
25 Joseph Nash creted upon the acounpt of Joseph Lovell	00	16	00
25 Joseph Lovell debt to severell good dll to his wife[461]	01	02	5
Joseph Lovell debt 5 peck of salt [?] him selef	00	08	9

Notes

James Richards, His Daybook, and the Economic History of New England

1 Winifred B. Rothenberg argued in her 1992 book, *From Market-Places,* that farm daybooks were an artifact of the 1750s. See Rothenberg, *From Market-Places*, 54, 64.
2 See Rothenberg, *From Market-Places,* 63, for a discussion of the lack of double-entry bookkeeping in New England. Most extant daybooks, ledgers, account books, or diaries are similar to that kept by Richards. Thomas Minor of Connecticut is the only farmer known to have kept a detailed diary of his daily activities. See Anderson, "Thomas Minor's World," and Miner and Stanton, *The Diary of Thomas Minor.*
3 Clark, *The Roots of Rural Capitalism,* 70.
4 McWilliams, *Building the Bay Colony,* 112–14.
5 Vickers, "Errors Expected," 1049.
6 Massachusetts Judicial Archives, Suffolk County Probate, Record Book, 17:216–17, 333, Massachusetts State Archives (hereafter Suffolk County Probate, Record Book).
7 Vickers, "Errors Expected," 1037, 1039, 1045.
8 Adams, *Proceedings on the Two Hundred and Fiftieth Anniversary,* 3–69.
9 *Encyclopedia of Massachusetts,* 344–45.
10 Main, "The Distribution of Consumer Goods," 155.
11 William had received twenty-five acres of land on Westerneck in 1636 including two acres of saltmarsh. In 1663, he received another twenty acres near the Braintree line. Much of this was woodland. See Chamberlain, *History of Weymouth,* 1:195, 200–201 (hereafter *History of Weymouth*).
12 In 1695, James purchased some land from Joseph Green. See James Richards's Daybook, page 24, line 12, herein (hereafter JRDB). In 1707, he sold "a great deal of waterside" to John Green "for his moor." See JRDB, page 209, lines 6–7. In April 1708, James purchased "a small quantity of land" from the town because the town began selling off common land in the flats and the Old Cedar Swamp. He also purchased three quarters of an acre of land for five pounds in May 1709. See Weymouth Town Book, 1:239, 241, 244. He sold a piece of land to John Vinson in 1701 and purchased thirteen acres of land adjoining his orchards in 1702. See Deeds, Wills, etc., vol. 4, "James Richards to John Vinson," Weymouth Historical Society. The deeds for the purchase of the thirteen acres are in the possession of one of James's descendant. James received a land grant in 1709 from the town, possibly of land in the Old Cedar Swamp, of which the town had voted to divest itself in February 1708. See *History of Weymouth,* 2:539, 541. In 1713, two years after James died, the town divided the old cedar swamp on the Hingham line because people were illegally taking lumber and rocks from the common area. They split the land into shares to be given to each household. Widow Ruth Richards received two shares of half an acre each. See Weymouth Town Book, 1:257–59.
13 Suffolk County Probate, Record Book, 17:216–17, 333.
14 The probates for this sample are taken from the Suffolk County Probate Records held in the Massachusetts State Archives, Massachusetts Judicial Archives. See Suffolk County Probate,

Record Book, 1:364–66; 3:35–37; 6:38–39, 460–63, 476–79, 842–44; 7:248–50, 278–81; 8:47–48, 181, 208; 9:83–84, 124; 243–44, 1449; 10:261–67; 11:83–85, 159–60, 162–63; 12:116–17, 296–97, 316–18, 325; 13:301, 369, 705–6; 14:82–84, 111–14, 131–32, 416; 15:183–86, 212–13, 350–52; 16:145–48, 174–76, 282–85, 470; 17:206–7, 216–17, 333, 432–33; 18:108–10, 152–53, 501; 20:56–59, 129, 206–8, 329–30, 391–96, 428–33; 21:177–78, 199–201, 552–55, 667; 22:42, 128; 23:242, 264–65, 281, 372; 24:46–47, 214–18, 223–24; 26:308–10, 424–25; 28:23–26; 29:323; 30:101–2, 442–43; 31:397–99; 32:19–20, 49, 64–65.

15 Saint George, "'Set Thine House in Order,'" 2:172.

16 Bedell, "Archaeology and Probate Inventories," 226.

17 Suffolk County Probate, Record Book, 17:216–17, 333; Bedell, "Archaeology and Probate Inventories," 226–27.

18 Suffolk County Probate, Record Book, 21:177–78; 18:152–53.

19 James gave his only surviving daughter, Ruth Richards Lovell, one hundred pounds. He left his wife, Ruth, his house and lands that passed to his only son, Benjamin, upon her death. See Suffolk County Probate, Record Book, 17:216–17, 333; 32:64–65; 36:101–2.

20 See, for example, Bidwell, "Rural Economy in New England"; Bidwell and Falconer, *History of Agriculture;* Earle, *Home Life in Colonial Days*; Tryon, *Household Manufactures*; Frank, "Social Change and the Family"; and Reid, *Economics of Household Production.*

21 Kulikoff, "The Transition to Capitalism in Rural America," 122–26.

22 See, for example, Loehr, "Self-Sufficiency on the Farm"; Hartz, *The Liberal Tradition in America,* 89; Grant, *Democracy in the Connecticut Frontier Town of Kent*; Lemon, "Household Consumption in the Eighteenth Century"; Lemon, *The Best Poor Man's Country*; Lemon, "Spatial Order"; Innes, *Labor in a New Land*; and Martin, *Profits in the Wilderness.*

23 See, for example, Greven, *Four Generations,* 68; Mutch, "Yeoman and Merchant in Pre-Industrial America"; Mutch, "The Cutting Edge; Mutch, "Colonial America," 851, 861 n19; Merrill, "Cash Is Good to Eat"; Henretta, "Families and Farms"; Clark, "Household Economy"; and Sheridan, "The Domestic Economy."

24 Shammas, "How Self-Sufficient Was Early America?"; Pruitt, "Self-Sufficiency and the Agricultural Economy"; Rothenberg, "The Market and Massachusetts Farmers"; Rothenberg, *From Market-Places;* McCusker and Menard, *The Economy of British America,* 298–308; Bushman, "Family Security in the Transition from Farm to City"; Newell, "Economy."

25 Vickers, *Farmers and Fishermen,* 23; Kulikoff, *From British Peasants to Colonial American Farmers,* 205–6.

26 Kulikoff, "The Transition to Capitalism in Rural America," 128–29.

27 Newell, "The Birth of New England"; Greven, *Four Generations,* 42–44; Allen, *In English Ways;* Breen, "An Empire of Goods," 468–73; Kulikoff, *From British Peasants to Colonial American Farmers,* 7–38. These were some of the first historians to understand the importance of the European colonial context for the economic history of New England. Margaret Ellen Newell brought these insights together in her remarkable book *From Dependency to Independence.* See also Clark, "The View from the Farmhouse," 198–201; Bruegel, "The Social Relations of Farming"; Vickers, "Errors Expected"; and Clark, *The Roots of Rural Capitalism.*

28 Bushman, "Markets and Composite Farms," 364 (quotation). See also Bushman, "Family Security in the Transition from Farm to City," 238–43; McWilliams, *Building the Bay Colony;* and Donahue, *The Great Meadow,* xv.

29 Vickers, "Errors Expected," 1037; Bushman, "Markets and Composite Farms," 354, 371.

30 This description of Weymouth comes largely from *History of Weymouth,* 2:127, 130–55, 163–67, 170–71.

31 Rutman, *Husbandmen of Plymouth;* Donahue, *The Great Meadow.*

32 Donahue, *The Great Meadow,* xv; Long, "The Salt Marshes of the Massachusetts Coast."

33 Donahue, *The Great Meadow.*

34 Worlidge, *Systema Agriculturae,* 210–11.

35 Christopher Clark has made essentially the same argument for western Massachusetts between 1780 and 1820. See Clark, *The Roots of Rural Capitalism,* 30.

36 Rutman, *Husbandmen of Plymouth,* 61.

37 Cummings, *Rural Household Inventories.*

38 Suffolk County Probate, Record Book, 14:82–84, 131–32.

39 Rothenberg, *From Market-Places,* 61.

40 Saint George, "'Set Thine House in Order,'" 2:175–76.

41 Clark, *The Roots of Rural Capitalism,* 97.

42 Bruegel, "The Social Relations of Farming," 539.
43 Suffolk County Probate, Record Book, 21:286–87.
44 Bushman, "Markets and Composite Farms," 366–67.
45 William Richards left thirty bushels and twenty-three bags of malt when he died, which probably indicates that he had already started a small malting operation. See Suffolk County Probate, Record Book, 9:83.
46 Suffolk County Probate, Record Book, 17:216–17, 333; Cleverly, "A Moonlight Ramble."
47 *The Acts and Resolves,* 447.
48 *The Acts and Resolves,* 226, 236, 249–50, 277.
49 McWilliams, "Brewing Beer," 548–49; JRDB, page 54, line 14; page 65, line 15.
50 McWilliams, "Brewing Beer," 557–69.
51 Weeden, *Economic and Social History,* 168–69, 186, 193, 196, 198, 246–47, 398; Innes, *Creating the Commonwealth,* 234–35; *The Acts and Resolves,* 231.
52 Newell, "The Birth of New England," 51.
53 MacGregor and Wardener, *Salt Diet and Health,* 54–55.
54 Gedan, Silliman, and Bertness, "Centuries of Human-Driven Change"; *History of Weymouth,* 2:78, 85.
55 Ulrich, "Wheels, Looms, and the Gender Division of Labor," 3, 6; Ulrich, *The Age of Homespun,* 37, 103–5, 192–96.
56 Ulrich, "Wheels, Looms, and the Gender Division of Labor," 9.
57 See *History of Weymouth,* 2:533. For a brief description of fulling, see McWilliams, *Building the Bay Colony,* 128.
58 *History of Weymouth,* 2:77, 164.
59 *A Report of the Record Commissioners,* 11:3–4.
60 See McWilliams, *Building the Bay Colony,* 145–57.
61 *The Acts and Resolves,* 21, 121, 269, 343, 478, 492, 526.
62 McWilliams, *Building the Bay Colony,* 106–20.
63 McCusker, *Money and Exchange in Europe and America,* 117–21.
64 This discussion of credit in the English world is drawn largely from Muldrew, *The Economy of Obligation,* and Vickers, "Errors Expected." See also Finn, *The Character of Credit.*
65 Muldrew, *The Economy of Obligation,* 123.
66 Muldrew, *The Economy of Obligation,* 124.
67 Muldrew, *The Economy of Obligation,* 158.
68 See, for example, JRDB, page 71, lines 10–13; page 114, lines 6–8; page 171, line 15; page 176, lines 1–3; page 226, lines 27–28; and page 246, lines 10–11; Shammas, "How Self-Sufficient Was Early America?" 262–63; and Pruitt, "Self-Sufficiency and the Agricultural Economy," 354.
69 Clark, *The Roots of Rural Capitalism,* 70.
70 Deeds, Wills, etc. vol. 4, "James Richards to Moses Peneman."
71 McWilliams, *Building the Bay Colony,* 98; Vickers, "Errors Expected," 1046.
72 Russell, *A Long, Deep Furrow,* 116.
73 Vickers, *Farmers and Fishermen,* 221.
74 In some colonies, such as the West Indies and the Chesapeake, sugar and tobacco could act as currency. In New England, beaver skins, deer skins, wampum, maize, and even iron bars could be used as currency. Weeden, *Economic and Social History,* 314–15, 324–25.
75 Newell, *From Dependency to Independence,* 118; Weeden, *Economic and Social History,* 382.
76 McCallum, "Money and Prices in Colonial America," 145; Newell, *From Dependency to Independence,* 115.
77 Davisson, "Essex Country Price Trends," 146–48; McCusker, *Money and Exchange in Europe and America,* 132; *The Acts and Resolves,* 70–71, 296.
78 For a study of how merchants overcame the challenges of Massachusetts's currency problems, see Baxter, *The House of Hancock.*
79 Dow, *Everyday Life in Massachusetts Bay Colony,* 172; Newell, *From Dependency to Independence,* 129, 133; McCusker, *Money and Exchange in Europe and America,* 133.
80 Unfortunately, James Richards's daybook does not permit the kind of analysis of monetary and nonmonetary transactions that Daniel Vickers applied to Matthew Patten's account book. Almost all of James's transactions have a monetary value attached, and we cannot be certain how often money changed hands to satisfy credit obligations. See Vickers, "Errors Expected," 1039–45.
81 Bruegel, "The Social Relations of Farming," 544, 524.

82 This level of activity is comparable with the diary of the judge Matthew Patten from Bedford, New Hampshire, between 1744 and 1788. But Martha Ballard of Kennebec, Maine, only dealt with thirteen in July 1786. See Ulrich, "Martha Ballard and Her Girls," 208, and Vickers, "Errors Expected," 1051–54.

83 James E. McWilliams found the same pattern in his study of daybooks. See McWilliams, *Building the Bay Colony,* 118.

84 McWilliams, *Building the Bay Colony,* 116–17.

85 Rothenberg, *From Market-Places,* 149–74; Clark, *The Roots of Rural Capitalism,* 107.

86 Vickers, *Farmers and Fishermen,* 74, 17, 64; Kulikoff, *From British Peasants to Colonial American Farmers,* 228.

87 Kulikoff, *From British Peasants to Colonial American Farmers,* 239.

88 William Richards had already arranged for the support of James's older brothers. His younger brothers were sickly and both died shortly after their father did. See Kulikoff, *From British Peasants to Colonial American Farmers,* 239–40; Suffolk County Deeds, 8:410, Massachusetts State Archives; and Suffolk County Probate, Record Book, 11:162, 159–60, 9:124.

89 William must have died in May 1682. His will was not proved until July, when the inventory was taken. James's first child, Benjamin, was born nine months later in February 1683, suggesting that James and Ruth married in May 1682. If James's mother had been alive after 1692, she would have appeared in his daybook just like his mother-in-law, Mary Bicknell, but she is entirely absent. We do not know when she died, but it appears that James began his daybook in 1692 because he had finally inherited the estate his father had left him.

90 Vickers, *Farmers and Fishermen,* 37.

91 Suffolk County Probate, Record Book, 14:82–84, 131–32.

92 James made this note on the rawhide cover of the daybook amid other notations that are largely illegible. Mary Lamb (b. 1680) was the daughter of John and Mary Lamb from Braintree. She was about twenty years old when she began working for James. Her twin sister was Grace. See Holbrook and Holbrook, *Massachusetts Vital and Town Records,* 663.

93 There is no record of an Abiall Boutage or Bowditch being born to any of the Bowditchs living in Braintree or in any of the nearby towns. James had six transactions with a John Boutage, but they all occurred before Abiall began working for James, and James never records Abiall's service as a debit on John Boutage's account. But it is possible that Abiall was John Boutage's daughter. See JRDB, page 12, lines 12–13; page 18, lines 8–10; page 52, line 4; page 55, lines 5, 8; page 58, lines 9–10; page 160, line 27.

94 Suffolk County Probate, Record Book, 14:111–14.

95 Russell, *A Long, Deep Furrow,* 108, 111; Rothenberg, "The Emergence of Farm Labor Markets"; Lepore, *The Name of War.*

96 Kerber, "Separate Spheres, Female Worlds, Woman's Place"; Brown, "Beyond the Great Debates"; Ryan, "The Public and Private Good"; Spear, "The Distant Past"; Manion, "Historic Heteroessentialism"; Snyder, "Refiguring Women in Early American History"; Ulrich, *Good Wives;* Ulrich, *A Midwife's Tale*; Norton, *Liberty's Daughters*; Salmon, *Women and the Law of Property*; Brown, *Good Wives, Nasty Wenches, and Anxious Patriarchs*; Karlsen, *The Devil in the Shape of a Woman*; Sturtz, *Within Her Power*; Cleary, *Elizabeth Murray*; Miller, "Gender, Artisanry"; Norton, *Separated by Their Sex.* Gloria L. Main has argued that by the late seventeenth century, women were heavily involved in domestic production, and female labor was becoming more segregated from male labor. Main, "Gender, Work, and Wages," 62.

97 James McWilliams found a similar trend in *Building the Bay Colony,* 141–42.

98 Ulrich, "Martha Ballard and Her Girls," 212.

99 Muldrew, *The Economy of Obligation,* 158.

100 Ulrich, *Good Wives,* 37–46.

101 McWilliams, *Building the Bay Colony,* 119.

102 *History of Weymouth,* 1:258.

103 Riello, *A Foot in the Past,* 62, 205.

104 Bruegel, "The Social Relations of Farming," 535–36.

105 Ulrich, "Wheels, Looms, and the Gender Division of Labor," 15.

106 Bruegel, "The Social Relations of Farming," 542.

107 Weymouth Town Book, 1:164, 175, 186,197, 211, 213, 218, 223, 227, 230, 235.

108 Weymouth Town Book, 1:204–5, 233–34, 236–37.

109 See Hart, *Commonwealth History of Massachusetts*, 114; Fearing, *Weymouth Town Government*, 18; Weymouth Town Book, 1:186, 188, 189, 193–94; *The Acts and Resolves*, 66–67.
110 Brown, *Middle-Class Democracy*, 79–82.
111 Bruegel, "The Social Relations of Farming," 527–28; McWilliams, *Building the Bay Colony*, 85–88, 94.
112 Bruegel, "The Social Relations of Farming," 543.
113 Vickers, "Competency and Competition," 4; Pruitt, "Self-Sufficiency and the Agricultural Economy," 356, 363.
114 McWilliams, *Building the Bay Colony*, 120, 104; Norton, "The Evolution of White Women's Experience"; Vickers, *Farmers and Fishermen*, 221; Sweeney, "Gentlemen Farmers and Inland Merchants," 66–67, 73; Main, "The Standard of Living in Southern New England"; Main and Main, "Economic Growth and the Standard of Living," 42–43.
115 Bushman, "Markets and Composite Farms," 354, 371.

The James Richards Daybook, 1692–1711

116 This page contains internal doodling, which I have been unable to decipher. Left marginalia: 1111; internal notations: sine in and d?; my e me hae; 66, 34, 36, 60, 10.
117 This is his mother-in-law, Mary Porter Bicknell (c. 1638–c. 1693).
118 This Mary is probably James's sister-in-law Mary Bicknell (1678–1764).
119 Probably refers to one pound paper notes issued by the Massachusetts Bay Colony.
120 Probably Thomas Coates.
121 I have found no record of a son for Joseph Drake.
122 I have found no record of a son named William for William Pettee.
123 This is Ephraim Hunt (1650–1713).
124 This is Nathaniel Ford (1658–1733), James's brother-in-law, husband of Ruth's sister Joanna.
125 Jacob Nash (1640–1718).
126 George Whitey may have been from Braintree.
127 Benjamin Richards (1683–1733).
128 This apparently reads "received of your father secure money," which may indicate that James held money as security against future debts.
129 This is Thomas Reed (c. 1645–1719), husband of Sarah Bicknell Reed (c. 1651–1719). He was James's brother-in-law.
130 Benjamin Savil.
131 Probably damask.
132 Most likely James's brother Joseph.
133 James refers here to his sister-in-law Sarah, Joseph's second wife.
134 Thomas Coates was probably from Braintree.
135 Possibly a Bowditch. Several Bowditches lived in Weymouth.
136 Richard Phillips.
137 This may be Lieutenant Ebenezer White. The term "Cornat" could be a miswriting of "cornal." I have no information, however, that Ebenezer White ever become a colonel.
138 Mary Porter Pettee.
139 This refers to Thomas Porter (1672–1753), the only child of Thomas Porter (1650–72) and Sarah Vining Porter.
140 Probably Robert Adkins of Boston.
141 The name could be Johnathon Daisy or Days. He may have been a servant working for John Green.
142 I have only been able to identify one Elizabeth Bicknell alive at this time.
143 This refers to James's son, Benjamin, being hired out.
144 Probably Mary Phillips Humphrey (1661–1738).
145 This is probably Jonathan Torrey (1654–1718) rather than Lieutenant John Torrey (1673–1730), as Lieutenant Torrey would have been too young to be paying the minister's rate in 1697. See *History of Weymouth*, 4:679.
146 This is most likely the mother of Jonathan Mountford of Boston, who died around 1704.
147 James's wife, Ruth. He calls her "mother" in the daybook to distinguish her from their daughter, also named Ruth. In all other instances, he adds a last name to the title "mother."

148 This may be the Elizabeth Bicknell for whom James paid for six months of medical treatment and a funeral in or after 1694, but I have found no connection with Nicholas Phillips that would justify her mark being given on a bill of credit other than as a simple witness.
149 John Hupper or Hooper may have been from Boston.
150 George Whitey appears to have been the hired hand of Samuel Spear from Braintree.
151 John Bicknell's wife, Sarah (d. 1730).
152 Possibly John Bicknell.
153 Elsewhere James indicates that Lambur Desper was from Braintree, but he does not appear in the Braintree town records.
154 Quince.
155 A William Hearsey lived in Hingham at this time.
156 Probably Mary French Badlam (1662–c. 1718).
157 Uncle Shaw was John Shaw, brother of James's mother, Grace.
158 Deacon Edward Bates (1655–1725).
159 Jacob Tyler.
160 Elder John Rogers (1638–1709).
161 There are two possibilities for this Stephen French: Captain Stephen French (c. 1640–1717) or his son Stephen French (1664–1741).
162 Nicholas Salter may have been from Charlestown.
163 Isaac Hunt was probably from Braintree.
164 Probably Aunt Bayley, that is, Ruth Porter Bayley (1639–1717).
165 Probably Thomas Vinson (b. c. 1628).
166 Probably John Vinson, Sr.
167 Samuel's father was John Vinson, Sr.
168 Probably Uncle Vinson.
169 This could be Joseph Shaw (1643–1704) or Joseph Shaw (1664–1718).
170 Widow Nash.
171 William Trask lived in Braintree. See Bates, *Records of the Town of Braintree*, 146.
172 Peter Newcomb lived in Braintree. See Bates, *Records of the Town of Braintree*, 28, 29, 33, 37–39, 53, 62, 65, 75, 93.
173 John Cillbe, Killbee, Kilby, or Kilbey may have been from Boston.
174 Deacon Ebenezer Hovey (1680–1756).
175 Probably Benjamin Pratt (b. 1693), Joseph Pratt, Jr.'s (1665–1765) oldest son. He would have been six years old in 1699.
176 This may be John Hubbard of Boston, who served as county treasurer. See *A Report of the Record Commissioners*, 7:176; 8:168.
177 Probably veal.
178 Probably nails.
179 Catherine Richardson Simpkins, wife of Pilgrim Simpkins.
180 This is most likely William Feese, who appears elsewhere in the daybook. I have not been able to trace him, but since Moses Penniman lived in Braintree, it seems likely that Feese did as well.
181 Possibly John Long from Boston.
182 Probably clapboards.
183 Elizabeth Shaw Poole.
184 Mr. Tyler may be Samuel, William, or Andrew Tyler from Boston.
185 Possibly Samuel Bayley.
186 Ephraim Hunt (1650–1713).
187 Probably Mary Barnsdale, who was married to William. See *A Report of the Record Commissioners*, 9:178, 195.
188 Either John or Zachariah Green.
189 Benjamin Nash (1685–1724).
190 James Nash (b. 1678).
191 This probably refers to James's nephew Benjamin, son of Joseph Richards, rather than his own son, Benjamin. See *History of Weymouth*, 4:590–93.
192 This could either be Hannah Whitman French (1641–1720), wife of Captain Stephen French (c. 1640–1717), or Abigail Beal French (b. 1671), wife of Stephen French (1664–1741). See *History of Weymouth*, 3:234–36.
193 Ensign John Hunt (1646–1723).

194 There are two possible Thomas Kingmans: Thomas Kingman, Sr. (c. 1627–1705), and his son Thomas Kingman, Jr. (1670–1742).
195 Mary Phillips (1667–1749).
196 Deacon Joseph Dyer (1653–1704).
197 Ephraim Hunt (1650–1713).
198 This is probably Ephraim Hunt's son Samuel Hunt (1681–1729). See *History of Weymouth*, 3:313–15.
199 Ruth Quincy Hunt.
200 There are so many female Torreys alive at this time, it is impossible to tell which he means.
201 John Wild lived in Braintree. See Bates, *Records of the Town of Braintree*, 65, 72, 74, 75, 77, 88, 90, 93, 99.
202 Thomas Copeland of Braintree. See Bates, *Records of the Town of Braintree*, 33, 37, 49, 56, 59, 68.
203 William Copeland of Braintree. See Bates, *Records of the Town of Braintree*, 28, 33, 37.
204 John Copeland of Braintree. See Bates, *Records of the Town of Braintree*, 29, 37, 38, 40, 44, 46, 49, 52, 61, 75.
205 Probably Hannah Reed (b. 1689), daughter of Thomas Reed, Sr. (1645–1719).
206 This could be one of two Samuels—Reverend Samuel Torrey (1632–1707) or Samuel Torrey (b. 1676), the son of William Torrey (1638–1718).
207 Mary Nash Porter (b. 1675).
208 Lieutenant John Torrey (1673–1730).
209 James Smith, Sr., settled in Weymouth around 1639 and had four children there. His second son was Joshua, but in his will in 1673, he mentions Joshua as deceased, so it remains unclear who this is. See *History Weymouth*, 4:632.
210 Probably Joseph Allen of Braintree.
211 Nicholas Whitmarsh.
212 Joanna Bolter.
213 Possibly Lamber Desper.
214 Probably Arthur Powell of Braintree. See Bates, *Records of the Town of Braintree*, 44.
215 This could be the father of the William Trask, Jr., who appears in the Braintree town records describing his proprietary mark on his sheep's ears. See Bates, *Records of the Town of Braintree*, 146.
216 There are no children of record for Captain Samuel White in Weymouth. His brother Thomas White had a son named Samuel (b. 1676), but he would not have been designated junior. See *History of Weymouth*, 4:732.
217 Mary Whitmarsh Bates (1663–1715), daughter of John Whitmarsh (d. 1709) and Sarah Harding Whitmarsh. See *History of Weymouth*, 3:23; 4:759.
218 Probably Samuel French (b. 1668), son of Captain Stephen French (1640–1717).
219 Stephen French (1640–1717).
220 William Badlam
221 Smelt Brook.
222 Probably Joseph Richards's son James (b. 1680). See *History of Weymouth*, 4:590.
223 Elder John Rogers.
224 John Wilkinson was clearly a servant of Samuel Whitemarch. He does not appear in the records of Weymouth.
225 Samuel Andrews's wife was Elizabeth Ludden Andrews, widow of Joseph Ludden.
226 Abigail Shaw Davenport (b. 1672) was Richard Davenport's (1670–1761) first wife.
227 Mary French Badlam (1662–c. 1718).
228 The Haydens appear to have been mostly a Braintree family. See *History of Weymouth*, 3:262–64, and Bates, *Records of the Town of Braintree*, index, s.v. "Hayden."
229 Sarah Nash Drake, the only daughter of James and Sarah Nash. See *History of Weymouth*, 3:206; 4:421–22.
230 Probably Susanna Short.
231 Samuel Hollis (c. 1680–1740).
232 John Hunt (b. 1687), first child of Captain John Hunt, who moved to Braintree after 1698.
233 It is difficult to tell who Sergeant Whitman is. Ensign John Whitman died in 1692, and none of the other Whitmans from Weymouth seem to have held military titles. See *History of Weymouth*, 4:753–55.
234 Richard Thayer belonged to the populous and important Thayer family of Braintree. See Bates, *Records of the Town of Braintree*, 22, 38, 49, 53, 55, 57, 87, 93, 95.
235 Edward Derby (1665–1723).

236 Lydia Holbrook, the wife of Sergeant Samuel Holbrook (b. 1644).
237 Probably Ebbett Brimsmead Hunt (d. 1712).
238 Theophilus Curtis was a prominent citizen of Braintree. See Bates, *Records of the Town of Braintree*, 28, 30, 35, 37, 29, 42, 45, 53, 55, 57, 62, 65, 70, 71.
239 Possibly Morris Trufant.
240 Probably meaty tongues.
241 Scotch cloth.
242 Cock of hay.
243 William Pratt (1673–1714).
244 This is probably a Hannah Pratt, though I have not found a daughter of William Pratt (1659–1713) of that name. See *History of Weymouth*, 4:504.
245 This refers to Benjamin Richards working on Easterneck in Weymouth, which was east of James's property.
246 Ebenezer Thayer was a prominent resident of Braintree. See Bates, *Records of the Town of Braintree*, 37–39, 42, 49, 52, 53, 65.
247 Samuel Thayer was a resident of Braintree. See Bates, *Records of the Town of Braintree*, 37.
248 Possibly either John or Ephraim Hunt.
249 A John Hayden appears in the Braintree town records in 1717. See Bates, *Records of the Town of Braintree*, 90.
250 Sarah Hunt Pratt (1640–1729).
251 This could either be Deliverance Byram Porter (d. 1720), wife of John Porter, Sr. (d. 1717), or Margaret Ford Porter, wife of John Porter, Jr. (1667–1723). See *History of Weymouth*, 4:485–87.
252 Possibly Joanna Alcock Hunt (1660–1746), wife of Colonel Ephraim Hunt. See *History of Weymouth*, 3:313.
253 Deborah Torrey (d. 1729).
254 Stephen French, Jr. (1664–1741), son of Captain Stephen French (c. 1640–1717).
255 Mary Nash Porter.
256 John Arnold (b. 1655).
257 Some members of the Tower family came to Weymouth from Hingham in the late seventeenth century. Samuel may have belonged to that family. See *History of Weymouth*, 4:696.
258 Mr. Brigham may have been from Boston.
259 Probably Samuel Wentworth of Boston.
260 Marcy Secole may have been a servant for Thomas Bicknell.
261 James indicates that Daniel Willard was from Braintree. He does not appear in their records unless he was the Mr. Willard paid by the town in 1700. Bates, *Records of the Town of Braintree*, 47.
262 Samuel Bryant may have been from Scituate.
263 Alice Nash (c. 1685–1751).
264 James Lovell, Jr. (1667–1718).
265 Sarah Bicknell Reed.
266 Elizabeth Poole Lovell (1674–1717).
267 Probably James Lovell, Sr. (1633–c. 1705).
268 James's brother John.
269 John Porter, Jr. (1667–1723).
270 Probably Micajah Torrey (1643–1711), son of Captain William Torrey (1608–90).
271 Probably William Feese.
272 This is most likely William Richards (1685–1712), son of James's brother John Richards (1650–95) and Sarah Pratt Richards (1650–1727). See *History of Weymouth*, 4:590.
273 Abigail Dyer Nash (b. 1647).
274 Nicholas Salter may have worked for Jacob Nash. This would explain why several of the following entries under Jacob Nash indicate that the items were purchased for Nicholas Salter and often delivered to Salter's wife.
275 John Hadman may also have worked for Jacob Nash.
276 A Samuel Willes worked as a baker in Boston in 1713. *A Report of the Record Commissioners*, 11:197.
277 Minister Torrey, probably Deacon Micajah Torrey.
278 Edward Derby's first wife, Ruth Whitmarsh Derby (1667–1704).
279 Captain Samuel White (1642–99).
280 John Hunt (d. 1761) of Braintree. See *History of Weymouth*, 3:314.
281 Major John Hunt (1646–1723).
282 James's son, Benjamin.

283 A Benjamin Lincoln lived in Braintree in the mid-eighteenth century, and there was a Lincoln family in Weymouth at the end of the century, but I have found no information on a Benjamin. See Bates, *Records of the Town of Braintree*, 357–58, and *History of Weymouth*, 3:369.
284 Probably Hannah Rogers Pratt Bayley.
285 James paid town rates in Braintree because he owned ten and half acers of salt marsh there.
286 Probably Mary French Badlam (1662–c. 1718).
287 John Shaw, Sr. (1630–1704), was James's maternal uncle.
288 The term "shilwork" remains unidentified.
289 Possibly Edward Bates or Edward Derby. James did business with both of them.
290 Probably Joseph Coals or Coles. A Henry Cole apparently lived in Weymouth for a short time in the 1670s and 1680s, but I have not been able to identify any Coles living in Weymouth in 1694.
291 A Mary Flood lived in Boston during this period.
292 Richard Phillips.
293 The manuscript is damaged, making it impossible to identify this individual.
294 The manuscript is damaged, but this is probably Thomas Kingman.
295 Joseph Allen lived in Braintree. See Bates, *Records of the Town of Braintree,* 24–77.
296 James Richards nephew Joseph Richards, Jr. (1676–1710).
297 Probably Joseph Richards's second wife and Joseph, Jr.'s stepmother, Sarah (b. c. 1657). See *History of Weymouth*, 4:590.
298 Ephraim Pratt lists a daughter named Hannah Hines in his will. See *History of Weymouth*, 4:504.
299 Several men named Needham lived in Boston at this time.
300 I have been unable to find any Marcy or Mercy Ford in Weymouth or Braintree at this time. There are several Marys, and this may refer to one of them.
301 James spells this as "galick" or "garlick," "holan," "holun," "holum," "halon," "halloone," and "scolun." I have been unable to identify this cloth.
302 There were several Mrs. Whites alive at this time, so it is impossible to tell who this is.
303 Sergeant William Reed (1688–1729).
304 James included some doodlings on the page, which I have removed for clarity. They are as follows: Sator, arepo, teret, opore, ratas, Sator, arepo, tenant, opera, rotas; thou then that binds, all that dwelleth in a deep fall.
305 Ephraim Hunt.
306 John Frathingham may have been from Charlestown.
307 Elizabeth Simms may have been from Charlestown.
308 Joseph Allen.
309 Possibly Ruth Fry Torrey (c. 1650–1724) or Mary Symmes Torrey (1678–1758).
310 Most likely Zachariah Bicknell's servant or slave.
311 Benjamin Ludden lived in Braintree. See Bates, *Records of the Town of Braintree*, 129–94.
312 Asparagus.
313 Possibly Mary Dyer White (1641–1716), wife of Captain Samuel White (c. 1642–99), whom James referred to as Samuel White, Sr., or Mary Pratt White, wife of Thomas White, Sr. (d. 1706), whom James called Thomas White, Sr. See *History of Weymouth*, 4:732.
314 There were several Neals living in Braintree at this time. Elder is most likely a title in the church rather than a name. See Bates, *Records of the Town of Braintree,* index, s.v. "Neal."
315 No Jacob Holbrook is listed as living in Weymouth or Braintree in the town records. This may be an alternate spelling of Ichabod Holbrook.
316 John Vining, Sr.
317 William Badlam, son-in-law of Captain Stephen French.
318 Joshua (b. 1696) was the second son of Zacharia Bicknell (b. 1667).
319 Plysh bricks may refer to a type of sugar brick.
320 Double-Ten Nails.
321 Isaac Poole.
322 Mr. Vesey or Veazie probably lived in Braintree. See Bates, *Records of the Town of Braintree*, index, s.v. "Veazie."
323 Sarah Orcutt.
324 This could be "wide cloth weaving," which might refer to the use of a wide loom.
325 Probably one of the members of the Wales family of Braintree.
326 Probably Edward Mortimer of Boston.
327 Possibly Stephen, John, or Peter Butler of Boston.

328 January.
329 Peter Thatcher (1677–1739).
330 Most likely Morris Trufant.
331 Jonathan Clark was probably from Braintree. See Bates, *Records of the Town of Braintree*, 122, 139.
332 Probably Anna Carver Richards (1675–1766).
333 Probably John or David Langdon of Boston.
334 Possibly Jeremiah Houtchine of Boston.
335 Matthew Pratt, Sr. (c. 1628–1713).
336 I have been unable to identify Widow Smith.
337 Goode Green may have been a child of John Green (1661–1734), but she does not appear in his 1734 will. Suffolk County Probate, Record Book, 30:442–43; 32:49.
338 Samuel Allen was probably from Braintree. See Bates, *Records of the Town of Braintree*, 52–53, 57, 68–69, 75, 90–95, 99, 102, 107–14, 151–56.
339 Solomon Townsend of Boston.
340 Probably Elisha Hutchinson of Boston.
341 Canterbery was probably the boy's last name.
342 Sarah Orcutt.
343 Sarah Turner Holbrook (1665–1739).
344 Lydia Whitman Thomas (c. 1678–1757).
345 Sarah Bicknell (1665–1730).
346 This could be Marah, Mary, or Mariah Tirrell, though I have been unable to identify one alive in Weymouth at this time.
347 Probably John's brother William Torrey, Jr. (1638–1718).
348 Probably William Drake (1661–1727).
349 Samuel White (1642–99).
350 Samuel White's African slave, named Frank.
351 "Wont of tally" means that Richards did not have an accurate count of the shingles.
352 Mary Green.
353 A large Wadsworth family lived in Boston at this time.
354 Colonel Ephraim Hunt had at least six sons to whom this entry may refer. See *History of Weymouth*, 3:314.
355 A Benjamin Allen appears in the records of Braintree; see Bates, *Records of the Town of Braintree*, 65–154. One was born in Boston in 1661; see *A Report of the Record Commissioners*, 9:78.
356 Probably Hannah Pratt.
357 Jonas Humphrey (1684–1761).
358 Joshua Torrey (1690–1776).
359 This entry reads in part, "Plowshare molds and the iron between them."
360 Some Lindalls lived in Boston at this time.
361 John French was from Braintree. See Bates, *Records of the Town of Braintree*, 18, 22, 25, 28, 30, 31, 36, 37, 46, 82, 106.
362 Richard Agers worked as a shipwright in Weymouth from 1698 to 1719.
363 William Badlam.
364 This could either be John Bates (d. 1746), son of Increase Bates (1641–1717), or Sergeant John Bates (1685–1770), son of Edward Bates (1655–1725). See *History of Weymouth*, 3:23–24.
365 Mary Reed Lovell (c. 1672–1745).
366 Sarah Green.
367 John Green, Jr., was the second son of John Green (1661–1734).
368 Richard Agers (d. 1719).
369 Richard Agers only had one son, also named Richard (1700–after 1750). *History of Weymouth*, 3:7–8.
370 The passage reads, "token of felling beach peas."
371 John Courser of Boston.
372 Possibly Jonathan Waldo of Boston.
373 Probably Solomon Townsend.
374 Henry Kingman (d. 1731).
375 John Bowditch.
376 This is Zipporah, wife of Frank "negro." They and their two children, Charles and Margaret, were owned by Samuel White. See Suffolk County Probate, Record Book, 14:82–84, 131–32.
377 Meagan may have been a servant girl living at Enock Lovell's house.
378 The phrase "his man" refers to a hired servant.

379 Ebenezer Vinson (1684–1764).
380 Probably Ebenezer Vinson.
381 Sara Kingman.
382 Probably Hannah Kingman.
383 Probably Hannah Bicknell.
384 Vinsons.
385 Zachariah Green was John Green's eldest son.
386 Possibly "thither."
387 Piece of paper.
388 Nathaniel Wales lived in Braintree. See Bates, *Records of the Town of Braintree*, 26–63.
389 Micah Pratt (1691–1758).
390 Striped linen.
391 Gwinops was apparently a family from Boston. James also spells their name Guinups and Gwimips.
392 Benjamin Poole (b. 1682).
393 This may refer to Micajah Torrey.
394 Probably Nathaniel Pettee (1688–1747).
395 Pages 192 and 193 were written by Nathanial Richards (1740–1822) in 1789 and so have been excluded from this text as they are not relevant to James Richards or his accounts.
396 James's great-grandson Nathaniel Richards wrote some accounts on this half-empty page. They have been omitted here.
397 Nathaniel Richards also made notes on the bottom of this page.
398 Possibly Thomas Pratt (1661–1744).
399 Possibly Zachary Gurney.
400 The use of the name "Frank Negro" indicates that he was a slave.
401 Probably Stephen Badlam (b. c. 1696).
402 Possibly David Farnum of Boston.
403 It is hard to say whether James refers to John Green's wife, Patience, or to John Green's mother, Elizabeth Whitman Green.
404 Probably James's wife, Ruth.
405 Possibly "Tylers."
406 Probably Samuel Bates, son of Deacon Edward Bates.
407 Many Willards lived in Boston where Mr. Willard kept a shop.
408 Mary Ripley (b. 1695).
409 I have been unable to locate Miltaick, though it could be Milton.
410 Possibly John Coombs from Boston, where he owned a wharf.
411 Probably a female servant working for John Green.
412 "Clark's son of Braintree" probably worked for Colonel Hunt.
413 John Rogers.
414 Stephen Badlam (b. c. 1696).
415 John Vinson, Jr. (c.1676–1756).
416 Mary Green.
417 All of the John Kingmans I have been able to find living in Weymouth at this period had either died or were not yet born in 1708. See *History of Weymouth*, 3:354–58.
418 Henry Kingman.
419 Most likely Joseph Hayden, who may have worked for Thomas Kingman.
420 John Randall, Jr. (1673–1730).
421 Mr. Combe.
422 I have been unable to locate any woman with the last name of Phillips related to Thomas Reed.
423 Mary Bicknell.
424 Probably Moses Penniman of Braintree.
425 Silence Humphrey (b. 1698).
426 His wife, Hannah Pratt (d. 1757).
427 Hannah Pray may have been a servant girl living with Enoch Lovell's family, possibly related to Ephraim Pray.
428 Mary Ford (b. 1684) and Lydia Ford (b. 1688).
429 Joshua Bicknell (b. 1696).
430 Possibly Samuel Greenwood.

431 Hundred.
432 Possibly Edward Richard.
433 Possibly James Varney of Boston.
434 Both "hlg" and "hlag" probably mean hog.
435 Probably William Richards, the son of James's brother John.
436 Hannah Bicknell (b. 1698).
437 Probably Ephraim Arnold from Braintree. See Bates, *Records of the Town of Braintree,* 135, 137, 141.
438 Nicholas Phillips, Jr. (1697–1744).
439 Probably Ichabod Holbrook's wife, Sarah Turner Holbrook.
440 Nicholas Phillips.
441 Possibly James or Peter Barber of Boston.
442 Peter Web was a prominent citizen of Braintree. See Bates, *Records of the Town of Braintree,* 37, 39, 53, 57, 67, 72, 74, 77, 80, 87, 89, 93.
443 It appears that Mary Green served in James's house for about a month before Abiall Boutage came. Abiall first appears in the daybook on March 29, 1709, and periodically until September 1710, a few months before James passed away.
444 Probably John Torrey.
445 William, Jr., and Thomas appear to have been the sons of William Manley, Sr. Later James indicates that William, Jr., lived in Bridgewater.
446 I have been unable to find a Widow Torrey living in Weymouth at the time. This may refer to the wife of the Mr. Torrey whose son was Timothy and who may have lived in Boston.
447 Probably blue linen.
448 Possibly the same person as Mr. Burrell.
449 Possibly Joshua Gee of Boston.
450 Probably Benjamin Brown of Boston.
451 Probably Lieutenant Jacob Nash.
452 Probably Mr. Greenwood.
453 Probably Mrs. Greenwood.
454 Probably Abraham Shaw.
455 John Shaw, Sr. (1630–1704).
456 Probably "crooking."
457 Ruth Ford may have been a servant in John Torrey's household.
458 Mary Gurney.
459 Anna Carver Richards (1675–1766), who married James's nephew Joseph Richards (1676–1710).
460 Either "a parcel of pears" or "a barrel of pears."
461 Ruth Richards Lovell (c. 1685–1766), James's daughter.

Appendix A

James Richards's Debtors, Creditors, and Associates

Note: This appendix contains the biographical information currently available for the individuals with whom James interacted in his daybook. It does not include those for whom very little or no information is available. If a name included in the daybook does not appear in this list, the author was unable to identify that person.

Adkins, Thomas. Boston-based brewer who purchased malt from James Richards. He held several positions for the town until he acquired a license to sell alcohol in 1711 so he could open a tavern. In 1698, James sold him ninety-eight bushels of malt for his brewery, which indicates that Adkins had been brewing beer for some time before he opened a tavern. He may be related to Robert Adkins, who purchased fifty-four bushels of malt from James in 1697. See *A Report of the Record Commissioners*, 7:215, 225, 243; 8:6; 9:183, 239; 11:126.

Agers, Richard (1700–aft. 1750). Weymouth cordwainer; son of Richard Agers (d. 1719) and Abigail Nash Agers (b. 1673). He married Susannah Colson in 1727. See *History of Weymouth*, 3:7–8.

Agers, Richard (d. 1719). Spelled variously Egor, Eagers, Degeres, and so on. Weymouth shipwright from 1698 to 1719. He married Abigail Nash (b. 1673), the daughter of Lieutenant Jacob Nash (1640–1717) and Abigail Dyer Nash (b. 1647). See *History of Weymouth*, 3:7–8.

Allen, Joseph. He was elected selectman in 1693 and remained prominent in Braintree affairs. See Bates, *Records of the Town of Braintree,* 24, 6, 28, 31, 32, 33, 37, 47, 52, 57, 62, 64–68, 72, 74, 77.

Andrews, Samuel (1688–1718). Born in Boston, he married Elizabeth Ludden, widow of Joseph Ludden. Samuel worked as a housewright in Weymouth between 1695 and 1702.

In 1699, he served on the committee to hire a schoolmaster. See *History of Weymouth*, 2:537; 3:13–14.

Arnold, John (b. 1655). He lived in Braintree until 1682, moved to Weymouth in 1682 and lived there until 1694, then moved to Boston. See *History of Weymouth*, 3:14.

Badlam, Mary French (1662–c. 1718). Daughter of Captain Stephen French (1640–1718). She was the second wife of William Badlam, who moved to Weymouth around 1690. See *History of Weymouth*, 3:17–18.

Badlam, Stephen (b. c. 1696). Son of William Badlam and Mary French Badlam (1662–c. 1718), Captain Stephen French's grandson. See *History of Weymouth*, 3:17.

Badlam, William. Married Mary French (1662–c. 1718), daughter of Captain Stephen French and Hannah Whitman French (1641–1720). See *History of Weymouth*, 3:17, 234–35.

Barnet or Barnut, Thomas. He was made a sealer of leather in 1721 and 1727 in Boston. See *A Report of the Record Commissioners,* 8:160, 215.

Basset, Mary. The wife of David Basset of Boston. She petitioned the selectmen on several occasions to be allowed to open an inn but was denied. See *A Report of the Record Commissioner,* 9:159; 11:52, 60, 75, 77.

Bates, Edward (1655–1725). Also known was Deacon Bates, he married Elizabeth Shaw Bates (1656–1748) of Boston, daughter of Anthony Shaw (c. 1628–1705) and Alice Stonard Shaw (c. 1630–after 1705). Bates was active in Weymouth society. In 1693, 1694, 1696, 1721, and 1722, he was elected selectman and in 1709 as town clerk. He also taught the children of the town between 1697 and 1699 in his own house. See *History of Weymouth*, 2:533, 535, 536, 537, 541, 545, 547; 3:23.

Bates, Increase (1641–1717). Married Mary Whitmarsh. See *History of Weymouth*, 3:23.

Bates, Samuel (1693–1752). Second son of Increase Bates and Mary Whitmarsh Bates. See *History of Weymouth*, 3:23.

Bates, Samuel. Son of Deacon Edward Bates (1655–1725) and Elizabeth Shaw Bates (1656–1748). He married Hannah Shaw. See *History of Weymouth*, 3:23.

Bayley, Aunt. Ruth Porter Bayley (1639–1717), sister of Ruth Bicknell Richards's mother, Mary Porter Bicknell (c. 1638–c. 1693). Ruth Porter married Thomas Bayley (d. 1691). She lived as a widow for twenty-seven years. See *History of Weymouth*, 3:65–67.

Bayley, Hannah Rogers Pratt (d. 1721). Second wife of Thomas Bayley (d. 1691), who had married James Richards's aunt Ruth Porter. This may be why James Richards delivered goods sold to Widow Hannah Bayley to Ebenezer and John Porter. See *History of Weymouth*, 3:65; 4:485–87.

Bayley, Mary. Widow of Thomas Bayley, Sr. (d. 1681). See *History of Weymouth*, 3:64–65.

Bayley, Samuel (d. 1711). Possibly the son of Thomas Bayley, Sr. (d. 1681), who came to Weymouth in 1644. Samuel received a land grant from the town in 1660 and had five children with his wife, Mary. See *History of Weymouth*, 3:65–66.

Bayley, Sarah (b. 1674). Thomas Bayley's (d. 1691) and Ruth Porter Bayley's fourth child. She married Joseph White of Braintree in December 1704. See *History of Weymouth*, 3:65.

Bayley, Thomas (d. 1691). Married Ruth Porter, James's aunt, in Weymouth on September 19, 1660. After Ruth died, he married widow Hannah Rodgers Pratt (d. 1721). In 1665, he was reprimanded by the town selectmen for cutting thatch with a scythe on town lands and fined twenty shillings. He served as fence viewer in 1677 and hay warden in 1670. See *History of Weymouth*, 2:525; 3:65.

Bayley, Widow. Probably Hannah Rogers Pratt Bayley (d. 1721), the second wife of Thomas Bayley. She had previously been married to Samuel Pratt (d. 1690). See *History of Weymouth*, 1:239; 3:65.

Beal, Abigail (b. 1671). Wife of Stephen French, Jr. (1664–1741). See *History of Weymouth*, 3:234–36.

Benson, Joanna (d. 1735). Daughter of Joseph and Sarah Benson of Hull; she was the first wife of Deacon Ebenezer Hovey (1680–1756). She died in Weymouth. See *History of Weymouth*, 3:298.

Bicknell, Benjamin (1694–1717). James Richards's nephew, son of John Bicknell (1654–1737) and Sarah Bicknell (d. 1730). See *History of Weymouth*, 3:79.

Bicknell, Elizabeth (b. 1673). Ruth Bicknell Richards's younger sister. James paid for her medical care in 1694 and her funeral, the date of which is unknown. The *History of Weymouth* claims that she married Simon Whitmarsh as his second wife and that she had children as late as 1701. Both accounts cannot be correct. See *History of Weymouth*, 3:78–79; 4:759.

Bicknell, Experience (b. 1665). Ruth's younger sister and Thomas's older sister. See *History of Weymouth*, 3:79.

Bicknell, Hannah (b. 1675). Younger sister of Ruth, she married Benjamin Shaw around 1690 and moved to Taunton around 1700. See *History of Weymouth*, 3:79; 4:614.

Bicknell, Hannah (b. 1698). Daughter of Zachariah Bicknell and Hannah Smith Bicknell (b. 1670). See *History of Weymouth*, 3:79.

Bicknell, John (c. 1623–1678). Married Mary Shaw (c. 1626–1658) in 1652. After her death, he married in 1658 Mary Porter (c. 1640–1682), who was the mother of Ruth Bicknell Richards. See *History of Weymouth*, 3:78–79.

Bicknell, John (1654–1737). James Richards's brother-in-law; James often refers to him as Brother John Bicknell. He married Sarah (1665–1730) in 1687. John was elected selectman in 1698. See *History of Weymouth*, 2:535–36.

Bicknell, Joshua (b. 1696). Son of Zachariah Bicknell and Hannah Smith Bicknell (b. 1670). See *History of Weymouth*, 3:79.

Bicknell, Mary (1678–1764). James Richards's sister-in-law, the youngest daughter of John Bicknell and Mary Porter Bicknell. She married Morris Trufant (d. 1740) from Marshfield around 1700. See *History of Weymouth*, 3:78–79; 4:697.

Bicknell, Thomas (1670–1718). Mary Porter Bicknell's fifth child. He moved to Middleboro after 1696. He married Ann Turner in 1696 in Hingham and died in Middleboro in 1718. See *History of Weymouth*, 3:79.

Bicknell, Zachariah (b. 1668). Married Hannah Smith (b. 1670). He moved to Rehoboth about 1705. See *History of Weymouth*, 3:79.

Bill, Jonathan. Served Boston as a tithingman, constable, and surveyor of the highways between 1685 and 1705. See *A Report of the Record Commissioners*, 7:177, 195, 205, 235; 8:26, 30 33; 11:45.

Bill, Samuel. Received permission to build a slaughterhouse on Peck Wharf in Boston in 1693. He was elected constable in 1698, but refused to serve. He purchased lambs, ham, cheese, butter, and asparagus from James Richards. He sent a pair of gloves to James

Richards by his African slave and returned the skin and wool of a wether he purchased in 1708. See *A Report of the Record Commissioners,* 7:214, 229; 8:76–78, 151; 9:159; 11:200, 223.

Blanchard, John (1660–1733). Married Abigail Phillips (d. 1724), daughter of deacon Nicholas Phillips. They had nine children in Weymouth. In 1709, he received a land grant from the town. See *History of Weymouth,* 2:541; 3:98.

Blanchard, Nathaniel (b. 1665). Married Dorothy Capen (b. 1673) of Dorchester. They lived in Weymouth until 1708, when they moved to Braintree. See *History of Weymouth,* 3:98–99.

Bolter, Joanna. Second wife of Thomas Bolter (d. 1690). His first wife, Experience Aldreide, died in 1671. See *History of Weymouth,* 3:124.

Boutage, Abiall. Came to serve in James Richards's house in March of 1709. She may have been related to the Boutage family of Braintree.

Brick, John. Became a clerk of the market in Boston in 1706, and in 1708, he received a license to sell rum in small casks from his shop and warehouse on Scarlet's Wharf. *A Report of the Record Commissioner,* 8:36; 11:74, 112.

Briggs, Remember. Son of Clement Briggs. He received land and money from both his parents in their wills. He received a land grant in 1664, married in 1685, and had three children in Weymouth. See *History of Weymouth,* 3:128–30.

Brimsmead, Ebbett (d. 1712). Second wife of the blacksmith Ephraim Hunt (c. 1610–86). See *History of Weymouth,* 3:313.

Burrell, Ephraim (1664–1726). Married Lydia (d. 1712). See *History of Weymouth,* 3:132.

Burrell, John (c. 1670–1731). Possibly married Mercy Alden from Taunton. See *History of Weymouth,* 3:133.

Burrell, Rebecca (d. 1719). Possibly wife of John Burrell, who fought in King Phillip's War in Captain Isaac Johnson's company in 1675. See *History of Weymouth,* 3:132.

Burrell, Widow. See Rebecca Burrell.

Carver, Anna (1675–1766). Married James Richards's nephew Joseph Richards (1676–1710) about 1700. They had six children. See *History of Weymouth,* 4:591.

Carver, David. Lived in Weymouth between 1701 and 1717. He apparently lived their earlier and may have been employed by William Pettee before his marriage. His first child was born in 1701. He married twice while in Weymouth, first to Ruth Whitmarsh and second to a woman named Hannah. Ruth died sometime between 1704 and 1709. See *History of Weymouth,* 3:154.

Clow, Ebenezer. Served on several Boston town committees and as a constable and selectman of Boston. He purchased lathe, shingles, and clapboard from James. See *A Report of the Record Commissioner,* 9:214, 221, 226; 8:140, 145, 154; 11:72, 123, 173.

Courser, John. Born in Boston to John and Margaret Courser in 1681. John managed to get himself excused from appointments as constable in 1727 and later as viewer of shingles and measurer of boards and planks. See *A Report of the Record Commissioner,* 9:154; 8:172, 215.

Davenport, Richard (1670–1761). Born in Boston, it is unclear when he lived in Weymouth, but he apparently moved from Weymouth to Bridgewater and later to

Sutton. He married first Abigail Shaw (b. 1672), then Abigail Newcomb. See *History of Weymouth*, 3:195.

Degere, Richard. See Agers, Richard.

Derby, Edward (1665–1723). Married Ruth Whitmarsh (1667–1704) and then Rebecca Sumner Hobart of Hingham, widow of Aaron Hobart. He moved between Weymouth and Braintree. He was elected selectman in 1717. His estate was valued at £830 18s 9d. See *History of Weymouth*, 2:544; 3:196–97.

Drake, Benjamin (b. 1670). Married Sarah Pool and moved to Taunton. See *History of Weymouth*, 3:205.

Drake, James (b. 1691). Son of William Drake and Sarah Nash. He apparently died young, though he was twelve years old when James employed him in 1703. See *History of Weymouth*, 3:206.

Drake, John (1658–1717). Married Rachel from Boston, who died in 1686. He then married Sarah King of Weymouth (1666–1727). See *History of Weymouth*, 3:205–6.

Drake, Joseph (1663–1719). Married a woman named Elishama who died in February 1717. He later married Lydia Kingman in May 1718. He served as a soldier in the 1690 expedition to Canada under Captain Ephraim Hunt. His sister Experience Drake (b. 1683) married William Richards (1685–1712), the nephew of James Richards, in 1706. See *History of Weymouth*, 3:205–6; 4:590.

Drake, William (1661–1727). Married Sarah Nash (b. 1699). He moved to Taunton about 1707. See *History of Weymouth*, 3:206; 4:423.

Dunbar, Peter. Lived in Hingham but had one child, Sarah, born in Weymouth in 1693. See *History of Weymouth*, 3:206.

Dyer, Benjamin (1688–1774). Married Sarah Sawyer (c. 1688–1773) of Hingham. See *History of Weymouth*, 3:211.

Dyer, John (1663–96). Married Mary Bicknell (d. 1677), daughter of John and Mary Shaw Bicknell, who was the half-sister of James Richards's wife, Ruth. Dyer was born in Weymouth and lived there until about 1672 when he moved to Boston. After Mary died, he married Elizabeth, who bore him five children, all born in Boston where he also died. He is listed as a cloth worker. See *History of Weymouth*, 3:210.

Dyer, Joseph (1653–1704). Married Hannah Frary (1659–1726) from Medfield. Joseph served as executor for his father's will in 1675 and on the town committee to rebuild the old meetinghouse in 1682. He was elected selectman in 1684, 1687, and 1693. In 1696, he was appointed, together with Edward Bates, to teach the children how to read, write, and cipher. See *History of Weymouth*, 2:523, 527, 529, 530, 535; 3:211.

Dyer, Mary (1641–1716). Wife of Captain Samuel White, who died in 1699. See *History of Weymouth*, 4:732.

Dyer, Thomas (b. 1651). Son of Deacon Thomas Dyer (c. 1612–76), who moved to Plymouth. See *History of Weymouth*, 3:210.

Dyer, Thomas (b. 1673). Son of John Dyer and Mary Bicknell Dyer. See *History of Weymouth*, 3:209–11.

Eyles, Hannah. See Eyles, Widow.

Eyles, Widow. Possibly Hannah Eyles, who James mentions throughout his daybook. He also mentions her in association with John Mountford of Boston, so she probably lived there.

Fisher, Cornelius. Lived in Weymouth between 1678 and 1679. He later lived in the part of Dedham that became Wrentham. See *History of Weymouth*, 3:225.

Ford, Brother. See Ford, Nathaniel.

Ford, Israel (1670–1736). Married Sarah Pratt (d. 1718). They had no children. His estate was valued at £385 18s 2d. Israel was the younger brother of James Richards's brother-in-law Nathaniel Ford. See *History of Weymouth*, 3:227–28.

Ford, Lydia (b. 1688). Along with Mary Ford (b. 1684), she was the daughter of James Richards's brother-in-law Nathaniel Ford and Joanna Bicknell Ford (1663–1739). See *History of Weymouth*, 3:227–28.

Ford, Nathaniel (1658–1733). Married Joanna Bicknell (1663–1739), daughter of John and Mary Porter Bicknell. Joanna was the sister of Ruth Bicknell Richards, James's wife. Nathaniel served as a tithingman in Weymouth in 1683. See *History of Weymouth*, 1:332; 2:528; 3:78–79, 227–28; 4:590–91.

Ford, Ruth (b. 1689). James Richards's niece, the daughter of Nathaniel Ford and Joanna Bicknell Ford. Ruth married Thomas Holbrook of Braintree. See *History of Weymouth*, 3:227–28.

Ford, Samuel (1656–1711). Son of Andrew Ford (1632–1692) and Eleanor Lovell Ford (1633–83). He married Sarah Pratt (b. 1660) about 1681. See *History of Weymouth*, 3:227.

Frank. Samuel White's (1642–99) African slave. Samuel owned a family of slaves—Frank, Zipporah, and their two children, Charles and Margaret. James Richards delivered goods to Frank and Zipporah twice on Mary White's behalf after Samuel died in 1699. See Suffolk County Probate, Record Book, 14:82–84, 131–32.

Freeman, James. Refused service as a constable in Boston in 1713. *A Report of the Record Commissioners*, 8:98.

French, Hannah Whitman (1641–1720). Wife of Captain Stephen French (c. 1640–1717). See *History of Weymouth*, 3:234–36.

French, Mary (1662–1718). Daughter of Captain Stephen French and Hannah Whitman French, and second wife of William Badlam, who came to Weymouth from Boston around 1690. See *History of Weymouth*, 3:17.

French, Samuel (b. 1668). Most likely the son of Captain Stephen French. Samuel had already built a house in Abington when his father made his will in 1718. See *History of Weymouth*, 3:234–35.

French, Captain Stephen (c. 1640–1717). Married Hannah Whitman (1641–1720). He served as deputy from Weymouth to the General Court in 1682. He called himself a yeoman in his will. French was one of the most prominent men in Weymouth. He served as selectman in 1653, 1656, 1670, 1673, 1675, 1679, 1681, 1684, 1709, and 1715 and constable in 1669, and was elected deputy to the General Court in 1702. In 1659, the town took a portion of his land to build a new highway. In 1687, a dispute he had with the town over some flats by the Back River was settled in his favor. In 1704, he joined the committee to draft new bylaws for the board of selectmen. See *History of Weymouth*, 2:504, 508, 509, 511, 518–20, 522, 523, 525, 526, 528, 529, 530, 537, 538, 540, 541, 543, 544, 545, 555, 556; 3:234–36.

French, Stephen, Jr. (1664–1741). Son of Captain Stephen French. He married Abigail Beal (b. 1671). He was not as active in town politics as his father. He worked on a committee to settle the minister's rate in 1719 and as trustee of the town rate in 1721. In 1730, he refused the offer to serve as deputy to the General Court. In 1734, he worked on the committee to draw up rules for catching the herring coming into the ponds. See *History of Weymouth*, 2:504, 508, 509, 511, 518–20, 522, 523, 525, 526, 528, 529, 530, 537, 538, 540, 541, 543, 544, 545, 555, 556; 3:234–36.

Gallop, Benjamin. Served as hog reeve in Boston, constable, clerk of the market, and scavenger. His petition to build a timber building was rejected in 1703. See *A Report of the Record Commissioner,* 7:213, 222, 229; 8:60, 103; 11:31, 68.

Gooding, John. The inspector of chimneys and brick masons in Boston in 1692 and 1693. See *A Report of the Record Commissioner,* 7:211, 213.

Green, John (1661–1734). Son of Joseph Green (d. 1700) and Elizabeth Whitman Green (d. 1720). He married Patience (d. 1736) in Weymouth. He served as constable in 1709 and was selected as a juror for the superior court in 1729. See *History of Weymouth*, 2:541, 554; 3:248–50.

Green, John, Jr. Second son of John Green (1661–1734) and Patience Green. He married Mary Humphrey (b. 1716) in 1745. See *History of Weymouth*, 3:250.

Green, Joseph (1658–c. 1733). Son of Joseph Green (d. 1700) and Elizabeth Whitman Green. He married Anne (d. 1711) in Weymouth. After Anne died, he then declared his intentions to marry Ruth Richards in 1712, probably James Richards's widow. They apparently did not marry as Ruth died in 1728 and Joseph Green married a Mary Angove from Marblehead in 1717 and then an Elizabeth Spear from Braintree in 1718. Joseph Green served on two town committees, one to oversee the location of roads in 1693 and the other to oversee the hiring of the schoolmaster in 1701. In 1708, he disputed the decision to purchase Zachariah Bicknell's land as a settlement of the schoolmaster as his land had also been under consideration. See *History of Weymouth*, 2:515, 533, 537, 539; 3:248–49; 4:590.

Green, Joseph (d. 1700). Moved from Plymouth to Weymouth in 1657 where he married Elizabeth Whitman (d. 1719). He was granted the right to dig a well in a small corner of his land in 1665. See *History of Weymouth*, 2:515, 533, 537, 539; 3:248–49.

Green, Mary. Second daughter of John Green (1661–1734) and Patience Green. It appears that Mary Green served in James Richards's house for about a month in 1709. See *History of Weymouth*, 3:249–50.

Green, Patience (d. 1736). Received one third of John Green's (1661–1734) estate after he died in 1730. They had six children in Weymouth. See *History of Weymouth*, 3:249–50.

Green, Sarah. Third daughter of John Green (1661–1734). See *History of Weymouth*, 3:250.

Green, Zachariah (d. 1743). John Green's (1661–1734) eldest son. See *History of Weymouth*, 3:249–50.

Green, Widow. Elizabeth Whitman Green (d. 1720), widow of Joseph Green (d. 1700). See *History of Weymouth*, 3:248–49.

Gurney, John (b. 1658). Married Elizabeth Green (b. 1664), daughter of Joseph and Elizabeth Whitman Green. See *History of Weymouth*, 3:252.

Gurney, Joseph (b. 1664). Son of Richard Gurney (d. 1719) and Rebecca Taylor and the brother of Zachariah Gurney. See *History of Weymouth*, 3:251–52.

Gurney, Zachariah (c. 1660–1732). Son of Richard Gurney (d. 1719) and Rebecca Taylor. Not much is known of his wife, Mary, except that she may have died in Weymouth in 1736. See *History of Weymouth*, 3:252.

Harding, John (d. 1682). Came to Weymouth around 1640. See *History of Weymouth*, 3:254.

Harvey, Peter. Moved to Weymouth about 1695, but it is unclear how long he remained. His son Samuel remained in Weymouth until his death in 1733. See *History of Weymouth*, 3:257.

Holbrook, Cornelius (1662–1742). Son of Captain William Holbrook (c. 1627–99); lived in South Weymouth. He married Margery in 1686, who died after only a few years of marriage. He then married Experience (d. 1742), with whom he had six children. See *History of Weymouth*, 3:270–73.

Holbrook, Ichabod (1662–1718). Married Sarah Turner (1665–1739) from Scituate in 1688, with whom he had six children. See *History of Weymouth*, 3:271.

Holbrook, Jacob. Probably lived in Weymouth or Braintree. This may be an alternate spelling of Ichabod Holbrook.

Holbrook, Thomas (b. 1624). Born in England to Thomas Holbrook, who migrated at seventy-seven years of age to Massachusetts. Holbrook lived in Braintree and Scituate and married Joanna Kingman, daughter of Henry Kingman. See *History of Weymouth*, 3:268.

Holbrook, Captain. This could refer either to William Holbrook (c. 1627–99) or John Holbrook (c. 1622–99). Both were captains. See *History of Weymouth*, 3:268–70.

Holbrook, Widow. Lydia, the widow of Sergeant Samuel Holbrook (b. 1644). See *History of Weymouth*, 3:270–71.

Hollis, John (c. 1645–1700). Married Elizabeth Priest. He served in King Phillip's War under Captain Isaac Johnson at Dedham. In 1685, the town granted Hollis the orchard and land he had fenced along the highway. See *History of Weymouth*, 2:529; 3:288.

Hollis, Samuel (c. 1680–1740). A weaver, he lost his first wife, Sarah, while she was still young and married his second wife, Abigail, about 1710. See *History of Weymouth*, 3:288–89.

Hooper, John. Married Mary Litchfeeld in Boston in 1690. He worked as a worsted comer who purchased wool from James Richards and was elected watchman in 1710. See *A Report of the Record Commissioner*, 8:13, 118; 9:193.

Hovey, Deacon Ebenezer (1680–1756). Married Joanna Benson (d. 1735) of Hull. After she died at Weymouth, he married Sarah King of Norton. He was a blacksmith. See *History of Weymouth*, 3:298.

Humphrey, James (1665–1718). Married Margaret Torrey after the premature death of his first wife in 1698. He served as selectman of Weymouth in 1709, 1711, 1715, and 1717. He was the first treasurer of the town to receive a salary (forty shillings) in 1711 and served as clerk. See *History of Weymouth*, 2:541–42; 3:302–4.

Humphrey, Jonas (1684–1761). Married Martha (d. 1712) of Weymouth and then Mary Neal of Braintree (d. 1766). See *History of Weymouth*, 3:304.

Humphrey, Mary Phillips (1661–1738). Married Jonas Humphrey (1655–89). She later moved to Braintree and married Peter Newcomb. See *History of Weymouth*, 3:303.

Humphrey, Nathaniel (1652–1700). Son of Deacon Jonas Humphrey (1620–98). Nathaniel was born in Dorchester and died in Weymouth. He was elected selectman in 1693. See *History of Weymouth*, 2:533; 3:302–4.

Humphrey, Samuel (b. 1649). Born in Dorchester and married and died in Weymouth after living some time in Rhode Island. He married Mary Torrey (b. 1656) of Scituate. He served as tithingman in 1683. In 1686, the town gave the house, orchard, and land that Humphrey was then occupying to Pastor Samuel Torrey. In 1696, Humphrey was elected selectman. See *History of Weymouth*, 2:528–30, 535; 3:302–3.

Humphrey, Silence (b. 1698). Daughter of James Humphrey (1665–1718), she married David How of Weymouth in 1720. See *History of Weymouth*, 3:304.

Humphrey, Widow. There are at least three widows Humphrey in Weymouth around the turn of the eighteenth century—Martha, widow of Deacon Jonas Humphrey (1620–98); Elizabeth, widow of Nathaniel Humphrey (1652–1700); or Mary Phillips Humphrey, widow of Jonas Humphrey (1655–89). See *History of Weymouth*, 3:302–3.

Hunt, Daniel (b. 1689). Son of Captain John Hunt (1646–1724) and Ruth Quincy Hunt (1658–1748). See *History of Weymouth*, 3:313.

Hunt, Ebbett Brimsmead (d. 1712). The second wife of the blacksmith Ephraim Hunt (c. 1610–86). See *History of Weymouth*, 3:313.

Hunt, Ephraim (1650–1713). One of the most prominent men in Weymouth. He married Joanna Alcock (1660–1746) from Roxbury in about 1678. He served as captain of an expedition to Canada in 1690. He is referred to by James Richards and in the town records as major by 1694. He was titled lieutenant colonel in the town records in 1699. He became a colonel in 1706 and served as a counselor to Governor Joseph Dudley between 1703 and 1713. He served as selectman in 1691, 1694, and 1696. He also served on the rate committee and on a committee to draft new bylaws for the selectmen. Because of a failure to furnish troops in 1703–4, he was censured by the governor. See *History of Weymouth*, 2:532, 533, 535, 537,538, 541; 3:313–14.

Hunt, John (1646–1723). Married Ruth Quincy (1658–1748) of Braintree. He was elected constable in 1681 and served on the committee to repair the old meetinghouse in 1682. He was elected selectman in 1683 and perhaps 1717, though the *History of Weymouth* indicates that he moved to Braintree sometime after 1698. He also apparently became an ensign, a major, and a captain. See *History of Weymouth*, 2:526, 528, 544; 3:313.

Hunt, John, Jr. (b. 1687). Son of Captain John Hunt (1646–1723) and Ruth Quincy Hunt (1658–1748). He was born in Weymouth. See *History of Weymouth*, 3:313.

Hunt, Joseph (b. 1670). Born in Weymouth but apparently lived in Milton. See *History of Weymouth*, 3:313.

Hunt, Samuel (1681–1729). Graduated from Harvard College in 1700 and became schoolmaster of Weymouth in 1701. He moved to Dunstable in 1707 to become minister and then later to Dartmouth, where he died. See *History of Weymouth*, 3:313–15.

Hunt, Sarah (1640–1729). Daughter of Enoch Hunt (d. c. 1647) and Dorothy Hunt (d. 1652). She married Matthew Pratt (1628–1713). See *History of Weymouth*, 3:312; 4:501–2.

Hunt, William (b. 1655). Son of Ephraim Hunt and Ebbet Brimsmead Hunt. He married Mary Bradford of Kingston. He later moved to Martha's Vineyard. See *History of Weymouth*, 3:314.

Jackson, Edmond. Moved among Braintree, Weymouth, and Abington from 1691 to 1724. Two of his six children were born in Weymouth. His father lived in Boston. See *History of Weymouth*, 3:332.

Kilby, John. Served as a tithingman in Boston and a clerk of the market, though he refused an appointment as assessor. He purchased cheese, butter, and cabbages from James Richards. See *A Report of the Record Commissioners*, 7:213, 217; 8:23, 98; 9:170, 180, 201, 239, 245, 248.

King, Esther Bayley (d. 1700). Daughter of Thomas Bayley, Sr. (d. 1681). She married John King (d. 1688) around 1647. See *History of Weymouth*, 3:64, 350–51.

King, Hezekiah. Son of John King, Jr. He called himself a husbandman. There is no record of when Hezekiah was born, but he was apparently still alive in 1710. See *History of Weymouth*, 3:351–52.

King, Mary Shaw (b. 1659). Wife of Hezekiah King and daughter of John Shaw (1630–1704). See *History of Weymouth*, 3:352; 4:612.

King, Samuel (c. 1640–1711). Married Experience Phillips (1641–1717), daughter of Deacon Nicholas Phillips. He was elected constable in 1682. See *History of Weymouth*, 2:526; 3:351.

King, Widow. See Esther Bayley King.

Kingman, Hannah. Probably a spinster who died in Weymouth in 1730. There was another Hannah Kingman, but she was the daughter of Thomas Kingman, Sr., who was born in 1666 and married Gideon Tirrell around 1688. It is unlikely James Richards would have referred to her as Hannah Kingman after her marriage. See *History of Weymouth*, 3:355, 360; 4:656–57.

Kingman, Henry (d. 1731). Son of Thomas Kingman, Sr. (c. 1627–1705) and Rebecca Kingman. He married Elizabeth Sargent in 1709. See *History of Weymouth*, 3:355–58.

Kingman, John (b. 1664). Son of John Kingman (c. 1632–c. 1690), who lived in Bridgewater. See *History of Weymouth*, 3:356.

Kingman, Sarah. Daughter of Thomas Kingman, Sr. (c. 1627–1705), and Rebecca Kingman. She married John Vinson, Jr. (1676–1756), about 1696. See *History of Weymouth*, 3:715.

Kingman, Thomas, Sr. (c. 1627–1705). Married Rebecca and was a large landowner and prominent resident of Weymouth. Kingman was fined twenty shillings six pence in 1662 for not appearing to mend the highway. In 1699, he was elected constable. See *History of Weymouth*, 2:511, 518; 3:355–57.

Kingman, Thomas (1670–1742). Son of Thomas Kingman, Sr. (c. 1627–1705). He married Mercy Randall (d. 1737) and later Mary Humphrey Burrell, widow of John Burrell. See *History of Weymouth*, 2:511, 518; 3:355–57.

Lash, Robert. He and Mary Lash had their first child in Boston in 1695. On April 28, 1701, Lash received permission from the town selectmen to build a timber building. In

June 1702, he purchased 2,100 shingles from James Richards. See *A Report of the Record Commissioners*, 9:222; 11:3–4.

Lovell, Elizabeth Poole (1674–1717). Married James Lovell, Jr. (1667–1718) in 1694. See *History of Weymouth*, 2:541; 3:394.

Lovell, Captain Enoch (1670–1746). Probably a cobbler as he frequently sold and repaired shoes for James Richards and his family. Enoch married Mary Reed (c. 1672–1745), daughter of Thomas Reed (c. 1645–1719) and Sarah Bicknell Reed. Lovell formed part of a group who in 1715 received permission to trade fish at Cape Sable. They received some land with a beach at the mouth of the Fore River for that purpose. In 1721, Lovell was elected moderator of Weymouth. In 1723, he was elected selectman. In 1725, he was assigned to a committee to work with the owners of local mills to create a passage for fish to Whitman's Pond and then to organize the catching of the herring as they made their way to the pond. See *History of Weymouth*, 2:543, 545, 547, 549–50, 552, 554, 556; 3:394–95.

Lovell, James, Sr. (1633–c. 1705). Married Anna, the mother of his first eight children, and then Jane, the mother of his last daughter. He was fined twenty shillings six pence in 1662 for failing to help in mending the highway. In 1664, he was appointed to survey the Hingham/Weymouth boundary. He became involved in a land dispute in 1670 and was arrested and fined nineteen shillings "for abusive language to the selectmen and snatching a deed from the hands of Lieutenant Holdbrook." In 1676, the selectmen appointed him to inspect the town inhabitants suspected of keeping houses of entertainment without a license, and in 1682, he worked on the committee to restore the old meetinghouse. He also served as selectman in 1673, 1675, 1683, 1684, and 1693. See *History of Weymouth*, 2:511, 512, 513, 514, 515, 518, 519, 522, 523, 526, 527, 528, 529, 533; 3:393–94.

Lovell, James, Jr. (1667–1718). Son of James Lovell, Sr., and Anna. He married Elizabeth Poole (1674–1717). He was constable in 1709. See *History of Weymouth*, 2:541; 3:394.

Lovell, Joseph (1684–1723). Married Ruth Richards (c. 1685–1766), daughter of James Richards and Ruth Richards. See *History of Weymouth*, 3:395.

Lovell, Mary Reed (c. 1672–1745). Married Enoch Lovell (1670–1746) in 1697. See *History of Weymouth*, 3:394.

Ludden, James (b. 1689). Son of Benjamin Ludden (d. c. 1690) and Eunice Holbrook Ludden. See *History of Weymouth*, 3:412–13.

Manley, William (d. 1717). Lived in Weymouth between 1676 and 1687 but apparently moved to Easton, where he died. See *History of Weymouth*, 3:413–14.

Mortimer, Edward. Engaged in some manual labor in Boston and served as a scavenger twice. He also sought a license to sell strong drink in 1709, but was denied. See *A Report of the Record Commissioners*, 7:125, 203, 229; 8:27; 11:46, 91, 93.

Mountford, Jonathan. Son of Edmond Mountford and Elizabeth Mountford (d. c. 1704). He was a Boston businessman who did considerable business with James Richards. He was elected constable of Boston in 1703 and 1709, though he refused to serve the second term. He was also elected tithingman in 1707 and 1709 and clerk of the market in 1710. See *A Report of the Record Commissioners*, 8:26, 42, 46, 59–60, 69; 9:146.

Nash, Alice (c. 1685–1751). Daughter of Lieutenant Jacob and Abigail Dyer Nash. She married Captain William Reed (1682–1753) in 1708. See *History of Weymouth*, 4:570.

Nash, Benjamin (1685–1724). Son of Lieutenant Jacob Nash and Abigail Dyer Nash. He married Rebecca Tirrell of Abington in 1713. See *History of Weymouth*, 4:424.

Nash, Lieutenant Jacob (1640–1718). Married Abigail Dyer (b. 1647), daughter of Deacon Thomas Dyer (c. 1612–76), one of the most prominent men in Weymouth at the time. Jacob also became a prominent citizen of Weymouth. He served as selectman in 1681, 1684, and 1687 and as representative to the General Court in 1689 and 1690. In 1676, he contracted with the town to build a new corral in return for six pounds and the old corral. In 1682, he built a new meetinghouse in return for £280 and the old meetinghouse. See *History of Weymouth*, 2:520, 523, 527, 529–31, 537, 538, 541, 543; 3:209–10; 4:422.

Nash, James (b. 1678). Son of Lieutenant Jacob Nash and Abigail Dyer Nash. He moved to Abington in 1710. See *History of Weymouth*, 4:422.

Nash, John (1671–1749). Married Mary (d. 1739). He was the son of Lieutenant Jacob Nash and Abigail Dyer Nash. See *History of Weymouth*, 4:422–23.

Nash, Lieutenant Joseph (1669–d. after 1735). Married Phebe Marsh (1676–1728), then Hannah Sturges (d. 1734), then Hannah Vinson, widow of Samuel Vinson. Nash served on the committee to hire a schoolmaster in 1701. See *History of Weymouth*, 2:537; 4:423.

Nash, Mary (b. 1675). Daughter of Lieutenant Jacob Nash and Abigail Dyer Nash. She married Samuel Porter (d. 1725) around 1698. See *History of Weymouth*, 4:488.

Nash, Simeon. Son of Joseph Nash. He lived with his uncle Lieutenant Jacob Nash after his father died until he moved to Abington in 1715. See *History of Weymouth*, 4:422.

Nash, Thomas (1681–1724). Seventh child of Lieutenant Jacob Nash and Abigail Dyer Nash. He married Mary Jackson (b. 1696) in 1714. See *History of Weymouth*, 4:422.

Nash, Widow. Possibly Alice, the wife of Lieutenant James Nash. See *History of Weymouth*, 4:421–22.

Orcutt, Andrew (b. c. 1667). Son of William Orcutt. He was a wheelwright. Born in Scituate, he married Frances Ward (1670–1737) from Hingham. See *History of Weymouth*, 4:447.

Orcutt, Benjamin (1678–1770). Son of William Orcutt. Brother of Joseph Orcutt and Andrew Orcutt. All three brothers were born in Scituate and moved to Weymouth around 1700. Benjamin worked as a tanner and farmer in Weymouth. See *History of Weymouth*, 4:447–48.

Orcutt, Joseph (b. 1672). Son of William Orcutt. He was baptized in Scituate. He purchased land in Weymouth and lived there between 1704 and 1714. He married a woman named Sarah. See *History of Weymouth*, 4:448.

Orcutt, Sarah. Wife of Joseph Orcutt. She lived with him in Weymouth between 1704 and 1714 and had five children while living there. See *History of Weymouth*, 4:448.

Penniman, Moses. Moses was part of the large and influential Penniman family of Braintree. See Bates, *Records of the Town of Braintree*, 67, 70, 75.

Pettee, Benjamin (1687–1710). Son of Joseph Pettee (1639–92) and Sarah Whitman Pettee. He died at sea in 1710. See *History of Weymouth*, 4:461.

Pettee, James (b. 1686). Son of William Pettee and Mary Porter Pettee (1663–1746). See *History of Weymouth*, 4:461.

Pettee, John (1679–1758). Son of Joseph Pettee (1639–92) and Sarah Whitman Pettee. He prematurely took over many of his deceased father's responsibilities at age thirteen per James's daybook. See *History of Weymouth*, 4:461.

Pettee, Joseph (1677–1759). Weaver and son of Joseph Pettee (1639–92) and Sarah Whitman Pettee. See *History of Weymouth*, 4:462.

Pettee, Mary. Wife of Joseph Pettee (1677–1759). She gave birth to nine children while living in Weymouth. She apparently died before her husband. See *History of Weymouth*, 4:462.

Pettee, Nathaniel (1688–1747). Son of William Pettee (1661–1728) and Mary Porter Pettee (1663–1746). He married Mary Stowell (d. 1740). After her death, he married Ann Porter in 1741. Nathaniel inherited his father's land and house in 1728. See *History of Weymouth*, 4:461–62.

Pettee, Samuel (b. 1657). Son of William Pettee (d. 1679). He married Mary around 1685 and apparently moved to Canton. See *History of Weymouth*, 4:461.

Pettee, Thomas (1688–1714). Son of William Pettee (1661–1728), he married Mary Stowell (d. 1740) about 1714. See *History of Weymouth*, 4:460–62.

Pettee, Widow. Most likely Sarah Pettee, widow of Joseph Pettee (1639–92). See *History of Weymouth*, 4:461.

Pettee, William (1661–1728). Son of William Pettee (d. 1679). A weaver, he married Mary Porter (1663–1746) around 1685. He served on the town committee to settle a school in Weymouth in 1709 and purchased some town land in 1708. See *History of Weymouth*, 2:516, 537, 549; 4:460–62.

Phillips, John. Son of Richard Phillips and Mary Packard Phillips. He married Elizabeth about 1690. See *History of Weymouth*, 4:466–67.

Phillips, Joshua. Could be either Joshua Phillips (b. c. 1685), son of Benjamin Phillips (d. 1687) and his wife, Anne, or Joshua Phillips (b. 1689), son of Joshua Phillips (1662–90) and his wife, Amy. See *History of Weymouth*, 4:466–67.

Phillips, Mary (b. 1690). Daughter of Nicholas Phillips (1664–1751). She married Samuel Badlam in 1716. See *History of Weymouth*, 3:18; 4:467.

Phillips, Nicholas, Sr. (1664–1751). A husbandman whose estate was worth £333 15s 11d. He married Mary Phillips (1667–1749). See *History of Weymouth*, 4:467.

Phillips, Nicholas, Jr. (1697–1744). Only son of Nicholas Phillips, Sr. (1664–1751), and Mary Phillips (1667–1749). He married Judith Savil (b. 1694) in 1728. See *History of Weymouth*, 4:467–68.

Phillips, Richard (c. 1641–1695). Eldest son of Deacon Nicholas Phillips (c. 1611–72). He married Mary Packard of Bridgewater and later Elizabeth (Edson) Kingman, widow of John Kingman. In 1673, Phillips served as constable. In 1680, he became the clerk of the market and the selectmen gave him scales, weights, and measures to perform his duties. In 1683, he was elected selectman and referred to as Sergeant Phillips. Upon his death, his estate was valued at £242 11s. See *History of Weymouth*, 2:522, 525, 528; 4:465–66.

Phillips, Widow. Most likely Amy Drake (b. 1666), wife of Joshua Phillips (1662–90). See *History of Weymouth*, 4:467.

Phippeny, Widow. From Boston, she received a license to sell beer and cider in 1680. This could also be the woman James calls "mother Phippeny." See *A Report of the Record Commissioners*, 7:139.

Poole, Benjamin (b. 1682). Son of Joseph Poole and Elizabeth Shaw Poole (1655–1748). See *History of Weymouth*, 4:475.

Poole, Captain Joseph (c. 1656–1706). Married Elizabeth Shaw Poole (1655–1748), maternal cousin of James Richards and daughter of John Shaw, Sr. (d. 1704), and Alice Phillips Shaw. He called himself a carpenter and said in his will that he was apprehensive of the "near approach of death by a dangerous disease." Poole served on the committee to repair the meetinghouse in 1682. The selectmen fined him five shilling for "entertaining" Sarah Downing contrary to their orders and five shillings for each week he continued to do so. In 1704, he was elected selectman. See *History of Weymouth*, 2:527, 528, 529, 538; 4:475.

Poole, Isaac (b. c. 1650). Son of Edward Poole (d. 1664) and Sarah Pinney. His first wife was Elishama with whom he had four children. He then married Margaret. Isaac, moved to Taunton in 1708 and sold off his land in Weymouth to Joseph Green, William Hunt, and John Nash. See *History of Weymouth*, 4:475, 612.

Poole, Samuel (b. 1686). Son of Joseph Poole and Elizabeth Shaw Poole (1655–1748). He married Sarah Nash (b. 1688) in 1710 and moved to Abington. See *History of Weymouth*, 4:475–77.

Porter, John, Sr. (d. 1717). Married Deliverance Byram (c. 1638–1720). He was appointed to the committee to repair the meetinghouse in 1682. See *History of Weymouth*, 2:526; 4:486.

Porter, John, Jr. (1667–1723). A cooper whose estate was valued at £871 6s. He married a Mary or Mercy (d. 1709) in 1693 and a Margaret Ford in 1709. He was appointed to survey the town line between Weymouth and Hingham and elected selectman in 1720 and 1722. He was also known as Sergeant Porter. He was the son of John Porter, Sr., and Deliverance Byram (c. 1638–1720) and James Richards's cousin on his mother's side. See *History of Weymouth*, 2:543, 545, 547; 4:485–88.

Porter, Samuel (d. 1725). Son of John Porter, Sr. He married Mary Nash (b. 1675) in 1698 and moved to Abington in 1725. See *History of Weymouth*, 4:486–87.

Porter, Thomas (1672–1753). Only child of Thomas Porter (1650–72) and Sarah Vining Porter. He moved from Weymouth to Taunton about 1701. See *History of Weymouth*, 3:78–79; 4:487, 489.

Pratt, Brother. Must be one of the brothers of Sarah Pratt Richards (c. 1650–1727), who married James's brother John Richards (1650–95). It could be either Matthew (c. 1628–1713), John (c. 1636–1716), or Joseph (1637–1720). See *History of Weymouth*, 4:500–504.

Pratt, Ebenezer (c. 1674–1752). Married three times to Martha (d. 1720), Waitstill Washburn, and Hannah (?). Pratt received a land grant from the town of Weymouth in 1709, and in 1722 he was granted the "pew on the east side of the rate door" in the church for the fee of four pounds five shillings. See *History of Weymouth*, 2:541–46; 4:506–7.

Pratt, Ephraim (c. 1675–1748). Married Phebe (d. 1736) and inherited his father, Joseph's homestead in Weymouth. See *History of Weymouth*, 4:503–4, 508.

Pratt, Hannah (d. 1757). Wife of William Pratt (1673–1714). They married around 1700. See *History of Weymouth*, 4:505.

Pratt, Lieutenant John, Sr. (1636–1716). Son of Matthew Pratt (d. 1673) and Elizabeth Pratt. He married Mary Whitman in 1656. They had no children. See *History of Weymouth*, 4:500–503.

Pratt, John, Jr. (1663–1744). Son of Samuel Pratt (1640–79) and Hannah Rogers (d. 1715). He had three wives. See *History of Weymouth*, 4:506.

Pratt, John (b. 1668). Son of Joseph Pratt (1637–1720) and Sarah Judkins Pratt (1645–1726). He married Mercy Newcomb (1665–1721). See *History of Weymouth*, 4:503–7.

Pratt, Joseph, Sr. (1637–1720). Married Sarah Judkins (1645–1726). He was the son of Matthew (d. 1673) and Elizabeth Pratt, some of the earliest settlers in Weymouth. He was not as active as his brother John, but he did serve on the meetinghouse repair committee in 1682 and the road relocation committee in 1693. See *History of Weymouth*, 2:526–27; 4:500, 503–4.

Pratt, Joseph, Jr. (1665–1765). Married Sarah Benson of Hull with whom he had twenty children. After Sarah died, he married Anna Richards (d. 1766) in 1721. He moved to Bridgewater in 1705, where he passed away. See *History of Weymouth*, 4:507.

Pratt, Matthew, Sr. (c. 1628–1713). Married Sarah Hunt (1640–1729). He and his wife apparently became deaf and dumb due to some illness they experience toward the ends of their lives. See *History of Weymouth*, 4:501–2.

Pratt, Matthew, Jr. (1665–1746). Married Susana Porter (1665–1761) in Weymouth and moved to Abington around 1713. See *History of Weymouth*, 4:504–5.

Pratt, Micah (1691–1758). Son of Matthew Pratt (1665–1746) and Susannah Porter Pratt (1665–1761). He moved to Taunton and then to Abington. See *History of Weymouth*, 4:504–5.

Pratt, Samuel (1670–1728). Weaver. He married Patience Chard (b. 1671). He moved to Taunton around 1710. See *History of Weymouth*, 4:506.

Pratt, Thomas (1661–1744). A deacon in the church in Weymouth before moving to Braintree in 1705. See *History of Weymouth*, 4:504.

Pratt, William (1659–1713). Married Elizabeth Baker (1655–1728) of Dorchester in 1680. He moved to Dorchester in 1690, where he was ordained ruling elder of a group from Massachusetts sent to settle in South Carolina in 1695. He returned to Weymouth because he did not like the climate in South Carolina and then moved to Bridgewater in 1705. He died in Easton. See *History of Weymouth*, 4:504.

Pratt, William (1673–1714). Son of Matthew Pratt, Sr. (c. 1628–1713), married Hannah (d. 1757). See *History of Weymouth*, 4:505.

Prout, Joseph. A prominent man in Boston politics. He entered service to the town in 1687 as an overseer of the wood corders and served continuously as tithingman, constable, selectman, town treasurer, and town clerk. He held the last two positions for about fifteen years. *A Report of the Record Commissioners*, 7:192, 197, 202, 205, 211–14, 222–25, 233–37, 241–43; 8:3, 35, 41, 46, 49, 56, 59, 89, 142; 11:7, 10, 12, 18, 25, 27, 34, 39, 40, 42.

Randall, John, Sr. (1635–1717). A wheelwright who moved among Weymouth, Braintree, and Abington. He died in what is now Easton. See *History of Weymouth*, 4:559.

Randall, John, Jr. (1673–1730). Married Susannah Benson (d. 1761) about 1696. He had special skill as a wheelwright. See *History of Weymouth*, 4:560.

Randall, Thomas (c. 1638–1711). Married Joan Drake (b. 1628) and then Hannah Briggs, widow of Clement Briggs. Randall lived in Weymouth until around 1685 and then moved to Taunton North Purchase (Easton), where he died. See *History of Weymouth*, 4:560.

Reed, Hannah (b. 1689). Daughter of Thomas Reed, Sr. (c. 1645–1719), and Sarah Bicknell Reed (c. 1651–1719). She married John Hunt (b. 1687) in 1714. See *History of Weymouth*, 4:569–70.

Reed, John (1679–1757). Married Sarah Whitmarsh (b. 1694) in 1715. Reed was the son of James Richards's cousin Sarah Bicknell Reed (c. 1651–1719). See *History of Weymouth*, 4:571.

Reed, Mary (1672–1745). Thomas Reed's (c. 1645–1719) second child and James Richards's niece. She married Enoch Lovell in 1697. See *History of Weymouth*, 3:394; 4:570.

Reed, Phillip (b. 1674). James says that Phillip Reed was from Braintree, but a Phillip Reed was born to Phillip and Hannah Reed in 1674 in Weymouth. See *History of Weymouth*, 1:250.

Reed, Samuel (1681–1739). Son of Thomas Reed (c 1645–1719). He married Abigail White (b. 1682) and lived in West Abington near the Weymouth town line. They apparently had no children. See *History of Weymouth*, 4:572.

Reed, Sister. Probably Sarah Bicknell Reed (c. 1651–1719), wife of Thomas Reed (c. 1645–1719). See *History of Weymouth*, 4:569–70.

Reed, Thomas (c. 1645–1719). Married Sarah Bicknell (c. 1651–1719). Reed served on the committee to restore the old meetinghouse in 1682 and the committee to hire a schoolmaster for the town in 1701. See *History of Weymouth*, 2:526; 4:569–70.

Reed, Thomas, Jr. (1671–1719). Son of Thomas Reed (c. 1645–1719) and nephew of James Richards. Reed, Jr., married Hannah Randall (1680–1767). When he died, his estate was valued at £216 16s. See *History of Weymouth*, 4:571.

Reed, William (c. 1650–c. 1706). Married Esther Tomson (d. 1705) of Middleboro in 1675. He became a fence viewer in 1677 to inspect the fences "lying beyond the river." In 1681, 1687, and 1696, he was elected selectman. In 1693, he worked on the committee assigned to reconstruct the town roads, and in 1699 and 1701, he served on the committee to build a school and hire a schoolmaster. See *History of Weymouth*, 2:526, 530, 533, 535–37; 4:569.

Reed, Sergeant William (1688–1729). Son of Thomas Reed (c. 1645–1719) and Sarah Bicknell Reed (c. 1651–1719). He married Jane Torrey (d. 1730) in 1716. See *History of Weymouth*, 4:572.

Richards, Benjamin (1683–1733). Oldest child of James Richards (1658–1711) and Ruth Bicknell Richards (1660–1729). He married Joanna Hunt (d. 1712). Benjamin was only about ten years old when he began being hired out to work for pay. He built on the estate his father left him so that when he passed away in 1734, he owned over 103 acres of land and had acquired prestigious material possessions including five gold rings and a chest of drawers. His estate was valued at over £2,705. See Suffolk County Probate, Record Book, 17:216–17, 333; 32:64–65; 36:101–2; *History of Weymouth*, 4:591.

Richards, Edward. No relation to James Richards, Edward lived in Boston and was appointed hog reeve in 1708 and fence viewer in 1726. See *A Report of the Record Commissioner,* 8:46, 203.

Richards, James (b. 1680). Son of Joseph Richards (c. 1653–96) and his first wife, Susan Richards (d. 1682). See *History of Weymouth,* 4:590.

Richards, John (1650–95). James Richards's older brother. He married Sarah Pratt (c.1650–1727) in 1670. John served as a fence viewer (1674–75, 1675–76, 1681–82, 1682–83, 1683–84), selectman (1685–86), tithingman (1686–87), constable (1687–88), and waywarden (1686–87). When he died, his estate was valued at £202 13d. See Weymouth Town Book, 1:128, 130, 149–50, 153, 158, 171–72, 174, 178; Suffolk County Probate, Record Book, 11:162.

Richards, Joseph (c. 1653–96). James Richards's older brother. Joseph married Susan (1654–82). After her death, he married Sarah (b. c. 1657) with whom he had five children. He served as fence viewer (1681–82, 1687–68, 1693–94), tithingman (1682–83), and constable (1686–87). Joseph left twenty acres of land with an estate worth £156, 3s. See *History of Weymouth,* 4:589–90; 1:153, 157, 172, 180, 195; Suffolk County Probate, Record Book, 11:159–60.

Richards, Joseph, Jr. (1676–1710). Son of Joseph Richards and Susan Richards. He married Anna Carver (1675–1766) about 1700. See *History of Weymouth,* 4:590–91.

Richards, Mary (b. 1697). Daughter of James Richards and Ruth Bicknell Richards. James noted the birth of Mary in his daybook, and her birth was recorded in the Weymouth town records, but she does not appear in James's 1710 will, so she apparently died as a child. See *History of Weymouth,* 1:258, 4:590–91.

Richards, Ruth (c. 1685–1766). Daughter of James Richards and Ruth Bicknell Richards. See *History of Weymouth,* 3:395; 4:590–91.

Richards, Ruth Bicknell (1660–1729). Daughter of John Bicknell (c. 1623–79) and Mary Porter Bicknell (c. 1638–c. 1693). She married James Richards in 1682, and they had three children: Benjamin (1683–1733), Ruth (c. 1685–1766), and Mary (b. 1697). See *History of Weymouth,* 3:78–79; 4:590–91.

Richards, Sarah Pratt (c. 1650–1727). Wife of John Richards. She survived John and administered his estate. See *History of Weymouth,* 4:590, Suffolk County Probate, Record Book, 2:162.

Richards, Sarah. Second wife of Joseph Richards (c. 1653–96). James also called her Sarah, Sr. See *History of Weymouth,* 4:590.

Richards, Sister. Possibly Sarah Pratt Richards, wife of John Richards; Sarah, second wife of Joseph Richards (c. 1653–96); or Mary Williams Richards, wife of William Richards, Jr. (c. 1656–83). See *History of Weymouth,* 4:589–90.

Richards, William, Sr. (d. 1682). James Richards's father. William immigrated to Plymouth in the 1630s, moved to Scituate in 1635, and to Weymouth by 1640, where he received several land grants. He married Grace Shaw around 1650. Together they had five sons: John (1650–95); Joseph (c. 1653–96); William, Jr. (1656–83); James (1658–1711); and Benjamin (1660–83). William received a land grant of some twenty-five acres in Weymouth about 1643 and another of twenty acres in 1663. He served as town constable (1660–61), hayward (1663–64), and fence viewer (1665–66, 1669–70). He was appointed tithingman in 1682 but died before he could complete his term. In 1645, he was exempt from the regulation to secure his hogs and in 1680 received another grant of land that had previously belonged to John Kings, Jr. In 1662, he chose to pay a fine rather than appear to mend the highway as ordered by the selectmen. He prospered in Weymouth. Upon his death in 1682, he left thirty-eight acres of land and a total value in property of £144 15s. In his will, he gave three pounds each to his sons John, Joseph, William, and Benjamin. The rest he gave to James after his widow, Grace, died on condition that James care for her until her death. See *History of Weymouth*, 4:589; Morse, *Genealogical Register*, 71; Weymouth Town Book, 1:25, 36, 38–39, 79, 92, 101, 114, 163; Suffolk County Probate, Record Book, 6:38–39; 9:83–84.

Richards, William (1685–1712). Son of John Richards and Sarah Pratt Richards, and brother of Bathsheba Richards (1674–1752). William married Experience Drake (b. 1683) in 1706. See *History of Weymouth*, 4:590.

Richards, Widow. Mary Williams Richards, the widow of William Richards, Jr. (c. 1656–83). See *History of Weymouth*, 4:590.

Ripley, Josiah (1667–1743). Born in Hingham, he came to Weymouth around 1690. See *History of Weymouth*, 2:948–49; 4:602–3.

Ripley, Mary (b. 1695). Daughter of Josiah Ripley (1667–1743) and Joanna Ripley (d. 1743). She married Samuel Green (d. 1724) in 1717. See *History of Weymouth*, 3:250; 4:602–3.

Robbison, George. Son of George and Elizabeth Robbison of Boston. He married Sarah Maverick in 1698. See *A Report of the Record Commissioners*, 9:62, 152, 237, 244.

Roberts, John. A boat builder from Boston who served as hog reeves in 1684 and 1718 and constable in 1694. He refused appointment as a constable in 1711 and requested a license to sell alcohol that was rejected in 1714. *A Report of the Record Commissioners*, 7:165, 217; 8:77, 129; 11:82, 121, 211, 213, 219.

Rogers, Elder John (1638–1709). Son of Deacon John Rogers (d. 1660), he married Mary Bates (d. 1683), daughter of Elder Edward Bates and Susannah Bates. Rogers was the "ruling elder of First Church in Weymouth." In 1665, he was elected constable and in 1679 and 1693 selectman. In 1682, he served on the meetinghouse repair committee. In 1694, he served on the board of assessors to assess town rates and protect the town from unjust country rates. In 1704, he was titled Elder Rogers and served on the committee to draft new bylaws for the board of selectmen. See *History of Weymouth*, 2:515, 525, 527, 533, 534, 538; 4:605.

Savil, Benjamin. Lived in Braintree and served as selectman there. See Bates, *Records of the Town of Braintree*, 26, 29, 30, 31, 37, 40, 47, 49, 52, 56, 59, 60, 67, 71, 72, 74, 77, 83.

Shaw, Abigail (b. 1672). Married Richard Davenport. She died sometime between 1700 and 1707. See *History of Weymouth*, 3:195.

Shaw, Abraham (1657–1706). Son of John Shaw, Sr. (1630–1704) and Alice Phillips Shaw. See *History of Weymouth*, 4:612.

Shaw, Abraham (b. 1685). Son of John Shaw, Jr. (1653–1718). See *History of Weymouth*, 4:613.

Shaw, Grace (1621–c. 1697). James Richard's mother. She was baptized in Halifax, England, on August 15, 1621. She came to Massachusetts with her father, Abraham Shaw, who settled in Dedham and worked as a clothier. She married William Richards (d. 1682). See *History of Weymouth*, 4:611.

Shaw, John, Sr. (1630–1704). James Richards's maternal uncle, the brother of his mother, Grace Shaw Richards. He married Alice Phillips (1632–85). In 1664, Shaw was appointed to survey the Hingham town line. In 1667, he was elected constable and fence viewer. In 1681, he was elected selectman and joined the committee for the repair of the old meetinghouse. See *History of Weymouth*, 2:514, 517, 524, 526, 527; 4:612.

Shaw, John, Jr. (1653–1718). Also known as Deacon Shaw because he was the deacon of First Church. A weaver, he married Hannah Whitmarsh (1661–c. 1735). He was elected selectman in 1709 and 1715. See *History of Weymouth*, 2:541, 543; 4:612–13.

Shaw, Joseph (1643–1704). Son of Joseph Shaw (1618–54) and Mary. He married Sarah (d. 1716). See *History of Weymouth*, 4:612.

Shaw, Joseph (1664–1718). Son of John Shaw (1630–1704) and Alice Phillips. He married Judith Whitmarsh (1669–1760) and moved to Bridgewater about 1696. See *History of Weymouth*, 4:612–13.

Shaw, Mary (b. 1691). Daughter of John Shaw (1653–1718) and Hannah Whitmarsh Shaw (1661–c. 1735). She married Jacob Lovell of Barnstable in 1713. See *History of Weymouth*, 4:613.

Shaw, Nicholas (1662–1717). Married Deborah Whitmarsh (b. 1659), daughter of Nicholas and Hannah Whitmarsh. In 1707, Shaw purchased land from the town and in 1715 was appointed, along with John Porter, to survey the town line between Weymouth and Hingham. See *History of Weymouth*, 2:540, 543; 4:614–15.

Smith, James, Sr. Settled in Weymouth around 1639 and had four children there. See *History Weymouth*, 4:632.

Smith, James, Jr. Married his second wife, Mary Brandon, at Weymouth in 1659; they had five children. See *History of Weymouth*, 4:633.

Speer, Samuel. A prominent resident of Braintree where he served as constable, tithingman, and selectman. See Bates, *Records of the Town of Braintree*, 26, 30, 37, 46, 53, 56, 59, 60, 63, 77.

Taylor, John (c. 1646–1714). Received a couple land grants from the town of Weymouth and was appointed to dig graves in 1667. See *History of Weymouth*, 2:506, 512, 513, 516, 519; 4:641.

Thatcher, Peter (1677–1739). Son of Thomas Thatcher (c. 1645–86). Thatcher "graduated from Harvard College in 1696 and served as minister of the North Parish of Weymouth from 1707–1718." See *History of Weymouth*, 4:642.

Thomas, Lydia Whitman (c. 1678–1757). Married Captain John Thomas (d. 1714) in 1701 after apparently serving him for several years as a maid. See *History of Weymouth*, 4:649–50.

Tirrell, Gideon, Sr. (1664–1730). Born in Boston and died in Weymouth. In 1693, the selectmen of Weymouth awarded Tirrell land along the river in the town commons to set up a fulling mill and one acre of land in damages for land seized to relocate the town's roads. In 1704, he served on the school committee with James Richards. Tirrell received further grants of land from the town in 1707 and 1709. In 1726, 1728, and 1729, he was elected representative to the General Court. See *History of Weymouth*, 2:533, 538, 541, 551, 553, 554, 555; 4:656.

Tirrell, Gideon, Jr. (1693–1766). Son of Gideon Tirrell (1664–1730). See *History of Weymouth*, 4:656–57.

Tirrell, William (1658–1727). Moved to Weymouth with his father, also named William, in 1672. He married Abigail Pratt (b. 1662) in 1680 and moved to Abington in 1705, where he lived until his death. See *History of Weymouth*, 4:655–56.

Torrey, Lieutenant John (1673–1730). Married Mary Symmes (1678–1758). Torrey's estate was valued at £1,069 16s 7d. He represented Weymouth at the General Court in 1719 and became a selectman in 1720, 1722, 1723, and 1728. In 1722, he joined a committee to survey the town. In 1728, along with John Randall, he was authorized to prosecute all trespassers who cut wood on the town commons. After his death in 1730, he was replaced as town clerk by Joseph Torrey. See *History of Weymouth*, 2:545, 546, 549, 553, 554; 4:679–80.

Torrey, Jonathan (c. 1654–1718). A husbandman, he married Ruth Fry (c. 1650–1724). He should not be confused with Lieutenant John Torrey (1673–1729). He was the son of Captain William Torrey (1608–90). In 1690, he was assigned the responsibility of keeping track of disorderly youths in the galleries of the Weymouth meetinghouse and reporting their names. See *History of Weymouth*, 2:531; 4:679.

Torrey, Joseph (c. 1679–1723). Son of William Torrey (1638–1718) and Deborah Torrey (d. 1729). He married Elizabeth in 1706. See *History of Weymouth*, 4:679–80.

Torrey, Joshua (1690–1776). Son of Jonathan Torrey (c. 1654–1718). He married Jane Lovell (d. 1752) in 1717. See *History of Weymouth*, 4:681.

Torrey, Micajah (1643–1711). Son of Captain William Torrey (1608–90). He married Susana (d. 1720). In 1682, the town compensated him for taking land for a new road. He served as selectman in 1682. See *History of Weymouth*, 2:526, 539.

Torrey, Reverend Samuel (1632–1707). Married to Mary Rawson (d. 1692). He served as minister of Hull between 1656 and 1664 and minister of First Parish of Weymouth between 1664 and 1707. Torrey replaced Rev. Thomas Thatcher in Weymouth and was widely recognized as an able minister. In 1684, the town granted him some land and in 1686 allowed him to fence in the town burying yard. In 1697, he was allotted £106 for his maintenance. See *History of Weymouth*, 2:497, 514, 529, 530; 4:678.

Torrey, Samuel (b. 1676). Son of William Torrey (1638–1718). See *History of Weymouth*, 4:678.

Torrey, William, Jr. (1638–1718). Son of Captain William Torrey (1608–90). He married Deborah (d. 1729) about 1668. He served as constable in 1672 and was appointed to investigate "houses of entertainment" in Weymouth in 1676. He served as a fence viewer in 1677. See *History of Weymouth*, 2:520, 523–24; 4:678–79.

Tower, Benjamin (b. 1686). Son of Benjamin Tower and Deborah Tower of Hingham. He married at Weymouth Margaret with whom he had three children. Shortly after she died in 1717, he moved to Scituate where he married Bethiah Woodward (b. 1685). See *History of Weymouth*, 4:696.

Townsend, Solomon. Married Elizabeth Jarvis in 1698 in Boston. In 1710, he was harboring a woman named Widow Ranger from Wrentham, and the selectmen of Boston ordered her to be removed from the town. He did some roadwork and boundary work for Boston before he was made clerk of the market in 1712. See *A Report of the Record Commissioners*, 9:123, 127, 218, 244; 8:95.

Trufant, Morris (d. 1740). Married Mary Bicknell (1678–1764). He came to Weymouth around 1700. See *History of Weymouth*, 4:697.

Turner, Jacob. Lived in Weymouth from 1693 to 1723. He married Jane Vining (b. 1672), daughter of John Vining and his second wife, Mary Reed Vining. Jane was the sister of John Vining, Sr. (1662–1737), who married Naomi Bicknell (1657–1719), and so would have been James Richards's sister-in-law. See *History of Weymouth*, 4:702, 706.

Turner, Sarah (1665–1739). Daughter of John Turner and Ann James of Scituate. She married Ichabod Holbrook (1662–1718) about 1688. See *History of Weymouth*, 3:271.

Tyler, Jacob. Lived near William Richards in 1682. See *History of Weymouth*, 2:526.

Vining, Benjamin (b. 1684). Son of John Vining (1636–85) and Mary Reed Vining (d. 1717). See *History of Weymouth*, 4:705–6.

Vining, John (1636–85). Married Margaret Read (1636–1659) and then Mary Reed (d. 1717). He was active in Weymouth politics. He served as fence viewer in 1660, constable in 1666, selectman in 1673, and on the committee to repair the old meetinghouse in 1682. See *History of Weymouth*, 2:509, 515, 516, 522, 526, 540; 4:705–6.

Vining, John, Sr. (1662–1737). Son of John Vining (1636–85) and Mary Reed (d. 1717). James Richards often refers to him as Brother Vining because he married Naomi Bicknell (1657–1719) around 1686. Naomi was the daughter of John Bicknell and Mary Shaw, James's maternal aunt. Their daughter Mary (1690–1718) married Ephraim Richards, James Richards's nephew (son of his brother John). That made her simultaneously Richards's cousin, Ruth Richards's half-sister, and a niece by marriage. Vining served as selectman in 1715, 1716, 1726, 1729, 1730, and 1735. See *History of Weymouth*, 2:543, 544, 551, 554, 555, 557, 558; 4:591, 706.

Vining, John, Jr. (1687–1746). Married Elizabeth Richards (c. 1682–after 1746), who is often listed as the daughter of James Richards. I have been unable to confirm the existence of Elizabeth as the daughter of James. She does not appear in his will. See *History of Weymouth*, 4:590–91, 706–7.

Vining, Widow. Mary Reed Vining (d. 1717), wife of John Vining (1636–85). See *History of Weymouth*, 4:705–6.

Vinson, Ebenezar (1684–1764). Married Jane Drake (1687–1754). He was a yeoman farmer and served on the committee to distribute sixty thousand pounds of credit to be divided among the inhabitants of Weymouth in accordance with their taxes in 1728. See *History of Weymouth*, 2:553; 4:716–17.

Vinson, John, Sr. James Richards referred to him as Uncle Vinson because John's son Samuel Vinson married Hannah, Ruth Bicknell's sister. John came to Weymouth before 1675 and married Sarah about that time. See *History of Weymouth*, 4:715–16.

Vinson, John, Jr. (c. 1676–1756). Son of John Vinson, Sr. Married Sarah Kingman, daughter of Thomas Kingman and Rebecca Kingman about 1696. See *History of Weymouth*, 4:715.

Vinson, Samuel (1680–1731). Son of John Vinson, Sr. He married Hannah Bicknell, sister of Ruth Bicknell. See *History of Weymouth*, 4:715–16.

Vinson, Thomas (b. c. 1628). Married Martha Shaw (1632–1704), the sister of Grace Shaw, James Richards's mother. See *History of Weymouth*, 4:611.

Webb, Elisha. Married Lydia Seottow in 1692 in Boston. He was appointed clerk of the market in 1701, constable in 1702, and sealer of leather in 1708 and 1709. See *A Report of the Record Commissioner*, 9:236, 11:9, 30, 32, 46, 60.

White, Benjamin (b. 1684). Son of Ebenezer White (1648–1703) and Hannah Phillips White. He married Ruth Reed (d. 1724). See *History of Weymouth*, 4:733–34.

White, Joseph. James may refer to one of the Joseph Whites born in Weymouth to Thomas White, Sr., or Ebenezer White, but it is impossible to tell. See *History of Weymouth*, 4:731–33.

White, Lieutenant Ebenezer (1648–1703). Married Hannah Phillips, daughter of Deacon Nicholas Phillips (c. 1611–72), in 1671. Their first child, Ebenezer (1672–1756), graduated from Harvard College in 1692. Ebenezer, Sr., was elected selectman of Weymouth in 1687 and 1691. He served as selectman until 1693, when he was put on a committee to reconstruct the roads of the town. He was elected as selectman again in 1694 and 1696. James referred to him as Colonel White in his daybook. See *History of Weymouth*, 2:530, 532, 533, 535; 4:464–65, 732–33.

White, Mary Pratt. Wife of Thomas White, Sr. (d. 1706). See *History of Weymouth*, 4:732.

White, Captain Samuel (1642–99). Married Mary Dyer (1641–1716). He was elected constable in Weymouth in 1666. In 1673, the selectmen hired him to clapboard the side of the meetinghouse and lay a new pine floor. He also served as deputy to the General Court in 1679. James referred to him as Mr. White, Sr. See *History of Weymouth*, 2:516, 522; 4:732.

White, Thomas, Sr. (d. 1706). Married Mary Pratt. His estate was worth £444 7s 6d. He became constable in 1673 and fence viewer in 1677. See *History of Weymouth*, 2:522–25; 4:732.

White, Thomas, Jr. (b. 1675). Son of Thomas White, Sr. He lived at least some of the time in Braintree at Monatiquot. It is difficult to separate in the town records Thomas White, Sr., and Thomas White, Jr., from the first Thomas White to come to Weymouth. Possibly a glazier. See *History of Weymouth*, 4:732–33.

White, Widow, or "Mrs. Snr. White." Possibly Mary Dyer White (1641–1716), wife of Captain Samuel White, whom James referred to as Samuel White, Sr. Or it could be Mary Pratt White, wife of Thomas White, Sr. (d. 1706). See *History of Weymouth*, 4:732.

White, Widow, Jr. Possibly Mary White (d. 1716), widow of Captain Samuel White (c. 1642–99), or Mary Pratt White, widow of Thomas White (d. 1706). The fact that James uses the phrase "junior" suggests that it is probably Mary Pratt White. See *History of Weymouth*, 4:732.

Whitman, Abiah (c. 1646–1728). Married Mary Ford (d. 1715). He served as constable in 1682 and was elected selectman in 1683, 1687, and 1691. See *History of Weymouth*, 2:526, 528, 530, 532; 4:754.

Whitman, John, Jr. (1668–1751). Married Dorothy Pratt (d. 1733). It is impossible to untangle John Whitman, Sr.'s activities from those of John Whitman, Jr., in the town records. See *History of Weymouth*, 4:752–54.

Whitman, John (b. 1681). Son of Abiah Whitman (1646–1728) and Mary Ford Whitman (d. 1715), who lived in North Purchase. He later settled in Easton. See *History of Weymouth*, 4:754.

Whitmarsh, Ebenezer (1658–1718). Married Christian Bayley (1661–1732). He moved to Abington, where he died. His son Ebenezer (b. 1688) was his second son of that name. The first died at a young age. Ebenezer, Jr., also moved to Abington. See *History of Weymouth*, 4:760.

Whitmarsh, Ezra (1670–1754). Married Bathsheba Richards (1674–1752), daughter of John Richards (c. 1650–95) and Sara Richards in Boston by Cotton Mather. Whitmarsh was elected selectman of Weymouth in 1715, 1720, 1721, and 1726. He worked on the committee to hire a minister in 1719, the committee to distribute loans from the General Court to the men of Weymouth in 1721, the committee to survey the town in 1722, the committee to create a passage for the fish into Whitman's pond, and the committee to create lawful deed of the fishway through the mill dam for the town in 1736. In 1722, he went to the General Court as the representative of Weymouth in a case regarding the creation of a new township. See *History of Weymouth*, 2:540–41, 543, 545–47, 550, 551, 553, 554, 556; 4:760.

Whitmarsh, John. This could either be John Whitmarsh, Sr. (d. 1709), or his son John Whitmarsh, Jr. (b. 1655). They were both alive in July 1709, when James recorded his transactions with Whitmarsh. John, Sr., died in November or December 1709. See *History of Weymouth*, 4:759–60.

Whitmarsh, Mary (1663–1715). Daughter of John Whitmarsh (d. 1709) and Sarah Harding Whitmarsh. See *History of Weymouth*, 3:23; 4:759.

Whitmarsh, Nicholas. Married Hannah Reed in Weymouth in 1658. In 1663, he had fifteen acres in twenty-seven lots. He received another land grant in 1682. See *History of Weymouth*, 2:513, 526.

Whitmarsh, Samuel (1665–1718). Married Hannah Pratt (b. 1670). He moved to Dighton about 1710. See *History of Weymouth*, 4:761.

Willard, Daniel. Both he and his wife appear in the daybook. They may have lived in Braintree. See Bates, *Records of the Town of Braintree*, 47.

Appendix B

Glossary of Terms

Alum. A mineral salt, sometimes combined with potash, that is used in dying and tanning animal skins and in some medicines. See *Oxford English Dictionary,* s.v. "alum"; Worcester, *A Universal and Critical Dictionary*, s.v. "alum."

Baize. A coarse woolen or cotton cloth used as a liner and for curtains. In warmer climates it was used for clothing such as ponchos and petticoats. It was commonly used for clothing in Britain. See Worcester, *A Universal and Critical Dictionary*, s.v. "baize"; *Oxford English Dictionary,* s.v. "baize."

Beach peas. An edible vining plant that grows on sandy or stony seashores. It produces a pod with tiny seeds that can be eaten raw when ripe or cooked.

Calico. A type of printed cotton cloth originating in Calicut, India. See Worcester, *A Universal and Critical Dictionary*, s.v. "calico."

Camlet. A thin cloth made of wool and silk. See Bailey, *An Universal Etymological English Dictionary*, s.v. "camlet."

Cards. Stiff brushes used to disentangle, clean, and align wool fibers in preparation for spinning the wool into thread.

Caster hat. A beaver hat. See Worcester, *A Universal and Critical Dictionary*, s.v. "castor."

Chadern. Appears to be either a form of measurement or a type of container in which coal was shipped.

Clapboard. A thin board used as siding on the exterior of houses. See Worcester, *A Universal and Critical Dictionary*, s.v. "clapboard."

Cock. A conical heap of hay. See *Oxford English Dictionary,* s.v. "cock."

Cock pin. In flintlock muskets, a cock pin was passed through a hole in the lock-plate, which allowed the cock or hammer to be held at half-cock. Eventually, this system was replaced by notches in the tumbler, which held the cock at half- and full cock. See Lenk et al., *The Flintlock*, 10.

Constable. Next in authority and importance to the selectmen, constables announced town meetings, "had charge of highways, levied fines, . . . collected rates, assisted tythingmen," and even walked before funeral processions. Service as a constable became so onerous that the men of Weymouth began trying to avoid it. So the selectmen began imposing a five-pound fee for refusal to serve, as stipulated by provincial law. See Hart, *Commonwealth History of Massachusetts*, 114; Fearing, *Weymouth Town Government*, 18; Weymouth Town Book, 1:186, 188, 189, 193–94; *The Acts and Resolves,* 66–67.

Crickthatch. Grass lands used for thatching roofs. "Towns along coastlines set aside certain parts of thatch banks in the marshes, as a supply for thatching houses." See Dow, *Everyday Life*, 19.

Crooking. Cutting grass or grain with a hooked stick in one hand and scythe in the other. This was done to allow workers to hold the grain or grass with the stick and cut it safely without getting their hands in the way of the scythe.

Current New England Money. In an attempt to overcome the scarcity of specie in the colony, the Massachusetts General Court began to coin its own currency in silver shillings and pence stamped with "N.E." for New England. These easily counterfeited coins were soon superseded in 1652 by the "pine tree" and "oak tree" coins, so named because of the images imprinted on them. They were coined in shillings, sixpence, and threepence. See Dow, *Everyday Life*, 167–68.

Damask. A type of woven cloth from Damascus. This cloth was originally made of silk and flax but later of cotton and wool. It is identified by flower designs either imprinted or woven into the cloth. See Worcester, *A Universal and Critical Dictionary*, s.v. "damask."

Double-ten nails. Probably refers to double-headed nails that were three inches long.

Drugget. Woolen fabric or wool mixed with silk used to make clothing. See Dow, *Everyday Life*, 74.

Duck. A strong canvas cloth made of hemp, linen, or cotton. See Worcester, *A Universal and Critical Dictionary*, s.v. "duck."

English hay. The practice of allowing native grasses to grow in fields or meadows before harvesting it.

Fanning. The process of winnowing threshed grain in preparation for storage or grinding. It was done using a basket to toss the threshed grain into the air so that the wind would carry away the chaff and other impurities such as stones, straw, dirt, weed seeds, or light immature seeds.

Fence viewer. Fence viewers enjoyed considerable authority in a society so dependent on livestock. As the land came under private ownership and domesticated livestock proliferated, the need to restrain animals from despoiling a neighbor's crops forced towns to name fence viewers to walk boundaries, set up markers, and enforce fencing regulations. In 1655, the General Court ordered the towns to create standing orders regarding fencing. Later that year, the Weymouth town selectmen ordered all grain fields and meadows to be fenced. See Fearing, *Weymouth Town Government*, 13; Russell, *A Long, Deep Furrow*, 106; Weymouth Town Book, 1:41, 49, 64, 66, 67, 175, 211.

Ferry Field. James purchased thirty acres of land near the ferry point on the Fore River, which he referred to as the Ferry Field. See Suffolk County Probate, Record Book, 17:333–34.

Filleting. A type of woven binding tape or ribbon. See *Oxford English Dictionary,* s.v. "filleting."

French-heel shoes. The term refers to large square heels popular for both men and women during the seventeenth and eighteenth centuries. High heels served as indicators of status in a hierarchical society. Riello, *A Foot in the Past*, 62, 205.

Fustian. A thick, durable cloth made of cotton and flax.

Glazier. A colonial glazier cut glass, glazed pottery, and even paper. See Bailey, *An Universal Etymological English Dictionary*, s.v. "glazier."

Gooseneck. Apparently refers to the iron hook affixed to a broom used onboard ships. See Worcester, *A Universal and Critical Dictionary*, s.v. "gooseneck."

Grape Islands. Fifty-four-acre island that sits just off the Weymouth town coast at Easterneck in Hingham Harbor. It was cultivated during colonial times and used as a source of stone. It became the site of a short engagement in 1775 between the colonials and British forces.

Hobby sheep. A ewe.

Hogsbutt. Two hogsheads or about 126 gallons.

Hogshead. A unit of liquid measure equal to sixty-three gallons; also a barrel. Worcester, *A Universal and Critical Dictionary*, s.v. "hogshead."

Hop. The flowering part of a plant used to add flavor to brewed malted alcoholic drinks. It became a highly profitable plant for New England farmers to grow after the 1630s. See Worcester, *A Universal and Critical Dictionary*, s.v. "hop"; McWilliams, "Brewing Beer," 552.

Hopple or hobble. A rope used to tie an animal's feet so as to restrict their movement. See Bailey, *An Universal Etymological English Dictionary*, s.v. "hopple."

Indian corn. Refers to maize to distinguish it from other European grains, called simply "corn." The term is still occasionally used in New England.

Jug. A "common pasture or meadow." See Bailey, *An Universal Etymological English Dictionary*, s.v. "jug."

Kersey. A coarse cloth made from long woolen fibers and usually ribbed. See *Oxford English Dictionary*, s.v. "kersey"; Worcester, *A Universal and Critical Dictionary*, s.v. "kersey."

Lamp oil. Possibly refined spermaceti oil.

Lean-to. A type of shed or an outbuilding whose rafters lean against a larger building. Lean-tos were often built on the backs of houses for summer cooking. See Worcester, *A Universal and Critical Dictionary*, s.v. "lean-to."

Licorice. A sweet-tasting root of the plant *Glycyrrhiza glabra*. It can be powdered or its juice can be evaporated and used to flavor drinks and make candy. Worcester, *A Universal and Critical Dictionary*, s.v. "licorice"; *Oxford English Dictionary*, s.v. "licorice."

Maile. A travel bag for carrying letters or other items. See Bailey, *An Universal Etymological English Dictionary*, s.v. "maile."

Malt. A grain, most frequently barely, which is soaked and germinated and then dried in a kiln. It is used to make beer, whiskey, and vinegar. Worcester, *A Universal and Critical Dictionary*, s.v. "malt."

Mate. An officer on a ship.

Monatiquot River. Flows into the Weymouth Fore River. It is spelled variously in the Braintree records Manatiquod, Menatiquod, and Menaticut. Constables were assigned specifically to this area. See Bates, *Records of the Town of Braintree*, 39, 40, 46, 52.

Mulata. A woman of mixed African and European descent.

Muslin. A fine cotton or linen cloth originally made in India. Worcester, *A Universal and Critical Dictionary*, s.v. "muslin."

Mutton Lane. A small lane southeast of Whitman's Pond.

Nantasket. A settlement on a chain of islands connected by sandbars that forms the eastern boundary of Hingham Bay. It was one of the earliest settlements in Massachusetts and was named after the tribe that lived there.

Neckcloth. Men wore different kinds of neckcloths such as cravats or socks. They could be made of linen, cotton, or silk, and they could be ruffled and tied in the front or plain. They could also be of many different colors. Neckcloths were the forerunners to modern ties. See Dow, *Everyday Life*, 80.

North Purchase. The 1668 purchase of land north of Taunton, which included the towns of Easton, Mansfield, and Norton.

Oakum. A fibrous and tarred caulking used to pack between the timbers of wooden ships to make them waterproof. Oakum was often made by unraveling old rope and soaking it in pine tar.

Osnaburg or osenberg. A coarse, plain cloth made from flax thread or yarn in Osnabrück, Germany.

Paper bills. Also called "charter bill," "colony bill," "paper money," or "province bill." In 1690, the General Court issued the first paper money in promissory notes of ten shillings, one pound, and five pounds. It took about a decade for paper money to catch on. Within the first year of their issue, they lost as much as thirty percent of their value, but they eventually became the most important medium of exchange. See Dow, *Everyday Life*, 172; Newell, *From Dependency to Independence*, 129, 133; McCusker, *Money and Exchange*, 133.

Petticoat stuff. The word "stuff" refers to thin woolen cloth with a slight texture often used as a lining. Petticoat stuff would be the lining on the inside of the petticoat. See Worcester, *A Universal and Critical Dictionary*, s.v. "stuff"; Bailey, *An Universal Etymological English Dictionary*, s.v. "stuff."

Piece of eight. Spanish coin valued in England at four shillings six pence. After 1687, Massachusetts set its value at six shillings, the same as the old Pine Tree shilling, thus inflating the value of the coins. James Richards consistently valued a piece of eight at six shillings. See Davisson, "Essex Country Price Trends," 146–48; McCusker, *Money and Exchange*, 132.

Pigeon shot. Shot made up of small balls used to shoot birds while in flight.

Piggins. A small wooden vessel used to hold liquids. See Bailey, *An Universal Etymological English Dictionary*, s.v. "piggins."

Pinions. Probably refers to bird wings or wing feathers. The other contemporary meaning was the teeth in the gears of a mechanism such as a clock. See Bailey, *An Universal Etymological English Dictionary*, s.v. "pinions."

"Plowshare mold and the iron between them." Plows with two moldboards turned up the earth on either side of the plow. The iron was the piece that attached the two moldboards to the sharp chisel in the front, which actually cut into the earth. Early moldboards were made of wood, and some had sheets of metal tacked to them to protect the wood. See Russell, *A Long, Deep Furrow*, 21, 24, 52, 102–3.

Pluck. The heart, liver, and lungs of an animal slaughtered for food. Worcester, *A Universal and Critical Dictionary*, s.v. "pluck" and "lights."

Quince. A tree-born fruit that looks like a pear with a rich yellow skin.

Quire. Quire refers to a small booklet of four sheets of paper folded so as to make eight leaves (usually called a "signature" today). It could contain printed material such as a small poem. See *Oxford English Dictionary,* s.v. "quire."

Rates. Taxes or fees payable by townsmen. These rates could be for county rates or taxes set by and payable to the crown or minister's rates to pay the minister's salary. The selectmen of the town could also collect town rates to pay for the expenses necessary for the upkeep of town properties, roads, meetinghouses, education, and care of the poor.

Romal. A silk or cotton handkerchief. See Dow, *Everyday Life*, 80.

Rose Hill. A small hill on James Richards's land west of the Great Hill.

Rundlet. "A cask for liquors from 3 to 20 gallons." See Bailey, *An Universal Etymological English Dictionary*, s.v. "rundlet."

Russel. Woolen fabric made in various colors and used for clothing. See Dow, *Everyday Life*, 80.

Salt hay. Hay cut from the grasses that grow in salt marshes.

Scotch cloth. An inexpensive soft cloth used for linens and window curtains. See Dow, *Everyday Life*, 81.

Seaweed. Used for food, fertilizer, medicine, and, when burned, as an alkali for making soap.

Selectman. Seven selectmen served as an executive committee for the town voters, who together formed the legislative branch of the town. They oversaw the common lands, land grants, assessment and collection of local and provincial taxes, rates, enforcement of orders from the General Court, and work of the various town officers who supported their activities. See Fearing, *Weymouth Town Government,* 10, 19–20; Weymouth Town Book, 1:213–15.

Serge. A quilted woolen cloth. Worcester, *A Universal and Critical Dictionary*, s.v. "serge."

Shirting. Cloth used for making shirts. Worcester, *A Universal and Critical Dictionary*, s.v. "shirting."

Smelt Brook. Flows out of Pond Meadow into the Fore River just across the Braintree town line.

Stadium. A Greek and Roman unit used to measure distance. It equals 125 paces or 625 feet. Worcester, *A Universal and Critical Dictionary*, s.v. "stadium."

Stay. A type of early bodice made stiff using whalebone. Stays were less concerned about shaping the female figure than in improving posture. Consequently, they were not tied as tightly as corsets would later be in the nineteenth century. See Worcester, *A Universal and Critical Dictionary*, s.v. "stays."

Surveyor of highways. Laying out and maintaining roadways became an increasing concern as the seventeenth century wore on. The Native American trails needed to be expanded to accommodate wheeled vehicles, adjoining towns had to agree on where to put the roads, and towns had to have the ability to take land for that purpose. Consequently, after 1639, Weymouth began appointing surveyors of the highways. The provincial legislature stipulated the responsibilities of highway surveyors in 1693. James Richards served as a surveyor of highways for four years (1702–3, 1703–4, 1704–5, 1707–8). By this time, a ferry had been established at the mouth of the Fore River, and a road crossed Smelt Brook further up the river. See Weeden, *Economic and Social History*, 110–16, 205–11, 408–11; Fearing, *Weymouth Town Government*, 14–15; *The Acts and Resolves,* 1:136.

Swan shot. Large pellets used in shotguns to shoot large game birds.

Tithingman. The tithingman's primary responsibility was to maintain "order in the meetinghouse." The selectmen appointed one tithingman for about ten families. They helped instruct the people and visited them in their homes. Some tithingmen were issued long "wands, a nob on one end and a fox tail on the other for use during Sunday meetings." Those who fell asleep or otherwise showed a lack of decorum during the meetings might either receive the gentle ticklings of the fox tail or the solid rap of the hard nob. James Richards served as the tithingman for the lower end of Weymouth below the Watch House Hill. Weeden, *Economic and Social History*, 279–80 (quotation); see also Hart, *Commonwealth History of Massachusetts*, 114.

Trimming. Adjusting the weight in the bottom of a boat so that it floats properly.

Venter. Any cavity, usually in a body.

Vetch. A flowering legume of the genius *vicia*. See *Oxford English Dictionary*, s.v. "vetch."

Warming pans. Usually made of brass and filled with hot coals to warm bedsheets at night.

Wether. A castrated ram. See Worcester, *A Universal and Critical Dictionary*, s.v. "wether."

Wormer. An iron corkscrew-shaped device used to remove unfired bits of cartridges or other debris from the barrel of a gun.

Worsted mohair. Mohair is a fine cloth similar to silk made from the hair of the Angora goat. Worsted refers to the method of producing the woolen yarn that made it finer, stronger, and sleeker, which made it very good for making clothing. See Worcester, *A Universal and Critical Dictionary*, s.v. "mohair" and "worsted."

"Your man." Refers to a servant or paid laborer.

Works Cited

Archival Sources

Massachusetts State Archive
Massachusetts Judicial Archives, Suffolk County Probate, Record Book, vols. 1–32
Suffolk County Deeds, vol. 8
Weymouth Historical Society
Luis A. Cook, "Quincy L. Reed," box 8
Deeds, Wills, etc., vol. 4
Weymouth Town Hall, Office of the Town Clerk
Weymouth Town Book, vol. 1

Published Sources

The Acts and Resolves, Public and Private, of the Province of Massachusetts Bay to Which Are Prefixed the Charters of the Province, vol. 1, *1692–1714*. Boston: Wright and Porter, 1869.

Adams, Charles Francis, Jr. *Proceedings on the Two Hundred and Fiftieth Anniversary of the Permanent Settlement of Weymouth with an Historical Address by Charles Francis Adams, Jr.* Boston: Wright and Potter, 1874.

Allen, David Grayson. *In English Ways: The Movement of Societies and the Transferal of English Local Law and Custom to Massachusetts Bay in the Seventeenth Century*. Chapel Hill: University of North Carolina Press, 1981.

Anderson, Virginia Dejohn. "Thomas Minor's World: Agrarian Life in Seventeenth-Century New England." *Agricultural History* 82, no. 4 (Fall 2008): 496–518.

Bailey, N. *An Universal Etymological English Dictionary, 25th edition*. London: B. Law, 1790.

Bates, Samuel E., ed. *Records of the Town of Braintree, 1640–1793*. Randolph, Mass.: Daniel H. Huxford, 1886.

Baxter, W. T. *The House of Hancock: Business in Boston, 1724–1775*. Cambridge, Mass.: Harvard University Press, 1945.

Bedell, John. "Archaeology and Probate Inventories in the Study of Eighteenth-Century Life." *Journal of Interdisciplinary History* 31, no. 2 (Autumn 2000): 223–45.

"Bibliography of Farm Diaries and Account Books." In *The Farm*, edited by Peter Benes, 170–87. Boston: Boston University, 1988.

Bidwell, Percy W. "Rural Economy in New England at the Beginning of the Nineteenth Century." *Transactions of the Connecticut Academy of Arts and Sciences* 20 (April 1916): 241–399.

Bidwell, Percy W., and John I. Falconer, *History of Agriculture in the Northern United States, 1620–1860*. Washington, D.C.: Carnegie Institution of Washington, 1925.

Breen, T. H. "An Empire of Good: The Anglicanization of Colonial America, 1690–1776." *Journal of British Studies* 25, no. 4 (October 1986): 467–99.

Brown, Kathleen M. "Beyond the Great Debates: Gender and Race in Early America." *Reviews in American History* 26, no. 1 (March 1998): 96–123.

Brown, Kathleen M. *Good Wives, Nasty Wenches, and Anxious Patriarchs: Gender, Race, and Power in Colonial Virginia.* Chapel Hill: University of North Carolina Press, 1996.

Brown, Robert E. *Middle-Class Democracy and the Revolution in Massachusetts, 1691–1780.* New York: Russell and Russell, 1955.

Bruegel, Martin. "The Social Relations of Farming in the Early American Republic: A Microhistorical Approach." *Journal of the Early Republic* 26, no. 4 (2006): 523–53.

Bushman, Richard Lyman. "Family Security in the Transition from Farm to City, 1750–1850." *Journal of Family History* vol. 6 (Fall 1981): 238–56.

Bushman, Richard Lyman. "Markets and Composite Farms in Early America." *William and Mary Quarterly*, 3rd series, 55, no. 3 (July 1998): 351–74.

Chamberlain, George Walter, ed. *History of Weymouth Massachusetts.* 4 vols. Boston: Wright and Porter, 1923.

Clark, Christopher. "Household Economy, Market Exchange and the Rise of Capitalism in the Connecticut Valley, 1800–1860." *Journal of Social History* 13 (1979): 169–89.

Clark, Christopher. *The Roots of Rural Capitalism: Western Massachusetts, 1780–1860.* Ithaca, N.Y.: Cornell University Press, 1990.

Clark, Christopher. "The View from the Farmhouse: Rural Lives in the Early Republic." *Journal of the Early Republic* 24, no. 2 (Summer 2004): 198–207.

Cleary, Patricia. *Elizabeth Murray: A Woman's Pursuit of Independence in Eighteenth-Century America.* Amherst: University of Massachusetts Press, 2000.

Cleverly, Thomas F. "A Moonlight Ramble through the Lower Plantation of Weymouth in 1750." *Weymouth Gazette,* April 9, 1886.

Cronon, William. *Changes in the Land: Indians, Colonists, and the Ecology of New England.* New York: Hills and Wang, 1983.

Cummings, Abbott Lowell, ed. *Rural Household Inventories: Establishing the Names, Uses and Furnishings of Rooms in the Colonial New England Home.* Boston: Society for the Preservation of New England Antiquities, 1964.

Daniels, Bruce C. "Economic Development in Colonial and Revolutionary Connecticut: An Overview." *William and Mary Quarterly*, 3rd series, 37, no. 3 (July 1980): 429–50.

Davisson, William I. "Essex Country Price Trends: Money and Markets in 17th Century Massachusetts." *Essex Institute Historical Collections* 103, no. 2 (April 1967): 144–85.

Donahue, Brian. *The Great Meadow: Farmers and the Land in Colonial Concord.* New Haven, Conn.: Yale University Press, 2004.

Dow, George Francis. *Everyday Life in Massachusetts Bay Colony*. Boston: Society for the Preservation of New England Antiquities, 1935.

Earle, Alice Morse. *Home Life in Colonial Days.* 1898. New York: Macmillan, 1945.

Encyclopedia of Massachusetts. New York: Somerset Publishers, 1984.

Fearing, Clarence W. *Weymouth Town Government: Its Beginnings and Development*. Weymouth, Mass.: Weymouth Historical Society, 1941.

Finn, Margot C. *The Character of Credit: Personal Debt in English Culture, 1740–1914*. Cambridge: Cambridge University Press, 2003.

Frank, Lawrence K. "Social Change and the Family." *Annals of the American Academy of Political and Social Science* 160 (March 1932): 94–102.

Gedan, K. Bromberg, B. R. Silliman, and M. D. Bertness. "Centuries of Human-Driven Change in Salt Marsh Ecosystems." *Annual Review of Marine Science* 1 (January 2009): 117–41.

Grant, Charles S. *Democracy in the Connecticut Frontier Town of Kent*. New York: Columbia University Press, 1961.

Greven, Philip J. *Four Generations: Population, Land, and Family in Colonial Andover, Massachusetts*. Ithaca, N.Y.: Cornell University Press, 1970.

Hart, Albert Bushnell, ed. *Commonwealth History of Massachusetts: Province of Massachusetts, 1689–1775*. Vol. 2. New York: States History Company, 1928.

Hartz, Louis. *The Liberal Tradition in America*. New York: Harcourt, Brace, 1955.

Henretta, James. "Families and Farms: Mentalité in Pre-Industrial America." *William and Mary Quarterly*, 3rd series, 35, no. 1 (1978): 3–32.

Holbrook, Jay, and Delene Holbrook. *Massachusetts Vital and Town Records*. Provo, Utah: Holbrook Research Institution, 2011.

Innes, Stephen. *Creating the Commonwealth: The Economic Culture of Puritan New England*. New York: Norton, 1995.

Innes, Stephen. *Labor in a New Land: Economy and Society in Seventeenth-Century Springfield*. Princeton, N.J.: Princeton University Press, 1983.

Jones, E. L., and E. J. T. Collins. "The Collection and Analysis of Farm Record Books." *Journal of the Society of Archivists* 3 (1965): 86–89.

Karlsen, Carol F. *The Devil in the Shape of a Woman: Witchcraft in Colonial New England*. New York: Norton, 1987.

Kerber, Linda K. "Separate Spheres, Female Worlds, Woman's Place: The Rhetoric of Women's History." *Journal of American History* 75, no. 1 (June 1988): 9–39.

Kulikoff, Allan. *From British Peasants to Colonial American Farmers*. Chapel Hill: University of North Carolina Press, 2000.

Kulikoff, Allan. "The Transition to Capitalism in Rural America." *William and Mary Quarterly*, 3rd series, 46, no. 1 (January 1989): 120–44.

Lemon, James T. *The Best Poor Man's Country: A Geographical Study of Southeastern Pennsylvania*. Baltimore: Johns Hopkins University Press, 1972.

Lemon, James T. "Household Consumption in the Eighteenth Century and Its Relationship to Production and Trade: The Situation among Farmers in Southeastern Pennsylvania." *Agricultural History* 41 (January 1967): 59–70.

Lemon, James T. "Spatial Order: Households in Local Communities and Regions." In *Colonial British America: Essays in the New History of the Early Modern Era*, edited by Jack P. Greene and J. R. Pole, 86–122. Baltimore: Johns Hopkins University Press, 1984.

Lenk, Torsten, et al. *The Flintlock: Its Origin, Development and Use*. New York: Skyhorse, 2007.

Lepore, Jill. *The Name of War: King Philip's War and the Origins of American Identity.* New York: Vintage, 1998.

Loehr, Rodney C. "Self-Sufficiency on the Farm." *Agricultural History* 26, no. 2 (April 1952): 37–41.

Long, Henry Follansbee. "The Salt Marshes of the Massachusetts Coast." *Historical Collections of the Essex Institute* 47, no. 1 (January 1911): 1–19.

MacGregor, G. A., and H. E. de Wardener. *Salt Diet and Health.* Cambridge: Cambridge University Press, 1998.

Main, Gloria L. "The Distribution of Consumer Goods in Colonial New England: A Subregional Approach." In *Early American Probate Inventories,* edited by Peter Benes, 153–68. Boston: Boston University Press, 1989.

Main, Gloria L. "Gender, Work, and Wages in Colonial New England." *William and Mary Quarterly,* 3rd series, 51, no. 1 (January 1994): 36–66.

Main, Gloria L. "The Standard of Living in Colonial Massachusetts." *Journal of Economic History* 43, no. 1 (March 1983): 101–8.

Main, Gloria L. "The Standard of Living in Southern New England, 1640–1773." *William and Mary Quarterly,* 3rd series, 45, no. 1 (January 1988): 124–34.

Main, Gloria L., and Jackson T. Main. "Economic Growth and the Standard of Living in Southern New England, 1640–1774." *Journal of Economic History* 48, no. 1 (March 1988): 27–46.

Manion, Jennifer. "Historic Heteroessentialism and Other Orderings in Early America." *Signs* 34, no. 4 (Summer 2009): 981–1003.

Martin, John Frederick. *Profits in the Wilderness: Entrepreneurs and the Founding of New England Towns in the Seventeenth Century.* Chapel Hill: University of North Carolina Press, 1991.

Mauss, Marcel. *The Gift: The Form and Reason of Exchange in Archaic Societies.* Translated by W. D. Halls. New York: Norton, 1990.

McCallum, Bennett T. "Money and Prices in Colonial America: A New Test of Competing Theories." *Journal of Political Economy* 100, no. 1 (February 1992): 143–61.

McCusker, John J. *Money and Exchange in Europe and America, 1600–1775.* Chapel Hill: University of North Carolina Press, 1978.

McCusker, John J., and Russell R. Menard. *The Economy of British America, 1607–1789.* 1985. Chapel Hill: University of North Carolina, 1991.

McWilliams, James E. "Brewing Beer in Massachusetts Bay, 1640–1690." *New England Quarterly* 1, no. 4 (December 1998): 543–69.

McWilliams, James E. *Building the Bay Colony: Local Economy and Culture in Early Massachusetts.* Charlottesville: University of Virginia Press, 2007.

Merrill, Michael. "Cash Is Good to Eat: Self-Sufficiency and Exchange in the Rural Economy of the United States." *Radical History Review* 3 (1977): 42–77.

Miller, Marla R. "Gender, Artisanry, and Craft Tradition in Early New England: The View through the Eye of the Needle." *William and Quarterly,* 3rd series, 60, no. 4 (October 2003): 743–76.

Miner, Sidney H., and George D. Stanton, Jr., eds. *The Diary of Thomas Minor, Stonington, Connecticut, 1653–1684.* New London, Conn.: Day, 1899.

Morse, Abner. *Genealogical Register of the Descendants of Several Ancient Puritans.* Boston: H. W. Dutton and Son, 1861.

Muldrew, Craig. *The Economy of Obligation: The Culture of Credit and Social Relations in Early Modern England.* London: Macmillan, 1998.

Mutch, Robert E. "Colonial America and the Debate about Transition to Capitalism." *Theory and Society* 9, no. 6 (November 1980): 847–63.

Mutch, Robert E. "The Cutting Edge: Colonial America and the Debate about the Transition to Capitalism." *Theory and Society* 9, no. 6 (November 1980): 847–63.

Mutch, Robert E. "Yeoman and Merchant in Pre-Industrial America: Eighteenth-Century Massachusetts as a Case Study." *Societas* 7 (1977): 279–87.

Newell, Margaret Ellen. "The Birth of New England in the Atlantic Economy: From Its Beginning to 1770." In *Engines of Enterprise: An Economic History of New England,* edited by Peter Temin, 11–68. Cambridge, Mass.: Harvard University Press, 2000.

Newell, Margaret Ellen. "Economy." In *A Companion to Colonial America,* edited by Daniel Vickers, 172–93. Oxford: Blackwell, 2003.

Newell, Margaret Ellen. *From Dependency to Independence: Economic Revolution in Colonial New England.* Ithaca, N.Y.: Cornell University Press, 1998.

Norton, Mary Beth. "The Evolution of White Women's Experience in Early America." *American Historical Review* 89, no. 3 (June 1984): 593–619.

Norton, Mary Beth. *Liberty's Daughters: The Revolutionary Experience for American Women.* Boston: Little, Brown, 1980.

Norton, Mary Beth. *Separated by Their Sex: Women in Public and Private in the Colonial Atlantic.* Ithaca, N.Y.: Cornell University Press, 2011.

Pruitt, Bettye Hobbs. "Self-Sufficiency and the Agricultural Economy of Eighteenth-Century Massachusetts." *William and Mary Quarterly,* 3rd series, 41, no. 3 (July 1984): 333–64.

Reid, Margaret G. *Economics of Household Production.* New York: Chapman and Hall, 1934.

A Report of the Record Commissioners of the City of Boston Containing Boston Births, Baptisms, Marriages, and Deaths [title varies], vols. 7–9, 11. Boston: Rockwell and Churchill, 1881–84.

Riello, Giorbio. *A Foot in the Past: Consumers, Producers and Footwear in the Long Eighteenth Century.* Oxford: Oxford University Press, 2006.

Rothenberg, Winifred B. "The Emergence of Farm Labor Markets and the Transformation of the Rural Economy: Massachusetts, 1750–1855." *Journal of Economic History* 48, no. 3 (September 1988): 537–66.

Rothenberg, Winifred B. "Farm Account Books: Problems and Possibilities." *Agricultural History* 58, no. 2 (April 1984): 106–12.

Rothenberg, Winifred B. *From Market-Places to a Market Economy: The Transformation of Rural Massachusetts, 1750–1850.* Chicago: University of Chicago Press, 1992.

Rothenberg, Winifred B. "The Market and Massachusetts Farmers, 1750–1855." *Journal of Economic History* 41, no. 2 (June 1981): 283–314.

Russell, Howard S. *A Long, Deep Furrow: Three Centuries of Farming in New England.* Abridged with forward by Mark Lapping. Hanover, N.H.: University Press of New England, 1976.

Rutman, Darrett B. *Husbandmen of Plymouth: Farms and Villages in the Old Colony, 1620–1692.* Boston: Beacon Press, 1967.

Ryan, Mary P. "The Public and Private Good: Across the Great Divide in Women's History." *Journal of Women's History* 15, no. 2 (Summer 2003): 10–27.

Saint George, Robert Blaire. "'Set Thine House in Order': The Domestication of the Yeomanry in Seventeenth-Century New England." In *New England Begins: The Seventeenth Century*, edited by Jonathan L. Fairbanks and Robert F. Trent, 2:159–83. Boston: Museum of Fine Arts, 1982.

Salmon, Marylynn. *Women and the Law of Property in Early America*. Chapel Hill: University of North Carolina Press, 1986.

Shammas, Carole. "How Self-Sufficient Was Early America?" *Journal of Interdisciplinary History* 13, no. 2 (Autumn 1982): 247–72.

Sheridan, Richard B. "The Domestic Economy." In *Colonial British America: Essays in the New History of the Early Modern Era*, edited by Jack P. Greene and J. R. Pole, 43–85. Baltimore: Johns Hopkins University Press, 1984.

Snyder, Terri L. "Refiguring Women in Early American History." *William and Mary Quarterly*, 3rd series, 69, no. 3 (July 2012): 421–50.

Spear, Jennifer M. "The Distant Past of North American Women's History." *Journal of Women's History* 16, no. 4 (Winter 2004): 41–49.

Sturtz, Linda L. *Within Her Power: Propertied Women in Colonial Virginia*. New York: Routledge, 2002.

Sweeney, Kevin M. "Gentleman Farmers and Inland Merchants: The Williams Family and Commercial Agriculture in Pre-Revolutionary Western Massachusetts." In *The Farm*, edited by Peter Benes, 60–73. Boston: Boston University, 1988.

Torry, Clarence A. *New England Marriages prior to 1700*. Baltimore: Genealogical Publishing, 2004.

Tryon, Rolla Milton. *Household Manufactures in the United States, 1640–1860: A Study in Industrial History*. Chicago: University of Chicago Press, 1917.

Ulrich, Laurel Thatcher. *The Age of Homespun: Objects and Stories in the Creation of an American Myth*. New York: Vintage, 2001.

Ulrich, Laurel Thatcher. *Good Wives: Image and Reality in the Lives of Women in Northern New England, 1650–1750*. 1980. New York: Vintage, 1991.

Ulrich, Laurel Thatcher. "Martha Ballard and Her Girls: Women's Work in Eighteenth-Century Maine." In *Diversity and Unity in Early North America*, edited by Philip D. Morgan, 201–26. New York: Routledge, 1993.

Ulrich, Laurel Thatcher. *A Midwife's Tale: The Life of Martha Ballard, Based on Her Diary, 1785–1812*. New York: Knopf, 1990.

Ulrich, Laurel Thatcher. "Wheels, Looms, and the Gender Division of Labor in Eighteenth-Century New England." *William and Mary Quarterly*, 3rd series, 55, no. 1 (January 1998): 3–38.

Vickers, Daniel. "Competency and Competition: Economic Culture in Early America." *William and Mary Quarterly*, 3rd series, 47, no. 1 (January 1990): 3–29.

Vickers, Daniel. "Errors Expected: The Culture of Credit in Rural New England, 1750–1800." *Economic History Review* 63, no. 4 (November 2010): 1032–57.

Vickers, Daniel. *Farmers and Fishermen: Two Centuries of Work in Essex County, Massachusetts, 1630–1850*. Chapel Hill: University of North Carolina Press, 1994.

Weeden, William B. *Economic and Social History of New England, 1620–1789*. Vol. 1. Boston: Houghton Mifflin, 1894.

Worcester, Joseph E. *A Universal and Critical Dictionary of the English Language*. Boston: Jenks, Hickling and Swan, 1854.

Worlidge, John. *Systema Agriculturae: Being the Mystery of Husbandry Discovered and Layd Open*. London: J. C., 1669.

Index

In many cases, it was difficult or impossible to distinguish between two people of the same name alive during the same period, for example Jr. and Sr. In these cases, there is a separate entry with just the name and no other distinguishing information.

Abington, Massachusetts, 306, 310, 312, 314–16, 320, 323
Adkins, Robert, 47, 301
Adkins, Thomas, 14, 62, 301
African slaves or servants, 25–26, 146, 182, 239, 248. *See also* Frank (Richard Ager's African slave); Frank (Samuel White's African slave); Zipporah (Samuel White's African slave)
Agers, Abigail Nash, 301
Agers, Richard (1700–aft. 1750), 192, 301
Agers, Richard (d. 1719), 25, 301; daybook entries, 96, 127, 187, 191–92, 239–40, 245, 263, 298n362
Alcock, Joanna, 309
Alden, Mercy, 304
Aldreide, Experience, 304
ale, 59, 78, 83, 107, 143, 145, 167
Allen, Benjamin, 181, 298n355
Allen, Joseph, 301; daybook entries, 85, 90, 129–30, 131, 145, 161, 284, 297n295
Allen, Joseph, Jr., 183
Allen, Joseph, Sr., 153, 160, 184, 251
Allen, Samuel, 168, 298n338
alum, 98, 260, 325
Amey, Mrs., 265
anchors, 105, 280
Andrews, Elizabeth Ludden, 89, 103, 301
Andrews, Samuel, 301–2; daybook entries, 82–83, 86–87, 89–90, 96, 104–5, 129, 159, 165–66, 185
Angove, Mary, 307
apples, 34, 43, 52, 134, 158–59, 175, 180, 285–86. *See also* cider and cider barrels
aprons, 151, 168
Arnold, Ephraim, 269
Arnold, John, 104, 123, 302
asparagus, 148, 260

Back River, 3, 6, *6*, 306
bacon, 38, 63, 120
Badlam, Mary French, 64, 90, 123, 302, 306
Badlam, Samuel, 285, 313
Badlam, Stephen, 240, 253, 264, 302
Badlam, William, 302, 306; daybook entries, 86, 151, 155, 163, 170, 173, 183, 188, 244, 252, 255, 267, 269
Bagley, Samuel, 19; daybook entries, 80, 112–14, 165, 226, 268, 294n185
Bagley, Samuel, Jr., 110
bags, 46, 123, 165, 173, 208
baize, 77, 80, 325
Baker, Elizabeth, 315
Ballard, Martha, 292n82
Barber, Mr., 271, 300n441
barley, 11, 13, *13*; daybook entries, 34–44, 46–52, 54, 56–61, 65–67, 69, 73, 76–78, 85, 98, 105–6, 111, 120, 124, 127, 133, 137–38, 144, 149, 151–52, 154–56, 158, 163–64, 166, 171, 185, 187, 191–93, 198, 201–3, 205, 210, 225–27, 232–33, 235–37, 242, 255–57, 262. *See also* seed barley
Barnet or Barnut, Thomas, 152, 302

Barnsdale, Mary, 81, 294n187
Barnsdale, Mr., 271
Barnsdale, Mrs., 130, 166, 271
Barnstable, Massachusetts, 24, 319
barrels, 245, 248, 250–51. *See also* cider and cider barrels
barter, 18–20
Basset, David, 302
Basset, Mary, 302
Basset, Mr., 257
Basset, Mrs., 240, 265
Basset household, 248
Bates, Ben, 267
Bates, Ebenezer, 253
Bates, Edward (Deacon), 302, 305; daybook entries, 37, 64–65, 89–90, 100, 109, 116, 122, 125, 127, 130, 143, 148, 154, 159, 172, 175, 211, 239, 244, 249, 251, 253–54, 265, 267, 278, 281, 297n289
Bates, Edward (Elder), 318
Bates, Elizabeth Shaw, 109, 302
Bates, Increase, 302; daybook entries, 63–64, 81, 90, 92, 100, 121, 127, 129, 196, 199, 272
Bates, John, 189, 298n364
Bates, Mary (d. 1683), 318
Bates, Mary Whitmarsh. *See* Whitmarsh, Mary (1663–1715)
Bates, Samuel (1693–1752), 302
Bates, Samuel (son of Edward and Elizabeth), 302; daybook entries, 82, 175, 239, 244, 249, 254, 265, 281
Bates, Susannah, 318
Bayley, Aunt (Ruth Porter), 19, 68, 157, 302
Bayley, Christian, 323
Bayley, Hannah Rogers Pratt (d. 1721), 122, 302–3
Bayley, Mary, 205, 302
Bayley, Mary (Samuel's wife), 302
Bayley, Samuel, 72, 132, 294n185, 302
Bayley, Sarah, 19, 157, 302
Bayley, Thomas (d. 1691), 42, 302–3
Bayley, Thomas, Sr. (d. 1681), 302, 310
Bayley, Widow, 34, 43, 122, 303
Bay Side Hotel, 7
beach peas, 193, 325
Beal, Abigail, 303, 306
beans, 104, 144, 257
bedcords, 46, 133
beef, 34–35, 38, 45, 47, 49, 56, 64, 88–90, 96, 100, 102, 108, 111, 114, 116–17, 120, 122, 125, 145, 162, 164–65, 253, 266–67
beer, 88, 100
beer production, 13–14, 327
bellies, 159, 213
Benson, Joanna, 89, 101, 303, 308
Benson, Joseph, 303
Benson, Sarah, 303
Benson, Susannah, 316
Bicknell, Benjamin, 138, 303
Bicknell, Elizabeth, 27, 50, 54, 294n148, 303
Bicknell, Experience, 57, 303
Bicknell, Hannah, 167
Bicknell, Hannah (b. 1675), 58, 211, 303, 321
Bicknell, Hannah (b. 1698), 269, 303
Bicknell, Hannah Smith, 247, 266, 303
Bicknell, Joanna. *See* Ford, Joanna Bicknell
Bicknell, John (1623–78), 21, 303, 305–6, 317, 321
Bicknell, John (Brother) (1654–1737), 2, 21, 22, 303; daybook entries, 39, 41, 44, 47, 49, 51, 59, 61, 63–67, 69–70, 76, 78–79, 85, 97, 99, 107–8, 127, 133, 136–38, 141, 143, 146, 151–52, 154, 157, 163, 170, 177, 181, 183, 189, 215, 232–34, 236–39, 244, 252, 254, 257, 260–61, 269–70, 273–76, 278, 280–86
Bicknell, Joseph, 270, 278
Bicknell, Joshua, 152, 263, 303
Bicknell, Mary (1678–1764), 27, 303, 321; daybook entries, 35, 53, 71, 110, 120, 124, 153, 260
Bicknell, Mary (d. 1677), 305
Bicknell, Mary Porter (Mother), 21, 27, 34–36, 292n89, 302–3, 306, 317
Bicknell, Mary Shaw (c. 1626–58), 21, 303, 305, 321
Bicknell, Naomi, 321
Bicknell, Ruth. *See* Richards, Ruth Bicknell (1660–1729)
Bicknell, Sarah (1665–1730), 61, 146, 170, 303
Bicknell, Thomas, 9, 17, 20, 22, 303; daybook entries, 35, 41–42, 45–46, 51, 54, 57, 68, 75–78, 94, 97, 101–2, 107, 119, 121–24, 165–66
Bicknell, Zachariah, 9, 19, 25, 29, 303, 307; daybook entries, 34, 38–39, 42, 45–46, 51, 61, 64, 66–68, 75–78, 85, 89, 94, 96–97, 105, 119, 121, 130, 138, 141, 143–44, 148, 151–55, 158, 168, 179–81, 184, 235–36, 239–40, 242, 245, 247, 254, 263, 266–67, 269
Bicknell, Zachariah (son of Zachariah), 138
Bill, Jonathan, 148, 303
Bill, Samuel, 16, 25, 128, 148, 243, 255, 257–58, 303–4
billing cloth, 196
bills of credit, 20, 27, 328; daybook entries, 139, 162, 167, 179, 194, 196, 203, 211, 220, 221, 248–49, 266, 287
bills of exchange, 20
biscuits, 65, 140, 145–46, 150, 166, 171, 211, 241, 243, 246, 257
black grape cloth, 105, 218, 231

Blanchard, Abraham, 46
Blanchard, John, 19, 157–58, 185, 209, 304
Blanchard, Nathaniel, 9, 53, 61, 62, 304
board nails, 65, 70, 84, 86, 98, 108, 133, 141–44, 149, 152, 154–55, 157–59, 165–66, 168–69, 171, 177–78, 180–81, 183, 188, 196, 205, 207, 211, 213, 218, 224, 231, 239, 250, 267, 280, 282, 285
boards, 122
boatman, 223
boats, 54, 57–58, 64, 87, 105, 153, 161, 173, 187, 244. *See also* sloops
boat sails, 80
bodices, 111, 201
Bolentine, John, 282
Bolter, Joanna, 86, 304
Bolter, Thomas, 304
bonnets, 218
book debts, 18, 20
Boston, Massachusetts: in daybook transactions, 38, 43, 44, 48, 52, 54, 58, 62, 68, 70, 75–76, 78, 80–82, 87, 92–93, 103, 115, 119, 122, 133, 135, 139–40, 148, 150–52, 158–59, 161, 165–66, 168, 170, 178–80, 191, 194, 201, 208–9, 211, 217–18, 223, 235, 239–43, 245, 247–51, 255, 257–59, 262–71, 273, 275–76, 278–80, 282–83, 285; goods sold to, 13–16; James Richards's associates in or from, 302–8, 310–11, 314–22; James Richards's networks and transactions in, 21, 23–24; mixed economy in, 20; skyline seen from Weymouth, 7; transport to and from, 11, 17, 22–23, 25, 29; Weymouth and, 3
Boston Harbor, 3, *23*
Boutage, Abiall, 26, 29, 292n93, 304; daybook entries, 216, 218, 277–78, 300n443
Boutage, John, 45, 51, 86, 89, 93, 292n93, 293n135
Boutage, William, 86
Bowditch, John, 198
Bradford, Mary, 310
Braintree, Massachusetts: in daybook transactions, 37, 42, 44, 58, 62, 66, 68, 76, 80–81, 83, 88, 96, 100–102, 105, 109–15, 119, 122, 141, 146, 148–49, 155, 165–67, 181, 183–85, 199–200, 214, 244–45, 251–52, 254, 257, 272, 277–78, 284; goods sold to, 22; James Richards's associates in or from, 301–2, 304–10, 312, 315–16, 318–19, 322–23; James Richards's land in, 3, 8, 14; Samuel White's land in, 8; Smelt Brook, 329; transport to and from, 9, 22–24
Brandon, Mary, 319
brass kettles, 112
breaking ground, 67
breeches, 82, 281
brewers, 259
Brick, John, 249, 252, 304
Bridgewater, Massachusetts, 22, 95–96, 110, 118, 123, 279, 304, 315, 319
bridles, 46, 141
Briggs, Clement, 304, 316
Briggs, Hannah, 316
Briggs, Remember, 43, 52, 121, 304
Brigham, Mr., 106, 296n258
Brigham, Mrs., 82
Brimsmead, Ebbett, 304, 309–10
Brinsdill, Benjamin, 277
Bristol County, Massachusetts, 52, 121
British East India Company, 16
British Imperial system, 18
broad hoes, 107, 119, 201
broom and pipes, 67, 70
brooms, 52, 57, 67, 82, 105, 107, 113, 143, 165–69, 251–52, 260, 263, 267, 273–74
Browne, Benjamin, 265, 278
Bryant, Samuel, 110, 296n262
building supplies trade, 15–16, 304
bullets, 82, 150, 189
Burrell, Ephraim, 19, 304; daybook entries, 67, 77, 82, 89, 113, 129, 157–58, 160, 205
Burrell, John, 304; daybook entries, 82, 89, 107, 123, 169, 171, 173, 179, 182, 253, 262, 278–80
Burrell, John (husband of Mary Humphrey), 310
Burrell, Lydia, 304
Burrell, Mary Humphrey, 310
Burrell, Mr., 278
Burrell, Rebecca, 304
Burrell, Widow, 82, 304
Butler (of Boston), 160, 298n327
Butler, Mr., 245, 285
butter, 44, 57, 61, 63, 74, 76, 100, 107, 118, 120, 125, 133–35, 139, 144, 159, 162, 173, 190, 198, 203, 257–59, 270–72, 274, 283
buttons, 181, 218, 231, 247
Byram, Deliverance, 56

cabbages, 34, 74, 159, 169
Cajun, 246
calf's bag, 107, 201, 258
calf skin or hides, 67, 106, 124, 212
calico, 16, 154, 201, 203, 213, 231, 325
calico aprons, 151, 168
calves, 40, 50, 58, 60, 107, 124, 207, 260–61
Cambridge, Massachusetts, 115
camlet, 123, 325
candles, 37, 42, 45, 46, 49–50, 53, 58, 62, 83–85, 93, 102, 104, 108, 111, 114–18, 121–25, 150, 162, 172–74, 182, 198, 254, 256, 269, 273–74, 276–77

cannon, 122
Canterbery (servant), 169, 261, 298n341
Canton, Massachusetts, 313
Capen, Dorothy, 304
cards, 4, 8, 12, 15, 191, 209, 211, 325
Caribbean islands, 14, 16
carting of goods, 16–17; daybook entries, 50, 57–58, 81, 86, 115, 121, 133, 173–74, 177, 199, 240, 242–45, 252, 260, 279
Carver, Anna, 166, 285, 304, 317
Carver, David, 304; daybook entries, 50, 78–79, 82–83, 89, 118, 120–21, 124, 135, 189, 192, 276
Carver, Hannah, 304
Carver, Ruth Whitmarsh, 121, 304
caster hat, 183, 325
cedars, 107, 160, 185
cedar swamp, 121
chadern, 325
Chard, Patience, 315
Charlestown, Massachusetts, 24, 246
charter bills, 328
cheese, 37, 38, 58, 63, 67, 73–74, 90, 99–101, 113, 120, 123, 133–34, 148, 162, 165, 169, 173, 179, 190, 200, 203, 205, 271, 274, 276, 281
chests, 170
chickens, 67, 113, 246. *See also* hens
cider and cider barrels, 49, 56, 84, 99–100, 114, 122, 187, 189, 201, 216, 255, 286
cinnamon, 140
clapboard nails, 84, 98, 105, 148, 188, 205, 207, 218, 239
clapboards, 8, 15–16, 17, 22, 325; daybook entries, 43, 77, 87, 97, 112, 115, 134, 139, 159, 167–68, 173, 194, 200, 204, 206, 208, 210, 212, 214, 216–17, 220, 222, 227, 230–31, 240–42, 246–47, 249–50, 252, 258, 261, 264, 275–80, 282–86
Clarck, Joseph, 110
Clarcke, Charles, 108
Clark, Jonathan, 166, 298n331
Clark's son of Braintree, 251, 299n412
cloth, 57, 89, 104, 125, 135, 181–82, 218, 223, 281. *See also specific cloth names; specific types of cloth*
cloves, 140
Clow, Ebenezer, 127–28, 191, 304
Clowe, Mr., 258, 265
coal, 76
Coals or Coles, Joseph, 125, 297n290
coats, 123, 257
cock pins, 108, 325
cocks of hay, 99, 325
colominko, 151
colonial economy: credit, currency, barter, and exchange, 18–20; family connections and, 21–22; labor of sons and daughters in, 24, 26; mixed husbandry and, 5–18; models explaining, 5; servants and slaves and, 24–26; women's roles in, 26–30
colony bills, 328
Colson, Susannah, 301
Combe, Mr., 257, 259
composite farming, 5–18, 21, 31
constables, 303–4, 306–7, 309–11, 313, 315, 317–22, 325–27; daybook entries, 122, 164, 167, 205, 207–9, 272
Coombs, John, 249, 299n410
Cooper, Betty, 54
Copeland, John, 83, 168
Copeland, Thomas, 83
Copeland, William, 83, 112
cords, 190, 201
cordwinders, 143, 172
corn, 39, 46, 49, 53, 63, 75, 87, 102, 104, 132, 144–45, 149–50, 152, 167, 172, 176–78, 180, 184, 187–89, 194, 202–3, 205, 239–42, 245, 249, 252, 277, 280, 282, 284. *See also* Indian corn; seed corn
corn and stalks, 49, 178
cotton, 62, 70, 111, 135, 140, 157–58, 161, 169, 172, 175, 178–79, 181–82, 184, 196, 198, 201, 205, 209, 213, 215, 223–24, 239, 248–50, 252, 262, 264, 267, 270–71, 273, 275, 277–78, 280, 282, 285
cotton cloth, 53, 57, 83, 218, 258
cotton wool, 43, 62, 63, 68, 70, 77, 82, 86, 97, 104, 107, 109, 113, 119, 132, 135, 150, 156, 161–62, 170, 175, 177, 203, 205, 207, 211, 213, 221, 268–69, 272–73, 277. *See also* sheep wool; wool
country pay or rate, 20, 167, 205, 207, 211, 236, 274
Courser, John, 194, 304
Courser, John (father of John), 304
Courser, Margaret, 304
cow hides, 72, 121, 201, 285
cows, 34, 40, 46, 86, 107, 124, 154, 207, 271. *See also* calves; heifers; steers
cow's belly, 89
credit economy. *See* colonial economy
crickthatch, 38, 177, 248, 326
crooking, 284, 326
crosscut saw, 94
cultivated fields, 6–9
cupboards, 69
currency system, 19–21, 291n74, 326
Current New England Money, 34, 326
curtains and valances, 58
Curtis, Theophilus, 97

Daese, Johnathan, 49, 293n141
damask, 326; daybook entries, 43, 54, 73, 82, 135, 168, 207, 218
Danford, Richard, 113
Darell, John, 249–50
Dartmouth, Massachusetts, 309
Davenport, Abigail Shaw, 89, 305, 318
Davenport, Richard, 66, 89–90, 103, 304–5, 318
daybooks, 1, 25–26, 289n1, 292n83. *See also* James Richards Daybook (1692–1711)
Dedham, Massachusetts, 306, 308, 318
Degere, Richard. *See* Agers, Richard (d. 1719)
Derby, Edward, 96, 109, 119, 125, 297n289, 305
Derby, Ruth Whitmarsh, 119, 305
Desper, Lamber, 24, 63–64, 86, 88, 96, 113–14, 294n153
Dighton, Massachusetts, 323
dishes, 209, 213
dogs, 43, 50
Donahue, Brian, 7
Dorchester, Massachusetts, 82, 304, 309, 315
double-ten nails, 153, 207, 213, 326
Downing, Sarah, 314
Drake, Benjamin, 89, 305
Drake, Elishama, 305
Drake, Experience, 305, 318
Drake, James, 56, 305
Drake, Jane, 321
Drake, Joan, 316
Drake, John, 82, 89–90, 305
Drake, Joseph, 37, 129, 150, 160, 305
Drake, Rachel, 305
Drake, Sarah Nash (b. 1699), 90, 305
Drake, William, 55, 56, 89, 129, 171, 305
drugget, 216, 326
duck, 326
Dudley, Joseph, 309
Dun, Goodman, 37
Dunbar, Peter, 47, 305
Dunbar, Sarah, 305
dung, 199
Dunstable, Massachusetts, 309
During, Widow (and son John), 62
Dyer, Benjamin, 128, 193, 225–26, 244, 253, 305
Dyer, Elizabeth, 305
Dyer, John, 43–44, 110, 305
Dyer, Joseph, 117, 123, 305
Dyer, Joseph (Deacon, 1653–1704), 82–85, 103, 295n196
Dyer, Mary, 120, 149, 153, 297n313, 305–6, 322
Dyer, Thomas, 136, 192
Dyer, Thomas (b. 1651), 305
Dyer, Thomas (b. 1673), 305
Dyer, Thomas (Deacon, c. 1612–1676), 305, 312
Dyer household, 138

earthen pots, 57, 139
Easterneck, 9, 105, 107, 296n245
Easton, Massachusetts, 24, 311, 315–16, 323, 328
eggs, 50, 66, 147, 169, 174, 178, 190–91, 239, 241–44, 246, 258, 266, 270, 277, 282, 284
elder blossoms, 139
English hay, 99, 166, 241, 326
Essex County, Massachusetts, 25
ethnic hierarchies, 24, 25
ewes, 125
exotic goods market, 16, 31
export economy, 16
Eyles, Hannah, 150, 305
Eyles, Widow, 305; daybook entries, 64, 86, 141–42, 167, 194, 269–70, 272

families: father and son relationships, 24–25; labor of sons and daughters, 24, 26; roles of women in, 26–30; transactions within, 22–23
fanning, 326
Farnum, David, 240–41, 299n402
Feese, William, 75, 77, 79, 99, 114, 294n180
fence, posts and setting, 52
fence viewers, 30, 303, 316–17, 319–22, 326
Ferry Field, *6*, 8–9, 12, 18, 326; in daybook entries, 41, 49–50, 66, 178
filleting, 77, 326
fish, 45, 49, 57, 75, 78, 80, 96
fishing line, 107, 122
flax, 67–68, 70, 73, 75, 82, 98, 100, 107, 132, 165, 168, 201, 203, 205, 207, 216
flints, 150, 189, 215
Flood, Mary, 29, 125, 297n291
Ford, Andrew, 306
Ford, Brother. *See* Ford, Nathaniel (Brother)
Ford, Eleanor Lovell, 306
Ford, Israel, 40, 46, 56–57, 234–35, 306
Ford, Joanna Bicknell, 306
Ford, Lydia, 29, 147–48, 263, 306
Ford, Marsey, 73, 135, 297n300
Ford, Mary (b. 1684), 29, 263, 306
Ford, Mary (d. 1715), 322–23
Ford, Nathaniel (Brother), 2, 15, 29, 306; daybook entries, 38–40, 44, 51, 53–54, 97, 129, 136–38, 143, 145, 147–48, 150, 153, 157–58, 160, 169, 175, 180, 187, 192, 232–33, 233–38, 240, 242, 251, 268, 276, 280, 282, 284–86, 293n124
Ford, Ruth, 143, 233, 284, 300n457, 306
Ford, Samuel, 116, 306
Ford, Sarah, 160, 262

Ford, Sarah Pratt (d. 1718), 306
Fore River, 3, 6, *6*, 9, 311, 326–27, 329
Framingham, John, 144, 297n306
Frank (Richard Ager's African slave), 239, 299n400
Frank (Samuel White's African slave), 25, 153, 173, 306
Frary, Hannah, 305
Freeman, James, 78, 159, 306
French, Abigail Beal, 82, 294n192
French, Hannah Whitman, 82, 294n192, 302, 306
French, John, 186, 198n361
French, Mary, 302, 306
French, Mrs., 103
French, Samuel, 86, 165, 183, 209, 211, 274, 306
French, Stephen, 79, 130, 276
French, Stephen (Captain), 4–5, 30, 302, 306; daybook entries, 67, 86, 103–4, 127, 129, 141, 145, 151, 155, 163, 168, 170, 173, 180, 187–88, 191, 196, 199, 240, 244, 252–53, 255, 260, 262, 264, 267–69, 274, 277, 285, 294n161
French, Stephen, Jr., 67, 104, 191, 255, 294n161, 303, 306–7
French-heeled shoes, 29, 53, 62, 102, 124, 207, 326
fulling, 15
funeral expenses, 50
fustian, 231, 326

Gallop, Benjamin, 249, 307
Garener, Simon, 58
garlick holan, 135, 201, 218, 231, 239, 259, 261, 274, 297n301
Gee, Joshua, 278–79
geese, 67
Gellile, Mr., 115
Gibson, John, 240
girdles, 218, 231
glass bottles, 68
glaziers, 179, 224, 327
gloves, 62, 258
Gold, John, 274
Gooding, John, 194, 243, 307
gooseneck, 133, 327
grain harvest failures, 13
Grant, Mr., 248, 250, 278
Grape Islands, 17, 24, 92, 187, 327
Great Hill, 6, *6–7*, *10*
Great Pond, 6, *6*
Green, Anne, 307
Green, Constable, 205
Green, Elizabeth (b. 1664), 307
Green, Elizabeth Whitman (d. 1720), 307; daybook entries, 49, 185, 241, 283–85, 299n403
Green, Goode, 100, 167, 298n337
Green, Hannah, 49
Green, John, 9–11, 16–18, 22, 26, 289n12, 307; daybook entries, 34, 49–51, 54, 65–66, 78, 83, 97, 119, 122, 142, 159, 165, 167, 169–72, 174–75, 178–79, 183, 185, 187–88, 190–91, 194, 196–99, 205, 207–8, 214, 225, 239, 241–47, 250–51, 253–87
Green, John, Jr., 22, 307; daybook entries, 81, 190, 197, 270, 272, 278, 286, 294n188, 298n367
Green, Joseph, 43, 57, 63, 80–81, 89–90, 96, 116, 289n12, 314
Green, Joseph (1658–c. 1733), 307; daybook entries, 83, 86, 116, 129, 132, 134, 141, 145, 162, 165, 199, 203, 252
Green, Joseph (d. 1700), 307
Green, Mary, 26, 175, 179, 199, 255, 274, 300n443, 307
Green, Mother, 241, 299n403
Green, Patience, 307; daybook entries, 54–55, 65, 89, 165, 169, 171, 174, 185, 241, 271, 283, 299n403
Green, Samuel, 318
Green, Sarah, 190, 277, 307
Green, Widow. *See* Green, Elizabeth Whitman (d. 1720)
Green, Zachariah, 307; daybook entries, 21, 81, 165, 214, 254–56, 263, 272, 276, 294n188
Greenwood, Mr., 266, 279
Greenwood, Mrs., 280
Greenwood, Samuel, 264
grindstones, 70, 72, 154, 168, 170, 180
guns, 67–68, 82, 86, 240
Gurney, John, 41, 118, 307
Gurney, Joseph, 78, 307
Gurney, Mary, 237, 285, 308
Gurney, Richard, 307–8
Gurney, Zachariah (Zachary), 307–8; daybook entries, 60, 69, 78, 89, 236, 251, 299n399
Gwinops family, 218, 285, 299n391

Haccut, Timothy, 61, 210
Hadman, John, 96, 117, 296n275
Halle, Solomon, 240
ham, 257
handkerchiefs, 61
Harding, John, 63, 308
Hart, Colonel, 175
Harvey, Peter, 46, 308
Harvey, Samuel, 308
hat cases, 216, 218, 277
hats, 82, 84, 133, 167–68, 179–80, 188, 194, 201, 215, 218, 245, 280. *See also* caster hat

hay, 34, 57–58, 66, 68, 80, 89, 99, 114, 124, 140, 146–47, 154, 156, 173–74, 177, 198, 209, 214, 244, 255, 275. *See also* salt hay
Hayden, John, 100, 102, 296n249
Hayden, Joseph, 90, 102, 255, 295n228
Hayward, Mr., 249–50, 259–60, 268–71, 273, 275
Hayward, Robbard, 169, 259
Hearsey, William, 63, 294n155
heifer hides, 106, 215
heifers, 46, 101, 124, 307. *See also* cows
hens, 171, 191, 200, 283
Hersy, James, 141
hides, 48, 49, 105–6, 160, 175, 201, 215, 273, 287. *See also* calf skin or hides; cow hides; heifer hides
hinges, 40, 43
Hingham, Massachusetts, 27, 289n12, 303, 305, 311–12, 314, 318–20; daybook entries, 50, 86
Hobart, Aaron, 305
Hobart, Rebecca Sumner, 305
Hobbe, Ebenezer, 132
hobbles, 82, 260
hobby sheep, 327
hogs, 44, 49–50, 141, 183, 266, 271. *See also* pigs
hogsbutt, 105, 327
hog's fat, 39, 64, 67, 81, 104, 121, 141, 175, 196, 247, 272
hogshead, 205, 247, 327
Holbrook, Captain, 123, 308
Holbrook, Cornelius, 308; daybook entries, 42, 44, 66, 82, 96, 104, 221
Holbrook, Experience, 308
Holbrook, Ichabod, 11, 308, 321; daybook entries, 35, 59, 60, 73, 90, 123, 151, 153, 155, 161, 249, 271
Holbrook, Jacob, 150, 209n315, 308
Holbrook, John, 26, 171, 180, 271, 308
Holbrook, Lydia (Widow), 22, 96, 104–5, 107–8, 308
Holbrook, Margery, 308
Holbrook, Sarah Turner, 123, 151, 253, 270, 308, 321
Holbrook, Thomas (b. 1624), 306, 308; daybook entries, 52, 63–64, 67–68, 91, 104, 130, 141, 146–47, 149, 168, 245, 254–55, 276, 280, 283
Holbrook, Thomas (father of Thomas), 308
Holbrook, William (Captain), 308
Holey, Mr., 127
Hollis, Abigail, 308
Hollis, John, 60, 64, 80, 86, 129, 308
Hollis, Samuel, 91, 308
Hollis, Sarah, 308
Holsey, Mr., 271, 281–83
Holsey, Mrs., 281
hooks, 40
Hooper, John, 308
hoops, 107
hopple or hobble, 327
hops, 327; daybook entries, 61, 65, 67–68, 82, 135, 168–69, 171, 174, 211, 224
horse and cart, 157, 172–74, 177–78, 241–46, 252, 260
horses and horse work, 48–50, 53, 160, 175, 177, 179, 188, 195, 198–99, 248, 257, 263–64
horse shoes and shoeing, 107, 115–16
Houtchine, Jeremiah, 167, 298n334
Hovey, Ebenezer (Deacon), 73, 303, 308
How, David, 309
Hubbard, John, 75, 89, 92, 294n176
Hull, Massachusetts, 24, 274, 303, 308, 315, 320
Humphrey, Elizabeth, 52, 309
Humphrey, James, 9, 12, 15, 308, 309; daybook entries, 37, 40, 44, 47–48, 51–52, 59–60, 64, 77, 79, 82–85, 104, 114, 127, 136–38, 149, 154, 156–60, 164, 167–68, 170–71, 180, 186, 192–93, 221, 232, 235–36, 238–40, 242, 247, 251, 261, 267
Humphrey, Jonas (1655–89), 308
Humphrey, Jonas (1684–1761), 65, 186, 308
Humphrey, Jonas (Deacon, 1620–98), 309
Humphrey, Martha (d. 1712), 308
Humphrey, Martha (widow of Deacon Humphrey), 309
Humphrey, Mary Phillips, 308, 309
Humphrey, Nathaniel, 15, 308; daybook entries, 40, 44, 52, 59–60, 89
Humphrey, Samuel, 51, 309
Humphrey, Silence, 261, 309
Humphrey, Widow, 309; daybook entries, 49, 51, 63, 86, 97, 99, 112
Hunt, Daniel, 143, 244, 262, 309
Hunt, Dorothy, 310
Hunt, Ebbett Brimsmead, 96, 304, 309–10
Hunt, Enoch, 310
Hunt, Ephraim (Colonel), 4–5, 29, 304–5, 309–10; daybook entries, 37, 38, 43, 44, 56, 81, 83–85, 96, 101–4, 120, 141, 150, 167, 180, 183, 185, 193, 225, 240, 248, 251–52, 267, 270. *See also* Hunt, Major (Ephraim or John)
Hunt, Isaac, 68, 107–8, 294n163
Hunt, Joanna Alcock, 44, 103
Hunt, John (1646–1723), 29, 309; daybook entries, 47, 80, 82–84, 92, 103–4, 115–16, 120, 122–24, 127, 129, 141, 143, 150, 152, 159, 167, 180, 262, 267–70, 273, 285. *See also* Hunt, Major (Ephraim or John)
Hunt, John (d. 1761), 120, 296n280

Hunt, John, Jr. (b. 1687), 92, 113, 116, 167, 309, 316
Hunt, Joseph, 34, 309
Hunt, Major (Ephraim or John), 102, 110, 113–14, 119, 121
Hunt, Ruth Quincy, 83, 92, 309
Hunt, Samuel, 83–84, 309
Hunt, William, 36, 310, 314
Hunt's Hill, 7
Hupper, John, 55, 294n149
Huslis, Mr., 258
Hustis, Mr., 282
Hutchinson, Elisha, 168, 298n340

Indian corn, 18, 26, 327; daybook entries, 34–40, 42, 45–46, 49, 50–51, 54, 100, 106, 112, 114–15, 119, 144, 148, 150–52, 158–59, 167, 169–70, 172, 184, 187, 199, 205–6, 239, 242, 244, 246, 256, 273, 283, 285
Indian meal, 44
Indian slaves or servants, 4, 26, 39, 68, 78, 131, 193, 264
indigo, 49, 108, 245, 260
international trade, 16
iron and iron products, 89, 92, 96, 109

jackets, 55, 119, 132
Jackson, Edmond, 47, 199, 310
Jackson, Mary, 312
Jackson, Mr., 127
James, Ann, 321
James Richards Daybook (1692–1711), 33–287; accounts reconciled and balanced in, 1–2; creation of, 1, 3, 5–6, 34, 292n89; economic history of New England and, 1–31; manuscript page from, *28*
jars, 168
Jarvis, Elizabeth, 320
Jonson, Mr., 128
jugs, 122, 240, 327

Kersey cloth, 327; daybook entries, 40, 53, 55, 104, 114, 116, 122
Kilby, John, 73–74, 283, 294n173, 310
King, Esther Bayley, 47, 310
King, Hezekiah, 37, 71, 310
King, John, 127, 310
King, John, Jr., 310
King, Mary Shaw, 310
King, Samuel, 310; daybook entries, 35–37, 45, 67–68, 71, 113, 179
King, Sarah, 308
King, Sarah (1666–1727), 305
King, Widow. *See* King, Esther Bayley
Kingman, Elizabeth Edson, 313
Kingman, Hannah, 82, 109, 209, 310
Kingman, Henry, 127, 197, 255, 308, 310
Kingman, Joanna, 308
Kingman, John (b. 1664), 147, 152, 255, 258–59, 284, 299n417, 310
Kingman, John (c. 1632–c. 1690), 310
Kingman, John (husband of Elizabeth Edson), 313
Kingman, Lydia, 305
Kingman, Rebecca, 310
Kingman, Sarah, 209, 310
Kingman, Thomas, 27, 29, 82, 145, 147, 175
Kingman, Thomas (1670–1742), 310; daybook entries, 193, 199, 254–55, 286, 295n194
Kingman, Thomas, Sr. (1627–1705), 111, 125, 295n194, 310
King Oak Hill, 6, *6*
Kings, John, Jr., 318
Kingston, Massachusetts, 310
knives, 70, 75, 101
Kulikoff, Allan, 5, 290n27

labor economy, 24–26
lace, 190, 218
laces, 216
lace thread, 223
Lamb, Mary, 25, 292n92
lambs and lamb meat, 34, 37, 42–43, 47, 49, 53, 56, 59, 62, 70, 72–73, 83–85, 88–90, 96, 100–102, 104, 112–14, 116–23, 125, 167, 170, 172, 176–79, 183, 190–91, 243, 250, 255, 262–63, 266
lamb skin, 113
lamp oil, 11, 327; daybook entries, 35, 63, 65, 98, 107, 141, 158, 174, 196, 203, 207, 282–85
land sold, 57, 100
Langdon, Mr., 167, 298n333
lard, 34
Lash, Mary, 310
Lash, Robert, 16, 115, 310–11
laths, 191, 204, 212, 220, 222, 241, 247, 258, 283, 286
lean-tos, 327
licorice, 68, 327
lime, 125, 253
Lincoln, Benjamin, 121, 297n283
Lindall, Mr., 186, 298n360
linen cloth, 51, 53, 57, 68, 73, 83, 150, 215–16, 218, 277
lines, 201, 258. *See also* fishing line
Litchfeeld, Mary, 308
Littlefield, Caleb, 155
livestock, 8–9
Long, John, 75, 93

Lovell, Anna, 311
Lovell, Elizabeth Poole, 111, 311
Lovell, Enoch (Captain), 9, 16, 22, 27, 311, 316; daybook entries, 48, 59, 60, 62, 71–72, 78–79, 85, 105–6, 111–12, 121, 124, 127, 129, 133, 135–38, 141, 146, 153–54, 156, 160, 172, 180, 189–90, 192, 197, 200–202, 207, 209, 215–16, 222, 225, 227, 232, 235–38, 243, 256, 263
Lovell, Jacob, 197, 201, 215, 225, 228, 238, 319
Lovell, James, 82, 114
Lovell, James, Jr., 111, 311
Lovell, James, Sr., 112, 311
Lovell, Jane, 311, 320
Lovell, Joseph, 16, 22, 311; daybook entries, 60, 78–79, 105–6, 127, 130, 136–38, 169, 178–81, 184, 186–87, 190–91, 194–97, 224, 239–43, 245, 248–53, 255–56, 258–62, 264, 266–73, 275, 277, 279–81, 283, 285–87
Lovell, Mary Reed, 22, 27, 72, 135, 190, 311
Lovell, Ruth Richards. *See* Richards, Ruth (c. 1685–1766)
Ludden, Benjamin, 30, 129, 148–52, 156, 158, 167–68, 172–76, 178–81, 186, 198, 213, 216, 235, 245–47, 249–51, 253, 297n311, 311
Ludden, Eunice Holbrook, 311
Ludden, James, 179, 247, 250, 252, 311
Ludden, Joseph, 301
lumber, 16

mace, 140
mackerel, 35, 38, 239, 266
maile, 327
malt, 327; daybook entries, 34–52, 54–60, 62, 63, 65–66, 68, 71, 73, 77–78, 82, 84, 89, 97, 100–101, 104–7, 110, 112, 119, 125–26, 131, 135, 137–39, 145, 147–49, 151, 153–57, 160, 162–63, 165–66, 168–73, 175, 177, 181, 183, 185, 187, 189–93, 197–99, 201–3, 205, 207, 209, 211, 214–15, 221, 223–26, 233, 235–37, 244, 253, 255–56, 258–61, 263–65, 267, 275–82, 284, 286
malt production and sales, 12–14, *13–14*, 291n45
maltster, 29, 228
man, "his" or "your," 25, 203, 224, 252, 258–59, 299n378, 330
Manley, Nathaniel, 287
Manley, Thomas, 130, 276, 279, 285–87, 300n445
Manley, William, 129–30, 270, 276, 280, 282, 287, 311
Manley, William, Jr., 276, 279, 287, 300n445
Mansfield, Massachusetts, 328
Marblehead, Massachusetts, 307
market historians, 5
market production on farms, 13
Marshfield, Massachusetts, 303
Martha's Vineyard, Massachusetts, 310
masons, 258
Massachusetts Bay, *17, 23*
Massachusetts General Court, 13, 20, 306, 312, 319–20, 322–23, 326, 328
mate, 327
Maverick, Sarah, 318
McWilliams, James E., 292n83
meadows, 3, 6–9
Medfield, Massachusetts, 305
Middleboro, Massachusetts, 303, 316
milk, 113, 200
Mill River, 6, *6*
Milton, Massachusetts, 247, 299n409, 309
minister's rate, 30; daybook entries, 51, 70, 97, 116, 164, 168, 205, 207, 211
Minor, Thomas, 289n2
mixed husbandry, 5–18, 21, 31
mohair, 247. *See also* worsted mohair
molasses, 49, 53, 62, 63, 68, 70, 72–73, 80, 82–84, 100, 104, 107–8, 112–13, 119, 133, 143, 147, 153–58, 161–62, 165–66, 172–75, 177, 190–91, 194, 198, 207, 215, 240, 242–44, 246, 263–64
Monatiquot River, 64, 86, 89, 327
money lent, borrowed, and exchanged, 34–50, 52, 54–55, 58–68, 70, 72, 75–77, 80–82, 84–88, 93, 95, 97–102, 104–11, 113–23, 125–26, 132–34, 138–39, 141, 143, 146, 148–49, 151–53, 155–58, 160–62, 164, 167–68, 171–74, 182–84, 189–90, 193–97, 199–200, 203–5, 207, 209–11, 215–16, 219, 221, 223–24, 228, 230–31, 236, 240–43, 245–48, 251, 253–57, 259–69, 271–73, 275–81, 283–87. *See also* Current New England Money; paper bills or money; pieces of eight
Mortemore, Mr., 129, 159, 297n326
Mortimer, Edward, 159, 297n326, 311
Mountford, Edmond, 311
Mountford, Elizabeth, 52, 75, 293n146, 311
Mountford, Jonathan, 22, 311; daybook entries, 65, 68, 71, 77, 97–98, 115, 142, 165, 169, 194, 197, 213–14, 217–18, 230–31, 239, 275, 293n146, 305
Mountford household in Boston, 141, 161, 168, 203, 221, 223, 262, 277
mowing, 35, 42, 43, 57, 61, 99, 119, 122–23, 155, 171, 175, 265
mulata, 25, 148, 199, 327
muslin, 16, 155, 213, 274, 327
mutton, 37–38, 45, 47, 49, 53, 56, 60, 62–64, 67, 70, 73, 80–85, 88–90, 93, 97–100, 102, 104, 105, 108–14, 116–24, 132, 181, 203, 252, 269, 284
Mutton Lane, 78, 327

nails, 23, 35, 43, 70, 75, 167, 179, 211, 239, 294n178. *See also* board nails; clapboard nails; shingle nails; shoe nails
Nantasket, 24, 187, 328
Nash, Abigail Dyer, 29, 117, 301, 311–12
Nash, Alice, 110, 311
Nash, Benjamin, 82, 110, 312
Nash, Jacob (Lieutenant), 29, 301, 311–12; daybook entries, 36, 37–38, 47, 68, 82–83, 110–11, 117–19, 127, 131, 141, 145, 148–49, 151, 153, 157–58, 160, 169, 173, 175, 177, 185, 187–89, 193, 196, 199, 253, 264, 275, 277, 279, 280, 282–84
Nash, James, 82, 110, 312
Nash, John, 171, 182, 193, 272, 312, 314
Nash, Joseph, 312; daybook entries, 64, 104, 127, 129–30, 169, 195, 224, 226, 240–42, 247–48, 252, 261, 283, 286–87
Nash, Mary (b. 1675). *See* Porter, Mary Nash (b. 1675)
Nash, Mary (d. 1739), 119, 312
Nash, Phoebe Marsh, 110, 312
Nash, Sarah (b. 1688), 314
Nash, Simeon, 312; daybook entries, 145, 147, 149, 151, 153, 157, 160, 171, 175, 177, 185, 187–89, 253, 273, 275, 277, 279–80
Nash, Thomas, 312; daybook entries, 36–37, 110, 117–18, 171, 273
Nash, Widow, 70, 312
Native American crops, 6
Native Americans, 26
Native American trails, 329
Navigation Acts, 14, 16
Neal, Mary, 308
Neals, Elder, 149, 297n314
neckcloths, 162, 179–80, 215, 217, 247, 328
Needham, Mr., 127, 129, 133–34, 266
needles, 43, 218. *See also* stocking needles
Newcomb, Abigail, 305
Newcomb, Mary, 315
Newcomb, Peter, 70, 152, 166, 294n172, 308
Newell, Margaret Ellen, 290n27
New England: currency in, 20, 291n74; economic history of, 1–31, 290n27; salt shortage in, 14
North Purchase, 24, 316, 323, 328
Norton, Massachusetts, 308, 328
nutmeg, 140, 151

oak tree coins, 326
oakum, 224, 264, 328
oak wood, 34, 37, 57, 60, 81, 112, 131, 160, 167, 184
oats, 35, 39–43, 49–50, 53–54, 59–60, 66, 75–76, 78, 85, 94, 105, 113, 116, 124, 132, 188, 192, 199, 201, 203, 215, 219, 221, 226, 251, 254–56, 274–76
oil, 35, 67, 70, 72–73, 80, 83–85, 89, 91, 93, 96, 98, 100, 102, 107, 112, 115, 135, 142–44, 149, 167–68, 190, 203, 207, 224, 284–87. *See also* lamp oil
Old Cedar Swamp, *6*, 16, 289n12
orchards, 7–8, 12
Orcutt, Andrew, 61, 210, 312
Orcutt, Benjamin, 312; daybook entries, 61, 130, 169, 184, 203, 210, 250, 267, 269, 273
Orcutt, Joseph, 22, 312; daybook entries, 61, 83, 141–42, 145, 148–49, 151–52, 154–58, 160–71, 173–75, 185–89, 198–99, 203–4, 209–13, 221, 233, 246, 279, 282
Orcutt, Sarah, 169–70, 312
Orcutt, William, 312
osnaburg or osenberg, 153, 213, 216, 218, 328

paper, 77, 162, 213, 215, 223, 241
paper bills or money, 20, 328; daybook entries, 34–35, 37–38, 84, 139, 150, 167, 179, 187, 201, 203, 207, 211, 219, 223, 239, 243, 248–50, 257, 262
pasture, 6, 7, 119
pasturing, 207
Pater, Samuel, 223
Patten, Matthew, 291n80, 292n82
pears, 285
peas, 69
Pemertin, Mr, 259
Penniman, Moses, 19, 312; daybook entries, 75, 148–50, 155, 182, 239, 260
Pen River, 6, *6*
pepper, 72, 88, 107, 215, 273
Pettee, Benjamin, 158, 312
Pettee, James, 103, 165, 189, 312
Pettee, John, 313; daybook entries, 39, 60, 103, 121, 175, 197, 234–35
Pettee, Joseph (1639–92), 312–13
Pettee, Joseph (1677–1759), 313; daybook entries, 40, 49, 59–60, 84, 104, 114, 127–30, 141, 149, 158, 167–68, 191–92, 196–97, 211, 226, 273, 279–81, 284, 287
Pettee, Mary (wife of Joseph), 205, 313
Pettee, Mary (wife of Samuel), 313
Pettee, Mary Porter, 47, 274, 312–13
Pettee, Nathaniel, 136, 138, 153, 192, 225, 238, 313
Pettee, Samuel, 89, 313
Pettee, Sarah Whitman, 312–13
Pettee, Simon, 105, 275
Pettee, Thomas, 313
Pettee, Widow, 39, 49, 313

Pettee, William (1661–1728), 304, 312–13; daybook entries, 37–38, 47, 49–50, 59–61, 83, 85, 89, 96, 103, 127, 136–38, 141, 143, 153, 162, 165, 171–72, 175, 177, 185, 189, 192–93, 197–98, 225–26, 233–38, 262, 274, 281
Pettee, William (d. 1679), 313
petticoats, 207
petticoat stuff, 261, 328
Phillips, Abigail, 304
Phillips, Amy Drake, 167, 313
Phillips, Anne, 313
Phillips, Benjamin, 313
Phillips, Elizabeth, 313
Phillips, Experience, 310
Phillips, John, 196, 209, 264, 270, 276, 285, 287, 313
Phillips, John (John's son), 287
Phillips, Joshua, 173, 209, 244, 246–47, 264, 313
Phillips, Joshua (1662–90), 313
Phillips, Joshua (b. 1689), 313
Phillips, Joshua (b. c. 1685), 313
Phillips, Mary, 129, 218
Phillips, Mary (1667–1749), 82, 313
Phillips, Mary (b. 1690), 190, 313
Phillips, Mary Packard, 313
Phillips, Nicholas (Deacon, c.1611–72), 304, 310, 313, 322
Phillips, Nicholas, Jr. (1697–1744), 270, 284, 313
Phillips, Nicholas, Sr. (1664–1751), 313; daybook entries, 51, 52, 54, 75, 82, 97, 127, 129, 137, 141, 155, 158, 169, 171, 183, 190, 259, 266, 270, 273, 282, 284, 286
Phillips, Richard, 45, 47, 125, 313
Phillips, Sister, 260, 299n422
Phillips, Widow, 167, 244, 313
Phippeny, Widow, 187, 314
pieces of eight, 20, 27, 328; daybook entries, 43, 45–47, 50, 53–54, 62, 65, 68, 77, 84, 87–88, 110, 113, 117, 119, 122, 124, 146, 152, 189, 211, 213
pigeon shot, 108, 215, 328
piggins, 266, 328
pigs, 34, 50, 67, 99–100, 122, 191, 275. *See also* hogs
pine, 57, 181
pine tree coins, 326, 328
pinions, 328
Pinney, Sarah, 314
pins, 167, 216
pipes, 64, 70, 80, 142, 144, 146, 160, 171, 174, 182, 184, 190–91, 196–97, 201, 207, 223, 245, 257, 264, 269, 273–74, 279–80, 284–85, 287
plowing, 41, 53, 55, 121, 188, 198–99, 216, 257
"plowshare mold and the iron between them," 186, 328
pluck, 12, 16, 328
plumes, 107, 283
Plymouth, Massachusetts, 95, 307, 317
plysh bricks, 153, 297n319
Pool, Elishama, 314
Pool, Isaac, 154, 182–83, 210, 314
Pool, Isaac, Sr., 186
Pool, Margaret, 314
Pool, Sarah, 305
Poole, Benjamin, 160, 221, 314
Poole, Edward, 314
Poole, Elizabeth Shaw, 79, 314
Poole, Joseph (Captain), 68, 76, 123, 250, 314
Poole, Samuel, 244, 246, 314
pork, 37–38, 46, 67, 80–81, 86, 102, 104, 108, 118, 125, 133, 152–53, 166, 168, 170–71, 173, 183, 199, 203, 205, 219, 242, 245, 251–52, 254, 262, 271, 279, 283
Porter, Ann, 313
Porter, Deliverance Byram, 103, 314
Porter, Ebenezer, 47, 302
Porter, John, 55–56, 58, 144–45, 302
Porter, John, Jr. (1667–1723), 314, 319; daybook entries, 47, 56, 64, 113, 123
Porter, John, Sr. (d. 1717), 9, 314; daybook entries, 63–64, 78–79, 93, 96, 103, 105, 118, 122–23
Porter, Margaret Ford, 103, 314
Porter, Mary. *See* Bicknell, Mary Porter (Mother)
Porter, Mary Nash (b. 1675), 85, 104, 312, 314
Porter, Mary or Mercy (wife of John, Jr.), 314
Porter, Ruth. *See* Bayley, Aunt (Ruth Porter)
Porter, Samuel, 85, 312, 314
Porter, Sarah Vining, 314
Porter, Thomas (1650–72), 314
Porter, Thomas (1672–1753), 48–49, 53, 82, 102, 293n139, 314
Porter, Thomas (John, Sr.'s son), 78, 113
posts, 167, 255
pots and pans, 169, 229
powder, 45, 61, 98, 105, 150, 155, 158, 160, 180, 189, 194, 197, 209, 215, 218, 243–45, 249–51, 262, 269, 275, 277, 281, 283, 285–87
powder of steel, 185
Powell, Arthur, 86, 295n214
Pratt, Abigail, 320
Pratt, Benjamin, 73, 294n175
Pratt, Brother, 149, 177–78, 183, 193, 225, 238, 314
Pratt, Dorothy, 322
Pratt, Ebenezer, 19, 314; daybook entries, 43, 103, 115–16, 127, 129, 141–42, 150, 152, 154, 157, 162, 165, 167, 169, 172–74, 177–78, 184, 188–91, 198, 201–2, 232, 234, 236–37, 267, 278
Pratt, Elder, 236, 299n398
Pratt, Elizabeth, 315

Pratt, Ephraim, 314–15; daybook entries, 111, 113, 133, 167, 201–2
Pratt, Hannah, 133, 193, 247, 297n298
Pratt, Hannah (b. 1670), 323
Pratt, Hannah (d. 1757), 100, 181, 263, 315
Pratt, Hannah (wife of Ebenezer), 314
Pratt, Hannah Rogers. *See* Bayley, Hannah Rogers Pratt (d. 1721)
Pratt, John, 77, 96, 103, 110, 129–30, 138, 142, 146–47, 149, 158, 162, 249, 271
Pratt, John (b. 1668), 63, 315
Pratt, John, Jr. (1663–1744), 29, 315; daybook entries, 43, 47, 86, 146, 149, 159, 184, 186
Pratt, John, Sr. (Lieutenant, 1636–1716), 314–15; daybook entries, 89, 177–78, 236, 261, 275
Pratt, Joseph, 19, 67, 73, 85, 101, 129, 151, 155, 180, 184, 245–47, 250, 269–70, 273, 275
Pratt, Joseph, Jr. (1665–1765), 16, 315; daybook entries, 73–74, 78, 81, 89–90, 99, 132, 135, 200
Pratt, Joseph, Sr. (1637–1720), 314–15; daybook entries, 63, 67–68, 85, 133–34, 166
Pratt, Martha, 314
Pratt, Matthew, 54
Pratt, Matthew (d. 1673), 315
Pratt, Matthew, Jr. (1665–1746), 103, 315
Pratt, Matthew, Sr. (c. 1628–1713), 100, 167, 192, 310, 314–15
Pratt, Micah, 216, 315
Pratt, Phebe, 111, 314
Pratt, Samuel (1640–79), 315
Pratt, Samuel (1670–1728), 315; daybook entries, 54, 144, 155–56, 232–35, 245, 249
Pratt, Samuel (d. 1690), 303
Pratt, Sarah (b. 1660), 306
Pratt, Sarah (c. 1650–1727). *See* Richards, Sarah Pratt (c. 1650–1727)
Pratt, Sarah Benson, 72, 99, 315
Pratt, Sarah Hunt (1640–1729), 310, 315
Pratt, Sarah Judkins (1645–1726), 63, 315
Pratt, Susannah Porter, 315
Pratt, Thomas, 236, 299n298, 315
Pratt, Waitstill Washburn, 314
Pratt, William, 9, 74, 84, 85, 97, 99, 104, 126, 130, 137, 151, 153, 156–58, 160–61, 165–68, 170, 176, 180–82, 186, 189, 220, 223, 226, 232–33, 236, 248, 250, 255, 262–63, 265, 272
Pratt, William (1659–1713), 315
Pratt, William (1673–1714, son of Matthew), 60, 100, 315
Pratt, William (son of Joseph), 151, 180, 184, 273, 275
Pray, Ephraim, 64, 86, 101–2, 129, 257
Pray, Hannah, 22, 263
Prentis, Solomon, 115
Pretter, Mr., 179
Priest, Elizabeth, 308
promissory notes, 20
Prout, Joseph, 139, 315
province bills, 20, 328
pumpkins, 159

quinces, 63, 158, 328
quire, 77, 213, 329

Radman, John, 64
raisins, 177
rakes, 123
Randall, Constable, 272
Randall, Hannah, 316
Randall, John, 34, 82, 89–90, 137, 147, 153, 158, 255, 260–61, 263, 274–75
Randall, John, Jr. (1673–1730), 256, 316, 320
Randall, John, Sr. (1635–1717), 315; daybook entries, 86, 137–38, 193, 243, 255–56, 263, 265, 271–72, 275–77, 280
Randall, Mercy, 310
Randall, Thomas, 43, 53, 125, 316
Ranger, Widow, 320
rates, 20, 30, 306–7, 329; daybook entries, 58, 114, 122, 163, 167, 256. *See also* country pay or rate; minister's rate
Rawson, Mary, 320
Read, Margaret, 321
reckonings, 1–2
Reed, Hannah, 84, 316
Reed, John, 189, 215, 237, 267, 316
Reed, Mary (1672–1745), 22, 27, 41, 151, 311, 316
Reed, Mary (d. 1717), 321
Reed, Phillip, 95, 316
Reed, Phillip, Sr., 123
Reed, Ruth, 322
Reed, Samuel, 316; daybook entries, 55, 58, 60, 84, 225, 254
Reed, Sarah Bicknell (Sister, c. 1651–1719), 42, 111, 138, 201, 311, 316
Reed, Thomas, 96, 127, 163, 168, 232, 251, 260
Reed, Thomas (c. 1645–1719), 23, 311, 316; daybook entries, 41–42, 48, 55, 57–60, 77–78, 84–85, 97–98, 136–38, 163, 185, 192–93, 225, 234–35, 237–38, 258, 293n129
Reed, Thomas, Jr. (1671–1719), 316; daybook entries, 41, 42, 66, 77, 84, 103, 136, 191, 201, 233, 235, 238, 257, 265
Reed, William, 144
Reed, William (c. 1650–c. 1706), 37, 77, 97, 105, 144, 316

Reed, William (Captain, 1682–1753), 311
Reed, William (Sergeant, 1688–1729), 136, 192, 235, 237–38, 316
Reed, William, Jr., 146
Rehoboth, Massachusetts, 303
Richards, Anna (d. 1766), 315
Richards, Anna Carver. *See* Carver, Anna
Richards, Bathsheba, 318, 323
Richards, Benjamin, 3, 9, 22, 27, 290n19, 292n89, 316–18; daybook entries, 53, 97–98, 106, 187, 197, 235, 239, 242–43, 247, 249, 256, 282; labor of, 40, 50, 53, 57, 65, 67–68, 73, 92, 101, 107, 121–22, 143, 154, 240, 244
Richards, Benjamin (James's nephew), 82, 294n191
Richards, Deborah, 22
Richards, Edward, 196, 264, 279–80, 285, 317
Richards, Elizabeth (c. 1682–after 1746), 321
Richards, Ephraim, 321
Richards, Grace Shaw. *See* Shaw, Grace
Richards, James (1658–1711): birth of, 3; building supplies trade, 15–16, 304, 311; cloth business of, 15; community affairs involvement of, 21, 30, 329; credit relationships formed by, 12, 31; credits and debits, 1692–1711, 3, *4*; credit transfers recorded by, 19; daybook entries, 34, 51, 52, 54, 71, 95, 97, 118, 120–21, 124, 228; death of, 3; estate and probate inventory of, 3–4; exotic goods business, 16, 31; inheritance of, 318; landholdings of, 3, 8, 12, 15, 289n12; malt production and sales, 12–14, *13–14*, 291n45, 301; networks and personal relationships of, 21–31; resource and labor sharing by, 9–11; salt business, 14; sheep heads and pluck business, 16; social and economic relationships of, 2–3, 5–6; transactions (1692–1711), *2*, 2–3; transactions, seasonality of, 11–12, *11;* transportation of goods, 17–18. *See also* James Richards Daybook (1692–1711)
Richards, James (b. 1680), 89, 125, 271, 317
Richards, John (1650–95), 314, 317–18, 321, 323; daybook entries, 45, 112, 209
Richards, Joseph, 34–35, 43, 121, 124
Richards, Joseph (c. 1653–96), 317–18; daybook entries, 43, 47, 125
Richards, Joseph, Jr. (1676–1710), 22, 29, 304, 317; daybook entries, 80–82, 89, 99, 104, 109, 127, 129, 132, 144, 147–48, 161–64, 170, 172–75, 178, 182, 185–86, 198–99, 209
Richards, Jr. (of Boston), 250
Richards, Mary (b. 1697), 3, 27, 124, 317
Richards, Mary Williams, 317, 318
Richards, Mr. (of Boston), 266–67
Richards, Nathaniel, 231, 299n397
Richards, Ruth (c. 1685–1766), 3, 22, 26, 27, 290n19, 311, 317; daybook entries, 53, 71, 106, 178, 202, 287
Richards, Ruth Bicknell (1660–1729), 3, 21, 26, 29, 289n12, 290n19, 292n89, 294n147, 303, 305–7, 311, 316–17, 321; daybook entries, 53, 71, 106, 118, 120, 124–25, 242, 299n404
Richards, Sarah, 15, 111, 140, 215
Richards, Sarah (b. c. 1657), 43, 112, 132, 297n297, 317
Richards, Sarah Pratt (c. 1650–1727), 314, 317–18, 323
Richards, Sister, 297n297, 317; daybook entries, 78–79, 82, 90, 132, 151, 156
Richards, Susan (1654–82), 317
Richards, Widow, 318
Richards, William (1685–1712), 305, 318; daybook entries, 116, 129, 141, 165, 200, 252, 266–67, 268–73, 277–78, 300n435
Richards, William, Jr. (c. 1656–83), 317–18
Richards, William, Sr. (d. 1682), 3, 25, 289n11, 292nn88–89, 317–18
riding hoods, 49
Ripley, Joanna, 318
Ripley, Josiah, 318; daybook entries, 61, 64, 68, 90, 93, 97, 203, 210, 282
Ripley, Mary, 246, 318
Robbison, George, 166, 318
Roberts, John, 271, 318
Rogers, Hannah (d. 1715), 315
Rogers, John (Deacon), 318
Rogers, John (Elder), 67, 77, 89, 253, 318
romal, 247, 329
rope, 61, 154, 177, 223, 245
Rose Hill, *6–7*, 9, 10, 18, 329; daybook entries, 49, 75, 119, 173, 179, 244
Rose Hill Club, *10*
Rothenberg, Winifred B., 9, 289n1
Roxbury, Massachusetts, 309
rum, 45, 61, 68, 74–75, 86, 108, 149, 151–52, 155–56, 168, 171, 188, 229, 240–42, 245–46, 257, 261, 263, 272, 275, 283, 287
rundlet, 283, 329
russel, 231, 329
rye, 34, 43, 285

saddles, 279
salt, 14; daybook entries, 34–35, 37–38, 41, 44, 49, 55, 60–61, 63–65, 67, 68, 70, 72–73, 75, 80, 82–86, 88–91, 93, 96–100, 102, 104–5, 107, 109, 111–13, 115, 122, 133, 135, 137, 141–45, 147–55, 157,

salt: daybook entries (*continued*) 159–60, 165–68, 171–72, 174–75, 178–85, 187, 190–91, 201, 203, 205, 207, 209–11, 215, 219, 221, 223–24, 233, 239–41, 244–58, 261–72, 280, 285–87
Salter, Nicholas, 64, 68, 102, 109, 117, 191, 294n162, 296n274
salt grass, 35, 41–43, 57, 114, 119, 122–23, 155, 224, 265
salt hay, 329; daybook entries, 44, 47, 58, 66, 68, 145–47, 166, 199, 203, 255, 276
saltmarshes, 6, 8, 15, 114, 329
Sargent, Elizabeth, 310
satin, 213
Savil, Benjamin, 42, 318
Savil, Judith, 313
Sawyer, Sarah, 305
scarves, 82
Scituate, Massachusetts, 308–9, 312, 317, 320–21
Scotch cloth, 98, 133, 135, 190, 271, 281, 329
scraps, 61, 82, 108, 263
scythes, 46, 123, 171, 201, 207, 213–14, 223, 241–42, 259
seaweed, 17, 87, 329
Secole, Marcy, 107, 296n260
seed barley, 40, 65, 105, 125, 146, 166, 219
seed corn, 188, 194, 277
selectmen, 15, 30, 301, 302–6, 308–23, 329
Seottow, Lydia, 322
serge, 168, 329
serge coat, 112
servants and slaves, 25–26, 29, 303–4, 307; daybook entries, 25, 49, 88–89, 97, 147–48, 159, 185, 190, 201, 203, 218, 224, 248, 251–52, 258–59, 261, 263–64, 274. *See also* African slaves or servants; Indian slaves or servants
Shane, Abraham, 248
Shane, Joseph, 241
Shaw, Abraham, 16, 204, 224
Shaw, Abraham (1657–1706), 318
Shaw, Abraham (b. 1685), 318; daybook entries, 127, 191, 194–95, 197, 239, 241–43, 245–46, 248–49, 253–56, 258, 260–61, 265, 267–68, 274–75, 277, 280–87
Shaw, Abraham (Grace's father), 318
Shaw, Alice Phillips, 314, 318–19
Shaw, Alice Stonard, 302
Shaw, Anthony, 302
Shaw, Benjamin, 265, 283–84, 303
Shaw, Grace, 3, 21, 25, 292n89, 317–19, 322
Shaw, Hannah (wife of Samuel Bates), 302
Shaw, Hannah Whitmarsh (1661–c. 1735), 319
Shaw, John, 64, 77–78, 82, 86, 120, 286
Shaw, John, Jr. (1653–1718), 318–19; daybook entries, 41–42, 78, 130, 153, 157, 235, 243, 250, 256, 263, 276, 280–81
Shaw, John, Sr. (1630–1704), 310, 314, 318–19; daybook entries, 64–67, 109, 123, 196, 283, 286, 294n157, 300n455
Shaw, Joseph (1618–54), 319
Shaw, Joseph (1643–1704), 70, 294n169, 319
Shaw, Joseph (1664–1718), 319; daybook entries, 70, 239, 242, 260–61, 267–68, 271–72, 274, 286–87, 294n169
Shaw, Martha, 322
Shaw, Mary (b. 1691), 67, 263, 319
Shaw, Mary (c. 1626–58). *See* Bicknell, Mary Shaw (c. 1626–58)
Shaw, Mary (wife of Joseph 1618–54), 319
Shaw, Nicholas, 86, 199, 319
Shaw, Sarah, 319
sheep, 34, 37–38, 40, 42, 45, 47, 58, 63, 66–67, 70, 73, 76, 83, 86, 101–2, 108, 110–11, 113, 116, 120, 124–25, 133, 135, 183–84, 196–97, 201, 203, 208, 216, 221, 239, 267, 269, 273. *See also* lambs and lamb meat; mutton; wethers
sheep heads and pluck, 16; daybook entries, 38, 56, 63–64, 67, 70, 73, 83, 86, 88–90, 96, 100–102, 104, 108, 110–17, 120–21, 123–24, 135, 170, 284
sheep shearing, 22, 258–59, 269, 277–78
sheep skin, 100, 257, 269, 273
sheep wool, 36, 47, 55, 62–65, 67, 73, 82, 90, 100–104, 108–9, 111, 113, 116, 118–19, 121–22, 132, 135, 142, 148, 156, 161, 169–70, 182, 185, 201, 203, 205, 215, 219, 245–47, 257, 273–74, 281, 283–84. *See also* cotton wool; wool
shilwork, 123, 297n288
shingle nails, 77, 84, 154, 165, 167–68, 188, 213, 239
shingles, 63, 67–69, 71, 74, 76–77, 81–82, 87, 93, 97, 105, 108, 112–13, 115, 133–34, 139, 152, 156–57, 165, 167–70, 172, 174, 176, 178–79, 182, 185, 194, 199–200, 202, 204, 206, 208, 210, 212, 214, 216–17, 220, 222, 226, 228, 230–31, 240–41, 243, 245–46, 249–50, 257–60, 268, 270, 277–79, 282
Shipery, Mr., 140
Shipery, Mrs., 152
shirting, 40, 329
shoe nails, 43, 65, 70, 84, 97, 135, 166, 168–69, 207, 211, 213, 243, 245
shoes, 39, 48–49, 53, 62, 71, 86, 102, 104–6, 118–20, 123–24, 144, 165–66, 178, 187, 202, 215–16, 218, 253, 275. *See also* French-heeled shoes; wooden-heeled shoes
shoe strings, 215
shopkeepers, 245

Short, Susanna, 90
shorting, 39
shot, 61, 65, 98, 153–55, 158, 163, 180, 189, 211, 213, 229, 248–50, 281–82, 283–85. *See also* pigeon shot
sickles, 261
sieves, 154, 229
silk, 77, 84, 155, 161, 167, 205, 213, 231, 247
silk thread, 218
silver money, 37
Simms, Elizabeth, 144, 297n307
Simpkins, Catherine Richardson, 17, 75–76, 103, 118, 294n179
Simpkins, Pilgrim, 118
single-entry bookkeeping, 1, 289n2
slaves. *See* servants and slaves
sloops, 9, 24, 142, 165, 279
Smelt Brook, 6, *6,* 87, 113, 124, 205, 329
smelts, 65
Smith, Hannah. *See* Bicknell, Hannah Smith
Smith, James, 123
Smith, James, Jr., 51, 319
Smith, James, Sr., 319
Smith, Joshua, 48, 52, 85, 90, 203–4, 233, 235, 295n209
Smith, Widow, 34, 167, 298n336
soap, 65
social historians, 5
social status, 3–4
sowing crops, 41
Spear, Elizabeth, 307
Speer, Samuel, 37, 40, 42, 58, 106, 319
spinning and weaving. *See* weaving and spinning
stadium, 329
staples, 107
starch, 213, 218
stays, 174, 178, 329
steers, 209, 219, 266, 268
stick baskets, 39
stocking needles, 191
stockings, 283
stones, 92
Stowell, Mary, 313
straw, 256
Sturges, Hannah, 312
subsistence farming, 5, 6–7
suet, 66, 266
sugar, 68, 83, 86, 98, 111, 140, 142–48, 160, 167–68, 177, 190–91, 205, 207, 211, 221, 223, 231, 241, 253, 255, 257–59, 264, 266, 272, 275, 280
sundry goods, 177, 271
surveyors of highways, 29, 303, 329
Sutton, Massachusetts, 304–5
swamps, 6, 8, 16, 61, 121
swan shot, 159, 329
sword and belt, 82

Tailler, Raffe, 52, 61, 84, 104, 129, 210
tallow, 39, 83–84, 105, 110, 116, 158, 173, 201, 247
tar, 224
Taunton, Massachusetts, 24, 52, 121, 303–5, 314–16, 328
tax payments, 20, 30, 329
Taylor, John, 319
Taylor, John, Sr., 122
Taylor, Rebecca, 307–8
Thare, Benjamin, 269
Thatcher, Mr., 190
Thatcher, Peter, 164, 319
Thatcher, Thomas, 319–20
Thayer, Colonel, 142
Thayer, Ebenezer, 19, 81, 101, 296n246
Thayer, Richard, 96, 295n234
Thayer, Samuel, 101, 296n247
Thomas, Lydia Whitman, 17, 130, 170, 182, 319
thread, 213, 218, 231
thread lace, 218
thread tongs, 77
The Three Friends (sloop), 9, 24, 165
ticking, 171
Tirrell, Gideon, Jr. (1693–1766), 320
Tirrell, Gideon, Sr. (1664–1730), 310, 319; daybook entries, 15, 46, 89, 129, 144, 168, 203–4, 209
Tirrell, Hannah Kingman, 310
Tirrell, Marah, 171, 298n346
Tirrell, Rebecca, 312
Tirrell, William (1658–1727), 114, 123, 320
tithingmen, 30, 303, 306, 309–11, 315, 317, 319, 330
tobacco, 35, 39, 41, 45–46, 50, 54, 56–57, 61–63, 67–68, 70, 75, 82, 96, 100–102, 105, 109–12, 122–23, 132, 135, 150–51, 155, 165–68, 175, 177, 179, 188, 190–91, 197, 201, 203, 205, 207, 210–11, 221, 223, 245, 268, 272, 274–82, 284
Tomson, Esther, 316
tongues, 98
Torrey, Deborah, 104, 198, 320
Torrey, Elizabeth, 320
Torrey, Jane, 316
Torrey, John (Lieutenant, 1673–1730), 9, 11, 17–18, 29, 320; daybook entries, 51, 84–86, 103, 127, 137–38, 141–42, 145–47, 149–50, 158–59, 167–68, 170–75, 177–79, 181, 184, 186, 188–89, 191–95, 198–99, 201–2, 204, 207, 225, 233, 236–37, 241–46, 248, 250, 252–54, 256, 258, 260, 264–66, 272–76, 281–86

Torrey, John (son of John), 272, 276
Torrey, John (son of William), 167
Torrey, Jonathan (c. 1654–1718), 320; daybook entries, 51, 61, 86, 111, 114, 121, 123, 142, 166, 168, 177, 186–87, 232, 236, 252, 293n145
Torrey, Joseph, 127, 146, 183, 254, 266, 272, 320
Torrey, Joshua, 186, 320
Torrey, Margaret, 308
Torrey, Mary (b. 1656), 309
Torrey, Mary Symmes, 145, 297n309, 320
Torrey, Micajah (Deacon), 86, 89, 103, 113, 118–19, 123, 135, 137–38, 141, 147, 158, 163–66, 168, 189, 221, 238, 240, 256, 259, 261–62, 264–65, 269, 279, 296n270, 320
Torrey, Miss, 83
Torrey, Mr., 50, 103, 104, 160
Torrey, Mrs., 145, 150, 165, 167–68, 271, 279, 297n309
Torrey, Ms., 157
Torrey, Ruth Fry, 142, 145, 167, 297n309, 320
Torrey, Samuel (b. 1676), 85, 295n206, 320
Torrey, Samuel (Reverend, 1632–1707), 85, 98, 295n206, 309, 320
Torrey, Susana, 262, 320
Torrey, Timothy, 50
Torrey, Widow, 277, 300n446
Torrey, William (Captain, 1608–90), 320
Torrey, William (John's son), 258, 263, 273
Torrey, William, Jr. (1638–1718), 123, 167, 171, 184, 189, 204, 298n347, 320
Tounfin, Simon, 278
tow cloth, 61
Tower, Benjamin (b. 1686), 138, 320
Tower, Margaret, 320
Tower, Samuel, 104, 296n257
Townsend, Solomon, 168, 197, 280, 284, 320–21
tramels, 123
transportation costs, 50
Trask, William, 70, 86, 99, 187, 294n171, 295n215
trimming, 330
Trufant, Morris, 9, 303, 321; daybook entries, 65, 68, 78, 83–84, 97, 119, 142, 147, 153, 155, 165–67, 170, 172–73, 177–78, 181–82, 187, 191, 193, 196, 220, 226, 232–35, 242, 257–59, 263–66, 278, 280, 281, 282, 284, 286–87
Turner, Ann, 122, 165, 303
Turner, Jacob, 129–30, 162, 177, 179–80, 182, 321
Turner, John, 321
Turner, Sarah. *See* Holbrook, Sarah Turner
turnips, 34, 76, 100, 158–61, 163, 172, 180–81, 187, 198–99, 209, 241, 286
Tyler, Jacob, 52, 66, 321
Tyler, Mr., 79, 117, 294n184
Tyler, Mrs., 51, 59, 87, 114, 117–18
Tyler household, 179, 241, 242

Varney, James, 265
veal, 38, 60, 67, 70, 72, 75, 82, 90, 94, 100, 120, 147, 150, 239, 294n177
venter, 330
verbal orders, 19
Vesey, Mr., 143, 297n322
vetch, 35, 330
Vicers, Jorge, 187
Vickers, Daniel, 5, 25, 290n27, 291n80
Vining, Benjamin, 22, 124, 321
Vining, Jane, 321
Vining, John, 144–45
Vining, John (1636–85), 321
Vining, John, Jr. (1687–1746), 275, 321
Vining, John, Sr. (1662–1737), 321; daybook entries, 44, 51, 79, 96, 151, 172
Vining, Margaret, 234
Vining, Mary (1690–1718), 321
Vining, Mary Reed, 321
Vining, Widow, 167, 321
Vinson, Ebenezer, 321; daybook entries, 70, 127, 129, 203, 205, 219, 228–29
Vinson, Hannah, 312
Vinson, John, 16, 105, 137, 149, 155, 161, 203, 207, 209–10, 216, 219, 221–22, 286, 289n12
Vinson, John, Jr. (c. 1676–1756), 9, 310, 321; daybook entries, 89, 127, 129, 204, 207–10, 215, 221–22, 226, 244, 247, 255
Vinson, John, Sr. (Uncle), 22, 321; daybook entries, 70, 89, 127, 129, 169–70, 172–73, 189, 205–6, 208, 219–20, 241, 255, 294n167
Vinson, Samuel, 16, 312, 321; daybook entries, 65, 70, 127, 129, 168, 180, 182, 190, 202, 205, 207–8, 211–12, 216, 223, 227, 250, 294n167
Vinson, Sarah, 205, 321
Vinson, Thomas, 69, 294n165, 322
Vinson household, 213
Vinting, Blase, 64, 96–97

Wadsworth, Mr., 179, 298n353
Waldo, Jonathan, 194
Wales, Deacon, 158, 297n325
Wales, Nathaniel, 216, 299n388
walnut wood, 34, 75–76
Ward, Frances, 312
warming pans, 190, 330
weaving and spinning, 15, 38, 53, 66, 80, 83, 143. *See also* wide cloth weaving
Web, Peter, 272, 300n442
Webb, Elisha, 241, 322

Wentworth, Samuel, 106, 135, 296n259
Wessagussett Yacht Club, *10*
wethers, 16, 19, 303–4, 330; daybook entries, 39, 125, 167, 205, 257
Weymouth, Massachusetts: book debts in, 18; cow herds in, 9; credit economy of, 1, 8; currency available in, 20; in daybook transactions, 54, 121, 125, 214, 228; economic markets of, 3; exotic goods market in, 16; fencing in, 326; geographical features of, 3, 6; James Richards's associates in, 301–23; James Richards's birth in, 3; James Richards's relative wealth in, 4–5; James Richards's transactions with residents of, 24; map of town of, *6*; mixed husbandry system in, 8; seasonality and diversity of activities in, 12 servants and slaves in, 25–26; spinning and weaving in, 15; view of North Weymouth, *7*; women in, 30
whalebone, 207
wheat, 98
White, Abigail, 316
White, Benjamin, 83, 127, 284, 322
White, Ebenezer, 36
White, Ebenezer (1672–1756), 252, 322
White, Ebenezer (Lieutenant, 1648–1703), 47, 96, 293n137, 322
White, Hannah Phillips, 322
White, James, 284
White, Joseph, 184–85, 238, 268, 302, 322
White, Mary Dyer. *See* Dyer, Mary
White, Mary Pratt, 149, 297n313, 322
White, Mrs., 136
White, Mrs., Sr., 149, 234, 238, 244, 297n313
White, Mrs. Mary, 153
White, Samuel, 69, 83, 86, 89, 129, 166, 183, 185, 244, 295n216
White, Samuel (Captain, 1642–99), 322; daybook entries, 38, 46–47, 112, 120, 173
White, Samuel, Jr., 129, 141, 166, 185, 252
White, Sara, 207
White, Thomas, 47, 64, 89–90, 96, 129, 161, 165–67, 179, 183, 186, 199, 216, 224, 244
White, Thomas, Jr. (b. 1675), 17–18, 24, 322; daybook entries, 80–81, 91, 110, 165
White, Thomas, Sr. (d. 1706), 322; daybook entries, 66, 89, 96, 101, 105
White, Widow, 25, 322; daybook entries, 70, 104, 138, 277
White, Widow, Jr., 169, 224
White, Widow, Sr., 171, 199
Whitey, George, 40, 58, 293n126, 294n150
Whitman (no first name given), 209
Whitman, Abiah, 322–23; daybook entries, 38, 56, 124, 127–29, 142, 159, 172, 232, 236, 243, 245, 251, 262, 281
Whitman, Deborah Richards. *See* Richards, Deborah
Whitman, Ebenezer, 22
Whitman, Hannah. *See* French, Hannah Whitman
Whitman, John, 83, 140, 155, 159–60, 165, 250, 280
Whitman, John (b. 1681), 38, 323
Whitman, John (Captain, d. 1714), 319
Whitman, John, Jr. (1668–1751), 159, 161, 164, 322
Whitman, John, Sr., 322
Whitman, Mary, 315
Whitman, Sergeant, 93, 128, 175, 236, 239, 245, 248, 254, 257, 295n233
Whitman, Sister, 243
Whitman's Pond, 6, *6*, 311, 323
Whitmarsh, Deborah, 319
Whitmarsh, Ebenezer (1658–1718), 184, 267, 323
Whitmarsh, Ebenezer, Jr. (b. 1688), 184, 323
Whitmarsh, Ezra, 323; daybook entries, 69–72, 88–90, 99, 116–17, 122–23, 144, 159, 236, 243
Whitmarsh, Hannah (1661–c. 1735), 319
Whitmarsh, Hannah Reed, 319, 323
Whitmarsh, John, Jr. (b. 1655), 323
Whitmarsh, John, Sr. (d. 1709), 323
Whitmarsh, Judith, 319
Whitmarsh, Mary (1663–1715), 323
Whitmarsh, Mary (wife of Increase Bates), 64, 86, 141, 302
Whitmarsh, Nicholas, 29, 86, 89, 319, 323
Whitmarsh, Nicholas, Sr., 125
Whitmarsh, Samuel, 323; daybook entries, 89, 103, 178, 181, 244, 248–49, 251, 256, 259–60, 266, 268, 270
Whitmarsh, Sarah, 316
Whitmarsh, Sarah Harding, 323
Whitmarsh, Simon, 303
wide cloth weaving, 156, 297n324
Wild, John, 83, 109, 111, 271, 295n201
Wilkinson, John, 295n224
Willard, Daniel, 109, 296n261, 323
Willard, Mr., 245, 248, 249
Willard, Mrs., 76, 111, 249
Willes, Samuel, 117, 296n276
William (African slave), 146
Willis, Joseph, 241–42, 247
wine, 133, 287
winnowing, 76
women: relationships and transactions with, 26–30; social and economic roles of, 26, 30, 292n96

wood and timber, 34, 50, 58, 60, 75–76, 80, 84–87, 98, 111–12, 121–22, 124, 162, 166, 168, 187, 201, 242–45, 247, 252, 279. *See also specific names of woods*
wooden-heeled shoes, 29, 119, 194
woodlands, 7–8, 12, 16
Woodward, Bethiah, 320
Woodward, Smith, 243
wool, 60, 73, 89–90, 96, 112, 122, 160, 191, 211, 240, 242, 245. *See also* cotton wool; sheep wool
woolen/wooling cloth, 38–40, 49, 56, 122, 203
Worlidge, John, 8
wormers, 330
worsted mohair, 181, 218, 330
worsted ribbing, 185
worsted wool, 140
Wrentham, Massachusetts, 51, 306, 320

yarn, 83

Zipporah (Samuel White's African slave), 25, 199, 298n376